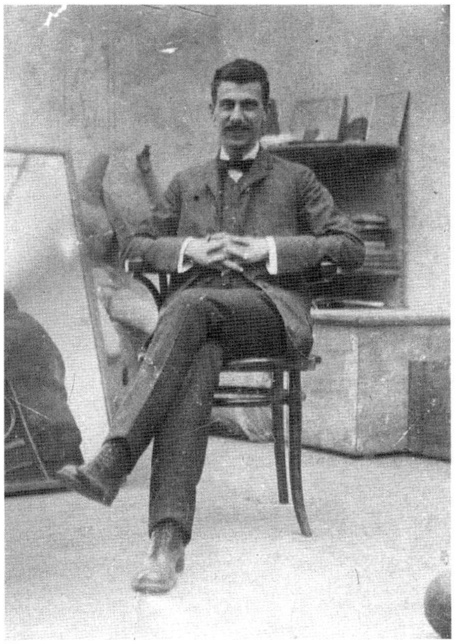

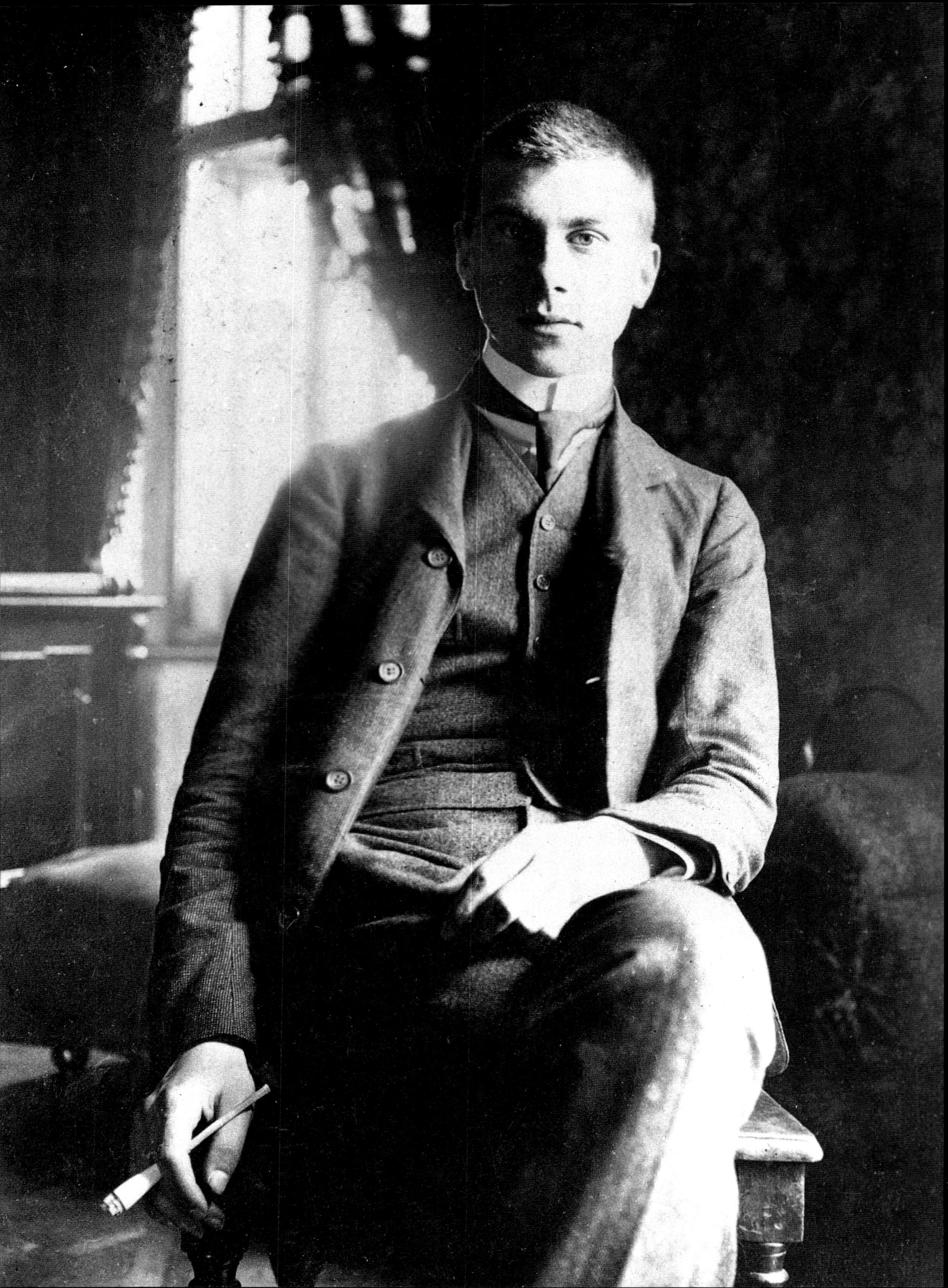

RICHARD GERSTL

Edited by Jill Lloyd and Ingrid Pfeiffer in collaboration with Raymond Coffer

With preface by Ronald S. Lauder, foreword by Renée Price,
and essays by Raymond Coffer, Jane Kallir, Diethard Leopold,
Jill Lloyd, Ingrid Pfeiffer, Maria Sitte, and Karol Winiarczyk

SCHIRN KUNSTHALLE FRANKFURT

RONALD S. LAUDER NEUE GALERIE
MUSEUM FOR GERMAN AND AUSTRIAN ART
NEW YORK

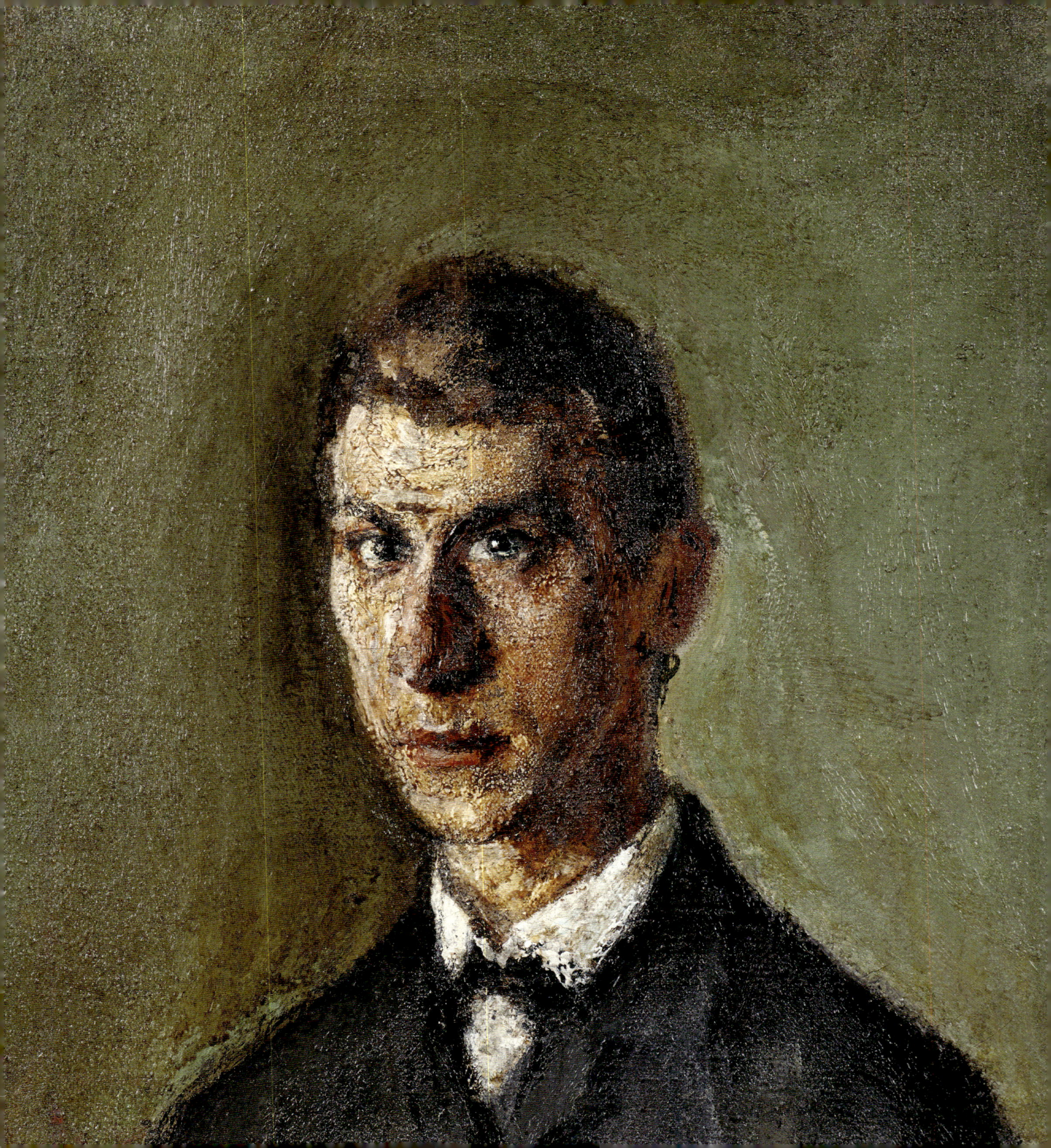

CONTENTS

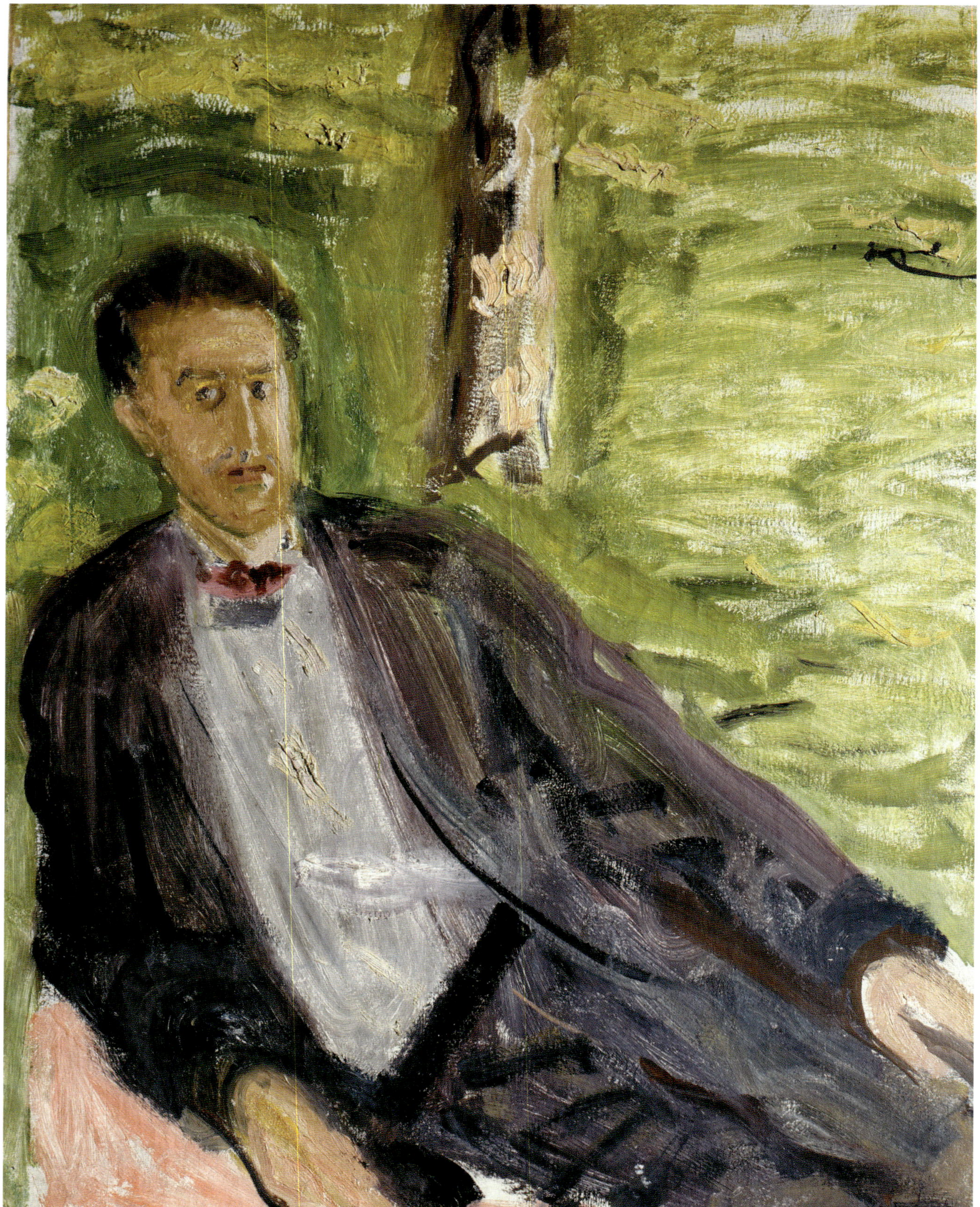

PREFACE

I discovered the art of Richard Gerstl some time after I became acquainted with the art of his Viennese contemporaries: Gustav Klimt, Egon Schiele, and Oskar Kokoschka. This is not so surprising, since Gerstl is far less known as an artist. In addition, very little of his art has survived to the present day.

But once I did get to see Gerstl, especially in a show at the Kunstforum in Vienna in 1993, I was completely taken with the work. Even though Gerstl died tragically young, his gifts were undeniable. He produced some of the strongest Expressionist painting and drawing imaginable. Gerstl belongs in the front ranks of any history of modern Austrian art.

On the rare occasions when the artist's work becomes available, whether privately or at auction, I make a point of trying to acquire it. To date, I have been fortunate to assemble a small selection of important Gerstl paintings. These are haunting works, and I am proud to include them in this major exhibition devoted to the artist. This is a show I have wanted to do for a long time, and seeing it come together in this way is very gratifying.

We have partnered with the Schirn Kunsthalle in Frankfurt to make this possible, and together we have realized an exhibition that conveys the strength and mystery at the heart of Gerstl's work. Major loans have been provided by several important Austrian art museums, including the Belvedere, the Leopold Museum, the Museum moderner Kunst, and the Wien Museum. I offer my sincere gratitude to all of them. We simply could not have done it without these great institutions. Jane Kallir of Galerie St. Etienne has provided special guidance during this process, and our curator and Neue Galerie board member Jill Lloyd has done a magnificent job as the curator. To all of them, I say thank you. Through this catalogue and the exhibition it accompanies, we are thrilled to be able to share the vision of Richard Gerstl.

RONALD S. LAUDER
President, Neue Galerie New York

Portrait of a Man (Green Background), summer 1908, oil on canvas. Private Collection

FOREWORD

The life of Richard Gerstl (1883–1908) was much too brief, but in his time as an artist he had a tremendous impact on the world around him. His psychologically complex work brought a special intensity to the art of turn-of-the-century Vienna. Although only about 70 surviving paintings and drawings are attributed to Gerstl, he managed to leave a lasting impression, and remains an early Expressionist artist of outsize influence and critical regard in the twentieth century.

Gerstl was a rebellious student at the Academy of Fine Arts in Vienna, and he clashed often with his conservative professor Christian Griepenkerl. Yet Gerstl could not be dissuaded from pursuing his own path. His stylized approach to portraiture led him to develop a highly distinctive form of Expressionist art. Gerstl claimed a closer affinity with avant-garde musicians of the day than with fellow artists, as he became an avid member of the circle around Arnold Schönberg. His love affair with Schönberg's wife, Mathilde, ended tragically, with Gerstl destroying much of his art and committing suicide. By 1931, his remaining work was re-discovered by gallerist Otto Nirenstein (Kallir) in Vienna and Gerstl was hailed as "the Austrian Van Gogh." One can only imagine the greater artistic heights Gerstl might have reached.

In order to realize this important exhibition, the first Gerstl exhibition in a U.S. museum, the Neue Galerie has partnered with the Schirn Kunsthalle in Frankfurt, a superb institution within the German art world. We wish to thank the former director of the Schirn and Neue Galerie board member, Max Hollein, for beginning the discussions on this partnership. We also offer our gratitude to the staff at the Schirn Kunsthalle, especially director Philipp Demandt and curator Ingrid Pfeiffer. The curator on behalf of the Neue Galerie presentation is Jill Lloyd, who has organized many important exhibitions here over the years, including "Munch and Expressionism," "Ferdinand Hodler: View to Infinity," "Van Gogh and Expressionism," "Christian Schad," and others. Dr. Lloyd is a dedicated and trusted ally of the Neue Galerie, and we offer her our sincere thanks.

We are very grateful for the support of numerous lenders to the exhibition. In particular, I wish to thank Mag. Hans-Peter Wipplinger, as well as Diethard and Elisabeth Leopold, of the Leopold Museum, Vienna, for their generosity in providing 13 key loans. Special thanks are also due to Dr. Stella Rollig of the Belvedere Museum, Vienna, as well as to Dr. Klaus Albrecht Schröder of the Albertina, Vienna and Dr. Karola Kraus of the Museum moderner Kunst, Vienna, for making several important works available. We also wish to thank Dr. Angelika Möser of the Arnold Schönberg Center Vienna together with Lawrence, Nuria and Ronny Schoenberg; Jane Kallir of Galerie St. Etienne; Elizabeth Szancer of the Ronald S. Lauder Collection; Michael Lesh of the Serge Sabarsky Collection; Ernst Ploil; Richard Grubman and Caroline Mortimer; and the collectors who prefer to remain anonymous.

Woman in a Feather Hat, early 1907, oil on canvas. Private Collection

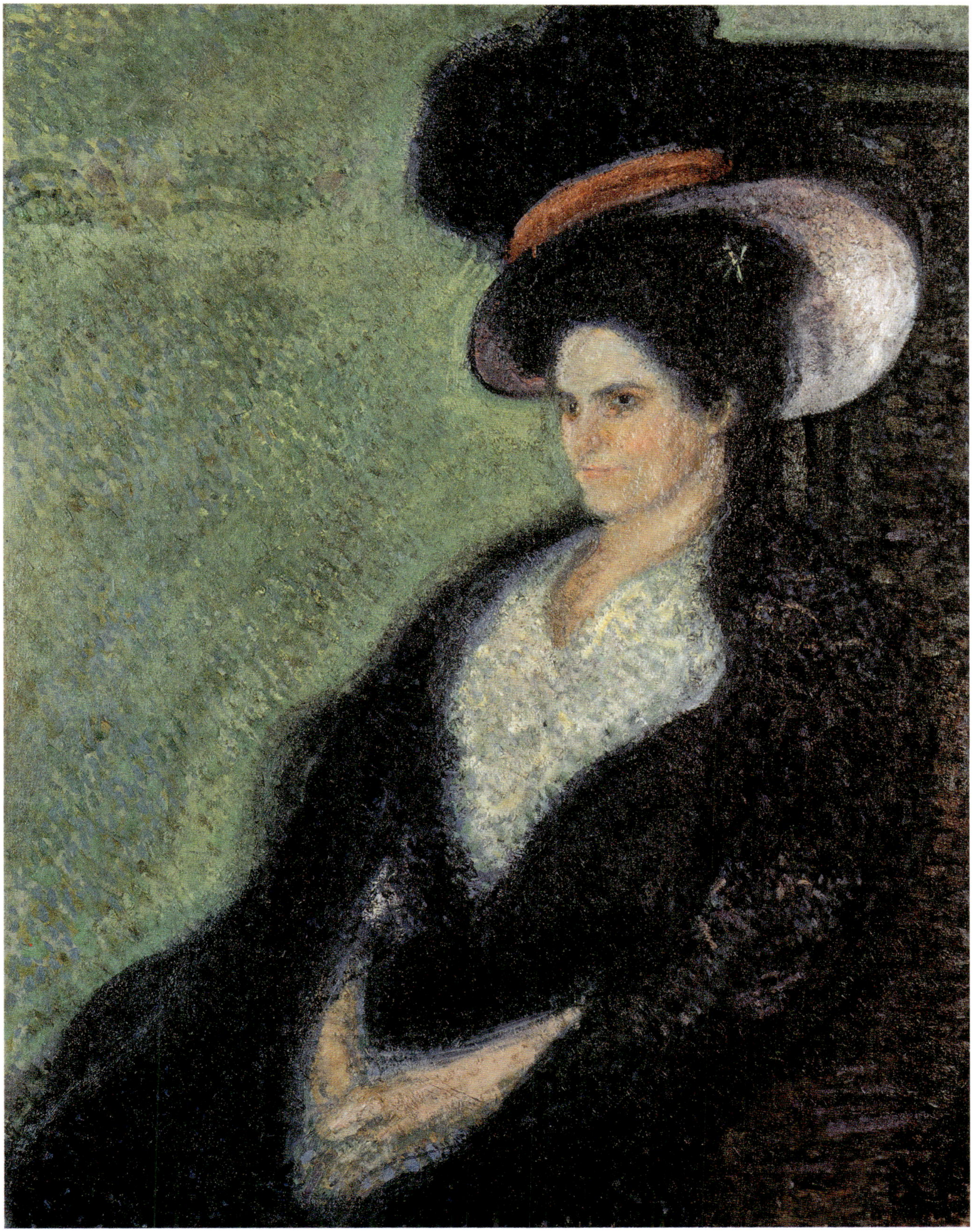

I would like to thank the contributors to this exhibition catalogue—Jane Kallir, Diethard Leopold, Jill Lloyd, Ingrid Pfeiffer, Maria Sitte and Karol Winiarczyk—for their thoughtful and original scholarly contributions. We would like to extend special thanks to Raymond Coffer, both for his essay and his revised chronology of Gerstl's paintings, which offers many new insights into the artist's work. Peter de Kimpe created the outstanding exhibition design, and Judy Hudson provided an elegant catalogue layout. Therese Muxeneder at the Arnold Schönberg Center gave us valuable help and advice. John Mauceri offered expert counsel on which Schönberg pieces to play in the galleries to complement the Gerstl exhibition. The Neue Galerie staff has played a vital role in assembling this exhibition, including Scott Gutterman, Deputy Director and Chief Operating Officer; Janis Staggs, Director of Curatorial and Manager of Publications; Liesbet Van Leemput, Curatorial Manager; Allison Needle, Chief Registrar and Director of Exhibitions; Julie Jung, Assistant Registrar; Erin Hauer, Graphics Manager; and Michael Voss, Head Preparator. The exhibition is supported in part by the President's Circle of the Neue Galerie New York.

Finally, we wish to thank our Board of Trustees and our President and Co-founder, Ronald S. Lauder, who has long recognized the importance of Richard Gerstl as a major artist. Mr. Lauder has graciously acquired several key works by Gerstl for the Neue Galerie collection, and was a strong advocate for this exhibition from the beginning. As always, we are grateful for his boundless support and shared vision for the Neue Galerie.

RENÉE PRICE

Director, Neue Galerie New York

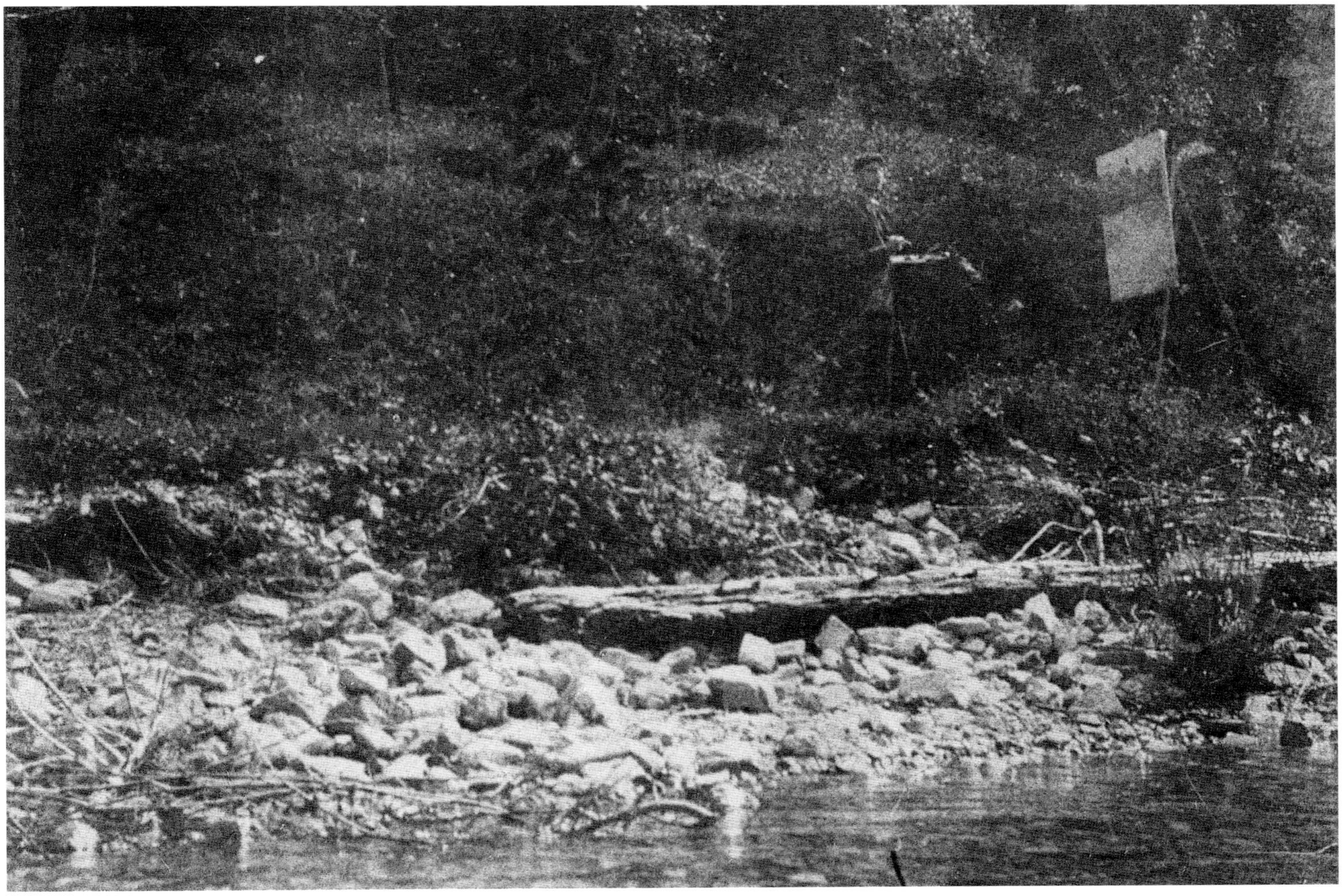

Gerstl painting on the shore of the Traunsee, Summer 1908. Archiv Otto Breicha, Vienna

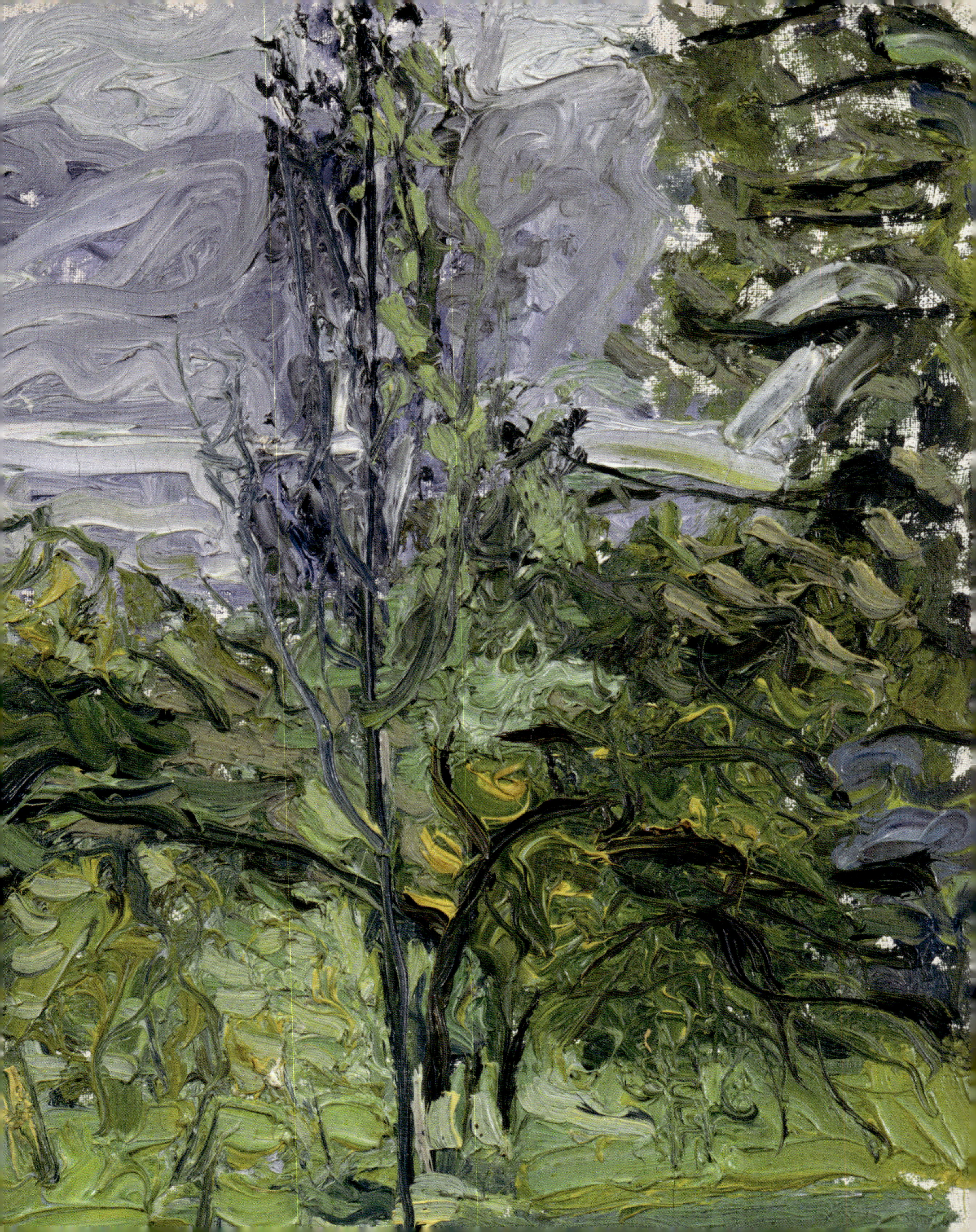

ACKNOWLEDGMENTS

Albertina, Vienna
Tanja Angermann, Vienna
Karen Angne, Munich
Arnold Schönberg Center, Vienna
Art Installation Design, New York
Belvedere, Vienna
Antonia Bryan, New York
Matti Bunzl, Vienna
Elliot Chiu, Washington D.C.
Raymond Coffer, London
Philipp Demandt, Frankfurt
Markus Denning, New York
Fay Duftler, New York
Sonja Eiböck, Vienna
Sabine Frohmader, Munich
Galerie St. Etienne, New York
Andrea Glatz, Vienna
Richard Grubman, Cambridge
Judith Hudson, New York
Jane Kallir, New York
Ingrid Kastel, Vienna
Peter de Kimpe, Amsterdam
Karola Kraus, Vienna
Diethard Leopold, Vienna
Elisabeth Leopold, Vienna
Leopold Museum, Vienna
Michael Lesh, New York
Jill Lloyd, Paris
Jane Michael, Munich
Eva Michel, Vienna
Caroline Mortimer, Cambridge
Angelika Möser, Vienna
Museum moderner Kunst, Vienna
Therese Muxeneder, Vienna
Oberösterreichisches Landesmuseum, Linz
Vlasta Odell, New York
Beverly Parsons, New York
Ingrid Pfeiffer, Frankfurt
Ernst Ploil, Vienna
Kornelia Pollek, Linz
Ellen Price, New York
Gerda Ridler, Linz
Jerry Rivera, New York
Stella Rollig, Vienna
Katharina Schendl, Vienna
Schirn Kunsthalle, Frankfurt
Lawrence Schoenberg, Los Angeles
Klaus Albrecht Schröder, Vienna
Franz Smola, Vienna
Maria Sitte, Frankfurt
Monica Strinu, Vienna
Elizabeth Szancer, New York
Wien Museum, Vienna
Karol Winiarczyk, Vienna
Hans-Peter Wipplinger, Vienna
Tom Zoufaly, New York

Small Landscape at Traunsee, August 1907, oil on canvas. Richard Grubman and Caroline Mortimer

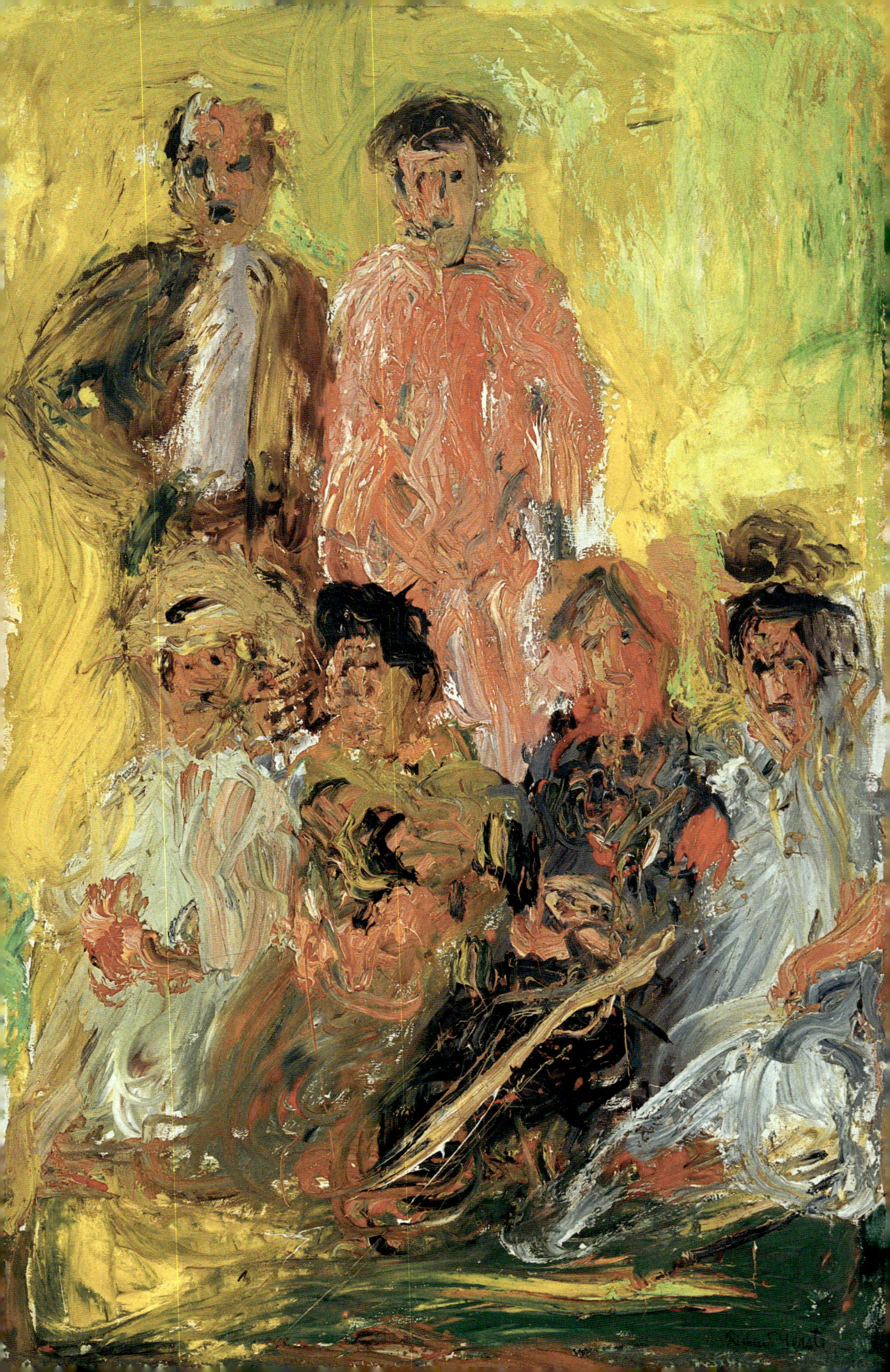

INGRID PFEIFFER

Richard Gerstl: An Overview

One wanted to be an artist around the turn of the century . . . there were so many who preferred being unhappy to not being a genius.[1]

Rudolf Kassner

1
Richard Gerstl, *Group Portrait with Schönberg*, late July 1908 (ca. July 23, 1908), oil on canvas. Kunsthaus Zug, Stiftung Sammlung Kamm

Who was Richard Gerstl, and why are so many artists and aficionados overwhelmed by storms of enthusiasm when his name is mentioned today, more than 100 years after his death? Gerstl died at the age of twenty-five and left behind an oeuvre of quite modest dimensions comprising some seventy identified works, of which only about sixty have survived. Yet he is described today as the "first Austrian Expressionist"[2] and mentioned in the same breath as Gustav Klimt, Egon Schiele, and Oskar Kokoschka as one of the most significant artists in Vienna in the early years of the twentieth century. Gerstl anticipated much of what would not be fully articulated until much later in the history of art. He died at his own hand in 1908, the year in which Kokoschka presented his first major exhibition in Vienna. And it was not until 1909 that Schiele first gained public attention with his remarkable works.

Gerstl's wild group portraits completed during the summer of 1908 [Cat. nos. 79–80] represent a radical departure from the style of his own era. Indeed, they actually call to mind the paintings of Willem de Kooning and the Abstract Expressionists of the 1950s.[3] "Richard Gerstl's 1908 portrait of the Schönberg family was not a painting, but an explosion, but since it took place in Austria, it was inaudible and has really remained invisible to this day," wrote the sculptor Fritz Wotruba in 1962.[4]

Was Gerstl the "archetype of the angry young man"?[5] A "neurotic Narcissus" who longed to be recognized in his brilliance, yet took every opportunity to let those around him know that they could not hold a candle to him, anyway?[6] According to some contemporaries, he was as self-assured and resolute as he was "nervous" and unstable, and thus entirely a child of his times. It is hardly possible to examine his art without reference to the circumstances of his brief life, which bore above all the indelible imprint of his ties with the equally radical composer Arnold Schönberg and the latter's wife Mathilde.[7]

That notwithstanding, the following discussion will focus above all on his portraiture, which is both heterogeneous and resistant to hasty interpretation, a group full of impressive highlights and pioneering innovations, but also of conventional elements—the output of an artist who was clearly still searching. The word "fragment" appears often even in the earliest reviews of the first exhibitions of Gerstl's works in Vienna and Berlin in 1931–32.[8] Only a single letter written by Gerstl has survived [Fig. 2], and there are no other written records that could shed light on his thoughts and ideas. He allegedly destroyed all written materials shortly before committing suicide. All we know about his opinions and attitudes is what we learn from the comments of a few contemporaries, most notably the recollections of his older brother, Alois,[9] and statements by fellow students and studio colleagues.[10]

Differentiation and Rebellion

According to those who knew him, Gerstl was firmly convinced of the quality of his own art and believed that he was pursuing "entirely new paths," as he emphasized in a letter in which he underlined the words by his professor twice. Nonetheless, he never exhibited his work during his lifetime, nor did he sell any of his pictures, although he received portrait commissions from friends. Yet even these portraits usually failed to please and remained in Gerstl's possession.[11] His progress in life was marked from the outset by rejection and relegation to the status of an outsider, from his school days to his brief academic career at Vienna's Academy of Fine Arts.[12] Although he attempted to identify kindred spirits among the artists in Vienna, Gerstl evidently found no one (at first) who was pursuing similar goals. The public did not begin to perceive Kokoschka (like Gerstl, an early Expressionist in Vienna) as an "*Oberwildling*" (super savage)[13] until after Gerstl's death. Gerstl was offered only three opportunities to participate in an exhibition in the course of his short career as a painter, and none of these was ever realized. In two cases, the responses of others were to blame, as they feared a scandal. It was Gerstl himself who turned down the third offer when he realized that Klimt had been invited to participate in the same exhibition.[14]

In order to illustrate the true extent to which Gerstl's attitude and style differed from that of his contemporaries, it will be helpful to take a brief look at the context in which they were embedded. Vienna differed in a number of ways from other major metropolitan centers of the art world, such as Paris and Berlin. The rapid progress of industrialization in the nineteenth century generated significant social tensions,[15] prompting many artists to abandon previously customary myths and allegories and look instead for new, more realistic images in order to describe the everyday circumstances of the different social classes.

That was not so in Vienna. The path from the overburdened history paintings of the "painter prince" Hans Makart led directly to the Vienna Secession, which, in spite of the innovations introduced by Klimt and the Wiener Werkstätte, ultimately remained a form of art for the upper class. In Klimt's art, nineteenth-century Symbolism was united with the pictorial programs of a strong artistic personality.[16] Although the Secession bore the clear imprint of a focus on social reform and education in its early years,[17] the idea of the *Gesamtkunstwerk*—the total work of art—faded as time passed. The costly materials and refined aesthetics ultimately appealed to an enlightened yet exclusive, extremely wealthy, and well-educated target group. The quasi-religious belief in the redemption of mankind by art[18] degenerated progressively into a mere matter of style.

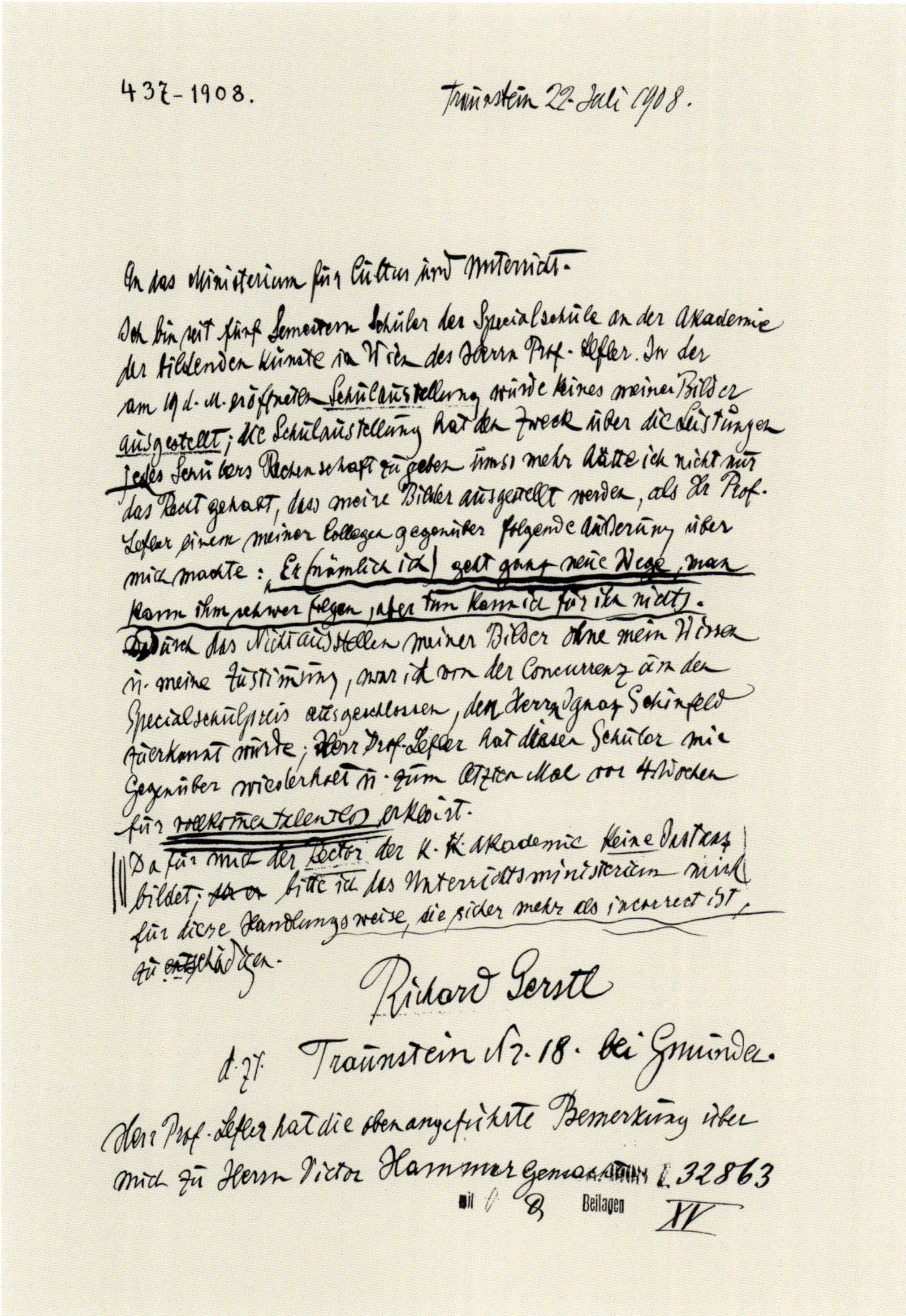
437-1908.

Traunstein 22. Juli 1908.

An das Ministerium für Cultus und Unterricht.

Ich bin seit fünf Semestern Schüler der Specialschule an der Akademie der bildenden Künste in Wien des Herrn Prof. Lefler. In der am 19. d. M. eröffneten Schulausstellung wurde keines meiner Bilder ausgestellt; die Schulausstellung hat den Zweck über die Leistungen jedes Semesters Rechenschaft zu geben umso mehr hätte ich nicht nur das Recht gehabt, dass meine Bilder ausgestellt werden, als Hr. Prof. Lefler einem meiner Collegen gegenüber folgende Äußerung über mich machte: Er (nämlich ich) geht ganz neue Wege, man kann ihm schwer folgen, aber tun kann ich für ihn nichts. Durch das Nichtausstellen meiner Bilder ohne mein Wissen u. meine Zustimmung, war ich von der Concurrenz um den Specialschulpreis ausgeschlossen, der Herrn Ignaz Schönfeld zuerkannt wurde; Herr Prof. Lefler hat diesen Schüler mir gegenüber wiederholt u. zum letzten Mal vor 4 Wochen für vollkommen talentlos erklärt.

Da für mich der Rector der k. k. Akademie keine Instanz bildet, bitte ich das Unterrichtsministerium mich für diese Handlungsweise, die sicher mehr als incorrect ist, zu entschädigen.

Richard Gerstl

d. Z. Traunstein Nr. 18. bei Gmunden.

Herr Prof. Lefler hat die obenangeführte Bemerkung über mich zu Herrn Victor Hammer gemacht.

Z. 32863 mit 0 Beilagen XV

2
Richard Gerstl, letter of complaint to the Ministery of Culture and Education, July 22, 1908.
Academy of Fine Arts Vienna, University Archive

3
Richard Gerstl, ca. 1902–03, photograph, Archiv Otto Breicha, Vienna

4
Richard Gerstl, *Fragment of a Full-Length Self-Portrait, Laughing*, detail, ca. 1904. Kunsthaus Zug, Stiftung Sammlung Kamm [Cat. no. 11]

Although Gerstl's oeuvre contains works that can be classified according to traditional genres, such as portraits, nudes, and landscapes, the manner in which they were realized indicates that he was intent upon exploring new terrain, both stylistically and psychologically. He rejected "everything that smacked of compulsion, discipline, and convention."[19] The contrast between Gerstl and the artists of the Vienna Secession could hardly be more pronounced, as the differences are reflected not only in aspects of style, but in matters of content as well. Gerstl did not deal with allegorical themes of the kind found in Klimt's art, and he had no interest whatsoever in applied art or graphic design; it was his fundamental attitude toward the concept of beauty that was of overriding importance. The theories advanced by members of the Secession were based on an entirely stylized, aesthetic approach to all areas of life, in contrast to which Gerstl's works are direct and devoid of symbolism and literary references.

We also find marked instances of dissonance in Gerstl's compositions—parallels to Schönberg's atonal music are clearly identifiable.[20] The "polemical core of his art," which embraced a new "aesthetics of ugliness"[21] and which can only be described with reference to a definition of "beauty," was a device Gerstl shared with many Expressionist artists. Kokoschka was later accused of taking a "barbaric plunge into ugliness," for example.[22] Gerstl presumably did not deliberately intend to shock people; he simply painted in opposition to certain rules, instinctively and without direct models—at least in his late gestural group portraits [Cat. nos. 79–80]. There is no evidence of the development of Expressionist theory in his case.

The rigid conservatism that prevailed in Vienna "posed no social questions and rejected the need for rethinking processes, preferring instead to ignore problems."[23] Accordingly, the profound sense of discontent that emerged under the influence of this widespread practice of repression

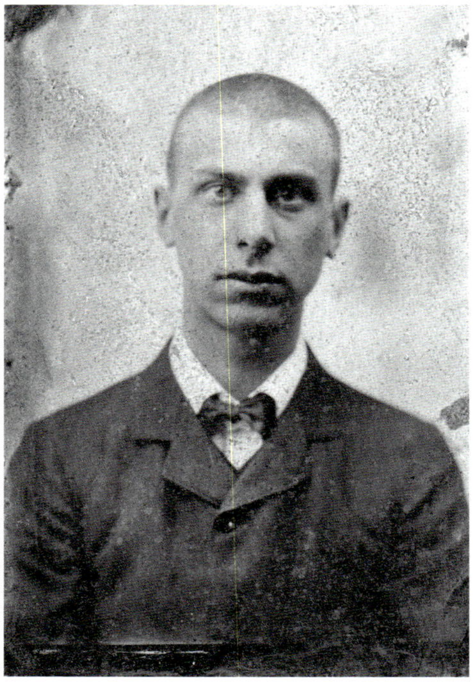

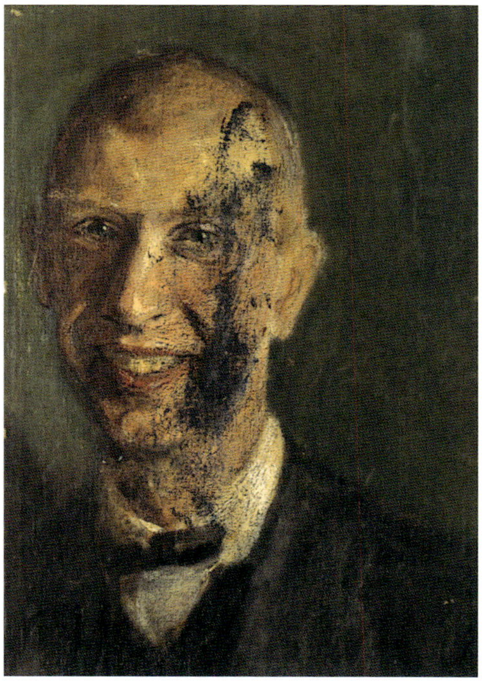

was discussed and categorized as pathological in Freud's writings on psychoanalysis. Gerstl was one of the few artists who purchased and read Freud's *The Interpretation of Dreams* immediately after its publication in 1900.[24] His interest in such authors as August Strindberg, Frank Wedekind, and Arthur Schnitzler also clearly indicates that he was concerned with the critical, realistic representation of existing relationships. In Austria, fissures and social tensions were addressed much earlier in literature than in art.[25] Gerstl appears to have registered the underlying tensions of his age in the manner of a seismograph.

Self-Appraisal and Self-Exposure

Gerstl realized some twenty self-portraits, seventeen of which have survived. In doing so he not only joined the ranks of other Expressionist and Austrian artists—as did Schiele and Kokoschka after him—but also followed a long tradition of artists from Rembrandt to James Ensor. All these artists regarded themselves as outsiders, at least at certain times, and reacted to their "banishment" from the world in which they lived with extreme forms of self-immersion. It is interesting to note that, unlike Gerstl, Klimt, a highly successful artist and a well-known public figure, refused to paint any self-portraits at all.[26]

It is appropriate in Gerstl's case not only to examine his painted and drawn portraits but also to view them in relation to the few photographs taken during the same period. During phases in which Gerstl felt well and at ease with himself, he wore his hair in a normal length and actually had what might have been regarded in those days as a "hairstyle." During more troubled periods, he had his hair cut short, "convict-style"[27] [Figs. 3–5]. Kokoschka later resorted to this kind of radical differentiation as well [Fig. 6].[28]

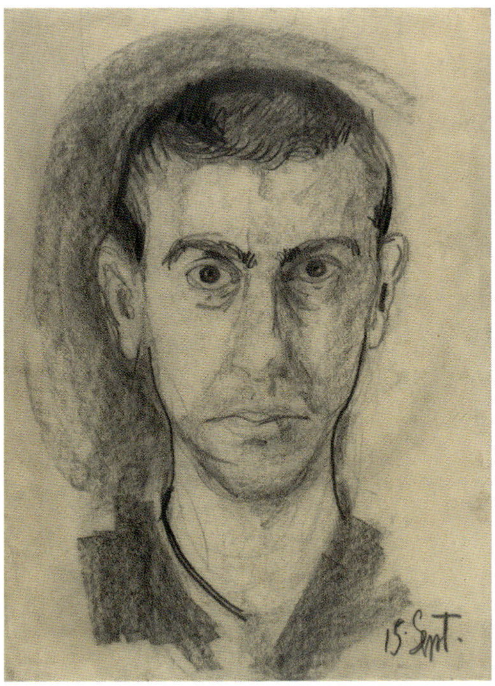

5
Richard Gerstl, *Self-Portrait*, September 15, 1907. Wien Museum [Cat. no. 60]

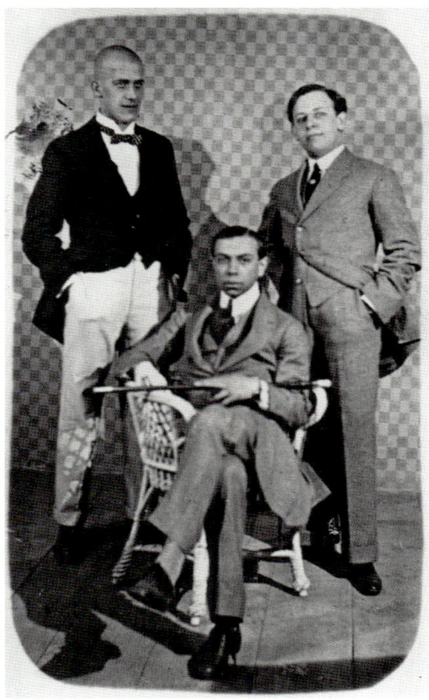

6
From left: Oskar Kokoschka, Max Oppenheimer (MOPP), and Ernst Reinhold, Vienna 1909, photograph, silver gelatin print on Baryta paper mounted on board. Universität für angewandte Kunst Wien, Kunstsammlung und Archiv, Oskar Kokoschka-Zentrum

7
Richard Gerstl, *Semi-Nude Self-Portrait*, 1902–04, oil on canvas. Leopold Museum, Vienna [Cat. no. 6]

In Gerstl's earliest self-portrait of 1902–04 [Cat. no. 6], which still exhibits the marked influence of Symbolism, he faces the viewer directly. The aura of the head against the atmospheric blue background, the radiant white body with the loincloth, and above all his intense gaze focused on the viewer are the most remarkable features of this "self-portrait as icon." A painter well-versed in art history, Gerstl dealt in this case with the iconography of Lazarus and Christ, the imagery of *Ecce Homo*. Here, the scorned artist-Christ exposes himself to the people. However, Gerstl cited and appropriated numerous props from a version of art history the young revolutionary had long since rejected. In spite of the fragility and vulnerability of the exposed body, this painting is an early, self-confident personal statement by an artist. The broad shoulders and the lucid, challenging gaze appeal for communication and almost for confrontation. In this and other self-portraits, Gerstl emphasized the asymmetrical placement of his eyes, which intensifies the sense of confrontation and challenge conveyed by this first self-portrait and early major work.

Several later self-portraits look as if Gerstl were experimenting with portraying himself in certain roles: as a dandy [Cat. no. 35]; as a traditional painter holding a palette and standing in front of a stove [Cat. no. 33]; and standing and in full figure, but in this case with an astoundingly reserved and insecure look on his face [Cat. no. 32]. He appears most radical, direct, and provocative in *Self-Portrait, Laughing* [Cat. no. 54], a major work completed in 1907. Here, the

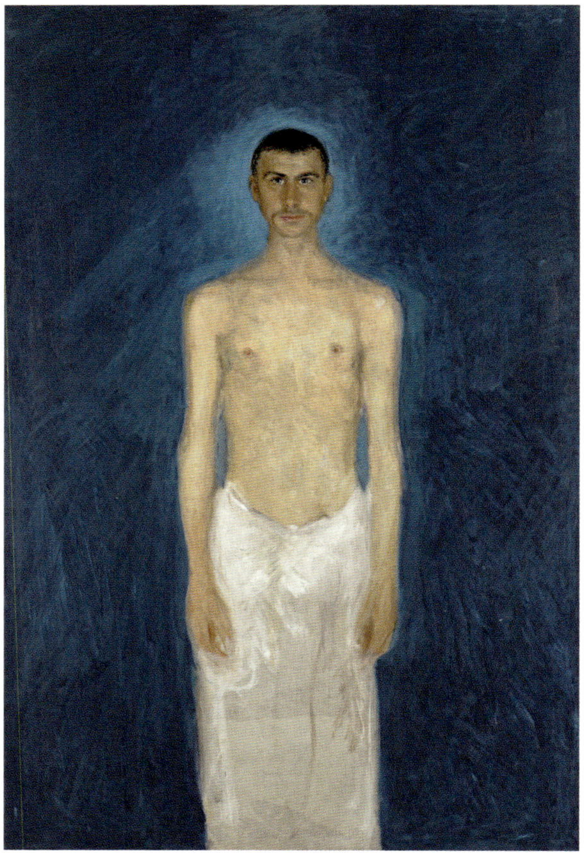

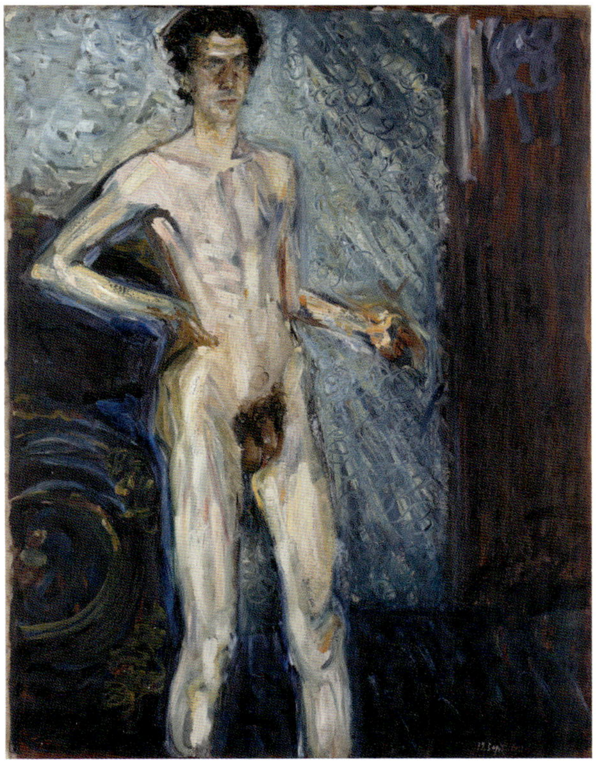

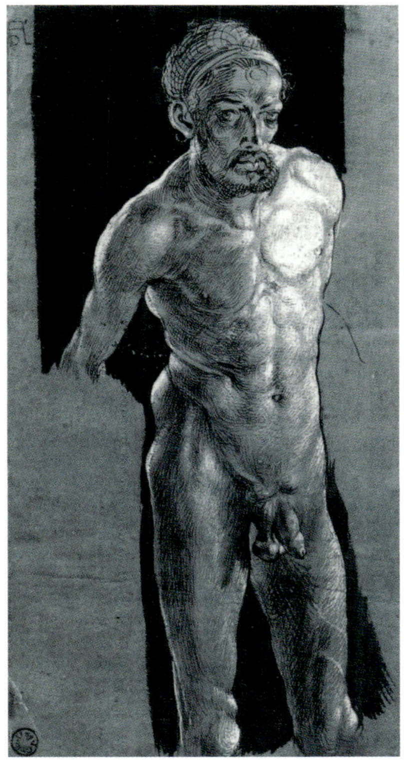

8
Richard Gerstl, *Nude Self-Portrait*, September 12, 1908, oil on canvas. Leopold Museum, Vienna [Cat. no. 86]

9
Albrecht Dürer, *Nude Study (Self-Portrait)*, Nuremberg years, ca. 1500–05, pen and brush on green primed paper. SWKK, Schlossmuseum, Weimar

10
Paula Modersohn-Becker, *Self-Portrait on Her Sixth Wedding Anniversary*, 1906, oil on board. Museen Böttcherstraße, Bremen, Paula Modersohn-Becker Museum

young man, often at odds with his outward appearance,[29] mocks and ridicules himself, the artist and fool with the almost crazed laugh—this also in keeping with a long tradition that extends from Rembrandt to Corinth.[30] Gerstl had already depicted himself with his head shaved long before in *Full-Length Self-Portrait, Laughing* [Cat. no. 11], which has survived only as a fragment. He later cut the painting apart and painted his portrait of *Alexander von Zemlinsky* [Cat. no. 77] on the reverse. This fragment, which Gerstl rejected as a "work," is a particularly revealing example of "auto-aggression,"[31] as Gerstl not only cut his figure, he also disfigured half of the face with paint—a disquieting and disturbing sight for viewers.

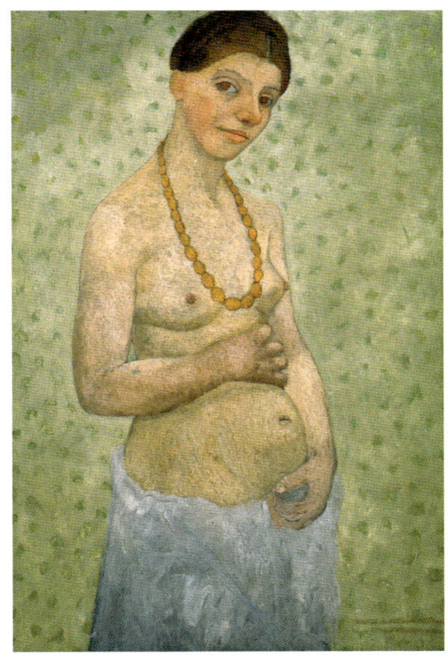

Gerstl's last self-portrait, executed in September 1908 [Cat. no. 86], has often been described as the radical finale of the series of self-portraits. It was radical because he painted himself completely nude[32]—the first major artist to do so since Dürer [Fig. 9]—and because in it he brought the painting style of his last creative phase to its final culmination. In this work, however, Gerstl refuses to communicate with the viewer; he turns to one side, his gaze dull and obscured. He would hang himself in his studio just a few weeks later.

Only one other contemporary artist has ever interpreted the nude self-portrait as radically as Gerstl. In 1907, Paula Modersohn-Becker painted herself as a pregnant woman with a naked torso [Fig. 10], a violation of two taboos at once by an artist who, virtually unnoticed by the art world, realized major innovations (and numerous self-portraits) and who did not attain the fame she deserved until after her premature death.

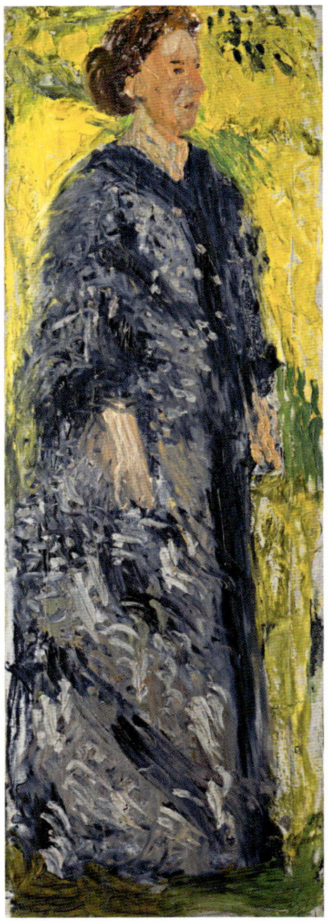

11
Richard Gerstl, *Mathilde Schönberg in the Garden*, July 1908, oil on canvas. Leopold Museum, Vienna [Cat. no. 78]

Klaus-Albrecht Schröder has described the dominant theme that emerges above all in Gerstl's self-portraits as the loneliness of the artist.[33] It occurs in the work of many other artists, including Rembrandt, Ensor, and Modersohn-Becker, in entire series of self-portraits, but Gerstl took it a step further, in that his actual and, more importantly, his perceived outsider status drove him to the last resort of suicide.

Gerstl and Women

Second in number only to his self-portraits are Gerstl's portraits of his mistress-to-be, Mathilde Schönberg, of which he did at least seven. Remarkable in these works above all are his restraint in the depiction of Mathilde and the absence of the passion and immediacy that characterize his intense self-portraits. Gerstl experimented with the style and iconography of the Mathilde motif for two years—from the stiff portrait of Mathilde and her daughter Trudi in the summer of 1906 [Cat. no. 16] to the highly unconventional interpretation of the ornamental style of the Wiener Werkstätte in *Portrait of Mathilde Schönberg in the Studio* [Cat. no. 67], to his obvious homage to Van Gogh in *Mathilde Schönberg in the Garden* [Cat. no. 78]. Gerstl also responded to the works of the Nabis artists Pierre Bonnard and Édouard Vuillard in the narrow vertical format typical of Japanese art that were on exhibit in Vienna in 1903.[34]

Yet in contrast to most of his contemporaries, Gerstl was not primarily a painter of women. In no other city was the theme of women treated so excessively in all conceivable variations—wife, whore, witch, vamp, Madonna, mother, etc.—as in the art of Vienna around 1900. Common to nearly all images of women (with either positive or negative connotations) was the idea that a woman is not an autonomous individual, but rather a symbol and a projection screen. To a certain extent, the real power struggle between the genders (the first women at universities and as instructors or influential clients), and the power of mothers (a theme in works by Klimt, Schiele, Gerstl, and Kokoschka), was reflected *ex negativo* in numerous works. It is no coincidence that a particularly large number of publications that propagated an especially negative and degrading image of women appeared in reaction to feminist tendencies shortly after the turn of the century.[35]

It has been demonstrated that Gerstl read and commented on Otto Weininger's anti-feminist book entitled *Sex and Character* (1903), but not a single one of the ideas proposed in Weininger's essay can be found in his artwork. He painted *Mathilde Schönberg* [Cat. no. 53], *Henryka Cohn* [Cat. no. 73], and *Smaragda Berg* [Cat. no. 22], the sister of Alban Berg and a gifted and successful pianist, with as much expressive power, love of detail, and respect as his male models. They wear progressive "reformist clothing" in these portraits, dresses that hang freely from the shoulder without corsets of the kind that were in vogue in Vienna around 1900, albeit mostly in artists' circles and less often in broader segments of society. Emilie Flöge, Klimt's long-standing girlfriend and muse, ran a large fashion boutique in Vienna and designed dresses of that kind.[36]

The subjects in Gerstl's portraits of women never look strange or threatening, nor do they ever look truly seductive. Even the only and presumably last of Gerstl's paintings of Mathilde as a nude figure [Cat. no. 87] is painted with extraordinary restraint, and the face is devoid of all distinctive features. Gerstl directed all of his destructive impulses towards himself and never sought to use women as projection screens for his own insecurities and neuroses, as did many of his contemporaries.[37]

His mother appears in an unfinished work [Cat. no. 84] that Gerstl began shortly before his death and abandoned with the explanation that it lacked verisimilitude. A number of scholars have insisted that Gerstl's close relationship to his mother was the source of his affinity for older women, and that Mathilde's features resembled those of his mother.[38]

The Quest for a Style

Painting with "meter-long brushes,"[39] scarifications on roughened surfaces, and traces left by the stem of the brush—all precursors of a gestural style of action art—are typical of Gerstl's experiments, which were practically without parallel in his time. He often worked without preliminary sketches, with great haste, sometimes gesticulating wildly, passionately, like the "full-blooded painter" he was.[40] Contrary to what was commonly taught during his lifetime, Gerstl worked without preliminary drawings or tempera sketches, and that, too, must have been viewed by his professors as a provocation.

The most confusing factor in the development of Gerstl's style between 1902 and 1908 is that it lacks a clearly recognizable sequential order, as would normally be expected. Instead, "progressive" phases alternate with periods marked by a more conventional style. The reasons for this are surely also rooted in Gerstl's biography. In order to please his clients—most notably the group of people associated with Arnold Schönberg—Gerstl opted for more conventional stylistic approaches than those he adopted in the works that were obviously painted only for himself. It has been said that Gerstl ordinarily avoided showing his works to studio colleagues or visitors.[41]

More than one-third of the surviving works by Gerstl are landscapes, most of which were painted at Traunsee in the summer of 1907. Gerstl painted the works in this series freestyle, so to speak, with thick applications of paint. They are full of "loops, strokes, spots, spirals, and whorls."[42] His earliest landscapes were panoramas with skies and horizons [Cat. no. 14], while the later ones often feature details in close-up rendered in a wild, gestural, pastose style, the very opposite of objects of meditation."[43]

Gerstl employed certain stylistic elements, such as short brushstrokes, for entire compositions and sometimes only in parts of a work, as for example in two major works completed in 1907, *Portrait of the Artist's Father, Emil Gerstl* [Cat. no. 18] and the portrait of his older brother entitled *Portrait of the Reserve Lieutenant Alois Gerstl* [Cat. no. 19]. Here he used solid areas for the figure of his brother, whose dark, sculptural body stands out even more distinctly from the shimmering interior bathed in sunlight. In other works, the short brushstrokes distributed liberally over the surface form ornamental patterns, as in *Portrait of Henryka Cohn* [Cat. no. 73], or evoke a disquieting eruptive effect as a pattern surrounding the head in *Self-Portrait, Laughing* [Cat. no. 54]. Although Pointillism "was briefly en vogue" in Vienna,[44] and Gerstl had undoubtedly visited the grand exhibition devoted to the history of Impressionism, he made brilliant use of the corresponding stylistic repertoire but did not commit himself to it for very long. Since Gerstl read a great deal and concerned himself constantly with aesthetic and philosophical theories,[45] there is no reason to assume that he failed to grasp the principles of Pointillism[46] and applied them only referentially and sporadically for that reason. Gerstl made use of the radiance of numerous brushstrokes in primary colors set close together in the aforementioned portrait of his father in order to lend greater emphasis to the theme of the light-bathed portrait in a window. Long, vigorous, energetic brushstrokes are dominant in many other works in which a different effect was to be evoked. Due to the lack of a clear line of stylistic development and the absence of dates, it remains difficult to view or grasp Gerstl's oeuvre as a coherent whole even today. Many aspects remain puzzling, and dates are based primarily on biographical sources.[47]

Did Gerstl regard "the act of painting as a battle"[48] in his late group portraits with Schönberg in the summer of 1908 [Cat. nos. 79–80]? Did he transpose "emotional arousal into the energy he needed to paint?"[49] The emerging independence of color that is already evident in the landscapes realized in the summer of 1907 [Cat. nos. 36–51] is intensified in these large, almost nihilistic group portraits to a degree of abstraction that Gerstl evidently found himself unable to pursue further. He returned to a less expressive style in the few works he completed in the autumn of 1908, shortly before his death [Cat. nos. 86–87].

The best and most unusual of Gerstl's works appear so fresh and immediate to us today because—regardless of the different styles, formats, colors, and compositions—they evoke a haunting and thus timeless effect. In the case of *The Sisters Karoline and Pauline Fey* [Cat. no. 12], critics have even spoken of "magic,"[50] as these two "beings" in their ghostly robes, without hands, feet, or real bodies, without real space or background, with their strange facial expressions and huge, black pupils, evoke an eerie, dreamlike effect. They look almost surreal. Anyone who attempts to describe what and how Gerstl was painting here must begin by noting the things he didn't paint. Only by means of reduction is the magical effect created.

The whole dark-hued composition is reminiscent of works by Édouard Manet, whose portrait of *Jeanne Duval* [Fig. 13] Gerstl would have seen at the Impressionist exhibition at the Vienna Secession in 1903,[51] yet Gerstl went even further than Manet in eliminating details in the pattern of the dress and the interior structure of the body and the background. In his own time, Manet was constantly criticized for the ugliness, flatness, and lack of atmosphere of his compositions. Gerstl would have been exposed to even harsher criticism if he had presented such works in public.

Gerstl was not genuinely interested in matters of style. We know just how skillfully he could and would switch painting techniques if the subject demanded it. In the case of the portraits, we inevitably gain the impression that the shifts in style were always closely related to the individual subject and the way in which he chose to characterize the person. The translucence of the portrait of *Alexander Zemlinsky* [Cat. no. 77]—bright, with extremely loose, summary brushstrokes—describes a figure in the process of withdrawing. It blends into the background, and the face exhibits virtually no distinctive features, seeming to withdraw along with the figure.

Only the right hand holding the walking stick, which points ahead at an angle along a dominant dark line, anchors the bright field of the body in the surrounding space.

Zemlinsky is also seated in bright light to Schönberg's left and is only vaguely recognizable in *Group Portrait with Schönberg* [Cat. no. 80]. Apparently, Gerstl's relationship with Schönberg and his "disciples" was no longer entirely untroubled—as Schönberg appears here as a threatening figure himself. Gerstl painted his mouth and eyes as black holes. That has the look of an act of reckoning with someone who at this point in time (late July 1908)[52] was evidently no longer the idol he had once been. The last group portraits resemble caricatures of family photographs [Cat. no. 79], or perhaps even of portraits of friends. The autonomy of color and form transgressed the psychological and aesthetic limits imposed by the times. And what Gerstl hoped to accomplish with these works, which would never have been accepted for exhibition at that time, remains a mystery.

We know very little about Gerstl's motivation, and the many attempts at reconstruction on the basis of statements by third parties ultimately amount to no more than speculation. All that remains are the works themselves and the often overwhelming effects they evoke, which continue to captivate viewers today. As a seismograph, not only of social tensions but also of personal disasters, the painter offered his final reckoning in his works.

12
Richard Gerstl, *The Sisters Karoline and Pauline Fey*, March/April 1905, oil on canvas. Belvedere, Vienna

13
Édouard Manet, *Lady with a Fan (Jeanne Duval)*, 1862, oil on canvas. Museum of Fine Arts, Budapest

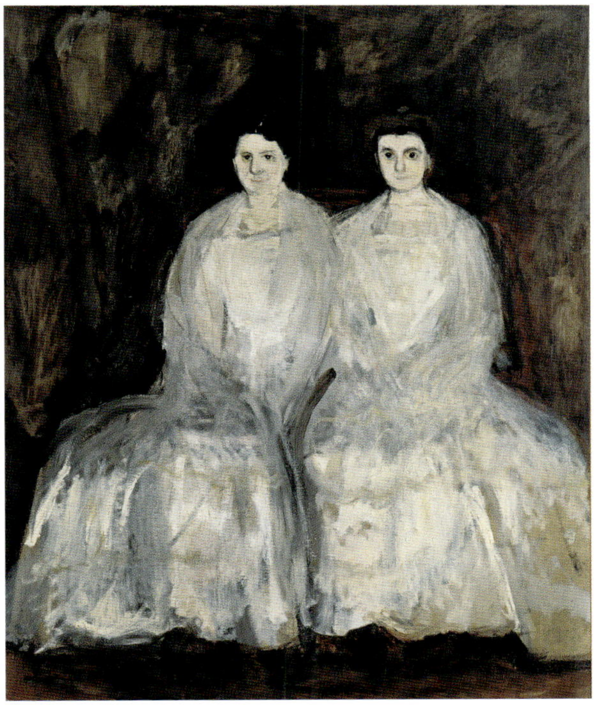

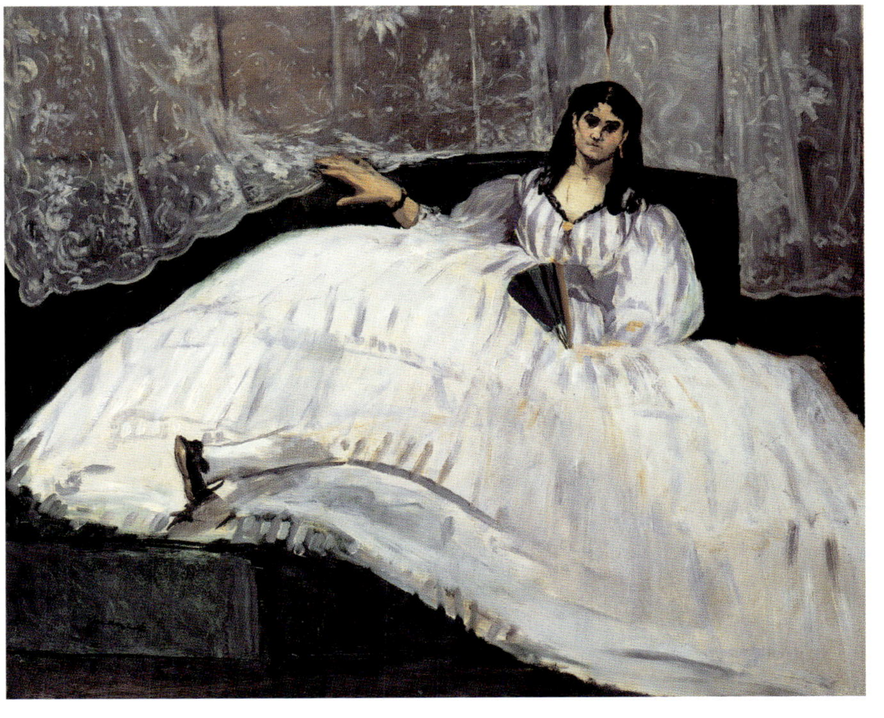

1 Rudolf Kassner, *Buch der Erinnerung* (Rentsch: Zurich, 1954), 123.

2 Raymond Coffer, *Richard Gerstl and Arnold Schönberg: A Reassessment of their Relationship (1906–1908) and Its Impact on their Artistic Works*, PhD diss., London, 2011, 2.

3 Jane Kallir, *Richard Gerstl, Oskar Kokoschka, Pioneers of Austrian Expressionism,* exh. cat. Galerie St. Etienne New York, 1992, 7.

4 Fritz Wotruba, "Wien erhält spät aber doch ein Museum des 20. Jahrhunderts," quoted from Matthias Haldemann, "Die Sammlung Kamm als Künstlersammlung. Wotrubas Dialog mit der Moderne," in: *Dialog mit der Moderne. Fritz Wotruba und die Sammlung Kamm* (Balmer: Zug, 1998), 40.

5 Antony Beaumont, *Alexander Zemlinsky: Biographie* (Zsolnay: Vienna, 2005), 246.

6 Diethard Leopold, "Der am Ast sägte. Richard Gerstl und das Phantasma des Künstler-Ich," in Tobias Natter (ed.), *Nackte Männer: Von 1800 bis heute*, exh. cat. Leopold Museum Vienna (Munich: Hirmer Verlag, 2012), 80.

7 See the article by Raymond Coffer in this catalogue, 38–44.

8 See the article by Jane Kallir in this catalogue, 46–50.

9 Alois Gerstl (1881–1961) was a bank clerk and an officer in the reserve. He is considered the most important source of personal information on Gerstl. He spoke with Otto Kallir-Nirenstein in 1931 and later with Otto Breicha. Cf. Otto Kallir, "Richard Gerstl (1883–1908) Beiträge zur Dokumentation seines Lebens und Werkes," in: *Mitteilungen der Österreichischen Galerie.* 18.1974, 125–193, and Otto Breicha, *Richard Gerstl, Bilder zur Person*, Salzburg, Verlag Galerie Welz 1991 and

Otto Breicha, *Gerstl und Schönberg—Eine Beziehung*, Salzburg, Verlag Galerie Welz 1993.

10 Including above all Waldemar Unger, his friend during his youth, of whom Gerstl painted two portraits, and his studio colleague Victor Hammer. Otto Kallir spoke with the latter around 1963, the records are held by the Galerie St. Etienne, New York. Unger's statements came through Gerstl's brother Alois and directly in conversation with Otto Breicha. Cf. Coffer 2011, 37.

11 "… nobody liked his pictures," wrote his studio colleague Victor Hammer; quoted and translated from Coffer 2011 (see note 2), 112.

12 Ibid., 59.

13 Ludwig Hevesi, *Altkunst—Neukunst: Wien 1894–1908* (Konegen: Vienna, 1909), 313.

14 Cf. Coffer 2011 (see note 2), 58.

15 Cf. Gabriele Koller, "Das Elend und der Schein. Wiener Gesellschaft um 1900," in: *Wien um 1900. Kunst und Kultur* (Christian Brandstätter: Vienna, 1985), 477–484.

16 Patrick Werkner, *Physis und Psyche: der österreichische Frühexpressionismus* (Herold: Vienna, 1986), 22.

17 Ibid., 41.

18 "The arts lead us to the ideal kingdom, in which we can find pure joy, pure happiness, and pure love." Text on the Klimt frieze at the Beethoven exhibition of the Vienna Secession 1902, quoted and translated from Werkner 1986 (see note 16), 22.

19 Werner Hofmann, *Moderne Malerei in Österreich* (Wolfrum: Vienna, 1965), 104.

20 See the article by Raymond Coffer in this catalogue, 38–44.

21 Klaus-Albrecht Schröder, *Richard Gerstl 1883–1908*, exh. cat. Kunstforum der Bank Austria, Vienna / Kunsthaus Zürich), Vienna 1993, 25.

22 Franz Servaes, "Ein Streifzug durch die Wiener Malerei," in: *Kunst und Künstler*, vol. 9, Berlin 1910–11, 587–598.

23 Eva Badura-Triska, "Die Früchte des Verdrängens. Radikale Körperkunst und gesamtkunstwerkhafte Erlösungskonzepte in der frühen Wiener Moderne und im Wiener Aktionismus," in: *Körper, Psyche und Tabu. Wiener Aktionismus und die frühe Wiener Moderne* (Walther König: Cologne, 2016), 11.

24 According to Victor Hammer in conversation with Otto Kallir, quoted and translated from Coffer 2011, 37.

25 Cf. André Schwarz, *Lustvolles Verschweigen und Enthüllen. Eine Poetik der Darstellung sexuellen Handelns in der Literatur der Wiener Moderne* (Marburg Verlag: Marburg, 2012).

26 Schröder 1993 (see note 21), 13.

27 Otto Breicha, *Richard Gerstl. Bilder zur Person: die Selbstdarstellungen und fotografischen Porträtaufnahmen Richard Gerstls* (Verlag Galerie Welz: Salzburg, 1991), 9.

28 Kokoschka depicted himself as a "wild man" with shaved head on the poster for the Berlin gallery Der Sturm. Cf. Werner J. Schweiger, *Der junge Kokoschka. Leben und Werk 1904–1914* (Christian Brandstätter: Vienna, 1983), 128.

29 "He was aware of how he looked, and he laughed about it; it was the laughter of desperation," explained Gerstl's friend and fellow student Victor Hammer in conversation with Otto Kallir, quoted and translated from Coffer 2011 (see note 2), 62.

30 Schröder 1993 (see note 21), 10–11.

31 Schröder 1993 (see note 21), 45.

32 That the naked male figure in the drawing located at Weimar Schlossmuseum was actually a self-portrait of Dürer was not established until 1906. Cf. Gemma Blackshaw, "The Jewish Christ: Problems of Self-Presentation and Socio-Cultural Assimiliation in Richard Gerstl's Self-Portraiture," in *Oxford Art Journal*, vol. 29, no. 1 (2006), 46.

33 Schröder 1993 (see note 21), 15.

34 Elfriede Wiltschnigg, *"Das Rätsel Weib." Das Bild der Frau in Wien um 1900* (Reimer: Berlin, 2001), 215–16.

35 See, for example, Paul Julius Möbius, Über den physiologischen Schwachsinn des Weibes (Marhold: Halle, 1900).

36 Flöge was a successful businesswoman and employed as many as eighty seamstresses. Cf. Anna Katharina Ganzenbacher, *Mieder und Reformkleid. Zum Wandel der Damenmode von 1900 bis 1918*, diploma thesis, Graz 2009, 86–90.

37 Weininger, who was of Jewish descent himself, equated Jewishness and femininity and constructed a hate-ridden hierarchy of moral-masculine versus urge-driven feminine attributes. His abstruse theories and his suicide at the age of twenty-three suggest the influence of deep-seated mental problems. Cf. Renate Berger, *Malerinnen auf dem Weg ins 20. Jahrhundert. Kunstgeschichte als Sozialgeschichte* (DuMont: Cologne, 1982), 73–78.

38 Wiltschnigg 2001 (see note 34), 216.

39 Wolfgang Born, "Richard Gerstl," in: *Belvedere. Monatsschrift für Sammler und Kunstfreunde*, vol. 10 no. 11, 1931, 155.

40 Werkner 1986 (see note 16), 70.

41 Based on a remark by Gerstl's studio colleague Victor Hammer, cited in Coffer 2011 (see note 2), 58.

42 Schröder 1993 (see note 21), 116.

43 Schröder 1993 (see note 21), 114.

44 G. Tobias Natter, "'Weltenstaub und wirbelnde Atome'—Zur Rezeption des Pointillismus in Wien," in: *Farben des Lichts. Paul Signac und der Beginn der Moderne von Matisse bis Mondrian*, exh. cat. Westfälisches Landesmuseum für Kunst und

Kulturgeschichte, Münster / Musée de Grenoble / Kunstsammlungen zu Weimar, Ostfildern 1996, 358.

45 According to Victor Hammer, cf. Coffer 2011 (see note 2), 37.

46 Schröder 1993 (see note 21), 28.

47 Cf. Coffer 2011 (see note 2), 3.

48 Wieland Schmied, "Widerschein und Dunkelheit," in: *Wien. Spektrum einer Stadt* (Biederstein Verlag: Munich, 1971), 281.

49 Werkner 1986 (see note 16), 70.

50 Ibid., 89.

51 Schröder 1993 (see note 21), 46 and Coffer 2011 (see note 2), 77.

52 Coffer 2011 (see note 2), 255.

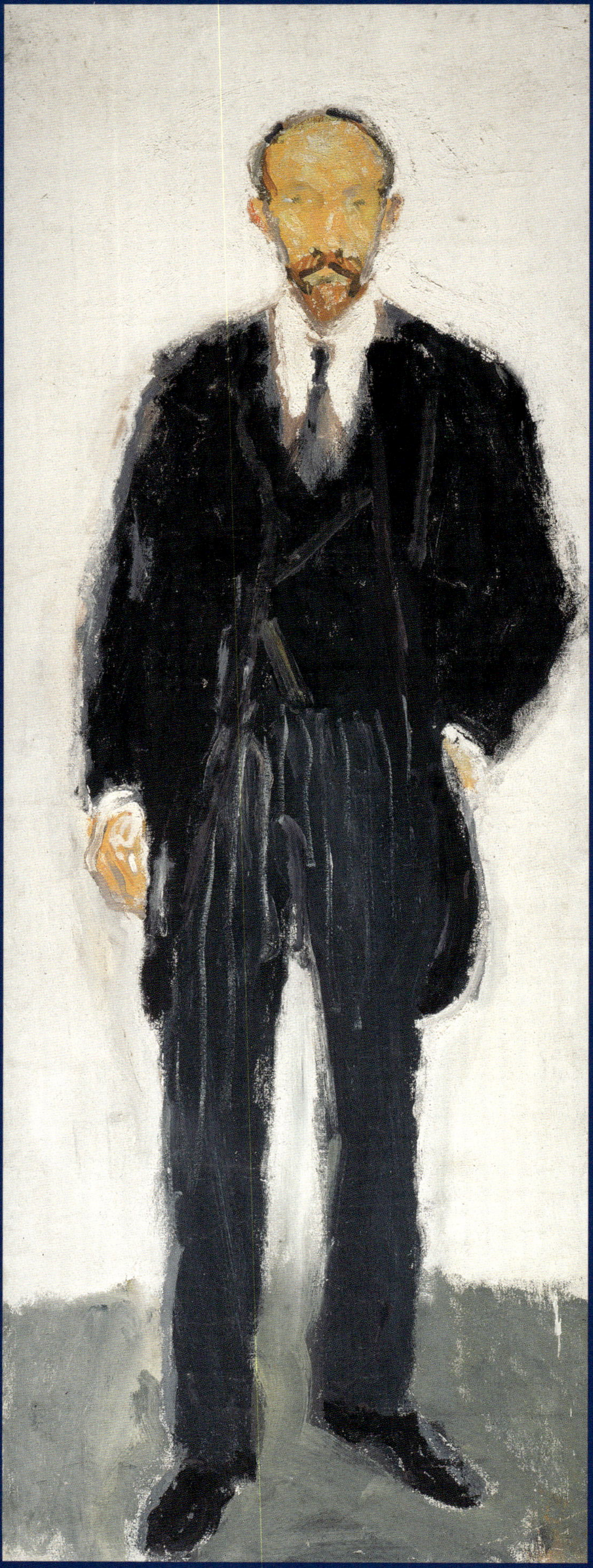

JILL LLOYD
KAROL WINIARCZYK

Richard Gerstl's Internationalism

Richard Gerstl has been described as "the most French" of the Viennese Expressionists;[1] he can be called, more accurately, the most international. Whereas his younger compatriots, Oskar Kokoschka and Egon Schiele, positioned themselves—at least initially—in relation to Gustav Klimt and the Vienna Secession, Gerstl proudly refused to exhibit his work alongside Klimt's,[2] rebelling with equal intensity against both his professors at the Vienna Academy of Fine Arts and the fashionable Viennese modernists associated with the Secession. Gerstl aligned himself instead with the inspirational figures of international modernism who were exhibited in Vienna in the early years of the twentieth century, taking his bearings, as we shall see, from Edvard Munch, Ferdinand Hodler, and Vincent van Gogh, among others.

What does this tell us about this highly talented young artist's ambitions and his relationship with Expressionism? In a very similar time frame to the Brücke artists in Dresden, who drew on exactly the same Post-Impressionist sources and "called together all youth [. . .] who embody the future [. . .] to fight for freedom of movement and life [. . .] in opposition to the older, established forces,"[3] Gerstl took a rebellious internationalist stance in an era when art, particularly of the academic kind, was closely aligned with the chauvinist establishment. Gerstl broke with Heinrich Lefler—the liberal Academy professor who was the only one of his teachers to recognize his talent—because he condemned the latter's involvement in the 1908 *Kaiserjubiläumshuldigungsfest*, believing that the celebration of Emperor Franz Josef's 60th jubilee (in which, incidentally, the young Kokoschka also participated), was to be avoided at all costs by anyone who called himself a genuine artist.[4] Gerstl adopted a self-consciously oppositional—and sometimes self-destructive—position at a moment when internationalism was associated with progressive, anti-establishment ideas. Although Gerstl would most likely have been unaware of parallel developments in Germany, internationalism was indeed a spirit of freedom that swept through the Expressionist movement, climaxing in the 1912 Sonderbund Exhibition in Cologne which proposed a grand survey of new European art rooted in Post-Impressionism. The *Blauer Reiter Almanac* (1911), edited by Vasily Kandinsky and Franz Marc and a key document of Expressionism, also embodied an essentially synthetic worldview, bringing together the art of different epochs and nationalities and forging a link between different art forms, especially painting and music. The almanach symbolized the idealistic aspiration of the Expressionist avant-garde to hold together a world that was increasingly threatened by the divisive nationalist tensions that eventually erupted in the apocalyptic destruction of World War I.

1
Richard Gerstl, *Professor Ernst Diez*, autumn 1906, tempera and oil on canvas. Belvedere, Vienna [Cat. no. 21]

Although Gerstl ended his short life well before these events, the synthetic worldview of Expressionism was rooted in turn-of-the-century Secession culture, which Gerstl both opposed and particpated in. The Vienna Secession not only mounted numerous exhibitions of modern European art, architecture, and design; it also fostered the dialogue between art and music. Arnold Schönberg, who befriended both Gerstl and Kandinsky, emerged from this world. The café culture of Vienna also nurtured the interchange of ideas between artists, musicians, and writers; these were places where the latest art magazines and reviews could be consulted, as was the art bookshop and gallery run by Hugo Heller, where Gerstl most likely purchased his first edition of Sigmund Freud's *The Interpretation of Dreams* (1899). He could also have visited talks, concerts, and exhibitions organized by Heller, including a previously unrecorded presentation of Edvard Munch's work.[5] Munch's 1894 *Portrait of Stanislaw Przybyszewski*, [Fig. 2] with its haunting head set against a thinly painted white background, which featured in Heller's show, may indeed have been one of the sources of inspiration for the painting style of Gerstl's 1906 *Professor Ernst Diez* [Cat. no. 21],[6] and for his self-portrait drawings.

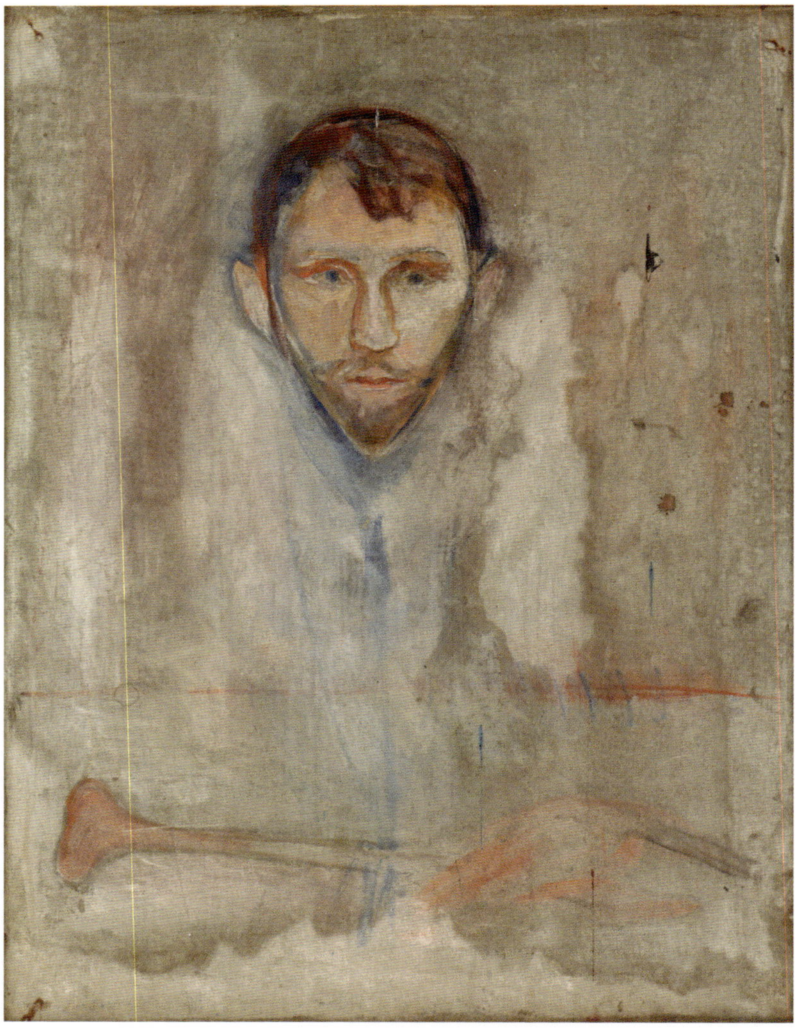

2
Edvard Munch, *Stanislaw Przybyszewski*, 1894, tempera on canvas. Munch Museum, Oslo

During the period 1901–04, when Gerstl broke off his studies at the Academy to pursue his passion for languages, philosophy, literature, and music, he aligned himself with the cutting-edge intellectual trends of his times. Not only Freud and Otto Weininger, but also fashionable Scandinavian and German authors such as Henrik Ibsen and Frank Wedekind caught his attention, alongside the music of his contemporaries, like Schönberg.[7] Gerstl's visual self-education followed suit, to the extent that echoes of international artists whom he saw in the Secession exhibitions clearly emerge in his work.[8] This essay explores Gerstl's main Post-Impressionist sources, bearing in mind that his assimilation of international modernism gave rise neither to paraphrase nor pastiche but rather to startlingly original reinterpretations, which often fuse more than one source of inspiration. Eventually, hand in hand with the biographical factors that are detailed elsewhere in this catalogue, Gerstl's stylistic experimentation resulted in the radical nonconformity of his 1908 figure paintings. For all the extreme originality of the works Gerstl painted in the months before his suicide, his revolutionary Expressionism was grounded in an intense engagement with international modern art.

Munch and Hodler

Gerstl's knowledge of Edvard Munch is a subject of debate among Gerstl experts, not least because this relates to the dating of a breakthrough work, Gerstl's *Semi-Nude Self-Portrait* [Cat. no. 6], in which the young artist presents himself to the world in a Christ-like or prophetic guise, stripped to the waist and surrounded by a nimbus of blue light. While Schröder suggests that the painting shows Gerstl adapting Munch's portrait style of the 1890s to "his own ends," taking paintings such as *Dagny Juell Przybyszewska* (1893) and *Self-Portrait in Hell* (1903) as his starting point, Raymond Coffer rightly points out that neither of these works by Munch was exhibited in Vienna nor readily available in illustration.[9]

Munch's fame had nevertheless spread quickly through the German-speaking world following the scandalous closure of his exhibition at the Association of Berlin Artists in 1892, which firmly established his reputation as a rebel.[10] His first major showing in Vienna was in 1904, when twenty of his paintings were included in the 19th Secession exhibition, alongside some thirty-one paintings by Ferdinand Hodler, which constituted the controversial Swiss Symbolist artist's breakthrough to international fame.[11] Although Coffer favors an earlier date for Gerstl's *Semi-Nude Self-Portrait* (1902–03), its frontal pose and haunting atmosphere certainly echo works by Munch that Gerstl would have seen at the 1904 Secession exhibition, such as *Puberty,* 1894, [Fig. 3], or in reproduction (*Inger in Black and Violet*, 1892 and *Self-Portrait with Cigarette*, 1895).[12] But the symbolic mood and frontal symmetry of Gerstl's nude self-portrait also relate to Hodler's *Young Man Admired by the Women* (1903), which has the added attraction of depicting a young man admired by a group of attractive women, or *Truth* (1903) [Fig. 5], where the girl's nudity blinds the half-shrouded males surrounding her. For all Gerstl's precocious originality, he had probably seen the Secession's 1904 presentation of Hodler and Munch before he painted his first self-portrait. Emerging from a period of study and reflection, it seems that Gerstl was boldly asserting his solidarity with the revolutionary international art of his times by identifying with Munch and Hodler.[13]

3
Edvard Munch, *Puberty*, 1894, oil on canvas. Munch Museum, Oslo

4
Richard Gerstl, *Semi-Nude Self-Portrait*, 1902–04, oil on canvas. Leopold Museum, Vienna

5
Ferdinand Hodler, *Truth*, (second version), 1903, oil on canvas. Kunsthaus Zürich, on loan from the City of Zürich

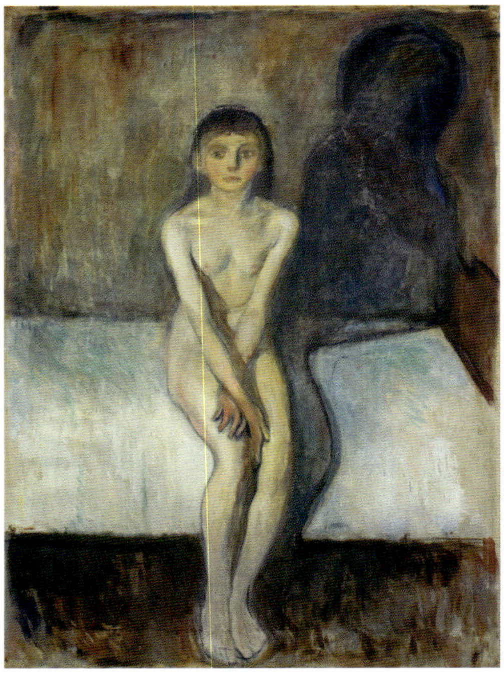

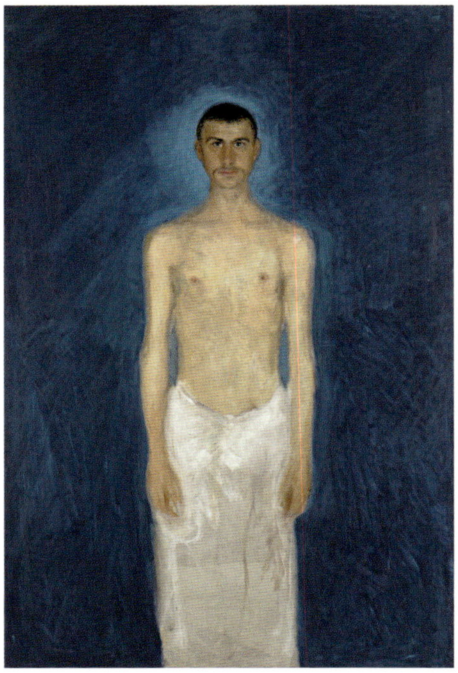

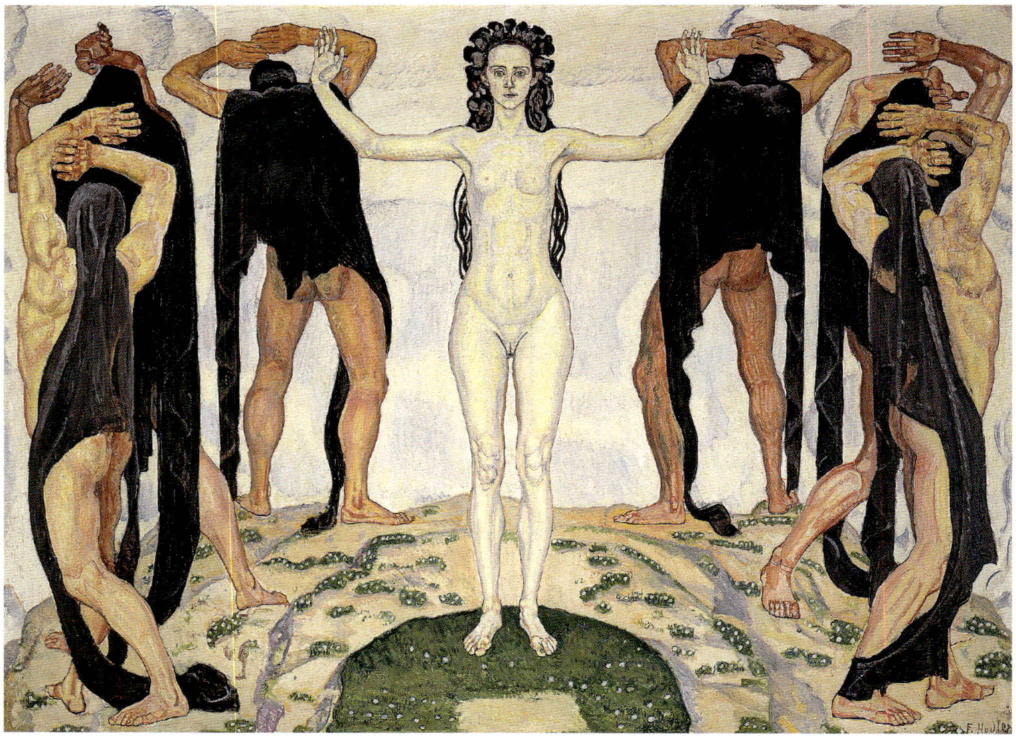

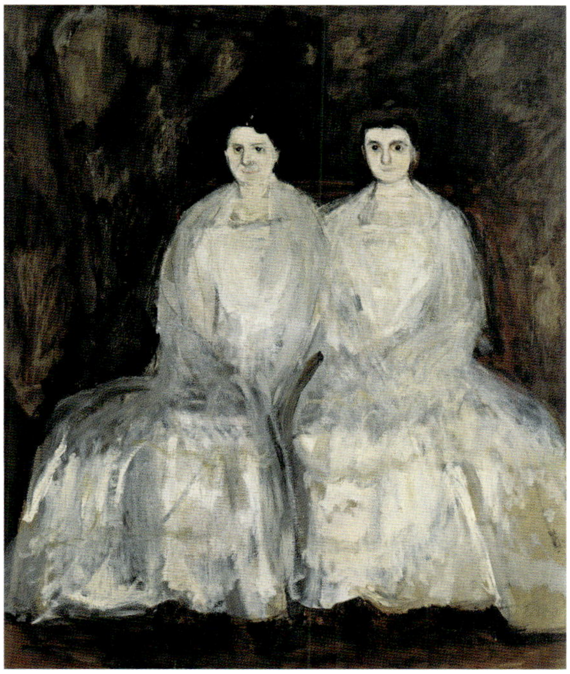

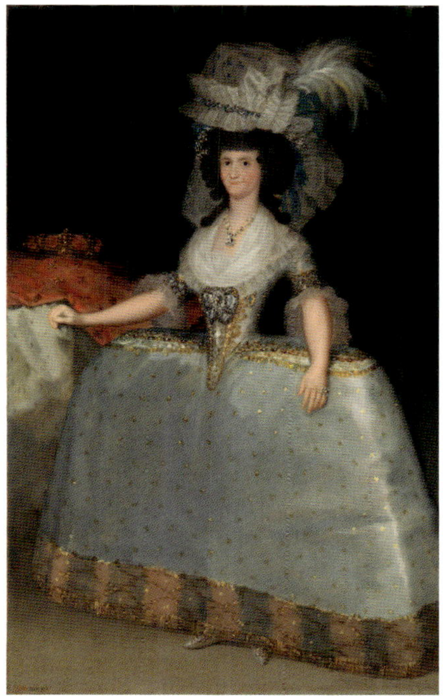

6
Richard Gerstl, *The Sisters Karoline and Pauline Fey*, March/April 1905, oil on canvas. Belvedere, Vienna [Cat. no. 12]

7
Francisco de Goya y Lucientes, *Queen María Luisa in a Dress with Hooped Skirt*, ca. 1789, oil on canvas. Museo Nacional del Prado, Madrid

Gerstl's other paintings that most clearly reflect the influence of Munch include *The Sisters Karoline and Pauline Fey* (1905) [Cat. no. 12], and *Professor Ernst Diez* (1906) [Cat. no. 21]. Both of these works also demonstrate an original fusion of Munch and other sources.[14] The bold gaze of the two sisters, together with their isolation in the surrounding space, strikes a distinct echo of Munch, recalling not only *Puberty* [Fig. 3] but also the blank forward stare of the faces in *Anxiety*, which had provoked widespread press attention when it was exhibited in Vienna in 1901.[15] However, the painterly treatment of the women's white dresses has also led to comparisons with Manet's *Portrait of Jeanne Duval* (1862), which Gerstl would have seen in January 1903 in the 16th Secession exhibition; this show was devoted to "The Development of Impressionism in Painting and Sculpture."[16] This exhibition included not only modern French and Belgian art, but also works by Velázquez and Goya, following the thesis developed by German art historian Julius Meier-Graefe that the rediscovery of Spanish art from the Golden Age was an essential ingredient of modern painting.[17] Gerstl's admiration for Zuloaga, Velázquez, and Goya is well documented[18]; in *The Sisters Karoline and Pauline Fey*, the women's stare, their painterly white dresses, and the looming, empty background all relate to stylistic characteristics of Spanish art (Velázquez, *Infanta Margarita Teresa in a White Dress*, ca. 1656, and Francisco de Goya, *Queen María Luisa in a Dress with Hooped Skirt*, ca. 1789) [Fig. 7].[19] Once again, it seems that Gerstl not only positioned himself in relation to the cutting-edge discourse surrounding international modernism, but also achieved compelling visual results through his highly original combination of diverse sources.

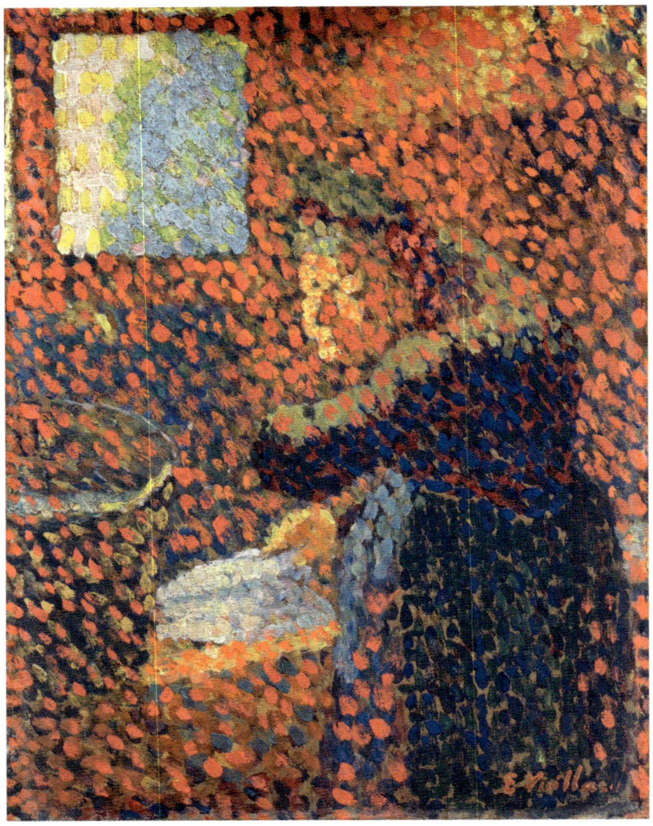

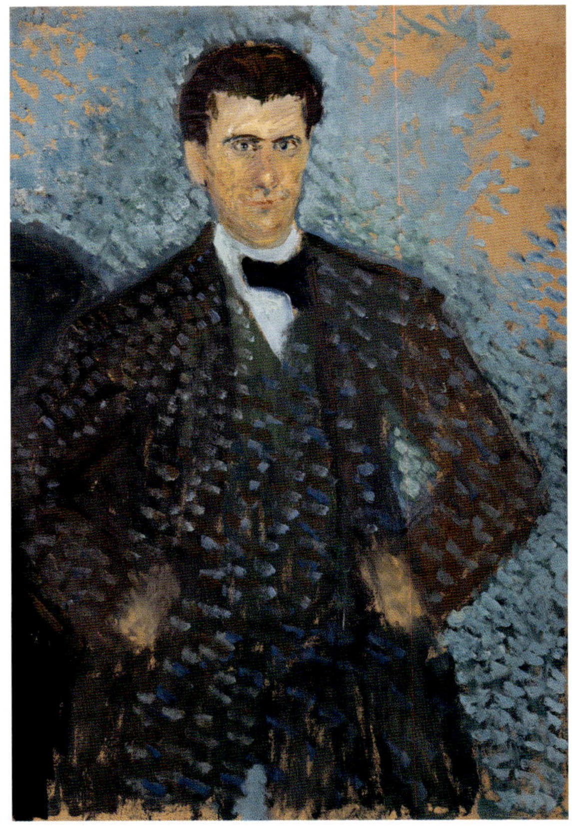

8
Édouard Vuillard, *Grandmother at the Sink*, ca. 1890, oil on board mounted on panel. Christie's Images Ltd.

9
Richard Gerstl, *Self-Portrait in front of a Blue-Green Background*, spring-summer 1907, oil on board. Tiroler Landesmuseum Ferdinandeum

French Art and Van Gogh

Alongside the fashionable European Symbolists Munch and Hodler, French art featured prominently in the Secession's exhibition program before 1905.[20] Gerstl was the only Viennese artist of the Expressionist generation old enough to have seen the 1903 Impressionism exhibition mentioned above, and the impact of artists shown on this occasion, including the Belgian Divisionist Théo van Rysselberghe and the French Nabis artist Édouard Vuillard, can be seen in the series of domestic portraits Gerstl painted in 1906. The Pointillist style evident in these paintings is acknowledged as an important stepping-stone in the artist's development.[21] Gerstl used broken brushwork and fragmented color not so much to analyze light scientifically (like Seurat and the French Neo-Impressionists), but rather to animate and pattern the surfaces of his paintings, and ultimately to challenge the boundaries between objects, figures, and surrounding space. A painting such as *Portrait of Mathilde Schönberg in the Studio* [Cat. no. 67] relates closely to Vuillard's practice of merging the figure and its surroundings through pattern and mixed, broken brushwork. Gerstl's reinterpretation of Neo-Impressionism as "a dynamic light event"[22] reached a climax in *Self-Portrait in front of a Blue-Green Background* (1907 [Cat. no. 35]), where flecks of blue strike up a forceful rhythm across the entire painting with the exception of the artist's face, recalling Vuillard's most radical experiments with broken color (for example, *Grandmother at the Sink*, ca. 1890 [Fig. 8]).

Gerstl's numerous self-portraits are central to his reinterpretation of Post-Impressionism, since he used them not only as a means of self-exploration but also to identify with the artists he most admired. *Self-Portrait with Palette* (1906–07 [Cat. no. 32]) depicts the young artist in confident professional guise reflecting his new-found self-assurance within Schönberg's circle. Standing in front of his earlier blue self-portrait that referenced Hodler and Munch, this new self-image echoes Munch's *Self-Portrait with Brushes* (1904), thus reaffirming Gerstl's identification with the rebellious yet highly successful Norwegian artist.[23] However, Gerstl identified most profoundly with Vincent van Gogh,[24] whose work made a major impact on many Expressionist artists when it was rediscovered in the early years of the twentieth century.[25] Arguably the most important single event for the birth of Expressionism was the travelling exhibition of Van Gogh's work seen by the Brücke artists in Dresden in November 1905, and then shown in a slightly different version at the Galerie Miethke in Vienna in January 1906. The same year, a selection of Van Gogh's letters was published in German, focusing attention on his life story and tragic suicide, which became potent factors in the "Expressionist" myth that quickly grew up around the Dutch artist.[26]

10
Vincent van Gogh, *Self-Portrait*, 1887, oil on board. Van Gogh Museum, Amsterdam

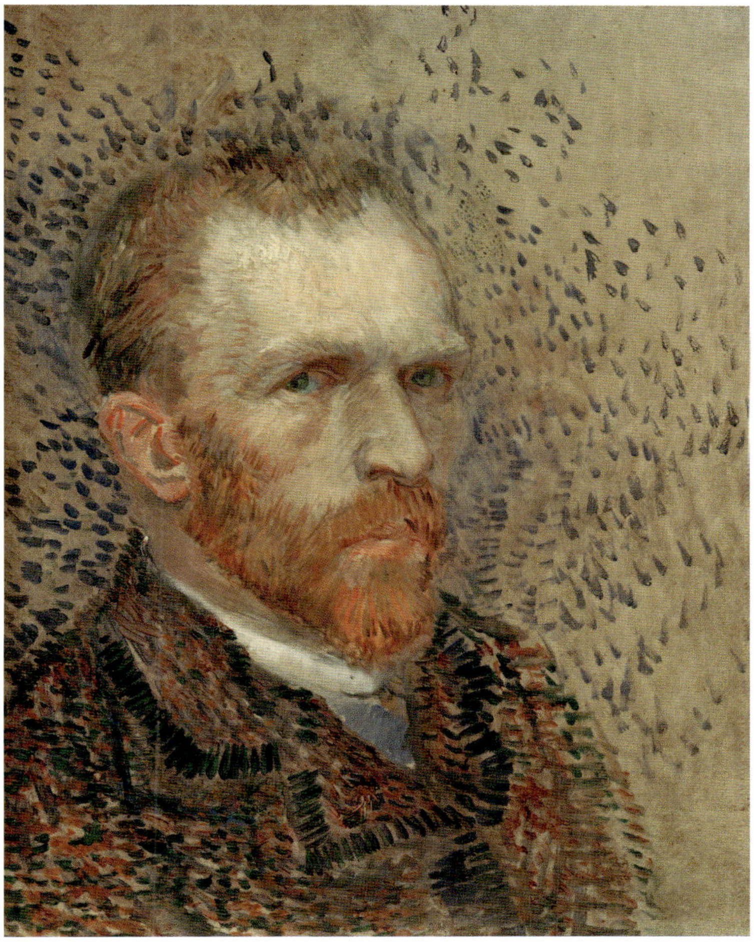

Gerstl responded to Van Gogh's paintings in a concentrated phase of self-portraiture characterized by a new psychological intensity.[27] Only two self-portraits by Van Gogh were shown at the Galerie Miethke, but one of them, *Self-Portrait* (1887 [Fig. 10]), features the same piercing gaze we find in Gerstl's *Self-Portrait* [Cat. no. 63] and in his two series of self-portrait drawings [Cat. nos. 26–29 and 59–62]. In the first series Gerstl experimented with Divisionist brushstrokes, which also feature in the dynamic blue markings around Van Gogh's head in the above-mentioned self-portrait, and then recur in Gerstl's own *Self-Portrait in front of a Blue-Green Background* [Cat. no. 35].[28] The unusual motif in Gerstl's *Self-Portrait in front of a Stove* [Cat. no. 33] may well echo another Van Gogh painting he saw at the Galerie Miethke, *Ward in the Hospital in Arles* (1889), which a contemporary reviewer described as depicting a "terrible bent black stove pipe . . . forcing one to think of the gallows."[29] Although Gerstl's self-portrait paintings show the artist's torso slightly twisted like Van Gogh's [Fig. 10], his drawings display the radical frontality we associate with Munch. Indeed, both Gerstl and more obviously Arnold Schönberg at a slightly later date [Cat. no. 7] pushed their frontal self-portrait drawings in the direction of the disembodied heads that often feature in Munch's paintings of the 1890s [Fig. 2].

These "fusions" of Munch and Van Gogh remind us that Gerstl was a young artist making bold imaginative leaps as he moved forward, not necessarily in a linear fashion but rather establishing creative connections among various visual stimuli. Making a link between Munch and Van Gogh was not simply a question of positioning himself in relation to the leading figures of international modernism—which the ambitious young Gerstl undoubtedly intended to do—but also of recognizing, with acute visual intelligence, the ground that these two great artists shared. The leading Munch scholar, Reinhold Heller, has recently described this common ground as an aesthetic of "ugliness," which involved both Munch and Van Gogh in transgressing stylistic rules such as harmony and consistency that were traditionally associated with beauty—and were still upheld as the guiding principles behind the Viennese Secessionist art that Gerstl rebelliously opposed. "For both Munch and Van Gogh," Heller writes, "despite differences in their approach, 'ugliness' became a newly valid means of enhancing their works' expressiveness." With particular reference to Van Gogh's famous *Night Café* (1888), Heller remarks that, like Munch, "he [Van Gogh] turned [. . .] to effects seemingly unskilled, primitive and ugly according to traditional criteria but emotively all the more powerful."[30]

No better words could be used to describe Richard Gerstl's radically unconventional works of 1908, painted during the last summer he spent with Schönberg and his circle in Gmunden before the dénouement of his affair with Mathilde (see the essay by Raymond Coffer in this catalogue, p. 58). In the late summer of the previous year, Gerstl was undoubtedly guided by Van Gogh's experimental painting style in landscapes such as *Vineyards with View of Auvers* (1890) that he had seen at the Galerie Miethke when he took a step further away from the motif than either Van Gogh or Munch would have contemplated (*Landscape Study* [Cat. no. 51]). The following spring and early summer he continued to make references to the international artists he admired—most obviously to Munch in his thinly painted *Mathilde Schönberg* [Cat. no. 53], to Vuillard in *Portrait of Mathilde Schönberg in the Studio* [Cat. no. 67], and to Van Gogh in his self-portraits. Gerstl's magnificent *Portrait of Henryka Cohn* [Cat. No. 73] is rightly described by Coffer as a calculated riposte to Gustav Klimt's supremely elegant *Portrait of Fritza Riedler*, which was exhibited at the Vienna "Kunstschau" in June 1908. Combining his different painting styles—the dynamic brushwork of Van Gogh, the decorative Pointillism of Vuillard, and the thinly painted abstract swathes of paint he found in paintings like Munch's *Portrait of Stanislaw Przybyszewski*—Gerstl indeed "purges" the decorative ornamentation of Klimt in *Henryka Cohn* with an aesthetic of "ugliness," consisting of "disintegrative, jagged brushwork, an unsettling, abstract background and an enveloping, mesmerizing mesh of black and red flecks."[31]

Gerstl's expressive fusion of international Post-Impressionist styles into a combative "anti-aesthetic" is one of the multiple factors that played into his last summer in Gmunden. Although there are still echoes of Munch's frontal group scenes such as *Anxiety,* and Van Gogh's wildly expressive brushwork in *The Schönberg Family* and *Group Portrait with Schönberg* [Cat. nos. 79–80], Gerstl's savage painting technique, combining paint squeezed straight from the tube with brutal use of the palette knife, takes the aesthetic of "ugliness" to previously unknown extremes. In the last summer of his life Gerstl assimilated his international sources into a highly original, experimental style that indeed places him at the vanguard of Expressionism.

1 See Breicha, quoted in Coffer 2011, 77: "unter den Wiener Malern seiner Zeit war Gerstl der französischste."

2 Gerstl turned down the opportunity of exhibiting in the prestigious Galerie Miethke because Klimt's work was scheduled to hang in the same space.

3 Program of the Brücke artists' group, 1906, carved as a woodcut by Ernst Ludwig Kirchner and distributed at the group's early exhibitions.

4 See Coffer 2011, 182, and Diethard Leopold, *Richard Gerstl*, Hirmer 2016, 13.

5 Only 600 copies of the first edition of Freud's *The Interpretation of Dreams* were printed in 1899, and Heller would certainly have been a major outlet for the book as he was an ardent supporter of Freud. He stocked all the latest art publications in his bookshop, where talks were held by Freud, Peter Altenberg, Arthur Schnitzler, Richard Dehmel, and Hermann Bahr, among others. His October 1906 exhibition of Edvard Munch also included a version of *The Kiss* and a *Study for Nude*. Heller was a very close friend of Zemlinsky, Ernst Diez, and Arnold Schönberg, who regularly performed in his concerts and presented the first exhibition of his paintings in Heller's art bookshop in 1910.

6 Schröder 1993, 32 writes of how the white background in *Ernst Diez* invades and dissolves the figure, affecting a "an Selbstauflösung grenzenden Entmaterialisierung."

7 See Coffer 2011, 37: "Weininger und Freud las [Richard] und [er] erkannte ihre Bedeutung gleich beim erscheinen" (Victor Hammer, 1974) and 41: "Ibsen [und] Wedekind interessierten [Richard] sehr," (Alois/Breicha/hand-written notes).

8 See Coffer 2011, 38: "As regards developments in the art world, Alois recalled that '[Gerstl] besuchte zwar die Ausstellungen.'" (Alois/ Breicha/hand-written notes).

9 Schröder 1993, 48, dates *Semi-Nude Self-Portrait* to 1905. Coffer re-dates the painting to 1902–03, responding to Alois Gerstl's recollection that it was painted when the artist was just nineteen years old. With specific reference to Munch's influence, Coffer quotes Hammer's recollection that Gerstl never expressed any enthusiasm for his work: "Von Munch [. . .] hat [Gerstl] mir gegenüber nie gesprochen." (Hammer, *Beiträge*, 142). See also Coffer 2011, 114: "Munch weiss ich nicht [. . .] Ich weiss nur, dass Zul.[oaga] ihm sehr gefallen hat." (Hammer, *Gespräch*, 1963). However, all these recollections were recorded many years after the events.

10 In the following years Munch rose to such fame that he was represented as the epitome of a young and reckless artist in the Austrian daily feuilletons. In 1901, his painting *Angst* made a deep impact when exhibited at the Vienna Secession, and in 1902 his etchings were well received. In 1904 his works were discussed widely in every newspaper and magazine. The first German translations of Ibsen and Strindberg were also illustrated by Munch's portraits. Indeed, Munch remained a focus of intense press interest until 1908, when the role of the renegade artist was taken over in the public perception by Oskar Kokoschka and Max Oppenheimer. For a more general discussion of Munch's importance for Expressionism, see *Munch and Expressionism*, ed. by Jill Lloyd and Reinhold Heller, Neue Galerie New York 2016.

11 Hodler, like Munch, had achieved notoriety when his breakthrough painting *Night* (1890) was removed by the mayor of Geneva from public exhibition.

12 Both paintings were illustrated in Hermann Esswein's, *Moderne Illustratoren*, Vienna 1904.

13 Wolfgang Born's inclination to date Gerstl's *Self-Portrait* to 1904 ("Richard Gerstl," in: *Belvedere, Zeitschrift für künstl. Kultur*, 10, Vienna 1931,153–157) may thus be correct. Certainly the painting breaks with the semi-academic style of other works dating from 1902–03 and is a stepping stone towards Gerstl's more radically modern style of 1905. The theme of the gaunt male nude was introduced by Georg Minne's *Fountain of Youth*, exhibited at the 9th Secession in 1901, which later greatly influenced both Egon Schiele and Oskar Kokoschka. But the Symbolist aura and frontality of Gerstl's self-portrait are more closely related to Hodler and Munch. Hodler's poster design for the 19th exhibition of the Vereinigung bildender Künstler Österreichs in 1904 also showed a male nude, which the artist had to clothe with a loincloth to avoid public scandal.

14 *Ernst Diez* has frequently been compared to Munch's *The Frenchman, Marcel Archinard* (1904), which although not exhibited in Vienna was illustrated in at least three publications before 1905: Max Linde, ed. Gottheiner, *Edvard Munch and die Kunst der Zukunft*, 1902–03, 25; Hermann Esswein, *Moderne Illustratoren*, 1904, 12; and *Kunst und Künstler*, 1904, 491. Once again, Gerstl may also be referring simultaneously to Manet, specifically to his *Self-Portrait with Cap (1878–79)*, also published in *Kunst und Künstler* 1904, 306. Goya's practice of placing his figures against a luminous empty background may also have inspired Gerstl.

15 Schröder 1993, 48, compares "die künstlerische Idee" of *The Fey Sisters* to Munch's *Mädchen am Meer* (1903–04), although it was not amongst the twenty paintings exhibited at the Secession in 1904. Breicha suggests that, "damals, anfangs 1905 stand [...] Gerstl unter dem Einfluß Munch's [sic] (aber ohne [. . .] "nachzuahmen")," observing that "Reife Frucht dieser Begegnung Munch-Gerstl ist das Doppelbildnis." (See Coffer 2011, 77)

16 Ibid.

17 Julius Meier-Graefe developed this argument in his *Entwicklungsgeschichte der modernen Kunst*, 1904, which was an important source for the Expressionists. Meier-Graefe wrote the preface of the 1903 Vienna Secession catalogue, and also gave a lecture titled "Bestrebungen und Ziele der Malerei und Plastik in der Gegenwart" in Vienna on 15 February 1903.

18 See Coffer 2011, 38, where he quotes Breicha (presumably from Alois): 'Daß Gerstl die Spanier (Velázquez und Goya) schätzte ist erwiesen." Diethard Leopold suggests that Gerstl's break in his studies at the Academy initiated a period of copying at the Kunsthistorisches Museum, with its spectacular collection of paintings by Velázquez (2016, 63), although he points out that very little is known about Gerstl's copying activities.

19 Goya, although not represented in the Kunsthistorisches Museum, was widely exhibited in Austria after 1901, when an exhibition of his work in Graz attracted more than 1,000 visitors. The 1903 Secession exhibition included six paintings and 60 works on paper. *Portrait of the Marquesa de Baena*, shown in the Secession, is most likely the painting from the Museo Zuloaga depicting the sitter reclining on a sofa against a dark background.

20 The international thrust of the Vienna Secession's exhibition program lasted from 1900 to 1905, when the so-called "Klimt Group", including the most significant and internationally renowned members of the Vereinigung, left the Secession.

21 See, for example, Jane Kallir, *Arnold Schönberg's Vienna*, New York 1984, 51.

22 Schroeder 1993, 29, interprets the colored brushstrokes across Gerstl's body as an attempt to visualize "Energieströme." The theme of

invisible fields of energy recurs in Strindberg's *Inferno* diaries (1894–97) and also in Edvard Munch's writings, for example with reference to *Separation* (1896), shown at the 1904 Vienna Secession, which he linked to "new energy in the atmosphere" (notes related to art and the *Frieze of Life*, Munch-Museet N43, folio 1r -1v).

23 This painting was illustrated in Hermann Esswein's *Moderne Illustratoren*, 1904, 14, from which Gerstl seems to have drawn several of his motifs echoing Munch (see also notes 12 and 14 above). The combination of Munch's status as a rebel and a famous, successful artist was also of great appeal to the Brücke artists in Dresden, who saw his work exhibited at the Saxon Art Association in 1906.

24 Victor Hammer recalled that Gerstl spoke positively of Van Gogh (Hammer, *Beiträge*, 143). See Coffer 2011, 106f.

25 Five paintings by Van Gogh were shown at the 1903 Impressionist exhibition at the Vienna Secession, including *The Plain of Auvers* (1890, F775), which was purchased by the Secession and presented to the newly founded Moderne Staatsgalerie (now Österreichische Galerie Belvedere). Gerstl's response to this purchase, which underlined Van Gogh's key importance in the eyes of the Viennese modernists, is seen in his own small landscape, *Grinzing* [Cat. No. 14]. The international orientation of Gerstl's landscape painting was probably encouraged by Simon Hollósy, whose painting school in Nagybánya Gerstl attended in the summers of 1900 and 1901.

26 These issues are discussed in depth in *Van Gogh and Expressionism*, ed. by Jill Lloyd and Michael Peppiatt, Neue Galerie New York 2007. A selection of Van Gogh's letters in German translation was first published in *Kunst und Künstler* in 1904.

27 Gerstl's affinity with Van Gogh was highlighted by Born in 1931 in his description of the artist as "ein österreichischer Van Gogh" (*Neues Wiener Journal*, September 29, 1931). Most subsequent writings on Gerstl have underlined Van Gogh's influence on Gerstl, see Coffer 2011 106.

28 An exactly parallel development, drawing inspiration from Van Gogh, can be seen in the work of the Swiss artist Cuno Amiet, who was exhibited alongside Munch and Hodler at the 1904 Secession and who joined the Brücke group in 1906. His *Self-Portrait in Pink* (1907) displays the same "abstract" brushwork slashing across the artist's torso.

29 Ludwig Hevesi in *Altkunst, Neukunst*, 1909, 526–529. This review was published the year after Gerstl's death is very typical of the hyperbole that features in discussions around Van Gogh at the time.

30 Reinhold Heller, "In part myself: Edvard Munch and Vincent van Gogh Compared," in: *Munch: Van Gogh*, Van Gogh Museum, Amsterdam and Munch Museum Oslo, 2015–16, 66–71. Schröder 1993, 25, also discusses Gerstl in relation to the concept of "Häßlichkeit" as an alternative to Secessionist ideals of beauty.

31 See the description by Raymond Coffer on p. 168 of the present publication.

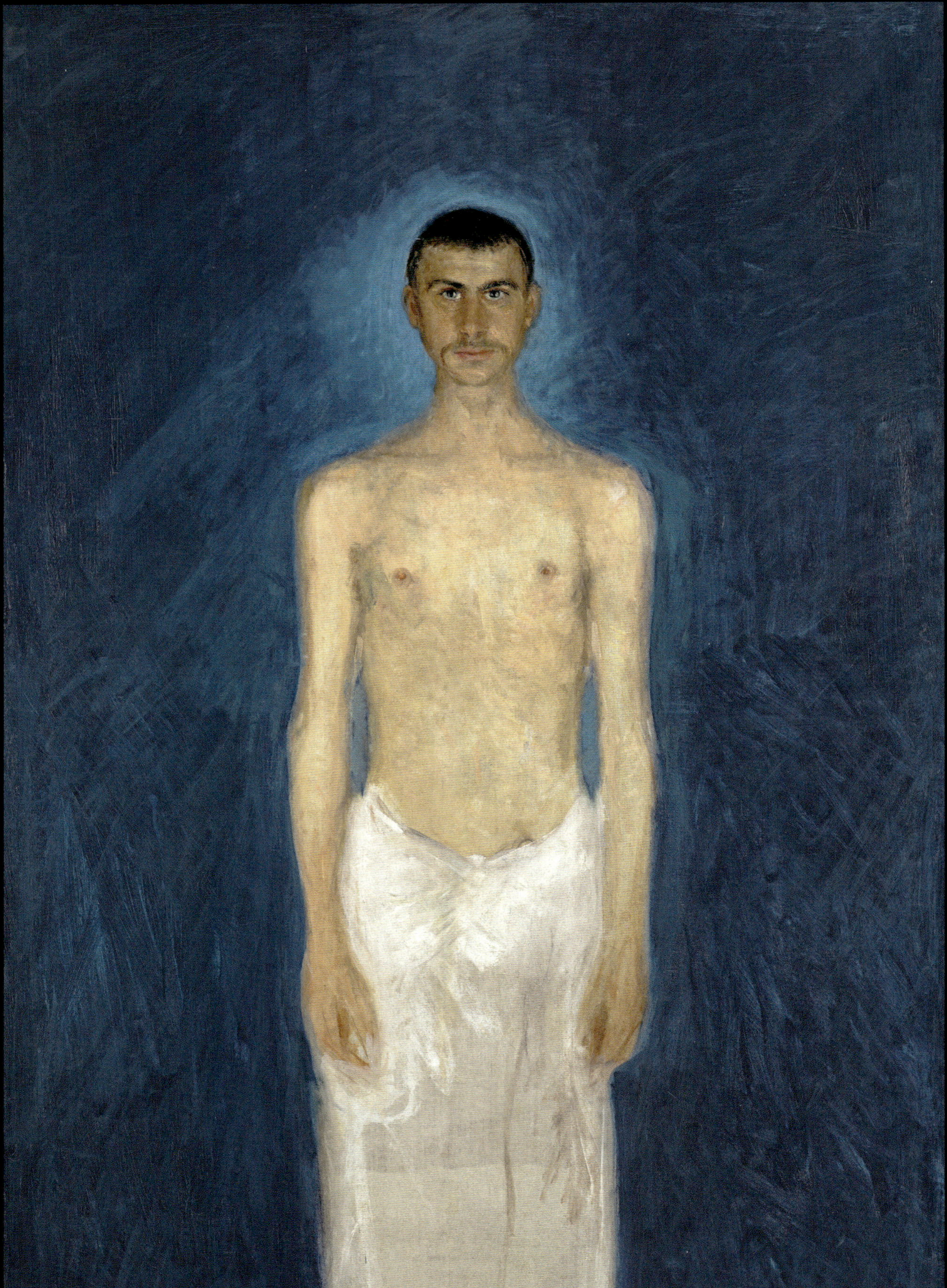

DIETHARD LEOPOLD

Richard Gerstl: *Semi-Nude Self-Portrait*

Richard Gerstl's *Semi-Nude Self-Portrait* [Cat. no. 6] is a singular work that presents a new definition of art. This painting may be regarded as an expression of a Symbolist concept of art[1] by virtue of the mysterious, non-representational background, the almost supernaturally radiant body enveloped by its surrounding aura, and the symmetrical, frontal presentation that gives the painting an especially meaningful resonance.

Yet the painting is a self-portrait, which considerably modifies its symbolic weight. The self-image projected by the artist, who presents himself here in the form of concrete truth while appealing to the viewer to respond to his gaze, is both heroic and sensitive. Its multiple layers of meaning are neither mysterious nor puzzling, but rather concrete and personal, which by no means rules out depth of meaning—although depth in this instance emerges in a dialogue between the work and the viewer. The painting sets a limit and a standard that lie somewhere between symbolic allusion and specific, process-based content.

Still, it is now customary among scholars to interpret this trailblazing new definition of self and also of art as evidence of a personal crisis. This biographically inspired misunderstanding can be traced to Gerstl's biographer Otto Breicha,[2] who calls attention to the central theme of the painting: "The subject and his image actually exhibit something of the essential character of a man who has risen from the dead," adding that "the image of 'Lazarus' was mentioned by those who had a prior interest in Gerstl's oeuvre,"[3] but unfortunately he cited no sources. It should be noted here that, for someone who rises from the dead, the moment of crisis is already in the past. The resurrected body may be regarded as evidence of indestructible or higher life, but it is no longer a symbol of past calamities. We are dealing in this case with a contradiction that appears repeatedly in the later literature devoted to Gerstl.

The obvious and subtle allusions to a resurrected individual—regardless of the nature of the death from which he has arisen—identify this painting as the legacy of an educated, sensitive painter in the tradition of European art. Whether it is an iconographic reference to Lazarus, who has been recalled from the realm of death, or to the resurrected Jesus Christ, ultimately makes no difference;[4] for the painting's status as a self-portrait makes us question, if not dismiss as irrelevant, such references to traditional iconography as a means of explaining the artist's intentions. What matters here, as Gerstl's convincingly depicted gaze tells us, is not the repetition, re-enactment, or reinterpretation—and certainly not the illustration—of a religious narrative. What

1
Richard Gerstl, *Semi-Nude Self-Portrait*, 1902–04, oil on canvas. Leopold Museum, Vienna

2
Oskar Kokoschka, *The Girl Li and I* from *The Dreaming Youths*, sheet 8, 1907–08, colored lithograph. Wien Museum

we have here is a more daring play on iconographic associations. Indeed, the painting breaks away from the traditions to which it alludes and opens the door to new horizons for art.

Particularly remarkable in this context is the unusual combination of recognizable self-portraiture in the artist's face and the disturbing transformation of his body, which clearly deviates from realistic depiction. We find similarly lean figures coupled with elongated limbs somewhat later in the art of the young Oskar Kokoschka [Fig. 2], in works by Egon Schiele [Fig. 3], and in the sculptures of Wilhelm Lehmbruck [Fig. 4]. All these artists depicted alienating alterations of the body that are reminiscent of the figures of young boys sculpted by George Minne [Fig. 5], whom the Vienna Secessionists so greatly admired.[5] In any event, the slender, elongated body captured in the process of dematerialization is a reflection of inner thoughts and emotions, and thus bears witness to the spiritual dimension of human existence.

In this aspect of the painting Gerstl strikes the nerve of his times, the essential features of which were just beginning to take shape and would find their way seventy years later into mainstream culture through the androgynous figure of Ziggy Stardust / David Bowie and the images of aliens in science-fiction films. This association is by no means coincidental. Aliens are always portrayed as intellectually superior to humans, which explains the emphasis on the eyes of these beings from space—an emphasis that becomes a central theme in all of Gerstl's self-portraits, above all in this first self-image. The combination of a transformed physique and a realistic portrait heightens the painting's intensity. The direct, unavoidable, deeply penetrating

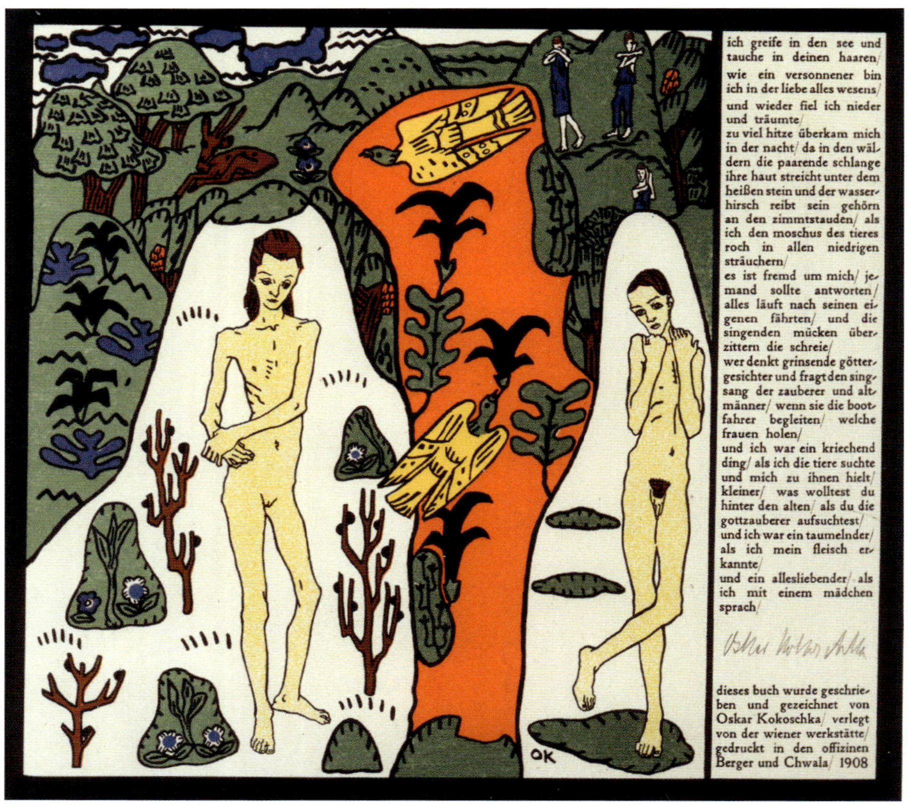

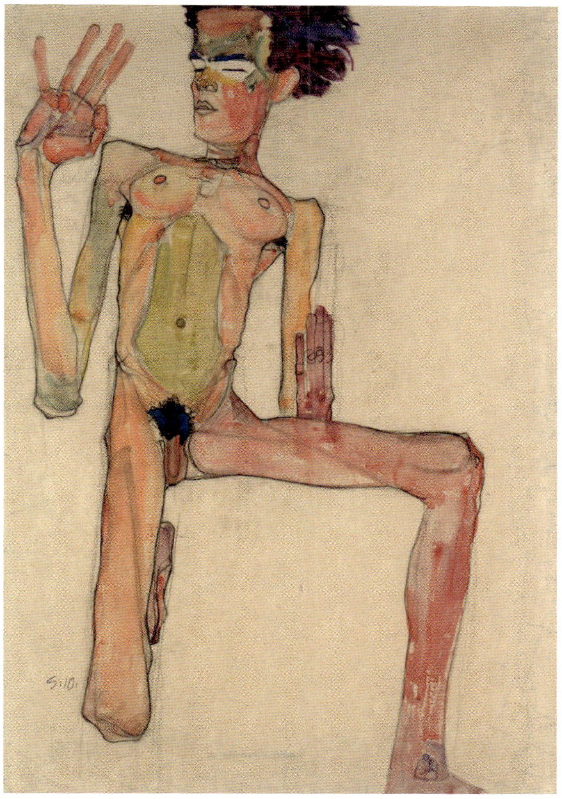

3

Egon Schiele, *Kneeling Nude, Self-Portrait*, 1910, black chalk and gouache on paper. Leopold Museum, Vienna

4

Wilhelm Lehmbruck, *Standing Youth*, 1913–14, bronze. Lehmbruck Museum, Duisburg

5

George Minne, *Solidarity*, 1897–98, Carrara marble. Private Collection, Vienna

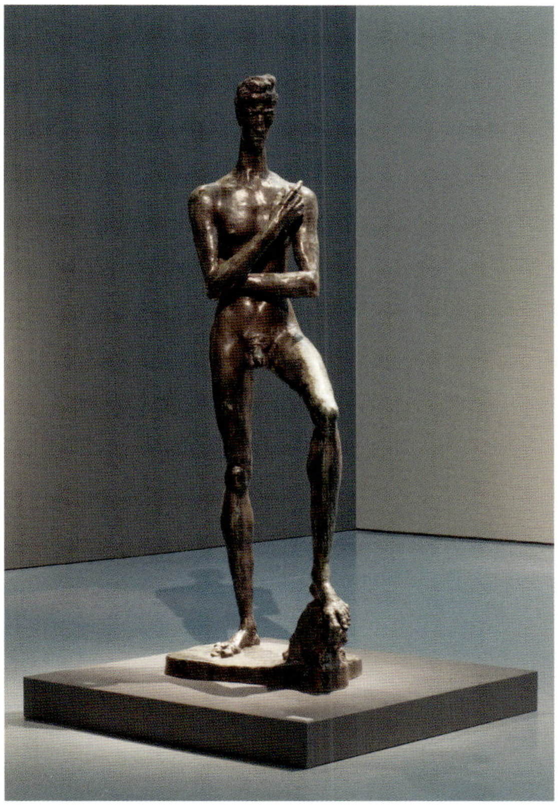

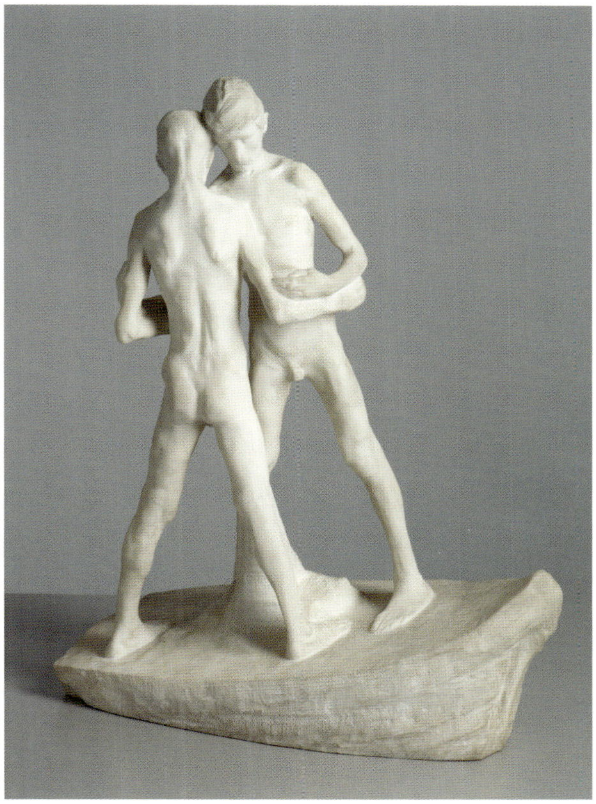

gaze cannot be adequately interpreted with reference to biography or iconography alone. What we see here is a new kind of artistic intention.[6]

Common to all interpretations of this painting is the realization that the subject's gaze is by far the most important element in the picture. It is a gaze which—if we respond to it — crosses boundaries, transcending the limits of the painting and the psychological barriers of communication with other people. We have a decision to make as viewers: do we respond to this encounter, or do we reject such intensity, for whatever reason? The difficulty involved in interpreting such a gaze is made more complicated in the literature on Gerstl by the fact that it is overloaded with both biographical and iconographic baggage.

Otto Breicha initially responded to the gaze, which he describes as "questioning, even penetrating, and, as in nearly all of Gerstl's portraits, so fixed on the viewer that some observers eventually find being stared at in this way unbearable." Subsequently, however, he attributed this disturbing effect solely to the painter's personality structure, claiming that the painting offers "obvious evidence of an (inner) crisis."[7]

Although Klaus A. Schröder unites these different levels of interpretation, his conclusion is not convincing: "Due to the formal expressions of pathos, the direct encounter between painting and viewer, the unavoidable reciprocal stare does not allow for dialogue or any form of communication. The repelling rigid frontality, the hieratic character of the strict pictorial symmetry, the unrealistic quality of the image, exclude in a psychological sense the viewer from the painting. Reduced solely to what is visible, the figure of the painter refuses to engage in the dialogue that potentially follows the act of looking into each other's eyes."

Schröder also locates the difficulty involved in interpreting the painting in the artist's psyche and his existential situation: "The archetypes developed in Christian iconography mutate into modern symptoms of suffering in Gerstl's self-portrait. . . . emptiness accounts for the effect of the marginal status of the total outcast."[8]

In the case of the Vienna Expressionists, there is undeniably a certain justification for approaching the interpretation of a work from the standpoint of the artist's personality. For the first time, interest in the self, in thoughts and experiences, plays a major role in the themes chosen by Gerstl, Kokoschka, and Schiele. Consequently, all three realized significant series of self-portraits. Yet it is important to make clear distinctions. Tracing the origin and meaning of a work of art to the biography and psyche of an artist is one thing; defining the ways in which artists use their psychological makeup, their thoughts and experiences in their works, or, to express it in modern terms, how they construct a persona and employ it effectively in their art, is something entirely different.

The same must be said with respect to analyses undertaken by art scholars. It is one thing to explain the contents of a work of art in terms of iconography; it is quite another to determine how a given work of art "interprets" its underlying iconography. The overall structure that must take into account content, form, and color speaks a totally different language, whose meaning cannot be adequately explained on the basis of pictorial tradition or the depicted subject alone.[9]

It is entirely possible that the young Gerstl created the almost overstated, self-assertive pose in which he appears as a semi-nude figure out of inner necessity in order to find his way out of unbearable circumstances. Yet by no means does the work of art reveal this driving force.

If such an interpretation is read into the work nonetheless, there is good reason to suspect that Gerstl's oeuvre is being interpreted *ex post*—that is, from the perspective of our subsequent knowledge of his suicide and/or of his experiences of rejection. Then, of course, everything is viewed as desperate, and precarious. In this scenario, the legend of the tragic artist—in short, the popular cliché cited by everyone who does not really know the artist at all—is confirmed.

Nonetheless, an unbiased understanding of a work of art can stand in glaring opposition to interpretations based upon biographical facts, which have a certain tradition in the case of Gerstl's early self-portrait, and are exemplified in Raymond Coffer's well-informed biographical study of the artist.

At the very beginning of Coffer's analysis, he describes the painting as "Gerstl's earliest artistic representation of rejection" and cites the notice of unsuitability for military duty, his dismissal from a painting school in Hungary, and his exclusion from the Academy as examples of rejection.[10]

Coffer notes the physical transformations performed by the painter in his self-portrait, yet he explains them in terms of biography as "an answer to his military examiners."[11] Coffer even attributes Gerstl's gaze and facial features, in which the central theme of the work is articulated, to character traits. And it comes as no surprise when he concludes that Gerstl's first self-portrait is defiant, proud, and narcissistic.[12] Yet had Gerstl really produced only a character study in this painting, it would have none of the intense, mysterious charm that has made it his most frequently reproduced work.

An unbiased understanding of Gerstl's early self-portrait, on the contrary, might involve approaching the painting with the hermeneutics of Nikolaus von Cues, that is, with "learned ignorance" or—to put it in modern terms—with a spontaneity refined by learning. We may perhaps find the direct and unavoidable gaze disturbing, but we sense neither necessity on the part of the artist nor the desire to shut himself away. "This specific gaze . . . shows that he sets no boundary between the *you* and the *I*, or—expressed more precisely—that he recognizes the boundary but is willing to ignore it. . . . The act of playing with these possible approaches to building a relationship, a game that relies on absolute freedom, is the *I* of the artist at this particular moment."[13]

If, as stated at the outset, an epoch-making work of art also proposes a new definition of art, then Gerstl defines not only his self but also art as well in this painting. He defines new possibilities for its existence and introduces several of the most important tendencies in the art of the century to come. In self-portraiture, concrete reality—the reality of existence stripped of all societal contingencies—replaces symbolic representation.[14] The artist becomes the medium for awaking reality to a more intense state. The artist commits himself to this intensification with his whole being, including his physical self. A work of art is a magical medium, an offer to experience a similar enhancement of the state of one's being on the side of the beholder. Meeting the artist—like with Russian orthodox icons or with performance artists like Marina Abramovic such as in her performance *The Artist is Present*—means meeting oneself, or, in Jungian terms, one's (larger than ego) Self. Egon Schiele's paintings of just a few years later, for example *Revelation* or *Self-Seer*, both from 1911, show a very similar intention. The artist does not shy away from depicting his body as transformed in a manner in keeping with his intellectual or even spiritual purpose. The Vienna Actionists, most notably Günter Brus [Fig. 6], found this approach inspiring and cited Richard Gerstl and Egon Schiele specifically as their predecessors. The Vienna Actionists not only depicted their bodies in a different way, as with the photographs of Rudolf Schwarzkogler, but they also transformed their bodies to extreme postures and put themselves into states of physical stress. The physical component is complemented by the underlying theme of sexuality, although this remains intangible.

Was Richard Gerstl asking too much? Was he suffering from a narcissistic inflation of the ego? Here again it is important to make a distinction. It may be that Gerstl asked too much of himself and that he was doomed by his own, hardly modest ambition. Yet on the other hand, this particular artist's self-portrait is recognized as one of the best and most visionary works of art produced in the early years of the twentieth century.

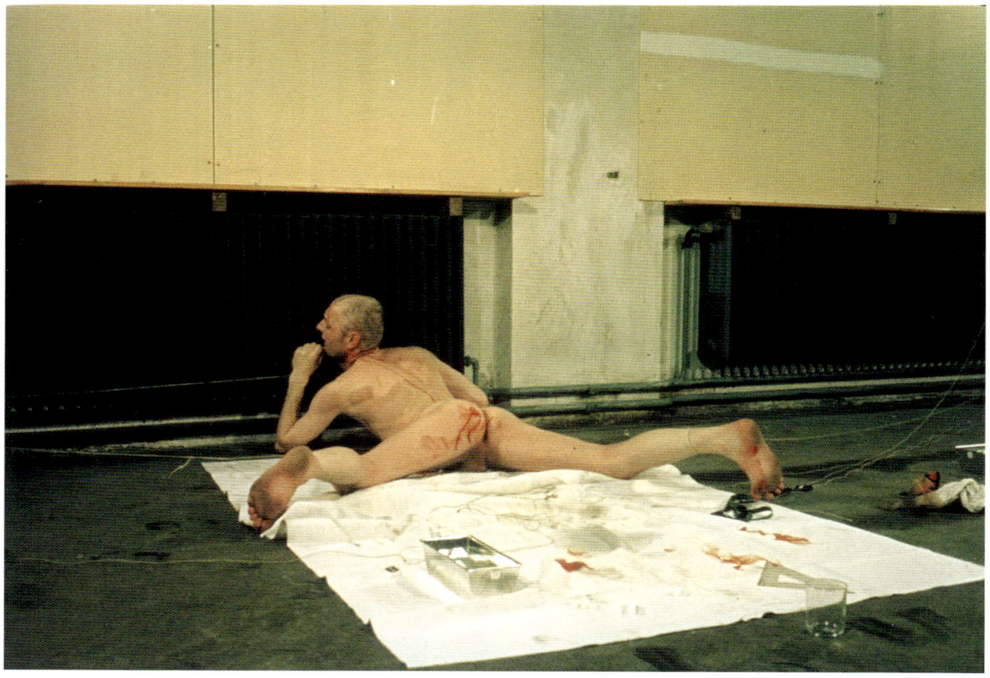

6
Günter Brus, *Breaking Test*, performed on June 19, 1970 at Aktionsraum 1 in Munich.

1 Cf. especially James Abbot McNeill Whistler, Edvard Munch, and Ferdinand Hodler, who were praised in art journals and newspaper arts sections as artists of a new generation.

2 Otto Breicha, *Richard Gerstl—Bilder zur Person. Die Selbstdarstellungen und fotografischen Porträtaufnahmen Richard Gerstls*, Salzburg 1991, 8.

3 Ibid.

4 This question is discussed at length in Klaus Albrecht Schröder, *Richard Gerstl, 1883–1908*, exh. cat. Kunstforum der Bank Austria, Vienna / Kunsthaus Zürich, Vienna/Zurich 1993.

5 And in much the same way in the art of Edvard Munch and Ferdinand Hodler, originally in that of El Greco, and even earlier in Gothic figures of saints.

6 The reference to religious icons seems appropriate to the extent that they also present a direct frontal view. Gerstl may have been familiar with this iconographic tradition from the religious mosaics he saw in Ravenna. We know at any rate that turn-of-the-century artists were aware of them, as reflected, for example, in works by Gustav Klimt. The icon's gaze is meant to serve the believer as a mirror of the divine foundation of the soul. In Gerstl's art, the gazes of the subject of the work of art and the viewer are secular and personal. The gaze is not a mirror of repeated recollection, but rather a medium for a potentially altering encounter. Cf. Diethard Leopold, *Richard Gerstl*, Munich 2016, 15–21. See also Heidi Blasl, *Die Selbstbildnisse Richard Gerstls im Kontext der Entwicklung des Selbstporträts*, diploma thesis, Katholisch-Theologische Privatuniversität Linz, 2009, 20.

7 Breicha 1991 (see note 2), 8.

8 Schröder 1993 (see note 4), 48–50.

9 Cf. Mikel Dufrenne, *The Phenomenology of Aesthetic Experience*, Evanston 1973, 123: "The aesthetic object does not speak to me *about* its subject. The subject itself speaks to me, and in the manner in which it is treated. The subject is an inevitable ingredient in the work not so much for its own sake as for the sake of the form which is given to it and by which it becomes expressive. . . . We shall emphasize strongly . . . the point that, in the case of the aesthetic object, what is signified is immanent in what does the signifying."

10 Raymond Coffer, *Richard Gerstl and Arnold Schönberg. A Reassessment of their Relationship (1906–1908) and Its Impact on their Artistic Works*, dissertation, University of London 2011, 63, 69, 71.

11 Ibid., 63.

12 Ibid., 71: "a defiant, proud and narcissistic restatement of self-worth."

13 Diethard Leopold, "Der am Ast sägte. Richard Gerstl und das Phantasma des Künstler-Ich," in: Tobias G. Natter and Elisabeth Leopold (eds.), *Nackte Männer von 1800 bis heute*, exh. cat. Leopold Museum, Vienna, Munich 2012, 77–87, here 81.

14 A comparison with Gustav Klimt's emphatically aesthetic *Nuda Veritas* realized several years provides an interesting contrast; see Leopold 2016 (see note 6), 15–16.

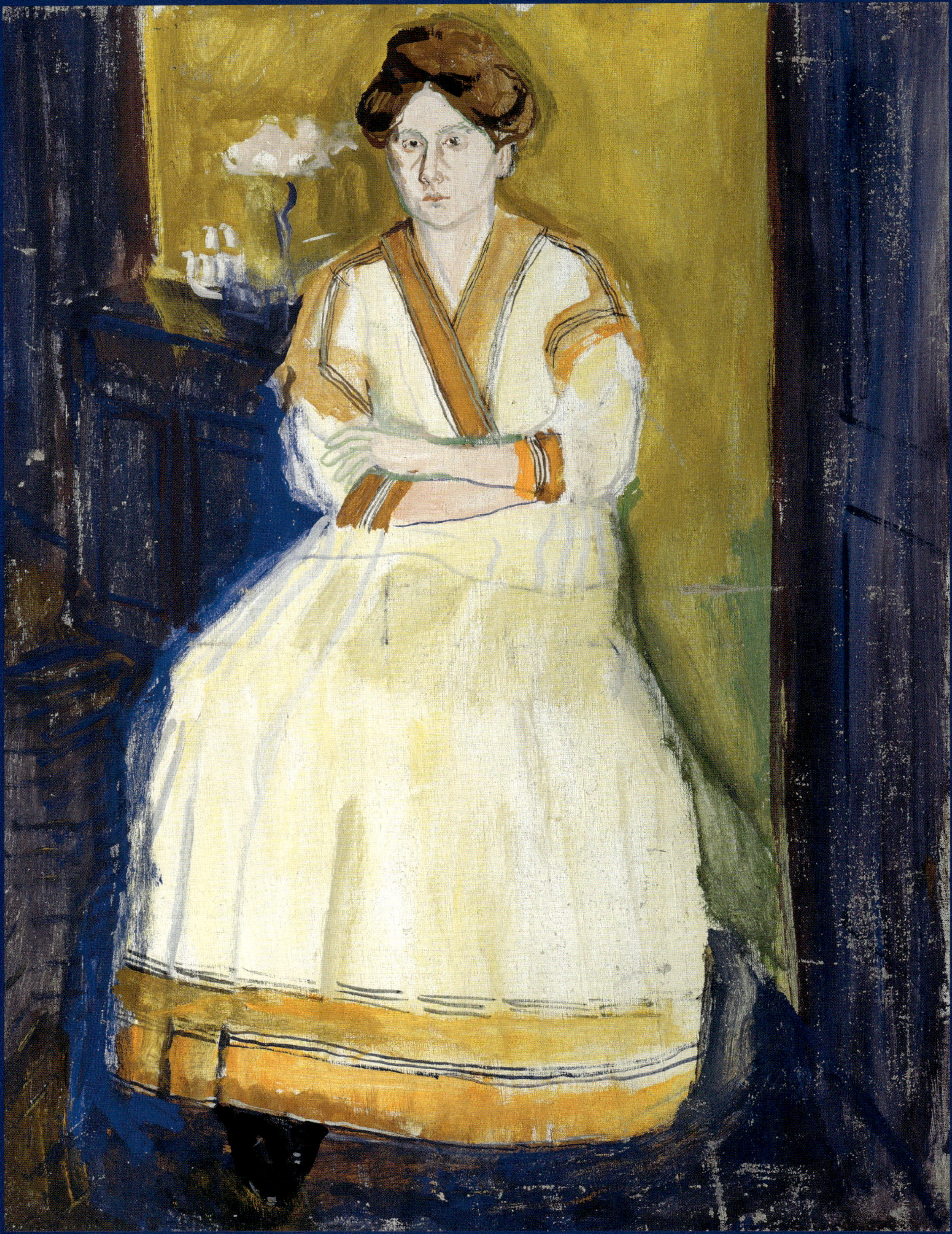

RAYMOND COFFER

A Song to the Siren: The Triangular Relationship between Richard Gerstl and Arnold and Mathilde Schönberg[1]

1
Richard Gerstl, *Mathilde Schönberg*, summer 1907, tempera on canvas. Belvedere, Vienna

When Richard Gerstl painted his full-length *Nude Self-Portrait,* in September 1908 [Cat. no. 86], just thirteen days had elapsed since his lover had returned to her husband. He was two days shy of his twenty-fifth birthday. Less than eight weeks later, he was dead.

As a *fin-de-siècle* version of the present-day selfie, it was nonetheless rare to find a male artist portraying himself naked at that time. And yet, despite its startling appearance, it was not until nearly twenty-three years after his death that the work was exhibited at the first-ever Gerstl show at Otto Nirenstein's (later Otto Kallir's) Neue Galerie in Vienna. Gerstl's older brother, Alois, told Nirenstein some of the background, but never disclosed the tragic liaison his brother had with Mathilde, the diminutive, intelligent and unassuming wife of the composer Arnold Schönberg [Fig. 2]. Indeed, it was only in 1967 that the veil of secrecy concealing the affair, loyally maintained by Schönberg's close circle, finally began to lift. This, then, is the story of how the final self-portrait of some twenty that Gerstl is known to have painted of himself came about.

Gerstl was born on September 14, 1883, to a powerful Catholic matriarch and a much older Jewish father. He grew to be a tall, reserved, introverted, and conceivably manic-depressive young man prone to mood swings, with an avowed desire to be a musician and a reputation for being difficult and confrontational [Fig. 3]. Consequently, he appears to have been plagued by rejection from a young age. He was also expelled from several educational establishments, amongst them Vienna's Academy of Fine Arts in 1901 and, later that summer, Simon Hollósy's painting school in Nagybanya after an injudicious episode with the wife of one of the Hungarian teachers. Perhaps most crushing, however, was having his desire to follow Alois into the army denied on account of his "physical weakness." Gerstl's reaction, other than suffering from a nervous stomach that would always plague him, was to represent his accumulated experience of rejection in his astonishing *Semi-Nude Self-Portrait* [Cat. no. 6], painted in his Hohe Warte studio sometime after his nineteenth birthday in 1902 or early 1903.[2] Together with his *Nude Self-Portrait,* these can be seen to act as bookends in the artist's representation of his favorite subject—himself.

A stay in a sanatorium in August 1904, just before Gerstl's twentieth birthday, was followed shortly after by a return to the Academy, where in spring 1905 and in utter rejection of everything that was being taught to him, Gerstl produced what was perhaps his first Expressionist work, *The Sisters Karoline and Pauline Fey* [Cat. no. 12]. It was a work that was to be instrumental in the twenty-two-year-old artist's formal introduction to Schönberg, for the double portrait so impressed

2
Arnold Schönberg in his home on the Liechtensteinstraße 68/70, 1907, photograph. Arnold Schönberg Center, Vienna

3
Richard Gerstl, ca. 1902–03, photograph. Archiv Otto Breicha, Vienna

the Academy professor, Heinrich Lefler that, a year later in early 1906, he not only offered Gerstl a place in his Special Landscape School, but was able to recommend his student to the thirty-one-year-old composer, who had been struggling to make ends meet from music and had decided to learn painting as an alternative source of income. Thus, in spring 1906, Schönberg, having probably been briefly introduced to Gerstl at a Mahler concert the previous December, invited the young artist into his tenement home in Alsergrund in Vienna's ninth district, just down the street from Gerstl's own family apartment. Gerstl's task was not simply to teach Schönberg and the twenty-eight-year-old Mathilde how to paint, but also to produce life-size portraits of the composer and his wife and daughter [Fig. 4].

The two domestic portraits [Cat. nos. 15–16] not only clearly incorporate the positive impact on Gerstl of Van Gogh's first major Vienna exhibition in January 1906, but also express his unfashionable disdain for his Viennese contemporaries, in particular Klimt, and the Secessionist manifesto. This may have impressed Schönberg, for he appears to have been taken with such a fellow non-conformist and unique talent—so much so that Gerstl was soon accepted by Schönberg's circle, including Schönberg's brother-in-law, Alexander Zemlinsky, and Schönberg's devoted set of students, amongst them Anton Webern and Alban Berg. Schönberg even appears to have facilitated commissions for Gerstl amongst his wider set, including Webern's cousin, Ernst Diez and Smaragda Berg, sister of Alban, so that the reserved Gerstl now found himself in the musical environment that he had always craved.

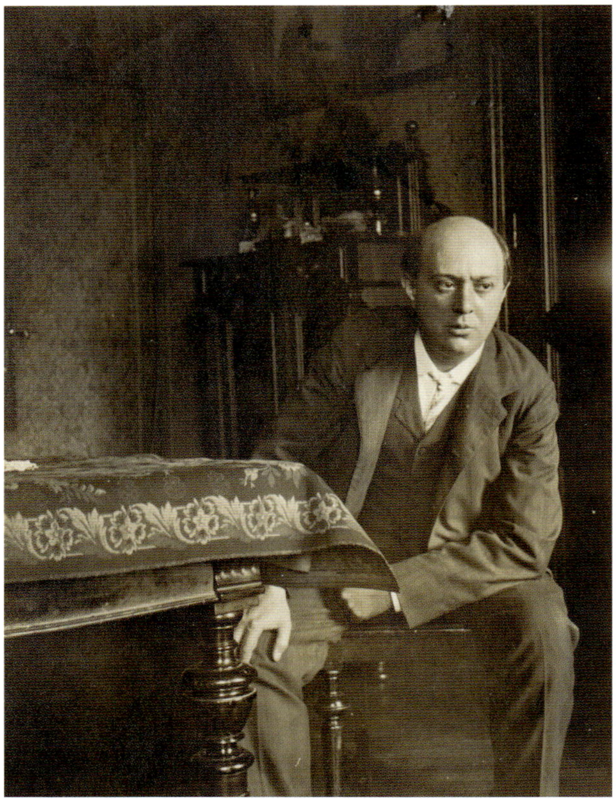

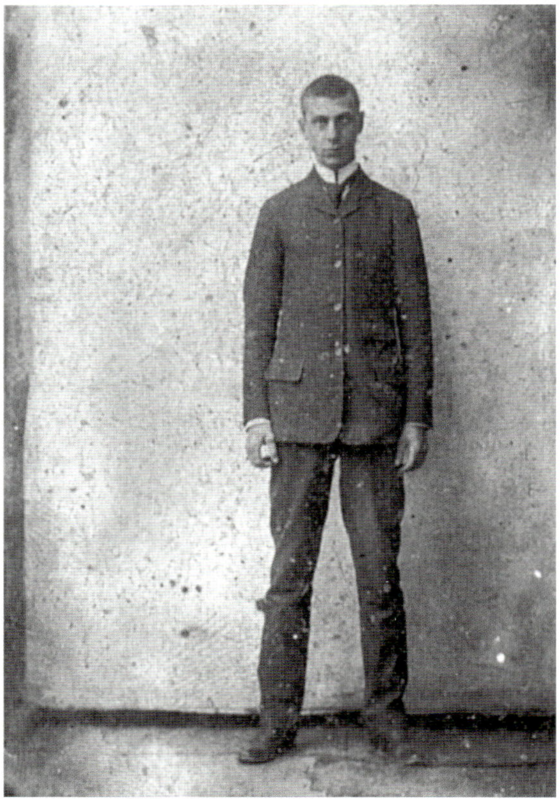

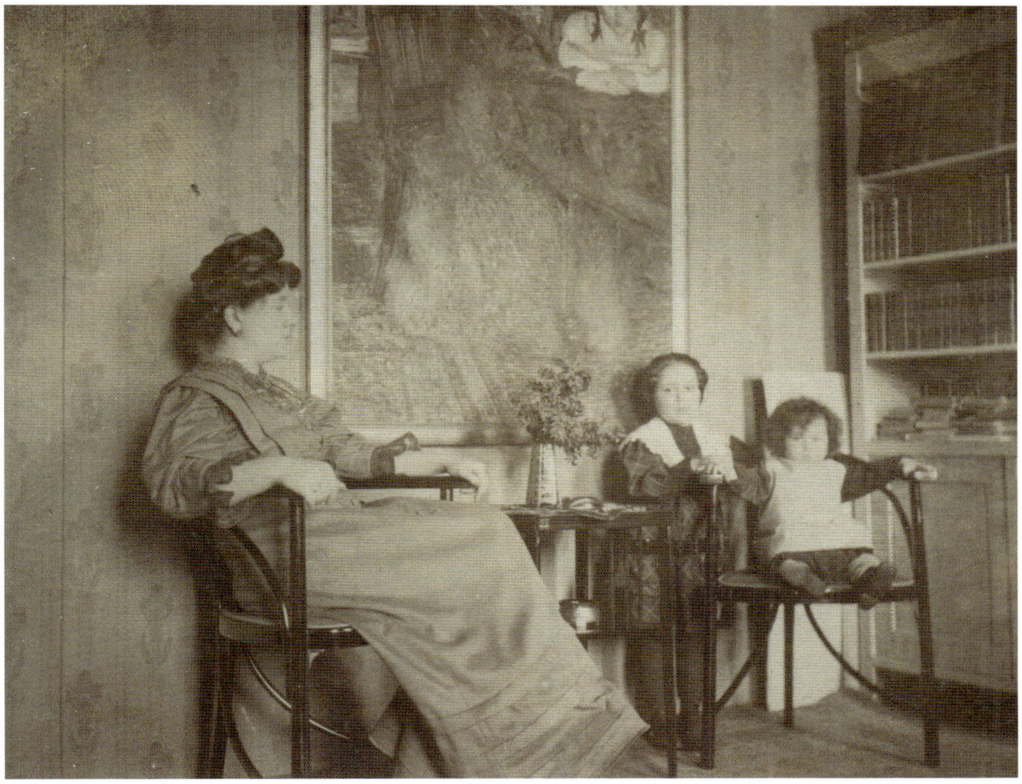

4
Mathilde Schönberg in the family apartment with Gertrud (Trudi) and Georg. Liechtensteinstraße 68/70. Gerstl's *Portrait of Mathilde Schönberg* hangs in the background. Private Collection / Courtesy Arnold Schönberg Center, Vienna

A key moment arrived in the New Year when, having found Schönberg threatening suicide after a disastrous series of concerts in February 1907, Gerstl is reputed to have diverted the composer from his avowed course by assuring him that "you are the greatest living artist that I know."[3] Their artistic and intellectual bond was now set, and Gerstl was invited to join Schönberg and his family for their long summer vacation in Gmunden, a picturesque spa town south of Salzburg [Fig. 5]. Here, Schönberg and his closest circle rented a number of farmhouses below the towering Traunstein on the eastern bank of Gmunden's beautiful glacier lake, the Traunsee [Fig. 6]. Gerstl settled into the Feramühle [Fig. 7], a mill and farmhouse close by the Schönbergs' accommodation, to spend July, August, and some of September with his new friends.

As he customarily did, Schönberg used the summer to compose, but discarded several pieces before finally turning to the first movement of his seminal *Second String Quartet* on September 1, 1907. Crucially, he would not return to the work until the following summer, again spent in Gmunden. For Gerstl, however, the summer would be one of extraordinarily swift transition, for he progressed from producing Pointillist landscapes influenced by Van Gogh, which he painted around his farmhouse, to a broader, almost abstract style, developing techniques in the process that would result in a series of startlingly innovative Expressionist portraits of the Schönberg circle the following summer.

Gerstl still found time, however, to paint the demure *Mathilde Schönberg* [Cat. no. 53] and, at the end of the vacation, a disturbing *Self-Portrait, Laughing* [Cat. no. 54]. However, while evidence

5

Gmunden on Lake Traun, ca. 1907–08, postcard. The town of Gmunden is visible in the front; the Traunstein is located at the edge of the lake. Below the Traunstein is the eastern bank, where Schönberg, Gerstl, and Schönberg's circle spent the summer of 1907 and 1908.

6

Preslgütl, Traunstein 24, ca. 1920, photograph. Private Collection

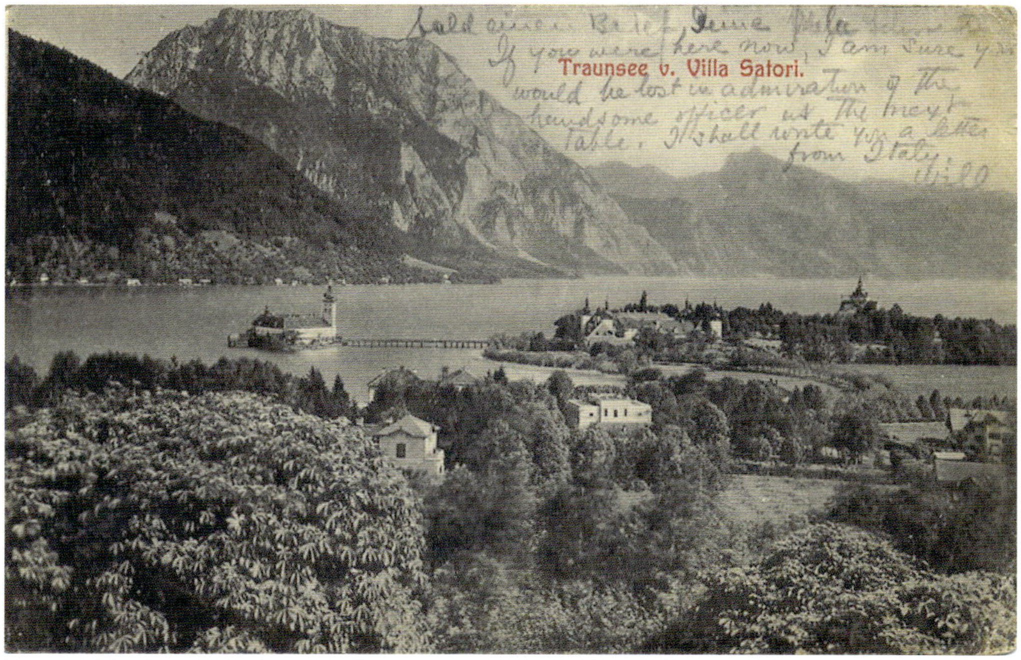

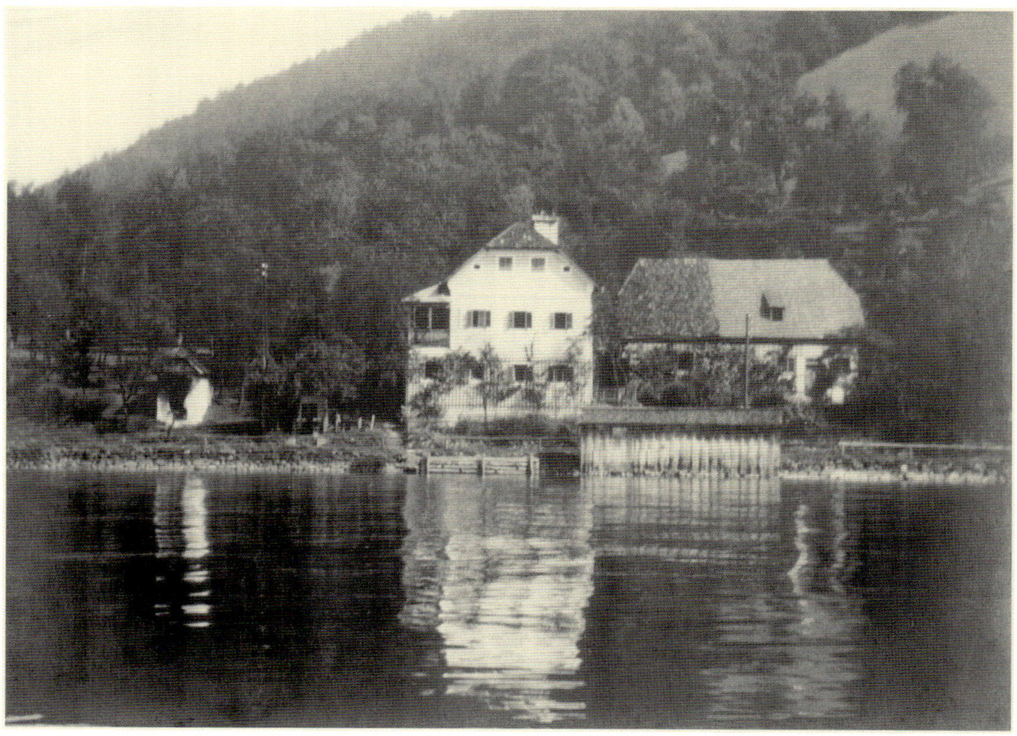

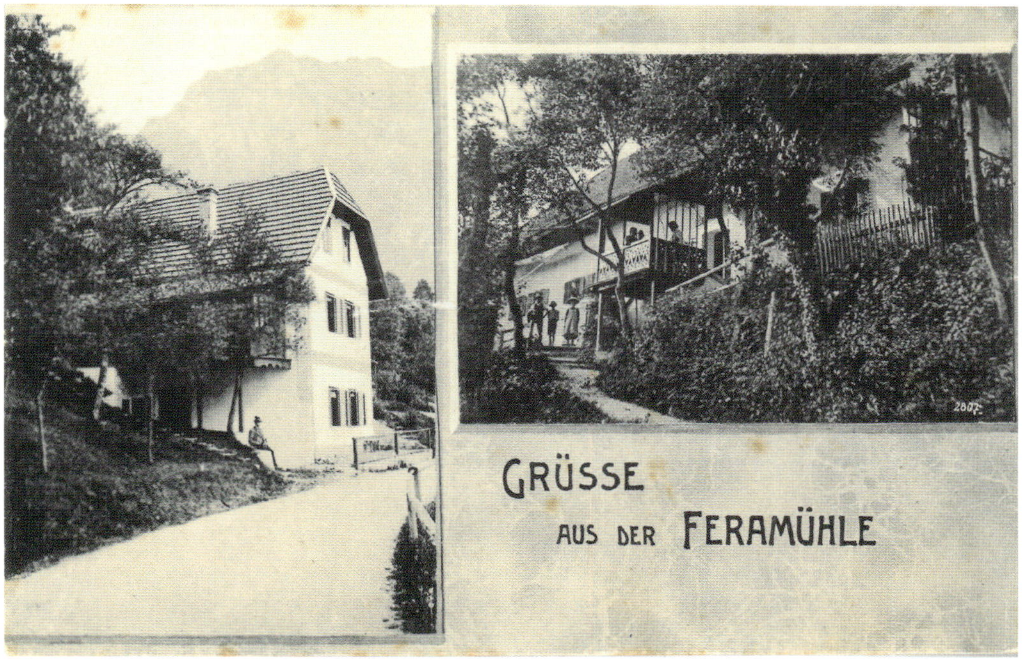

7
Postcard "Greetings from Feramühle," original prints, Phot. Anst. F. Heisig, Gmunden 1907. Private Collection

suggests that Mathilde was a woman with strong sexual desires,[4] there is no suggestion that she had already entered into a liaison with Gerstl, either at that time or in the months thereafter. Indeed, Schönberg had encouraged Gerstl to accompany his wife to concerts while he, who was having difficulty making ends meet as always, fought his publisher over income. Moreover, by February 1908, the "two chaps," or "*zwei Kerle*," as Schönberg described them, had taken a joint studio in Schönberg's building, where they shared paints, canvases, and other materials. Here Gerstl painted a series of large-scale portraits, including Mathilde, who, as Gerstl's second-favorite subject, presumably openly climbed the staircase to sit for the young artist [Cat. no. 67].

Finally, after a financially stressful few months, during which marital strains may have begun to emerge, Schönberg escorted his family back to Gmunden nearly a month earlier than usual. On June 7, 1908 he settled them into their idyllically situated and somewhat more comfortable summer farmhouse, Preslgütl. Typically, however, the perennially impecunious Schönberg had not yet acquired the funds to pay for the vacation, so he returned to Vienna two days later to do so, beginning an unprecedented eighteen-day separation from his family, during which he insisted that he and Mathilde exchange letters daily. While only Mathilde's scrawled, often illegible replies survive, they not only give a fascinating insight into their recurring marital conflicts and apparent discontents, but also strongly suggest that the greatest source of the Schönbergs' domestic tensions was their financial situation, and not that Gerstl, with whom Schönberg's personal relationship appears to have remained strong, might by then have become Mathilde's lover.

8
Handwritten copy by Karl Horwitz, dated July 4, 1908 of *Litanei* (Litany) from *Der siebente Ring* (The Seventh Ring) by Stefan Georges to Arnold Schönberg. Arnold Schönberg Center, Vienna

In fact, Schönberg again invited Gerstl to join him and his friends in Gmunden and, although the two had planned to travel together, Schönberg arrived alone on June 26 to find that members of his circle had already begun to congregate amongst the remote, secluded farmhouses on the eastern bank of the Traunsee. Gerstl was delayed and turned up in the late evening of Saturday 27, settling in again at Feramühle.

Once there, Schönberg appears to have been relaxed and convivial, taking a full ten-day break and determined, it would seem, to enjoy a family holiday with friends. Webern visited from Bad Ischl over the weekend of June 27, possibly carrying his treasured copy of Stefan George's recently published *Der siebente Ring* (The Seventh Ring). It may have been at this point that Schönberg became aware of two of the volume's poems, *Litanei* (Litany) and *Entrueckung* (Rapture), which, adapted for a soprano, would become the vocal third and fourth movements of his *Second String Quartet*, op. 10.

Though Schönberg may well have sketched the first few bars of *Entrueckung* while Webern was there, he was plainly in no rush to continue after Webern had departed, for he took over a week before writing to his student Karl Horwitz in Vienna, asking him to copy the poems and send them to Gmunden [Figs. 7–8]. Receiving them on July 5, Schönberg's jolly letter of thanks reflected his continuing good-humored mood, writing back in positive anticipation, "Now I can at last begin."[5] By July 11, he had completed *Litanei*, the prayer-like third movement.

A spell of warm, summery weather may have persuaded Schönberg to enjoy his family holiday, as he then took a near two-week break from composing, during which he continued to send out jovial correspondence to his students and displayed no sign that, deep into their vacation, any breach in the Schönbergs' marital relationship had, as yet, occurred.

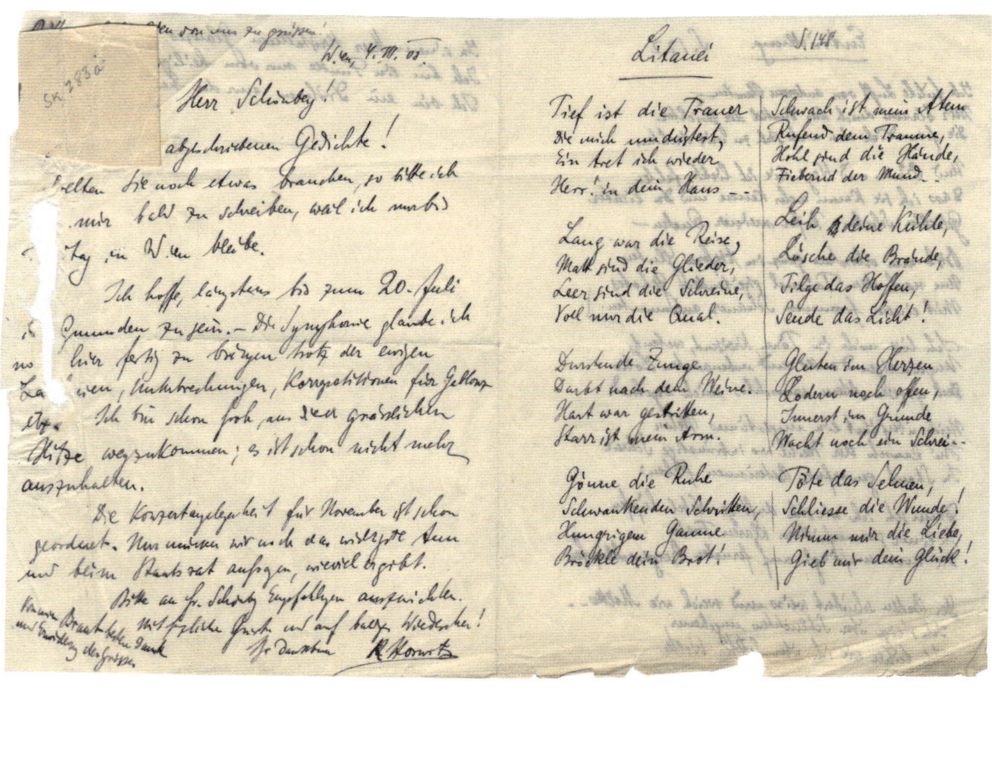
Litanei

Tief ist die Trauer
Die mich umdüstert,
Ein tret ich wieder
Herr! in dein Haus . . .

Lang war die Reise,
Matt sind die Glieder,
Leer sind die Schreine,
Voll nur die Qual.

Durstende Zunge
Darbt nach dem Weine.
Hart war gestritten,
Starr ist mein Arm.

Gönne die Ruhe
Schwankenden Schritten,
Hungrigem Gaume
Bröckle dein Brot!

Schwach ist mein Atem
Rufend dem Traume,
Hohl sind die Hände,
Fiebernd der Mund . . .

Leih deine Kühle,
Lösche die Brände,
Tilge das Hoffen,
Sende das Licht!

Gluten im Herzen
Lodern noch offen,
Innerst im Grunde
Wacht noch ein Schrei . . .

Töte das Sehnen,
Schliesse die Wunde!
Nimm mir die Liebe,
Gieb mir dein Glück!

Gerstl, on the other hand, took advantage of the good weather and, with unlimited access to his fellow holidaymakers on the grounds of the Schönbergs' farmhouse, began to paint life-size *plein-air* portraits, including those of Zemlinsky and Mathilde [Cat. nos. 77–78], catching them outside in apparent moments of spontaneity with the broad, almost disdainful brushstrokes that he had first employed the previous summer. Gerstl's mood, however, was soon to swing for, on July 22, he wrote a letter brimming with rage and indignation to the Ministry of Education, complaining that his works had been omitted from the Academy's summer exhibition, raising once more the recurrent specter of rejection.

His artistic reaction was to produce two astonishing group portraits over the next couple of days that incontrovertibly establish Gerstl as the earliest Austrian Expressionist. He first portrays the Schönberg family [Cat. no. 79], posing as one on their annual vacation, husband and wife nestled closely together, Georg on his mother's lap and Trude sitting in front of her father. Here, despite broad, impulsive brushstrokes and barely defined facial features, Gerstl not only maintains individual recognition, but evokes a sense of marital unity that defies any suspicion that the relationship between Arnold and Mathilde was under visible stress.

The second, a disturbing, impromptu life-size portrayal of friendship—Schönberg, Mathilde, Alex and Ida Zemlinsky, and, most likely, the honeymooning Horwitzs—was probably painted on July 23 or 24, 1908, with the artist, the seventh member of the group, conspicuous by his absence [Cat. no. 80]. Here, hardly subsuming his anger and feelings of rejection, Gerstl now stretched his techniques to a distorted extreme, employing broad, furious, brushstrokes and practically obfuscating faces to create nonetheless a respectful, even sympathetic vision of kinship.

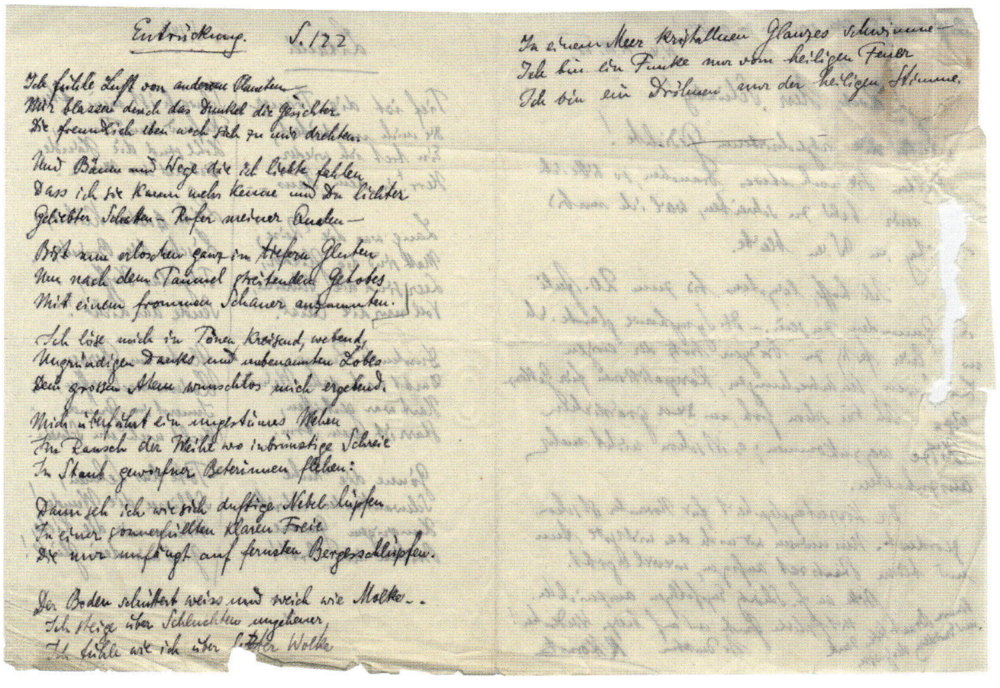
Entrückung. S. 122

Ich fühle Luft von anderem Planeten.
Mir blassen durch das Dunkel die Gesichter
Die freundlich eben noch sich zu mir drehten.
Und Bäume und Wege die ich liebte fahlen
Dass ich sie kaum mehr kenne und Du lichter
Geliebter Schatten – Rufer meiner Qualen –
Bist nun erloschen ganz in tiefern Gluten
Um nach dem Taumel streitenden Getobes
Mit einem frommen Schauer anzumuten.
Ich löse mich in Tönen, kreisend, webend,
Ungründigen Dankes und unbenamten Lobes
Dem grossen Atem wunschlos mich ergebend.
Mich überfährt ein ungestümes Wehen
Im Rausch der Weihe wo inbrünstige Schreie
In Staub geworfner Beterinnen flehen:
Dann seh ich wie sich duftige Nebel lüpfen
In einer sonnerfüllten klaren Freie
Die nur umfängt auf fernsten Bergesschlüpfen.
Der Boden schüttert weiss und weich wie Molke..
Ich steige über Schluchten ungeheuer,
Ich fühle wie ich über letzter Wolke
In einem Meer kristallnen Glanzes schwimme–
Ich bin ein Funke nur vom heiligen Feuer
Ich bin ein Dröhnen nur der heiligen Stimme.

9
Handwritten copy by Karl Horwitz, dated July 4, 1908 of *Der Entrueckung* (Rapture) from *Der siebente Ring* (The Seventh Ring) by Stefan Georges to Arnold Schönberg. Arnold Schönberg Center, Vienna

10
Richard Gerstl, *The Schönberg Family*, late July 1908, oil on canvas. Museum moderner Kunst Stiftung Ludwig Wien, Gift of the Kamm Family, Zug 1969

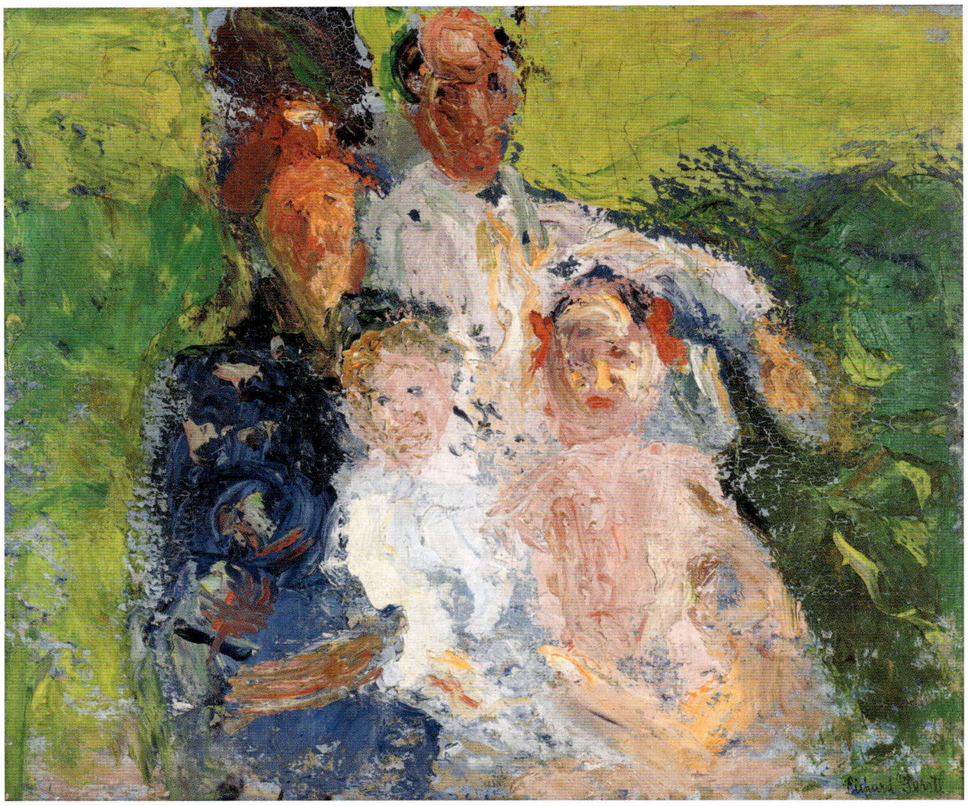

Schönberg, as the central subject of both paintings, could not have failed to recognize the extraordinary creative advances that Gerstl was making through both his liberated, unrestrained, visceral brushwork and its attendant dissolution of form. Perhaps inspired and invigorated by his friend's sheer force of originality, he emerged from his voluntary interregnum, and swiftly returned to his *Second String Quartet*. Indeed, by July 27, he had completed the second movement, the Scherzo, in whose trio Schönberg fleetingly introduces the line, "Alles ist hin" (All is lost) from the old Viennese street ballad, *Ach! du lieber Augustin* (Oh! You dear Augustin). This has led to much speculation that, despite Schönberg's explicit denial, such an unexpected musical quotation was either a reference to his marriage, or his imminent desertion of tonality in the fourth movement of his *Second String Quartet*, which Schönberg then finished three or four days later.

The fourth movement is a vocal setting of Stefan George's *Entrückung*, whose very first line, "Ich fühle luft von anderem planeten"—"I feel air from another planet"—has likewise been the subject of considerable speculation as to whether Schönberg was representing the breakdown of his marriage, or even signalling that Mathilde's infidelity had been the catalyst for his leap to atonality. The simple truth, however, is that, by the time Schönberg had finished composing his *Second String Quartet* in the last days of July 1908, and subsequently sent off the finished parts a couple of weeks later to Mahler's brother-in-law, Arnold Rosé, for rehearsal, Schönberg still had no reason to suspect any infidelity on his wife's part; indeed, her affair with Gerstl had probably not even commenced at that point.

In fact, it was not until August 26, nearly four weeks after finishing the composition, that Richard and Mathilde were discovered in a compromising situation in Feramühle. Schönberg's reaction was one of such violent shock that it beggars belief that he could have suspected beforehand. He refused to listen to Mathilde's exhortations, so she and Gerstl set off back to Vienna. Too late for the last train, the two stayed overnight in Stadt Frankfurt, a hotel in Gmunden. The night was warm, still, humid, and clear, and Schönberg, now desolate, set off on the long walk into the brightly lit main town on an unsuccessful expedition to find his wife, smashing his head against a tree in despair along the way. That night, perhaps a little tipsy, he sat on his veranda and wrote a heartbreaking, unfinished testament, in which he again threatened suicide, bemoaned his lack of success, and disowned his wife.

11
Richard Gerstl, *Group Portrait with Schönberg*, late July 1908 (ca. July 23, 1908), oil on canvas. Kunsthaus Zug, Stiftung Sammlung Kamm

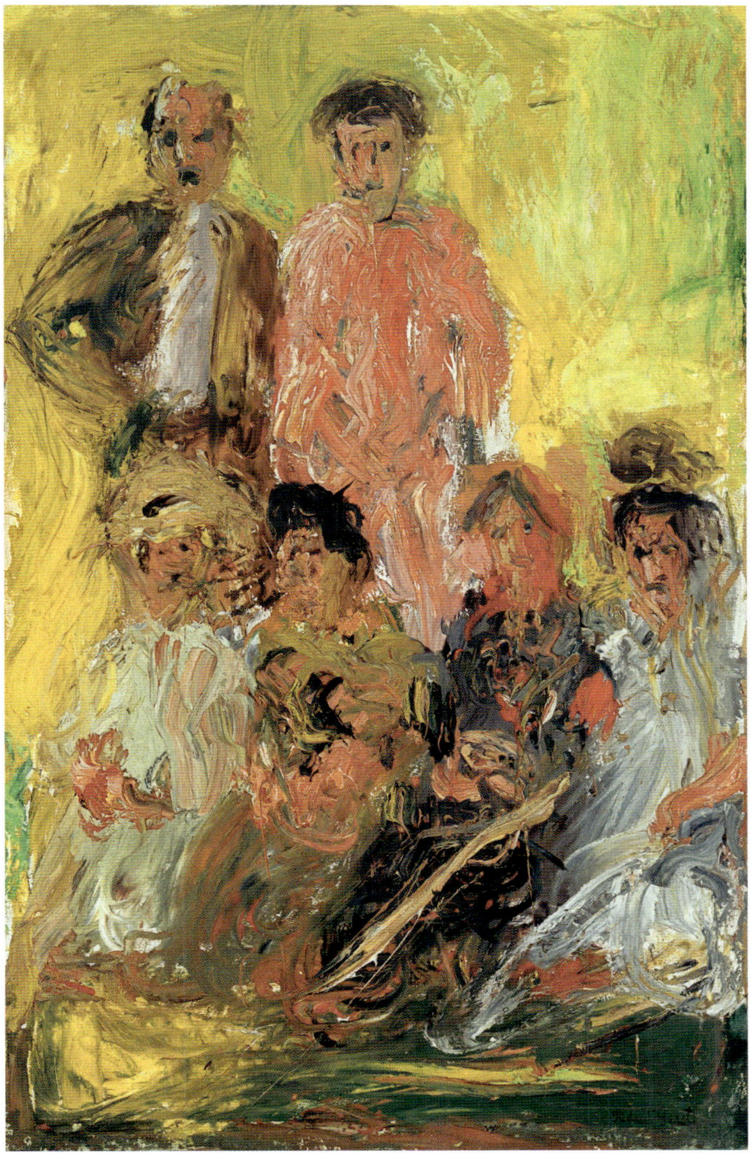

12
Certificate of registration for a place of business of Richard Gerstl, October 18, 1908, Vienna's ninth district, Liechtensteinstraße 20. Wiener Stadt-und Landesarchiv, Historische Meldeunterlagen

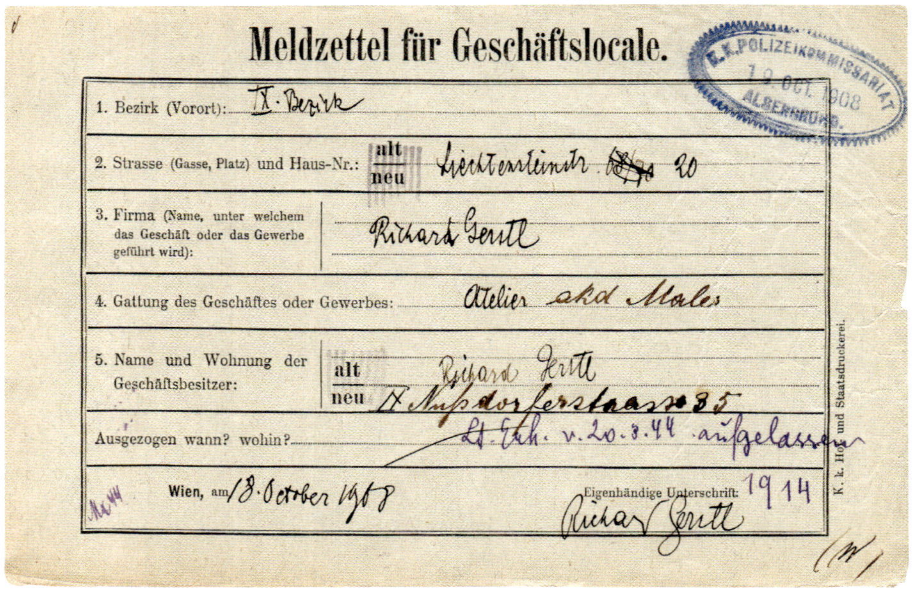

Meldzettel für Geschäftslocale.

1. Bezirk (Vorort): IX. Bezirk
2. Strasse (Gasse, Platz) und Haus-Nr.: alt / neu Liechtensteinstr. 20
3. Firma (Name, unter welchem das Geschäft oder das Gewerbe geführt wird): Richard Gerstl
4. Gattung des Geschäftes oder Gewerbes: Atelier
5. Name und Wohnung der Geschäftsbesitzer: alt Richard Gerstl; neu IX Nussdorferstrasse 35

Ausgezogen wann? wohin?

Wien, am 18. October 1908 — Eigenhändige Unterschrift: Richard Gerstl

K. k. Hof- und Staatsdruckerei.

The runaways, meanwhile, travelled to Vienna the next day, stopping briefly by the Schönbergs' apartment, where Mathilde hastily half-wrote a self-pitying letter of remorse. By late that evening, the lovers were installed in a pension in the northern suburb of Nussdorf. From here, Mathilde had her letter, now finished, hand-delivered to her husband, whereupon Schönberg reported his wife as missing. The registration of accommodation at the local police station quickly revealed her whereabouts, and to his great relief, Mathilde returned home on August 30.

Unable to re-enter his studio in Schönberg's building, expelled from the Academy following his vitriolic letter and with Mathilde gone, Gerstl returned to his family and began to paint, responding to rejection with his alarming *Nude Self-Portrait,* as he had previously done with *Semi-Nude Self-Portrait.* He thus came full circle in his inveterate search for self-representation and exploration of sexual self-awareness. The work was probably painted in his parents' living room, where, in his solitude, he displays himself fully naked against a blue aura, with his most powerful attributes—his sex, his head, and his paintbrushes—deliberately tinted in a far deeper tone than his sallow, skeletal frame. This, then, rather than an indication of pre-suicidal tendencies, is the depiction of an artist at the height of his powers, proudly exploiting his potency, having slept with the unhappy wife of a man who had not only become his friend but his colleague, too.

Indeed, thoughts of suicide could not have been further from Gerstl's mind, for on October 18, he gathered his paintings and paraphernalia, and, perhaps with a view to becoming a professional artist, took possession of a light, airy commercial studio on the top floor of 20 Liechtensteinstraße overlooking Freud's consulting rooms [Fig. 12]. Moreover, the flame in Mathilde's heart had not been extinguished, for she visited the new studio, where Gerstl painted her naked, and she, according to Gerstl's close student friend, Victor Hammer, satisfied his strong sexual needs.[6]

Then on November 4, Schönberg's students put on an invitation-only concert of their new works at the Musikverein. Anton Webern, Gerstl's friend, now became involved, and persuaded Mathilde to return "for the sake of the children." Leaving personal belongings behind in her lover's studio, she never saw him again. Excluded from the concert, Gerstl may have listened wistfully outside the hall, before returning to his studio, where, rejected by both his lover and his friends, he stood on a chair in front of his trusty mirror with a noose around his neck and a kitchen knife in his hand, before stabbing himself in the heart and hanging himself. His mother, who had become alarmed by the afternoon's events, sent her maid scurrying round at 5 pm. Too late, for Gerstl, having never exhibited in his life, was dead.

Schönberg panicked, fearing a scandal, but Maria Gerstl's Catholic sense of shame ensured that her son was buried quickly and without publicity. His paintings were packed off to the furniture warehouse from where, twenty-three years later, Alois would introduce them to Otto Nirenstein.

As for Schönberg, just six weeks later, on December 21, 1908, he saw the première of his *Second String Quartet*. Presumably Mathilde was by his side, for, although he never meant the work to be a song to the siren, he now rededicated it simply to "Meiner Frau" (My Wife) [Fig. 13].

13

Arnold Schönberg, *Second String Quartet,* op. 10, title page with dedication to his wife, before 1908. Library of Congress, Washington, D.C.

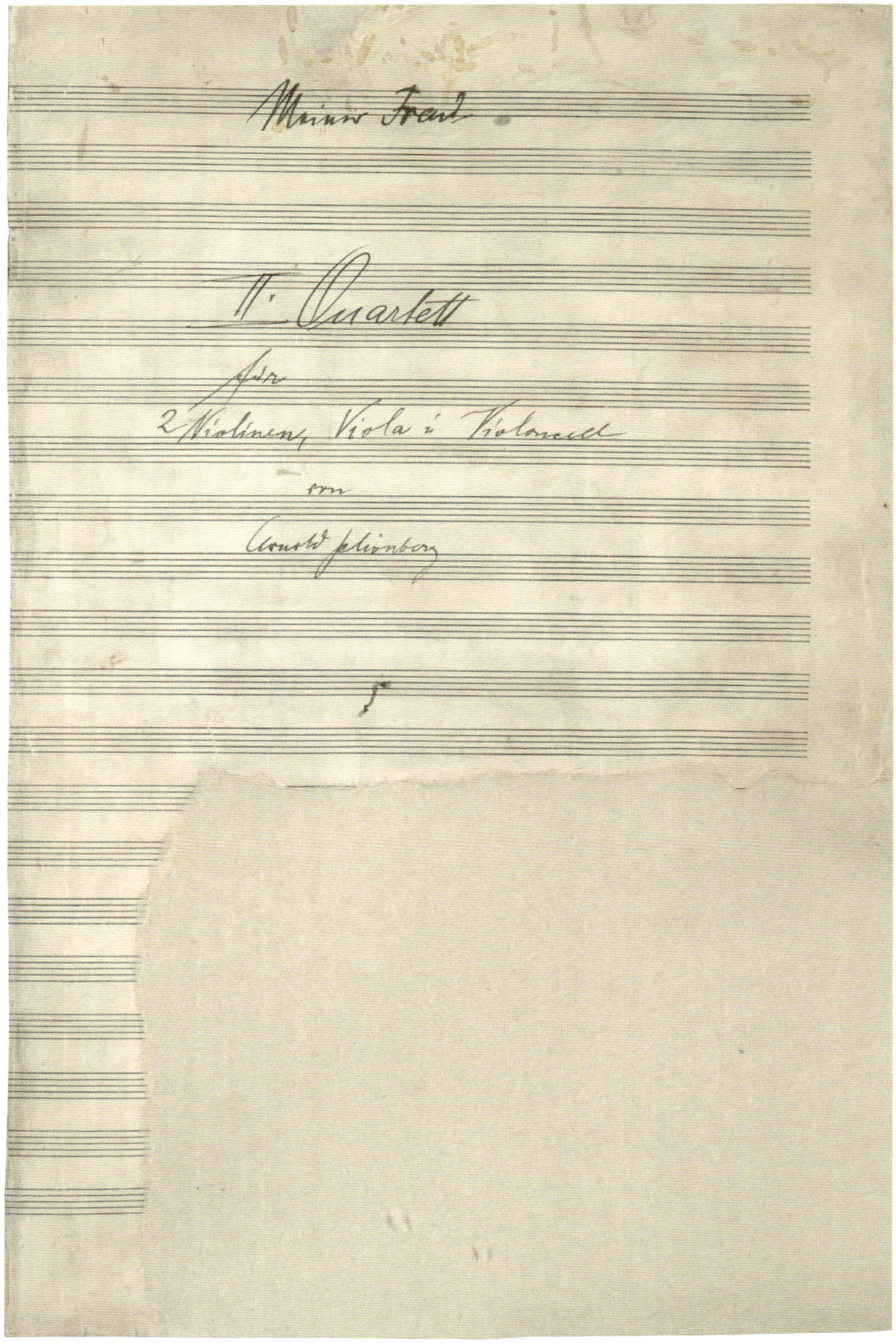

1 The details in this essay are drawn from the author's doctoral thesis, *Richard Gerstl and Arnold Schönberg: A Reassessment of their Relationship (1906–1908) and its Impact on their Artistic Works*, Raymond Charles Coffer, Institute of Germanic and Romance Studies, University of London, 2011, or see www.richardgerstl.com/thesis-2.

2 For a justification of the dating of this painting see Coffer p. 84 in present publication. Otto Breicha, who met and befriended Alois Gerstl in 1960, maintained in many memoranda, documents and essays, dating from to his first meeting with Alois to his death in 2003, as well as during many conversations with the author, that Alois was adamant that his brother, Richard, had painted his *Semi-Nude Self-Portrait* as a 19 year old, therefore either in late 1902 or early 1903.

3 Alois Gerstl's oral recollections, around 1961, Archiv Otto Breicha Archive.

4 Coffer 2011 (see note 1), 136–138 for details.

5 "Jetzt kann ich erst anfangen." Schönberg to Horwitz, July 5, 1908, Arnold Schönberg Center.

6 Victor Hammer to Otto Kallir, July 5, [1964], Victor Hammer Collection, Library of Congress.

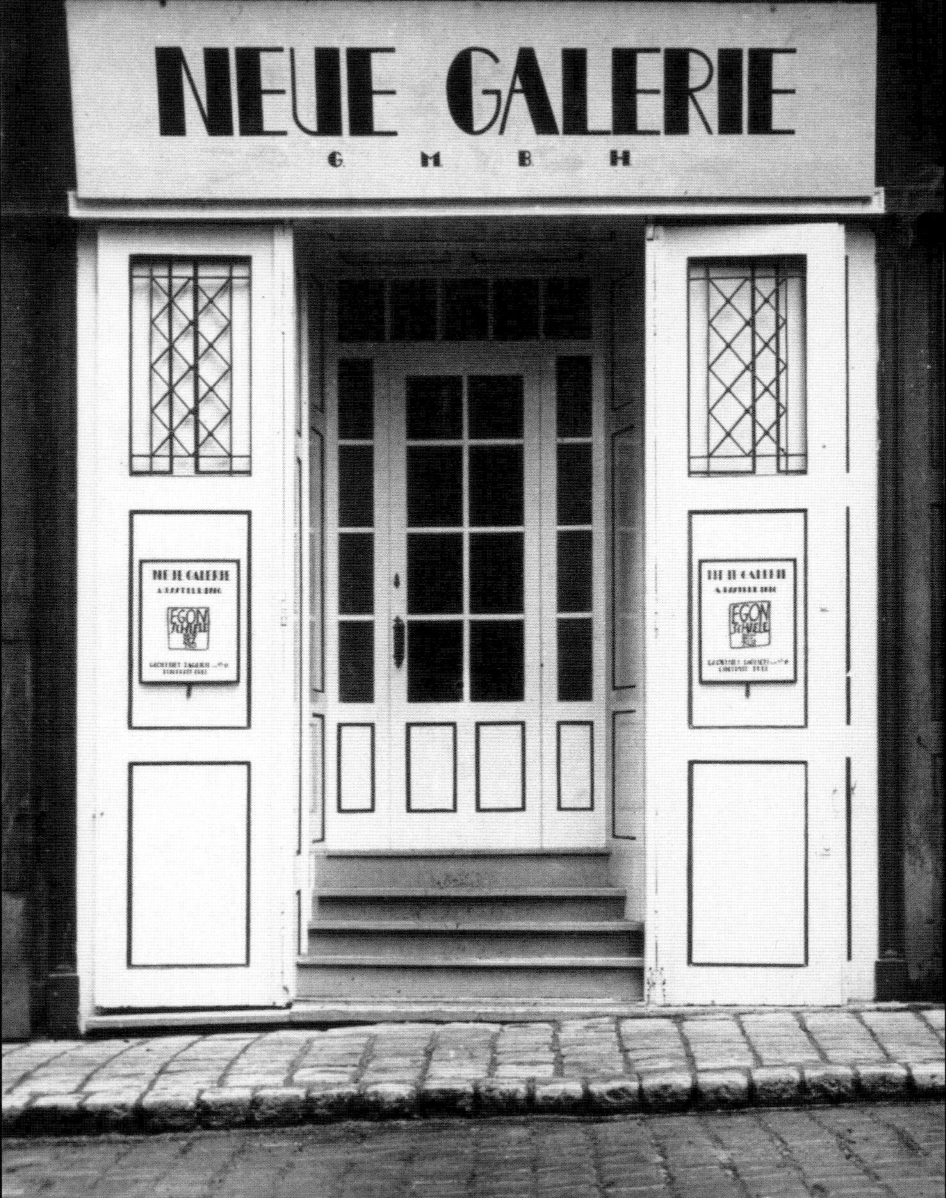
NEUE GALERIE
G M B H

JANE KALLIR

The Remarkable Discovery and Rediscovery of Richard Gerstl

On November 4, 1908, the twenty-five-year-old Austrian artist Richard Gerstl thrust a knife into his chest and hanged himself.[1] Prior to his death, Gerstl had hovered between a student existence and mature professional practice. His work had never been publically exhibited. This was due, in part, to the artist's reluctance to share his creations and to his contempt for contemporary artistic trends.[2] In 1907, he turned down an offer to exhibit at the prestigious Galerie Miethke when he learned that Gustav Klimt's work would also be shown. He also declined to exhibit at the Ansorge Verein, an interdisciplinary cultural group associated with Arnold Schönberg's circle.[3] However, Gerstl's semi-abstract brand of Expressionism was so atypical for anything being created in Austria at that time that even his supporters feared an exhibition would provoke a scandal.[4] Not immune to the sting of rejection, Gerstl complained bitterly when he was excluded from the Vienna Academy of Fine Art's 1908 student exhibition.[5]

Alois Gerstl, the artist's brother, claimed that Richard burned all the letters, notes, paintings and drawings in his studio before killing himself.[6] This statement is partly belied by the number of canvases that survived, including many in the studio.[7] Regardless, a number of personal documents were destroyed, along with most of the artist's works on paper—either by Richard or, as has been recently suggested, by his other brother, August, with whom he had a strained relationship.[8] Only nine significant drawings (on eight sheets of paper)—all of them self-portraits executed in a mix of ink, wash and watercolor—have to date been recorded.[9] And some twenty to twenty-five paintings, abandoned when Gerstl left Gmunden in the summer of 1908, are also believed to have been lost.[10] What remained was sent to storage at the warehouse of Rosin & Knauer in Vienna by Richard's family.

Twenty-three years later, in 1931, Alois Gerstl took a few of his brother's landscape studies to Vienna's Neue Galerie [Fig. 1]. Alois wanted to know whether the works were worth keeping or whether they should be thrown out.[11] The gallery, established by my grandfather, Otto Kallir [Fig. 2] in 1923, represented such contemporary Austrian artists as Oskar Kokoschka and Alfred Kubin, and played a central role in sustaining the posthumous reputation of Egon Schiele, who had died in 1918.

On the basis of the small landscapes, my grandfather agreed to accompany Alois to view the rest of the works at Rosin & Knauer. There, my grandfather recalled, he "found a great number of unstretched, rolled or folded canvases. . . . Many had been damaged by unprofessional

1
The Neue Galerie in Vienna (Grünangergasse 1), 1923, photograph. Courtesy Galerie St. Etienne, New York

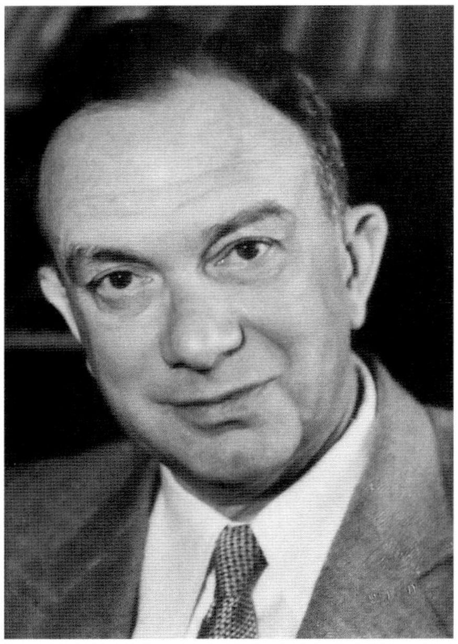

2
Otto Kallir, ca. 1949, photograph. Courtesy Galerie St. Etienne, New York

3
Estate stamp on the front side of Richard Gerstl, *Self-Portrait,* winter 1906–07 [Cat. no. 28]. Courtesy Galerie St. Etienne, New York. Every work from Gerstl's estate was marked with a stamp, signed, and numbered by Otto Nirenstein (Kallir).

handling, the canvases often torn, many pictures cut apart, everything dirty and dusty, so that one could hardly make out the colors. Nonetheless, this first encounter with the work of the unknown painter Richard Gerstl was an extraordinarily powerful one."[12] While he recognized that a great deal of effort and expense would be required to restore and promote the paintings, Kallir "immediately resolved to do everything possible to resurrect the name of this forgotten artist."[13]

A trained art historian who had recently published the first Schiele catalogue raisonné,[14] Kallir began by systematically examining and documenting Gerstl's surviving oeuvre. Each work was given a title, marked with an estate stamp [Fig. 3], numbered and photographed.[15] Alois helped identify many of the portrait subjects, but it was not easy to make sense of the artist's disparate production. "The often surprisingly uneven quality of Gerstl's paintings frequently puzzled me," Kallir recalled. "In contrast to Schiele, it is difficult to discern a consistent development with Gerstl. In his early as well as his late years, he produced both excellent as well as bad, almost kitschy pictures. They were all mixed up."[16] Although Kallir was impressed by many of the paintings he saw at Rosin & Knauer, some were so inferior, in his opinion, that he did not want to exhibit them. "I was a afraid that, in a first exhibition, the unevenness would confuse visitors and weaken the impact of the main works."[17]

In May 1931, Kallir purchased 34 paintings from Gerstl's estate and acquired an option to buy or consign the remainder [Fig. 4].[18] The rejects stayed at Rosin & Knauer or with Alois Gerstl.[19] By autumn, the selected works had been restored and were ready to be shown.

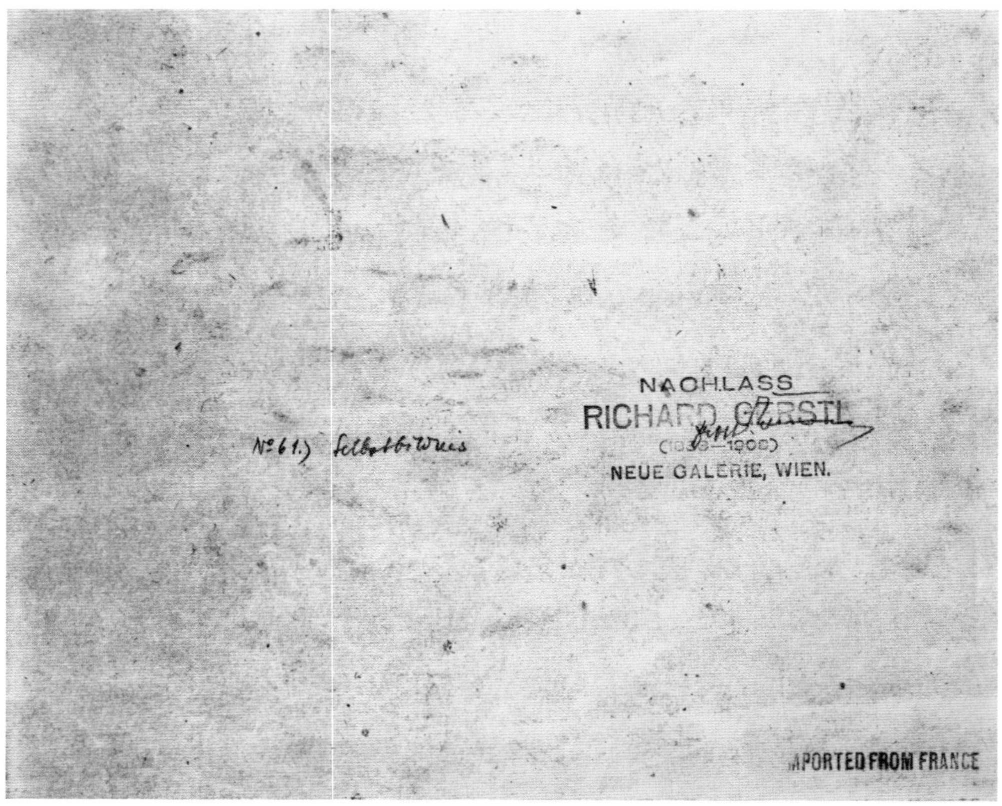

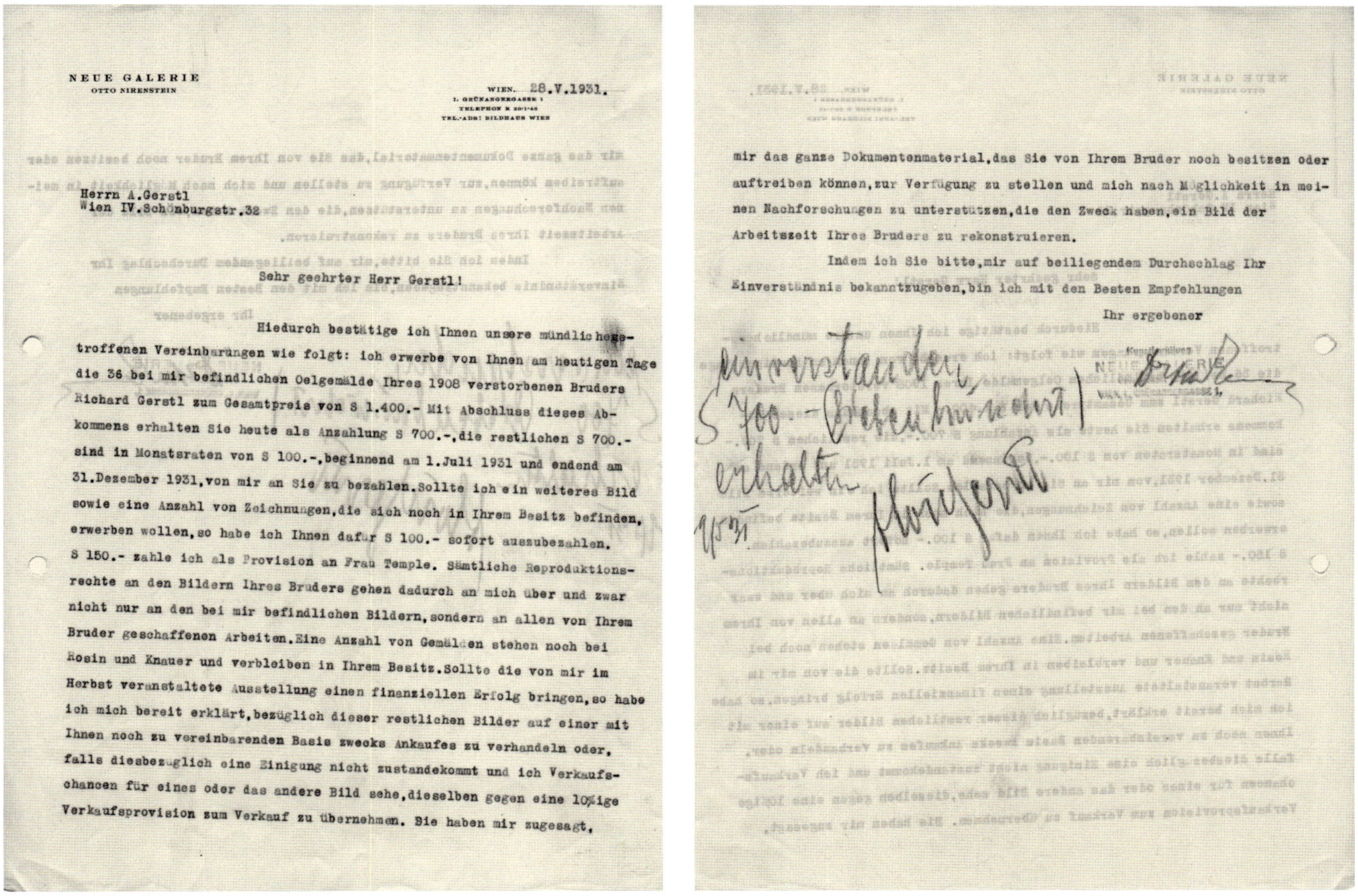

NEUE GALERIE
OTTO NIRENSTEIN

WIEN. 28.V.1931.
I. GRÜNANGERGASSE 1
TELEPHON R 20-1-48
TEL.-ADR: BILDHAUS WIEN

Herrn A.Gerstl
Wien IV.Schönburgstr.32

Sehr geehrter Herr Gerstl!

Hiedurch bestätige ich Ihnen unsere mündlich getroffenen Vereinbarungen wie folgt: ich erwerbe von Ihnen am heutigen Tage die 36 bei mir befindlichen Oelgemälde Ihres 1908 verstorbenen Bruders Richard Gerstl zum Gesamtpreis von S 1.400.- Mit Abschluss dieses Abkommens erhalten Sie heute als Anzahlung S 700.-,die restlichen S 700.- sind in Monatsraten von S 100.-,beginnend am 1.Juli 1931 und endend am 31.Dezember 1931,von mir an Sie zu bezahlen.Sollte ich ein weiteres Bild sowie eine Anzahl von Zeichnungen,die sich noch in Ihrem Besitz befinden, erwerben wollen,so habe ich Ihnen dafür S 100.- sofort auszubezahlen. S 150.- zahle ich als Provision an Frau Temple. Sämtliche Reproduktionsrechte an den Bildern Ihres Bruders gehen dadurch an mich über und zwar nicht nur an den bei mir befindlichen Bildern,sondern an allen von Ihrem Bruder geschaffenen Arbeiten.Eine Anzahl von Gemälden stehen noch bei Rosin und Knauer und verbleiben in Ihrem Besitz.Sollte die von mir im Herbst veranstaltete Ausstellung einen finanziellen Erfolg bringen,so habe ich mich bereit erklärt,bezüglich dieser restlichen Bilder auf einer mit Ihnen noch zu vereinbarenden Basis zwecks Ankaufes zu verhandeln oder, falls diesbezüglich eine Einigung nicht zustandekommt und ich Verkaufschancen für eines oder das andere Bild sehe,dieselben gegen eine 10%ige Verkaufsprovision zum Verkauf zu übernehmen. Sie haben mir zugesagt,

mir das ganze Dokumentenmaterial,das Sie von Ihrem Bruder noch besitzen oder auftreiben können,zur Verfügung zu stellen und mich nach Möglichkeit in meinen Nachforschungen zu unterstützen,die den Zweck haben,ein Bild der Arbeitszeit Ihres Bruders zu rekonstruieren.

Indem ich Sie bitte,mir auf beiliegendem Durchschlag Ihr Einverständnis bekanntzugeben,bin ich mit den Besten Empfehlungen

Ihr ergebener

“Richard Gerstl: A Painter’s Fate” opened at the Neue Galerie in Vienna on September 28, 1931.[20] “Never before had the first exhibition of an Austrian painter received comparable international attention,” Kallir remembered.[21] The *Neues Wiener Journal* dubbed Gerstl “an Austrian Van Gogh.”[22] He was hailed as an “amazing discovery” by the Österreichische Reichpost. “There will hardly be a second case in the history of art where such an artistic genius remained completely hidden, even though his painterly strength was unsurpassed by any of his contemporaries.”[23] “An artistic sensation of the first order has taken place in Vienna,” reported the *Kölnische Zeitung*. “A success unequaled by anything that has happened in the realm of art for the last century.”[24] “One of the most important artists of the early 20th century,” declared the *Kleines Volksblatt*. “On a par with … Manet and Van Gogh.”[25] “An apostle for the art of the future,” observed the *Neues Wiener Extrablatt*.[26]

The international resonance was so great that a few months after the Gerstl show closed in Vienna, Kallir sent it to the Galerie Caspari in Munich. From there, it traveled to the Galerie Gurlitt in Berlin, the Kölnischer Kunstverein in Cologne, and the Städtische Suermondt-Museum

4
Original contract between Alois Gerstl and Otto Nirenstein (Kallir), May 28, 1931. Courtesy Galerie St. Etienne, New York

in Aachen.[27] Just days after the Aachen exhibition opened, however, Adolf Hitler was appointed Chancellor of Germany. Although Gerstl was probably not well enough known to make it onto the official lists of banned artists, his Expressionistic style was incompatible with Nazi cultural dictates. After Hitler annexed Austria in 1938, Kallir, who was Jewish, sold the Neue Galerie in Vienna to his secretary, Vita Künstler, and fled to America.

Künstler's purchase was a rare example of a "friendly Aryanization." Künstler protected the gallery throughout the National Socialist years and voluntarily returned it to Kallir after World War II. Because Kallir began making arrangements to emigrate immediately after the *Anschluss*, and because many of the artists he represented were "degenerate" according to Nazi standards, he was able to take a significant inventory into exile.[28] Nevertheless, the scale of Gerstl's major oils made them impractical to transport. Kallir brought with him only one small painting and four of the self-portrait drawings. He regularly included these in group exhibitions at his New York Galerie St. Etienne, but he did not have enough works to introduce Gerstl to the American public properly.

In 1939, when Kallir established the Galerie St. Etienne, Austrian modernism was virtually unknown in the United States. Only Oskar Kokoschka, who was still alive, had any sort of international reputation. Despite repeatedly exhibiting the work of Egon Schiele, Kallir had no real success with the artist until 1957. Gustav Klimt was still largely unrecognized outside Austria in 1959, when the Galerie St. Etienne hosted his first American exhibition. Approximately twenty-two Gerstl paintings had survived the war in storage at the Neue Galerie in Vienna, but Kallir was not sure what to do with them.[29] In the early 1950s, the expense of transporting these large canvases to New York was no less of a financial risk than it had been in 1938. And in any case, Kallir doubted the Austrian government would grant him an export license. So in 1955, he sold his Viennese Gerstl inventory for the bargain price of $4,000 to the Galerie Würthle, which at the time was run by the sculptor Fritz Wotruba.[30] Kallir made only one condition: "that the paintings would be made available to me in the future for an exhibition in America."[31]

Ten years later, international awareness of Austrian modernism had improved considerably. In 1960, Kallir had helped organize the first American museum exhibitions of Schiele's work,[32] and in 1965, he convinced Thomas Messer, director of the Guggenheim Museum, to mount a major joint Klimt and Schiele show.[33] The following year, the Vienna Secession presented a large Gerstl retrospective.[34] Kallir tried desperately to convince the Secession's president, Walter Eckert, to send the show to America, even offering to cover part of the bill. But Eckert, for reasons unknown, demurred.[35] Wotruba also never granted Kallir's request to exhibit the Gerstl paintings in America.[36] Kallir, however, remained convinced that success for Gerstl must "come from abroad, as it did for OK [Oskar Kokoschka] and now for Schiele."[37]

Time has proven Kallir right. Gerstl first entered the international arena in 1956, when the art historian Werner Hofmann selected ten of the artist's paintings for inclusion in Austria's pavilion at the 1956 Venice Biennale.[38] But Gerstl's reputation really took off following a spate of "Vienna 1900" exhibitions,[39] which peaked in the mid 1980s with blockbuster presentations in Venice, Paris and New York.[40] To be sure, Gerstl was seldom singled out for special mention in reviews of those exhibitions, which were dominated by Klimt, Kokoschka and Schiele. Nevertheless, as the multivalent cultural and intellectual achievements of *fin-de-siècle* Austria began receiving more scholarly attention, Gerstl became ensconced in the literature.[41] His relationship with Arnold Schönberg made him ripe for an interdisciplinary approach, prompting comparisons between the composer's "emancipation of dissonance" and the painter's "emancipation of brushstroke."[42]

After Otto Kallir's death in 1978, the Galerie St. Etienne, under the directorship of Hildegard Bachert and myself, inaugurated a program of museum-scale loan exhibitions. Starting with "Austria's Expressionism" in 1981,[43] and again with "Arnold Schoenberg's Vienna" in 1985,[44] we brought for the first time some of Gerstl's most important canvases from Austria to the United States. As a private gallery, we were unable to mount a one-man show given the cost of securing foreign loans. In 1992, we featured Gerstl alongside Kokoschka and assembled 26 works for the exhibition "Richard Gerstl, Oskar Kokoschka." This was the largest American presentation until now of the artist's work.[45] The Kamm family in Switzerland, which had owned the Galerie Würthle during Wotruba's tenure, made good on the sculptor's promise and loaned seven works from their private collection. All three exhibitions at Galerie St. Etienne were widely acclaimed by the public and press, which recognized that borrowing so many Gerstls from European collections was "a considerable coup."[46]

One-man Gerstl shows, mounted at the Galerie Würthle in 1957 and 1966,[47] the Historisches Museum der Stadt Wien in 1983[48] and the Kunstforum der Bank Austria in 1993[49] were obviously easier to organize in Austria than elsewhere. In 1994, the latter exhibition traveled to the Kunsthaus Zürich, marking the first major presentation on Gerstl outside of Austria since the 1930s. The Kamm Family provided their Gerstl collection on long-term loan in 1998 to the Kunsthaus Zug, where the paintings are periodically exhibited or loaned to other institutions.[50] In 2001 the Austrian state built a museum to house the collection of Rudolf Leopold, who owned a significant number of Gerstl canvases.[51] Today, Gerstl's paintings are regularly on view in Vienna at the Belvedere (which purchased its first Gerstl paintings from the Neue Galerie in 1946[52]), the Leopold Museum, and the Wien Museum. The Neue Galerie New York featured Gerstl in its 2001 inaugural exhibition,[53] and his paintings have been displayed there ever since. Although his oeuvre is of a very limited number and mainly confined to Austrian collections, Gerstl's position alongside Klimt, Schiele and Kokoschka is now secure.

Scholarship on the artist developed in tandem with the artist's slowly growing reputation. Otto Kallir always hoped to produce a catalogue raisonné of Gerstl's works. In addition to his original catalogue of the estate, Kallir retained records of all the early exhibitions in Austria and Germany, photographs and a file of press clippings. In 1954 he asked Alois Gerstl to write a memoir about his brother, and in 1963 he obtained a similar document from the artist's erstwhile studio mate, Victor Hammer.[54] During the early 1960s, Kallir contacted Austrian art historian Otto Breicha, who also wanted to write a Gerstl catalogue raisonné. When it became evident that collaboration with Breicha would be impossible, in 1974 Kallir published his principal documents in the *Mitteilungen der Österreichischen Galerie*. In addition to the 63 works (some double-sided) that were in the original estate, "Richard Gerstl: Beiträge zur Dokumentation seines Lebens und Werkes" includes four further paintings that Kallir knew and considered authentic.[55]

Two interrelated problems have historically impeded Gerstl scholarship: the difficulty of dating the artist's work, and a paucity of information about his brief life. Gerstl himself dated only six works, four illegibly.[56] While additional dates can be deduced from the circumstances surrounding the execution of certain pieces, there is not enough information upon which to construct an overall chronology. It seems logical to posit a developmental trajectory that begins with relatively academic works, continues through Gerstl's pointillist phase and ends with the broad-stroke Expressionism ascribed to his final year or years.[57] But Gerstl's stylistic shifts could also have been influenced by violent moods swings.[58] Some have proposed to date the self-portraits according to the artist's hairstyle, which he is said to have cropped, like a convict, when he was depressed.[59] It is understandable that Kallir preferred to adhere to his relatively random original numbering rather than impose an order that would risk being even "more inexact."[60]

Breicha intended to develop a schema for dating Gerstl's work,[61] but evidently he gave up.[62] It was left to Klaus Albrecht Schröder to compile the first comprehensive Gerstl catalogue raisonné.[63] His book, published in 1993, doubled as the catalogue for the retrospective at the Kunstforum, of which he was then director. Schröder's research, enriched by a wealth of newly unearthed public and private sources, was subsequently augmented by Raymond Charles Coffer, whose 2011 doctorial dissertation, "Richard Gerstl and Arnold Schoenberg," offers the fullest account thus far of the artist's life and work.[64] Crucially, after Breicha's death in 2003, the art historian's family gave Coffer access to his unpublished papers.[65] As a result, Coffer's dating of Gerstl's work in many respects seems more plausible than the chronology proposed by Schröder.[66]

The present Gerstl exhibitions at the Schirn Kunsthalle and the Neue Galerie New York are the culmination of more than 85 years of work, begun by Kallir and advanced by each of his successors. Kallir concluded his 1974 "Dokumentation" with the hope that "perhaps in the future Richard Gerstl's name will be known beyond Austria's borders."[67] That day has come.

1 The Vienna police report lists the cause of death as "loss of blood from stabbing" (*Stickfluß*), while the city records list it as "hanging" (*Erhängen*). (Raymond Charles Coffer, "Richard Gerstl and Arnold Schönberg: A Reassessment of their Relationship (1906–1908) and its Impact on their Artistic Works," PhD thesis, Institute of Germanic and Romance Studies, University of London, 2011, 58.)

2 Victor Hammer, "Erinnerungen an Richard Gerstl," in Otto Kallir, "Richard Gerstl (1883–1908): Beiträge zur Dokumentation seines Lebens und Werkes," *Mitteiliungen der Österreichischen Galerie*, Vienna, 1974, 142.

3 Alois Gerstl, "Biographische Aufzeichnungen über Richard Gerstl," cf. Kallir 1974 (see note 2), 139.

4 Ibid. Alois Gerstl refers to an exhibition at the Hagenbund, which was apparently suggested by Gerstl's Professor at the Vienna Academy of Fine Arts, Heinrich Lefler. It is not clear whether the suggestion was made during Gerstl's lifetime or immediately after his suicide, in which case Lefler may have changed his mind because of the circumstances surrounding the artist's death (Coffer, 295, 297).

5 Coffer, 183.

6 Kallir 1974 (see note 2), 125.

7 Coffer, 295–96. However, as Kallir mentions (see note 12), a great many canvases had been cut before he became in involved with the estate, and the number of surviving fragments suggests that the artist may have slashed (rather than burned) his work.

8 Ibid., 47.

9 Cat. nos. 29, 27, 28 [not catalogued by Kallir], 26, 68, 59/60 [recto and verso], 61 and 62 are self-portraits. A small watercolor portrait of Trude Geiringer, painted in the sitter's *Stammbuch*, also survives [Cat. no 10].

10 Kallir 1974 (see note 2), 167; Coffer, 261.

11 As recollected by Hildegard Bachert, Kallir's partner at the Galerie St. Etienne.

12 "*Ich . . . and dort eine große Anzahl von meist unaufgespannten, gerollten oder zusammengefalteten Leinwanden . . . Zwar war viele durch die unfachgemäße Art der Aufbewahrung beschädigt, die Leinwanden oft geknickt, manche Bilder sogar in Teile zerschnitten, alle schmutzig und verstaubt, so daß man Farben kaum erkennen konnte. Trotzdem war der Eindruck dieser Begegnung mit dem Werk des unbekannten Malers Richard Gerstl ein außerordentlich starker*" (cf. Kallir 1974 "Dokumentation," 125). It is, however, clear that a number of the larger paintings were—and remain—on their original stretchers. Coffer (154–5) has identified a group of eleven smaller canvases, which he believes Kallir had mounted on board.

13 "*Ich war aber gleich entschlossen, alles daranzusetzen, um den Namen dieses Künstlers der Vergessenheit zu entreißen*" [Kallir 1974 (see note 2), 128].

14 Otto Nirenstein [Kallir], *Egon Schiele: Persönlichkeit und Werk* (P. Zsolnay: Vienna, 1930).

15 Unfortunately, the original negatives were destroyed by bombing during World War II. The contents of Gerstl's estate can thus be reconstructed only partly, based on the photographs and records that were preserved at the Neue Galerie [cf. Kallir 1974 (see note 2), 135].

16 "*Die überraschend ungleiche Qualität der Gerstl Bilder hat mich oft gewundert. . . .Bei Gerstl* [ist] *ja, zum Unterschied von Schiele, keine stete Entwicklung festzustellen. Er hat in frühen und späten Jahren hervorragende und schlechte, beinahe kitschige Bilder produziert. Das ging ganz durcheinander*," letter from Otto Kallir to Otto Breicha, January 10, 1962 (Galerie St. Etienne archive).

17 "*Ich fürchtete, daß diese Ungleichmäßigkeit bei einer ersten Ausstellung die Besucher verwirren und den Eindruck der Hauptwerke abschwächen würde*," cf. Kallir 1974 (see note 2), 129.

18 Ibid., 126–27. Apparently due to the success of the Neue Galerie's exhibition, an additional twelve or thirteen works were consigned in October 1931 (letter from Otto Nirenstein [Kallir] to Alois Gerstl, Oct. 29, 1931).

19 Kallir/Breicha, January 10, 1962. It seems Alois Gerstl retained a few paintings that Kallir never catalogued.

20 "Richard Gerstl: Ein Malerschicksal." Fifty-five works, including all the then-known self-portrait drawings, were on view when the show first opened. Twelve more paintings were added in October (see note 18). The exhibition ran through November 8.

21 "*Wohl nie zuvor [ist] das Werk eines österreichischen Malers bei seiner ersten Ausstellung solcher* internationalen *Beachtung begegnet*," Kallir 1974 (see note 2), 133. The show drew praise not just from within Austria and its former imperial territories, but also from critics in Germany, France and Holland.

22 Wolfgang Born, "Ein österreichischer van Gogh," *Neues Wiener Journal*, September 27, 1931.

23 "*[Eine] verblüffende Entdeckung. . . . Es wird in der Kunst kaum ein zweites Mal vorgekommen, daß ein künstlerisches Ingenium wie das Richard Gerstls völlig in der Verborgenheit verblieb . . . , obwohl Gerstl von keinem einzigen seiner malenden Zeitgenossen an malerischer Kraft übertroffen wurde*," V. Trautzel, "Ein unbekannter Meister," Österreichische Reichspost, September 30, 1931.

24 "*In Wien [hat sich] ein Ereignis zugetragen, das als künstlerische Sensation ersten Ranges anzusprechen ist . . . Es ist ein Erfolg, wie er auf dem Gebiete der Kunst im letzten Jahrhundert nicht zu verzeichnen war*," M.P., "23 Jahre nach dem Tode zum Genie erklärt: Eine künstlerische Sensation in Wien," *Kölnische Zeitung*, October 21, 1931.

25 "*[Einer] der bedeutendsten Maler des beginnenden XX. Jahrhunderts. . . . In der Nähe der . . . Manet und van Gogh*," "Ein Malerschicksal," *Kleines Volksblatt*, October 4, 1931.

26 "*Ein Apostel der kommenden Kunst*," St. Ventura, "Richard Gerstl," *Neues Wiener Extrablatt*, Oct. 15, 1931.

27 Galerie Caspari, Munich, January–February, 1932; Galerie Gurlitt, Berlin, June 14–mid July 1932; Kölnischer Kunstverein, Cologne, November–December, 1932; Städtisches-Suermondt-Museum, Museumsverein Aachen, January 1933.

28 For further discussion of Kallir's emigration and his early years in New York, see Jane Kallir, *Saved from Europe* (Galerie St. Etienne: New York, 1999).

29 Vita Künstler, who continued to run the Neue Galerie for Kallir after the war, mounted one-man Gerstl exhibitions in 1946 and 1947. Between 1946 and 1954, the Neue Galerie sold four paintings by the artist to the Belvedere (see note 52). In 1955 a further eighteen works were sold to the Galerie Würthle (see note 30).

30 In an unpublished draft of the introduction to his "Dokumentation," Kallir states that he offered his Austrian Gerstl inventory to Wotruba because he feared he would be unable to get an export license (Galerie St Etienne archive). In the published version, Kallir states that he sold these works because he could not afford to transport them to America (Kallir "Dokumentation,"

135). The price, $4,000, is mentioned in the unpublished draft and confirmed in a letter of August 26, 1954, from Fritz Kamm to Otto Kallir (Galerie St. Etienne archive). According to Christine Kamm (email to the author, August 7, 2016) the Galerie Würthle acquired a total of eighteen Gerstl paintings from Kallir.

31 "*Daß mir in Zukunft die Bilder für Ausstellungen in Amerika zur Verfügung stehen würden*," Kallir 1974 (see note 2), 135.

32 "Egon Schiele," Boston Institute of Contemporary Art, October 6–November 6, 1960; Galerie St. Etienne, New York, November 15–December 15; J.B. Speed Museum, Louisville KY, January 3–31, 1961; Carnegie Institute, Pittsburgh PA, March 2–April 2; Minneapolis Institute of Arts, April 19–May 21.

33 "Gustav Klimt and Egon Schiele," Solomon R. Guggenheim Museum, New York, Feb.–April 1965.

34 "Richard Gerstl," Wiener Secession, Vienna, and Tiroler Kunstpavillon, Innsbruck, June–July 1966.

35 Kallir "Dokumentation," unpublished draft.

36 Kallir noted, in an unpublished memo, that, "Once the sale was concluded, all my, almost yearly repeated requests for an American Gerstl exhibition were disregarded, mostly unanswered" (*Kaum war dieser Verkauf abgeschlossen, so blieben all meine, beinahe jährlich erneuten Bitten um eine amerikanische Gerstlausstellung unberücksichtigt, meist unbeanwtortet*) (Galerie St. Etienne archive).

37 "*Der Erfolg kam, so wie bei OK und jetzt Schiele, via das Ausland*," letter from Otto Kallir to Otto Breicha, July 15, 1961 (Galerie St. Etienne archive).

38 "La mostra Austriaca alla XXVIIIa Biennale de Venezia," summer 1956. Nine of the paintings came from the stock acquired from Kallir by the Galerie Würthle; the tenth, *Die Schwestern Frey* [Cat. no. 9], was loaned by the Belvedere.

39 Among the museum exhibitions that first introduced Gerstl to foreign audiences were "Vienna Secession: Art Nouveau to 1970," Royal Academy, London, January 9–March 7, 1971; "Kunst in Österreich 1900–1930," Kunstmuseum Luzern, July 14–September 8, 1974; "Experiment Weltuntergang: Wien um 1900," Kunsthalle Hamburg, April 10–May 31, 1981; "Vienna 1900: Vienna, Scotland and the European Avant-Garde," National Museum of Antiquities, Edinburgh, summer 1983.

40 "Le Arti a Vienna dalla Secessione alla caduta dell'impero asburgico," Palazzo Grassi, Venice, May 20–September 16, 1984; "Vienne 1880–1938: L'Apocalypse Joyeuse," Centre Georges Pompidou, Paris, February 13–May 5, 1986; "Vienna 1900: Art, Architecture and Design," Museum of Modern Art, New York, July 3–October 21, 1986.

41 Alessandra Comini, *The Fantastic Art of Vienna* (Khnopf: New York, 1978); Donald E. Gordon, *Expressionism: Art and Idea* (Yale University Press: New Haven, 1987); Almut Krapf-Weiler, *Wien um 1900: Kunst und Kultur* (Christian Brandstätter: Vienna, 1985); Rupert Feuchtmüller, Österreichs Aufbruch in die Moderne, 1880–1980 (Fritz Molden: Vienna, 1980); Nicholas Powell: *The Sacred Spring: The Arts in Vienna 1898–1918* (Studio Vista: London, 1974); Peter Vergo, *Art in Vienna, 1898–1918* (Phaidon: London, 1975).

42 Jane Kallir, *Richard Gerstl, Oskar Kokoschka*, New York, 1992, 11.

43 "Austria's Expressionism," Galerie St. Etienne, New York, April 21–May 30, 1981. Gerstl's monumental *Die Familie Schoenberg* [Cat. no. 79], borrowed from the Museum Moderner Kunst in Vienna and featured on the invitation, was the star of the show.

44 "Arnold Schoenberg's Vienna," Galerie St. Etienne, New York, November 13, 1984–January 5, 1985. The exhibition included eleven works by Gerstl, among them loans from the Historisches Museum der Stadt Wien (today Wien Museum) and an Austrian private collection.

45 "Richard Gerstl, Oskar Kokoschka," Galerie St. Etienne, New York, March 17–May 9, 1992. In addition to the Kamm family's loans, the exhibition included paintings from several Austrian private collections, the Historisches Museum der Stadt Wien (today Wien Museum) and the Tiroler Landesmuseum Ferdinandeum, Innsbruck.

46 John Russell, "Austria's Expressionism," *The New York Times*, April 25, 1981.

47 A small undated Gerstl catalogue with an essay by Heimo Kuchling was published by the Galerie Würthle in 1956 or 1957, either in connection with the Gerstl presentation at the Venice Biennale (see note 38) or to accompany an exhibition at Galerie Würthle. The latter exhibition has variously been dated to 1956 or June—July 1957, with most sources favoring 1957 (email from Christina Kamm to the author, September 13, 2016). A second Gerstl exhibition took place at Galerie Würthle in June—July 1966.

48 "Richard Gerstl," Historisches Museum der Stadt Wien, Vienna, December 1, 1983–February 26, 1984.

49 "Richard Gerstl, 1883–1908," Kunstforum der Bank Austria, Vienna, Sept. 21–Nov. 28, 1993; Kunsthaus Zürich, March 25–May 23, 1994.

50 After selling the Galerie Würthle in 1975, the Kamm family brought eight Gerstl paintings to their native Switzerland, all of which are now in the possession of the Stiftung Sammlung Kamm, a foundation established in 1998 and domiciled at the Kunsthaus Zug.

51 Rudolf Leopold acquired, through purchase or exchange, a total of eight Gerstl paintings from the Galerie Würthle and/or the Kamm family (email from Christine Kamm to the author, August 7, 2016).

52 *Selbstbildnis lachend* [Cat no. 54] and *Ernst Diez* [Cat. no. 21] were purchased from the Neue Galerie in 1946. The Belvedere subsequently acquired *Die Schwestern Frey* [Cat. no. 12] from the Neue Galerie in 1950, and *Mathilde Schoenberg II* [Cat. no. 53] from the Neue Galerie in 1954. In 1968, the Kamm family donated *Zahnradbahn auf den Kahlenberg* [Cat. no. 17] and *Doppelbildnis Mathilde und Gertrud Schoenberg* [Cat. no. 16]. (Email from Stefan Lehner, Belvedere, to the author, July 29, 2016).

53 "New Worlds: Austrian and German Art, 1890–1940," Neue Galerie New York, November 16, 2001–February 18, 2002.

54 Otto Kallir first asked Victor Hammer to write his Gerstl recollections in 1961 (Galerie St. Etienne archive).

55 See note 2. The additional four paintings are Cat. nos. 15, 16, 18, and 52 (Kallir "Dokumentation," 167). Schröder and Coffer, who both gave separate numbers to each side of double-sided works, came up with totals of 80 and 88 items respectively.

56 Coffer, 29.

57 Cat. nos. 74, 77, 78, 76, 79, 80, 81. Coffer dates these crucial paintings to 1908, while Klaus Albrecht Schröder (*Richard Gerstl 1883–1908*, Vienna, 1993, 92, 93, 108–13, 120–27) ascribes them to 1907. *Selbstbildnis (Akt in Ganzfigur)* [Cat. no. 86] is dated September 12, 1908, by the artist.

58 Although it is impossible to make an accurate posthumous diagnosis, it is evident that Gerstl was emotionally troubled and may have suffered from bipolar disorder (Coffer, 48–51, 265–68).

59 Wolfgang Born ("Richard Gerstl," *Belvedere, Zeitschrift für Kunst und Künstlerische Kultur*, Vol. 10, No. 11, 1931) was probably the first to associate Gerstl's shorn hair with his emotional decline and to date his four most Expressionistic self-portrait drawings [Cat. nos. 59–62] to the final weeks of the artist's life. This dating has generally been affirmed by subsequent scholars, including Schröder, but is disputed by Coffer (293–94).

60 "*Ungenauer*" (Kallir/Breicha, January 10, 1962).

61 Letter from Otto Breicha to Otto Kallir, July 18, 1962 (Galerie St. Etienne archive).

62 Coffer, 29.

63 See note 49.

64 See note 1.

65 Coffer, 27.

66 See notes 57 and 59. Coffer and Schröder have different hypotheses regarding the works abandoned in Gmunden in 1908 (see note 10). Schröder concludes that *all* Gerstl's paintings from that fateful summer were lost, while Coffer argues that only the landscapes were left behind (Coffer, 249–61).

67 "*Es ist zu hoffen, daß vielleicht in Zukunft der Name Richard Gerstl doch über die Grenzen Österreichs hinaus bekannt wird*," Kallir 1974 (see note 2), 136.

PAINTINGS AND WORKS ON PAPER

Raymond Coffer

1

PORTRAIT OF CARL ZENTZYTZKI/ BILDNIS CARL ZENTZYTZKI, ca. 1902

Oil on canvas
55.9 x 44.8 cm (22 x 17 5/8 in.)
Private Collection*

The 15-year-old Richard Gerstl entered the Academy of Fine Arts in Vienna in October 1898, where, as a reputedly difficult student, he clashed with his rigidly classical teacher, Professor Christian Griepenkerl; he was expelled for the first time in summer 1901. Perhaps wishing to demonstrate his youthful independence, he soon rented his first studio in Haubenbiglgasse in Unterdöbling, Vienna's nineteenth district, a 15-minute tram ride north of his family home at Nussdorferstrasse 35, in the ninth district. By the following year, however, he had moved to the nearby Therese-Krones-Haus, Hohe Warte 37, in Heiligenstadt (in the nineteenth district), the home of a 61-year-old bookshop manager, Carl Zentzytzki. Here, Gerstl took over the veranda room from his closest academy friend, the impecunious Victor Hammer, who had also left the school a few months earlier and could no longer afford the rent. In his new studio, it was natural for Gerstl to paint his landlord, whose portrait is among the artist's earliest existing works. It displays a fine, mature example of the type of perceptive portraiture that he would have been taught at the academy.

Annotation guide

* Catalogued by Otto Nirenstein (Kallir) but not exhibited at the 1931 Neue Galerie show

** Exhibited in 1931 at the opening on September 28, 1931

*** Exhibited in 1931 from October 17, 1931

**** Not known to Nirenstein (Kallir)

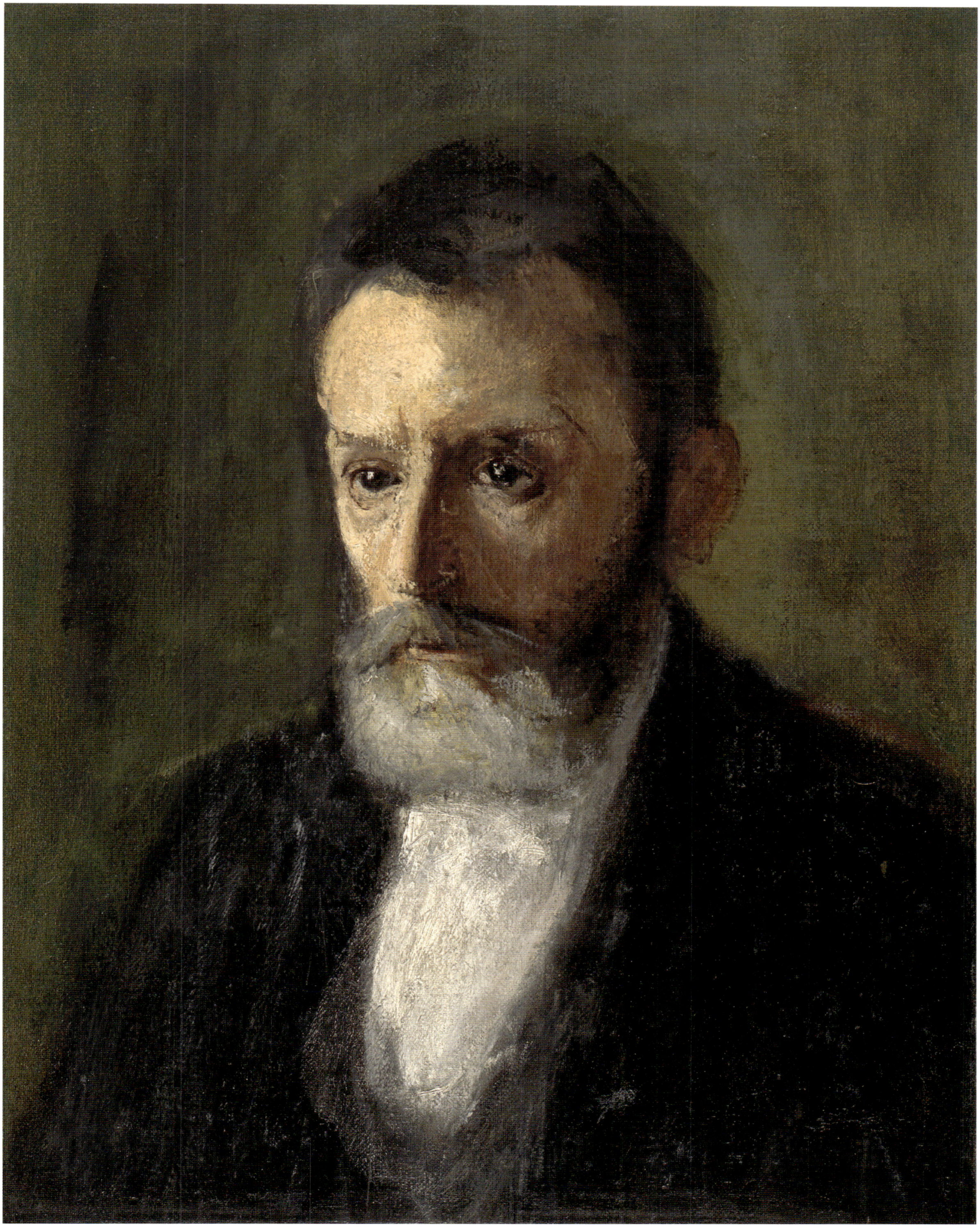

1

2

PORTRAIT OF RICHARD GERSTL'S COUSIN (ANNA BÄUMER)/BILDNIS DER COUSINE RICHARD GERSTLS (ANNA BÄUMER), ca. 1902

Oil on canvas
47 x 38 cm (18 ½ x 15 in.)
Private Collection, Vienna*

Gerstl's portrait of his cousin, Anna Bäumer, may have been painted around the same time as that of Carl Zentzytzki, although the freer, almost transparent brushwork of the subject's white blouse and neckwear demonstrates a more modern approach, suggesting his first shift away from his classical training. Anna Bäumer was born Anna Gerstl on April 24, 1868 (d. 1935); she married a Czech architect, Rudolf Bäumer, and the couple resided at Sensengasse 5 in Vienna's nineteenth district, a short walk from Gerstl's family home. Anna was therefore an accessible subject for the young and aspiring artist, and while it cannot be excluded that the portrait was painted in Therese-Krones-Haus like Zentzytzki's, it was likely executed conveniently in either her or Gerstl's apartment. This portrait is one of 62 works by Gerstl that were packed up and stored in the furniture warehouse of Rosin and Knauer in Vienna's ninth district directly after Gerstl's suicide in 1908, where they remained until his brother, Alois, offered them to Otto Nirenstein (later Kallir) in 1931.

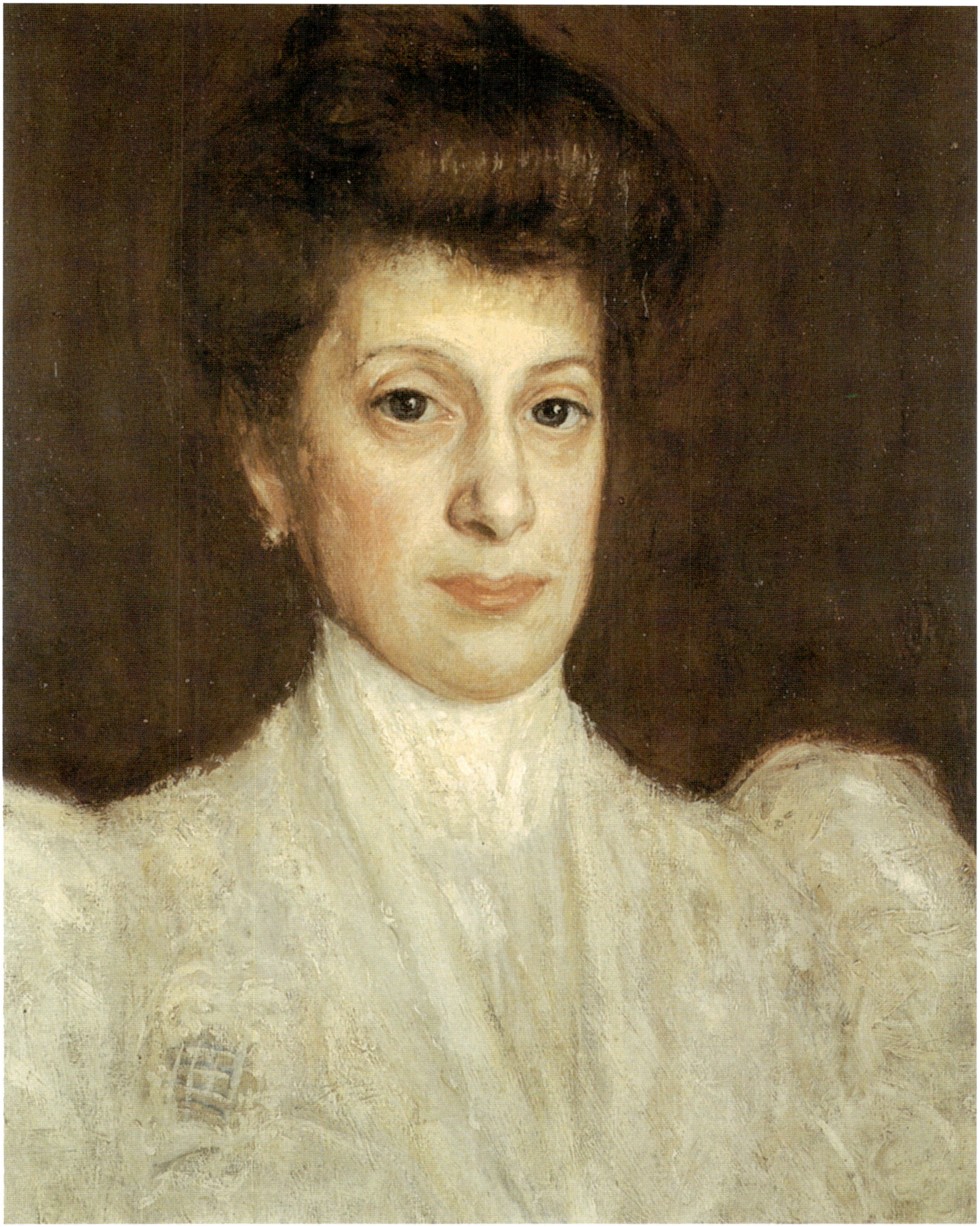

3

HEAD OF A WOMAN/FRAUENKOPF, ca. 1902

Recto: *Small Self-Portrait*, winter 1906–07 [Cat. no. 31]
Oil on canvas
47 x 37 cm (18 ½ x 14 ⅝ in.)
Kunsthaus Zug, Stiftung Sammlung Kamm**

Of almost identical dimensions to Gerstl's *Anna Bäumer*, and with many of the same academic characteristics, this portrait of an unknown woman can be ascribed to around 1902, when the artist would have been in his late teens. At that time he sought subjects known to him, perhaps in order to practice or hone his skills. While the identity of the woman in this picture remains a mystery, it is likely that she was associated in some way with Gerstl's family or close circle. The work displays a further evolution in Gerstl's development, not only in the looser depiction of the subject's attire but also in the way in which, in a rejoinder to conventional realism, the slight inclination of the head and the marginally differential eye sizes heighten the expressive impact of the subject. Whether for economic, practical or aesthetic reasons, Gerstl used the other side—as he did with other works—for the completely unconnected *Small Self-Portrait*, No. 26, which was painted in 1906–07.

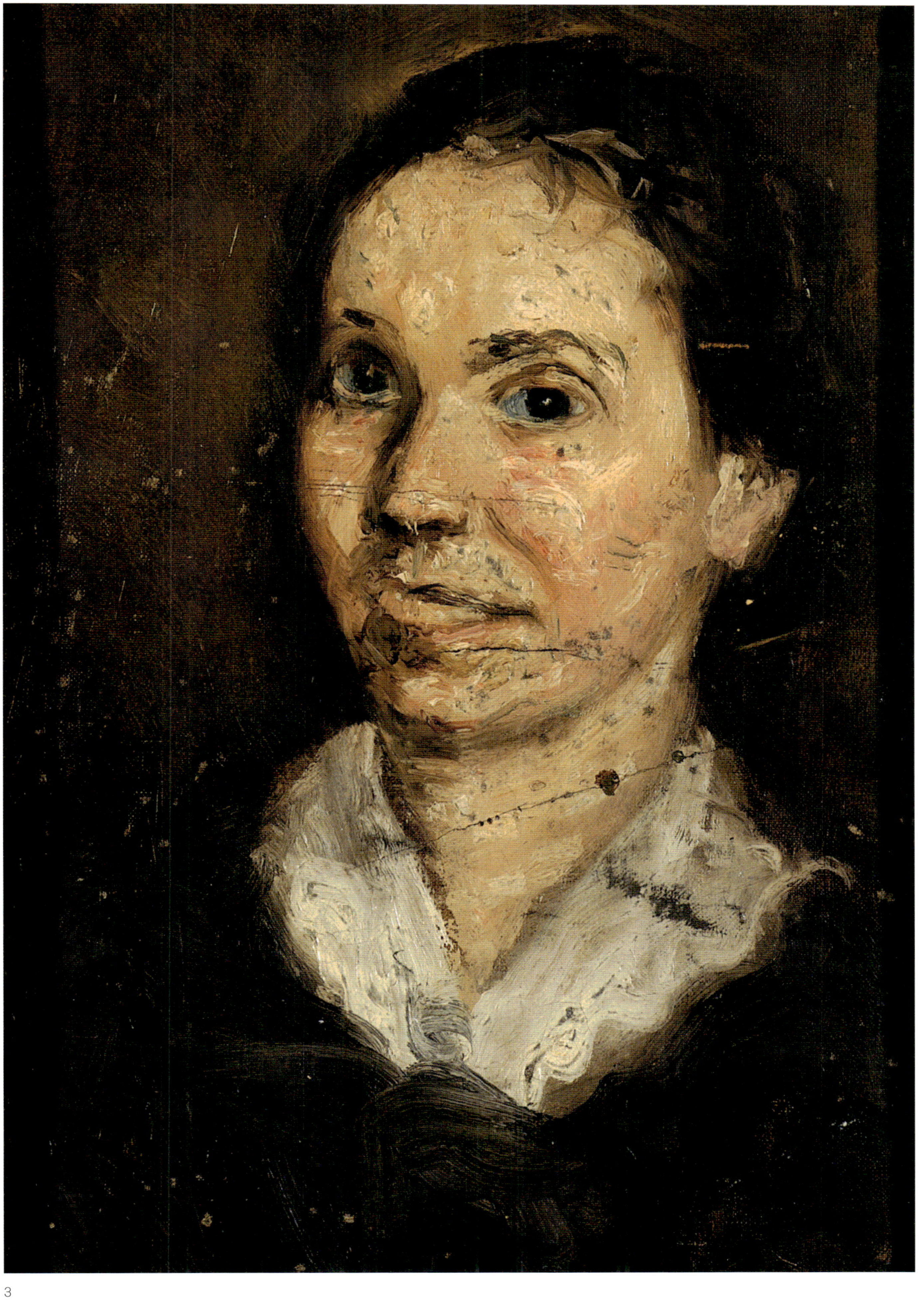

3

4

PORTRAIT OF WALDEMAR UNGER I/ BILDNIS WALDEMAR UNGER I, 1902–03

Oil on canvas
42 x 34 cm (16 ½ x 13 ⅜ in.)
Oberösterreichisches Landesmuseum Linz,
Schenkung Kastner****

Amongst other fundamentally "conventional" portraits that emanated from the period after Gerstl's expulsion from the Academy were two he painted of Waldemar Unger, his best friend from childhood. In a letter to Otto Breicha of February 15, 1960, Unger ascribed these as "2 paintings from my student days around 1900 (Unger entered Vienna University in 1901) that were painted during a summer holiday that the Gerstl and Unger families took together in Kritzendorf," a resort on the Danube, just 12 miles north of Vienna. Since Gerstl spent the summers of 1900 and 1901 at the renowned summer school of painting of the Hungarian Impressionist Simon Hollósy in Nagybánya, Hungary, he most likely painted *Portrait of Waldemar Unger I* in the summer of 1902, at which point he had clearly not yet shed his reliance on the classical realism that he had railed against at the Academy. The work is dated, slightly illegibly above the subject's left shoulder, as "October 190[?]," which suggests that Gerstl added the finishing touches to his friend's portrait that autumn.

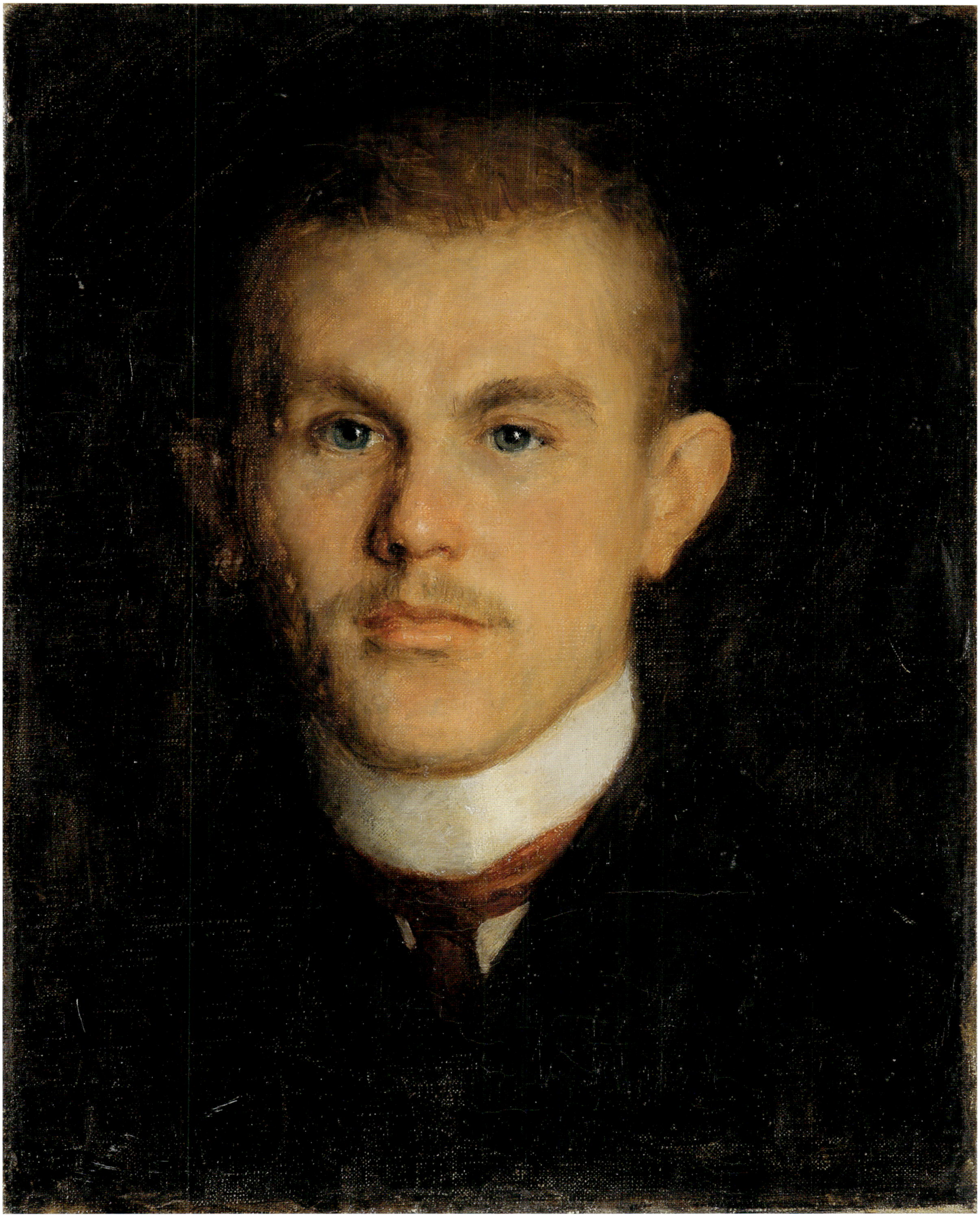

5

**PORTRAIT OF WALDEMAR UNGER II/
BILDNIS WALDEMAR UNGER II, 1902–03**

Oil on canvas
44 x 35 cm (17 ⅜ x 13 ¾ in.)
Private Collection, Milan****

Unusually, Gerstl both signed and dated *Portrait of Waldemar Unger II* and, while the date, found above the right shoulder, is somewhat illegible, Otto Breicha, who may have owned the work in the 1960s, recorded that the inscription reads "*Richard Gerstl 10. Febr, 1903.*" Gerstl also wrote on the frame, "10.2.1903 Herrn. Dr. Unger Floragasse 6," although, since Unger did not gain his doctorate until November 1907, this may have been added after that date, perhaps as a commemoration of his friend's degree. Nonetheless, the fact that this second portrait was dated some months after *Waldemar Unger I* may explain its lighter, less dense touch, suggesting that Gerstl used his friend's portraits to find an individual and more modern approach. He regularly made rapid advances in style and technique. The two Unger pictures still bear the characteristics of the three other early existing portraits, including their dimensions and some academic traits. However, as with *The Sisters Karoline and Pauline Fey* [Cat. no. 12], there is the sense of Manet's influence in *Waldemar Unger II.* In January 1903, nine of the French artist's works were shown at the Vienna Secession's seminal Impressionists exhibition, which Gerstl surely attended, perhaps in the weeks before he finished the work.

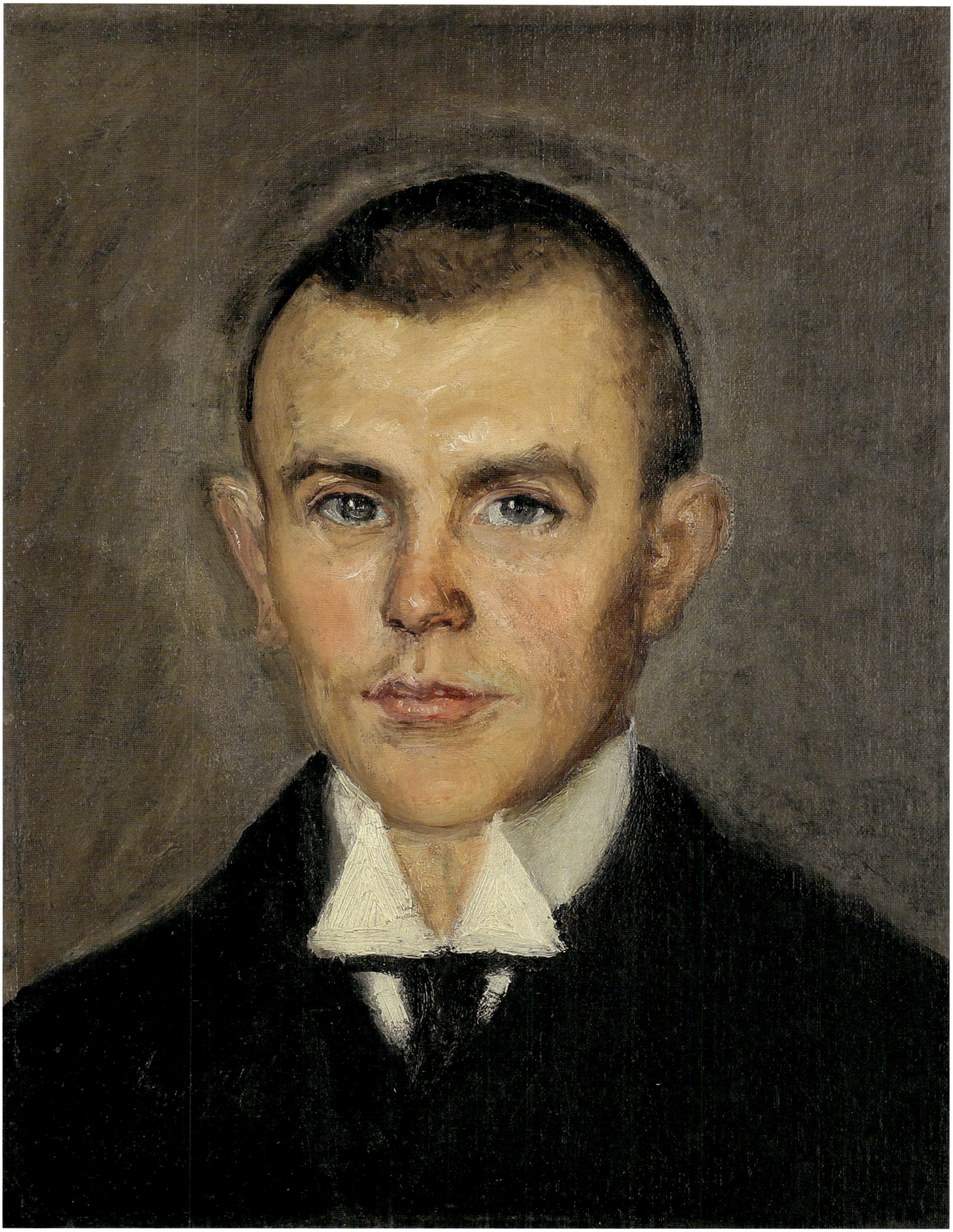

5

6
SEMI-NUDE SELF-PORTRAIT/ SELBSTBILDNIS ALS HALBAKT, 1902–04

Oil on canvas
159 x 109 cm (62 5/8 x 42 7/8 in.)
Leopold Museum, Vienna*

Gerstl is described as a reticent, moody individual, disaffected by his appearance and blighted by a persistent stomach disorder. He was often the victim, perhaps wilfully, of expulsion and disappointment, including having his desire to be an army volunteer denied on grounds of his weak physique. His repeated encounters with rejection appear to have found artistic expression in his self-portraits, the first being *Semi-Nude Self-Portrait*. According to Breicha, Alois Gerstl clearly recalled that it was painted by his brother at the age of nineteen, probably around late 1902 or early 1903, and thereby almost certainly in his Heiligenstadt studio. It can be seen not only as Gerstl's earliest self-representation of rejection, but also as a youthful, self-confident riposte to his army medical examiners, whose decision, again according to Alois, had left his brother noticeably depressed. Barely retaining his modesty with a flimsy knotted sheet that harks back to his transparent touch in *Anna Bäumer*, Gerstl's flaunts proudly his scrawny upper torso, arms too slim and long, an over-slender neck, shoulders uncommonly sloped and an almost pubescent waist and hips. His pale, exaggerated skinniness is emphasized by a graduated darkening of the face, although, for a man who claimed to possess an unusually large head, it is disproportionately small, amplifying the disturbingly piercing eyes and tight lips of "an extremely taciturn man," as Paula Fey [Cat. no. 12] described him. Gerstl's Christ-like pose, blue ephemeral aura and spectral halo have unsurprisingly given rise to *Ecce Homo* comparisons, although it is far more likely that *Semi-Nude Self-Portrait* was intended as a secular image of his personal redemption from the successive setbacks and rejections that had afflicted his adolescent years. Various art historians (including Lloyd and Winiarczyk, see p. 31 in this catalogue) have suggested that artists such as Edvard Munch and Ferdinand Hodler inspired Gerstl's first self-portrait, and that it is more likely that this work was painted after the Secession exhibition in January 1904, which included numerous examples of Munch's and Hodler's work. However, this show occurred a year after Alois recalled the work was completed. Furthermore, Victor Hammer claimed that, as opposed to other artists, Munch was never mentioned by Gerstl. As such, *Self-Portrait against a Blue Background* represents a unique juncture in Viennese art, perhaps influenced by little else other than the artist's expressive and entirely original imagination.

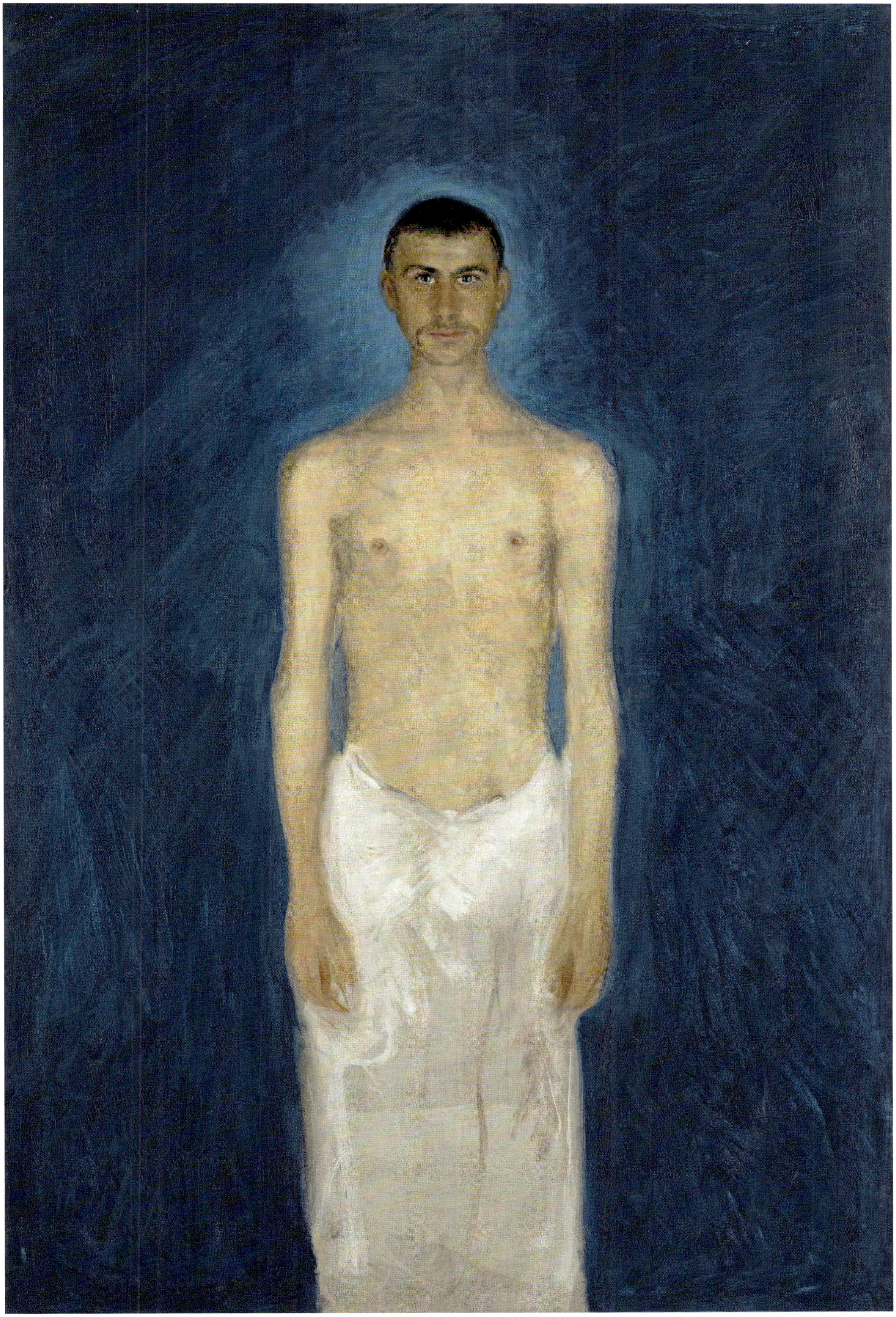

7

PORTRAIT OF MR. WANTSCHURA/
BILDNIS HERR WANTSCHURA, ca. 1904–05

Probably oil on canvas
Size unknown
Whereabouts unknown

8

PORTRAIT OF DR. BREITENFELD/
BILDNIS DR. BREITENFELD, ca. 1904–05

Probably oil on canvas
Size unknown
Whereabouts unknown

9

PORTRAIT OF BENEDICT KOSIAN/
BILDNIS BENEDICT KOSIAN, 1904–05

Probably oil on canvas
Size unknown
Whereabouts unknown

10

PORTRAIT OF A CHILD/
BILDNIS EINES KINDES, ca. 1904

Oil on canvas
70.5 x 50.5 cm (27 3/4 x 19 7/8 in.)
Whereabouts unknown**

The original work, which was exhibited at the Neue Galerie in 1931, has been lost. Nonetheless it is known that the boy portrayed in his *Portrait of a Child* was the son of a grocer whose shop was in the nineteenth district in the Hohe Warte area, where Gerstl had both of his early studios. Although only known through a black and white photograph, there is a clear progression in Gerstl's style. Certainly, as opposed to his early portraits, Gerstl begins here to exhibit a much greater freedom of brushwork as he portrays his subject's eyes in an expressionless stare, his hands almost merging into his body. Since this can be clearly dated after his early, more "academic" portraits, it is reasonable to assume that Gerstl's *Portrait of a Child* was painted in his second Hohe Warte studio at Therese-Krones-Haus, probably around 1904.

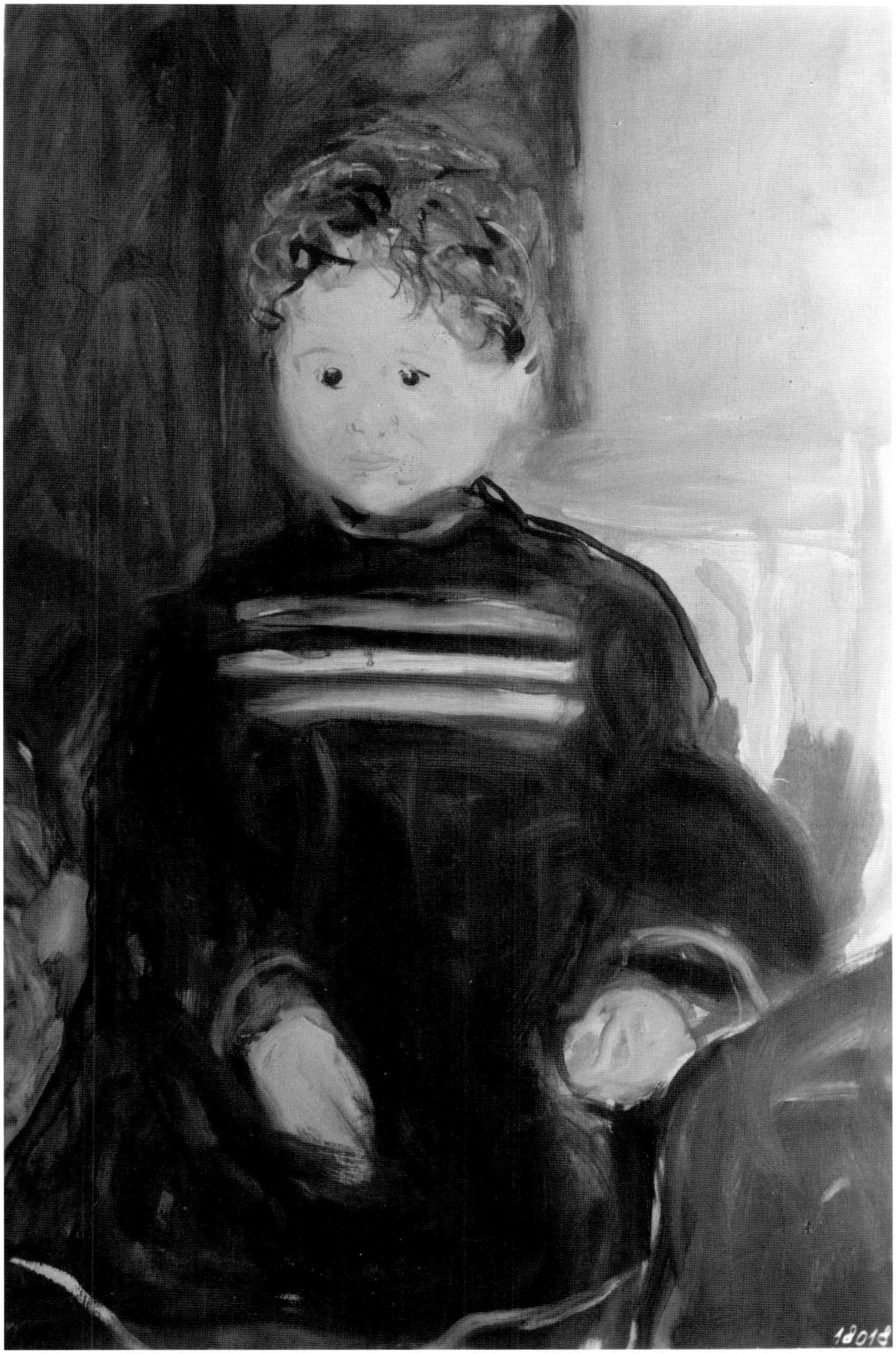

10

11

FRAGMENT OF A FULL-LENGTH SELF-PORTRAIT, LAUGHING/FRAGMENT EINES LACHENDEN SELBSTBILDNISSES IN GANZER FIGUR, ca. 1904

Recto: *Portrait of Alexander von Zemlinsky*, July 1908 [Cat. no. 77] and *Mathilde Schönberg in the Garden*, July 1908 [Cat. no. 78]
Oil on canvas
170.5 x 74.3 cm (67 1/8 x 29 1/4 in.)
Kunsthaus Zug, Stiftung Sammlung Kamm**

In an act that recalls his shearing of one of his pictures after a viewer's unwelcome remark, Gerstl deliberately defaced his full-length *Laughing Self-Portrait*, using a deep blue oil to obscure his features and dividing the canvas into two unequal halves. Although he used the versos for his portraits of *Alexander Zemlinsky* and *Mathilde Schönberg in the Garden* in Gmunden 1908, the fact that he was prepared to destroy his canvases may explain the lack of existing works from his early years. Probably painted in his veranda-room studio in Therese-Krones-Haus, a slim, elegant Gerstl portrays himself here against a cavernous void, wherein the tall, lanky artist, his hair closely shorn, fixes his smile in a false grimace. Gerstl's shaved look may have been acquired ahead of a sanatorium stay at the Städtische Bade- u. Heilanstalt in Baden bei Wien, where he arrived on August 13, 1904, most likely to receive therapy for his nervous stomach problems. This may explain the trepidation and despair that seem inherent in this complex and ambiguous impression of Gerstl's state of mind at that time, a work reminiscent, perhaps, of Munch's early full-length portraits, of which Gerstl may have recently become aware.

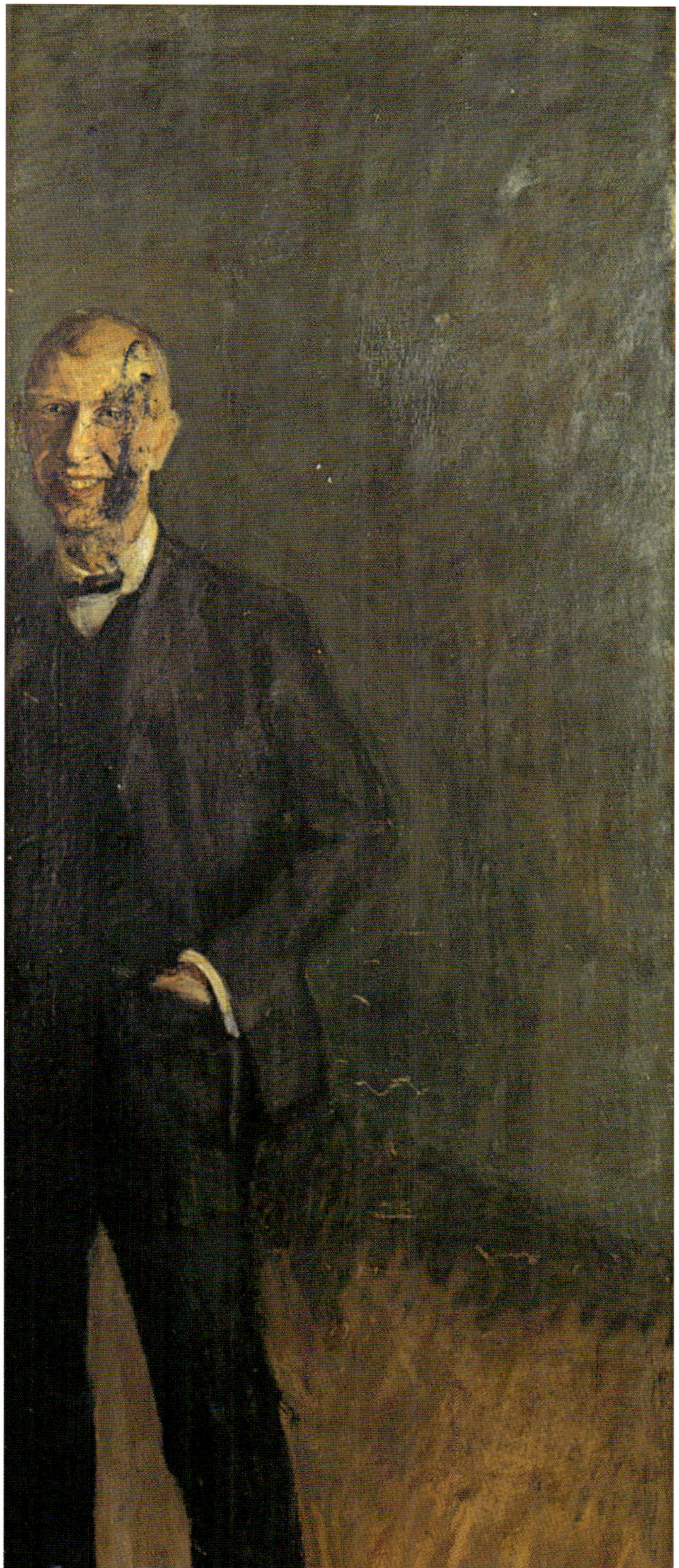

11

12

THE SISTERS KAROLINE AND PAULINE FEY/ DIE SCHWESTERN KAROLINE UND PAULINE FEY, March/April 1905

Oil on canvas
175 x 150 cm (69 ⅞ x 59 in.)
Belvedere, Vienna**

After his spell in the sanatorium, Gerstl rejoined Griepenkerl's class for the 1904–05 academic year, a period from which not a single painting exists other than this portrait of the Fey sisters. The younger sister, Paula, recalled that the Gerstl and Fey families were friendly and that Gerstl, who was of a similar age, painted them in their family home in Döbling, in Vienna's nineteenth district around March or April 1905, just after the *Fasching* (carnival) ball season. The composition was executed quickly and freehandedly, without pre-drawing, again betraying Gerstl's desire to accentuate the subject within an undefined, strong neutral setting (see *Semi-Nude Self-Portrait* and *Fragment of a Full-Length, Laughing Self-Portrait).* In a work again displaying clear affinities to Manet [see Cat. no. 5], Gerstl conjoins the sisters by their ball gowns, their hands almost invisibly but demurely crossed beneath their capes, gazing blankly with penetrating eyes across an empty room. The inscription of his address on the verso was presumably to ensure that the work was delivered back to his home, after which it remained in the family until shown at the opening of the Gerstl exhibition in 1931.

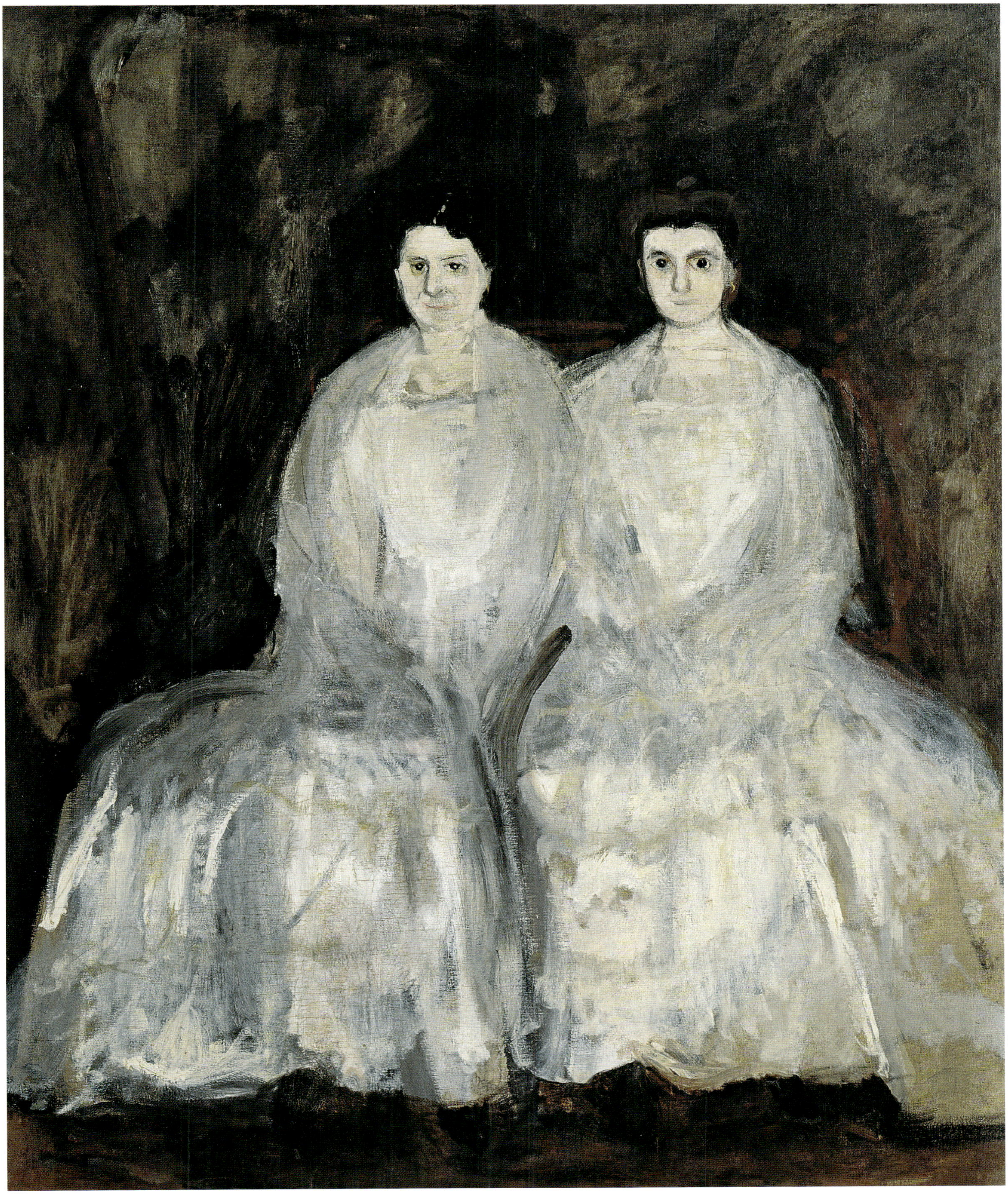

13

IDEALIZED PORTRAIT OF TRUDE GEIRINGER/ IDEALBILDNIS DER TRUDE GEIRINGER, February 10, 1906

Pencil, ink, watercolor on paper
19.5 x 12.4 cm (7 5⁄8 x 4 7⁄8 in.)
Private Collection, Courtesy Galerie St. Etienne, New York****

After Gerstl had been refused admission to the Academy for the 1905–06 winter semester having clashed once again with Griepenkerl, he appears to have turned his mind to teaching. Trude Neumann, later Geiringer, born February 1, 1890, may have been amongst his first students. The eldest daughter of a successful Jewish lawyer, she lived in an affluent area, close to the Opera, and attended the renowned Schwarzwaldschule for Girls. Gerstl sketched his idealized likeness of Trude in her *Stammbuch* (friendship album), in which messages and notes from her friends and family can be found. The sketch, which was almost certainly drawn in Trude's apartment at Kärntnerring 2, in the first district of Vienna, is dated, signed and bears the inscription, "Zur freundlichen Erinnerung an 10 Febr, 1906 Richard Gerstl" (To the friendly memory of 10 February 1906), so it may have been a gift to mark her recent sixteenth birthday. Looking far older than her years, however, Trude's image seems imbued with affection and beauty, which Gerstl contrives to enhance by catching an expressive sideways glance.

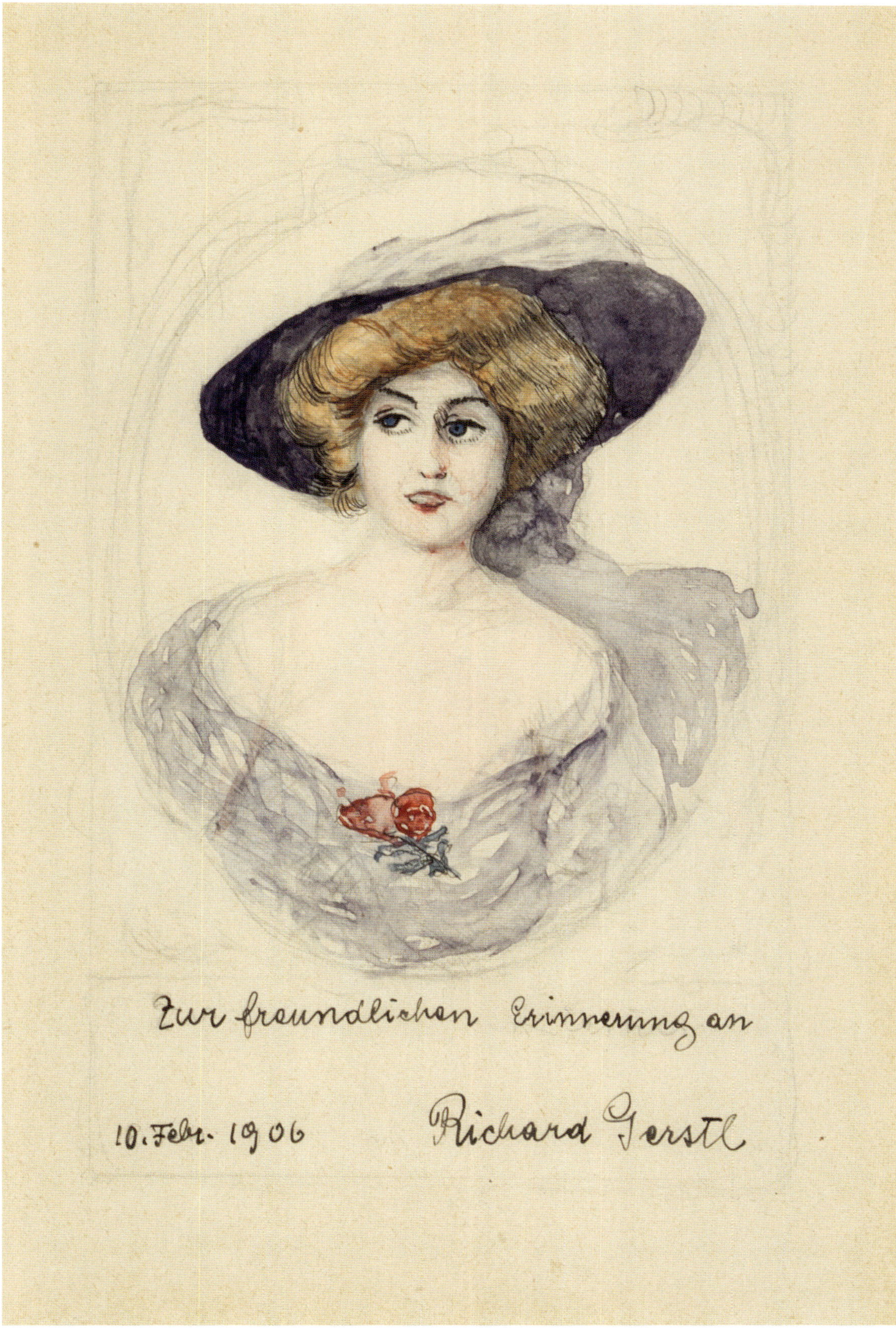
Zur freundlichen Erinnerung an
10. Febr. 1906
Richard Gerstl

13

14

GRINZING/GRINZING, spring 1906

Oil on canvas

29.7 x 40.2 cm (11 ¾ x 15 ⅞ in.)

Private Collection, Courtesy Galerie St. Etienne, New York*

By March 1906, Gerstl had returned to the Academy this time under the tutelage of Professor Heinrich Lefler, the head of its Special School of Landscape Painting. The latter had seen and recognized the qualities of Gerstl's *Fey Sisters* in Victor Hammer's studio, and had offered him the opportunity to join his class. Before then, however, Gerstl had attended Vienna's first-ever Van Gogh show, held at Galerie Miethke in Vienna from January 6–31, 1906, when 45 works—33 landscapes, three still lifes, seven portraits and two self-portraits—were exhibited. The event was significant for, of all the artists that Gerstl admired, Van Gogh had the greatest influence on the young artist's future output. This soon became clear in Gerstl's early landscape depicting the pastures above Grinzing, an area that he would have known well, since it was very close to the location of his studio in Heiligenstadt. Probably painted around spring 1906, just after he had joined Lefler's class, the work gives the impression of being an academic exercise, but also plainly owes something to Van Gogh's several views of the Auvers countryside, including his 1890 landscape, *Plain near Auvers,* exhibited as No. 25 at Miethke's show the previous January (see Lloyd and Winiarczyk, pp. 35 and 39, note 25).

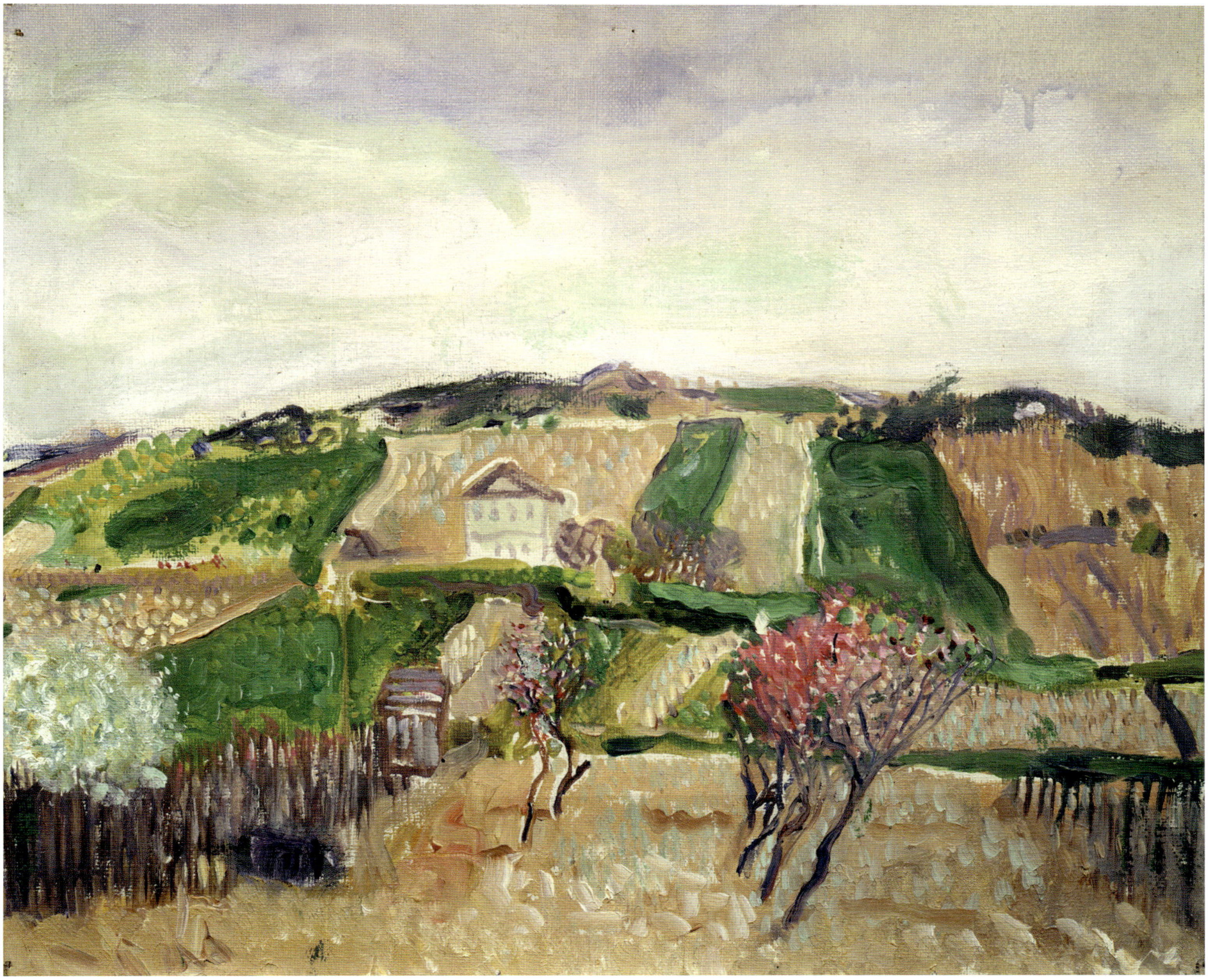

14

15

PORTRAIT OF ARNOLD SCHÖNBERG/ BILDNIS ARNOLD SCHÖNBERG,

spring-summer 1906

Oil on canvas

182 x 130 cm (71 ⅝ x 51 ⅛ in.)

Wien Museum, Vienna****

By the winter of 1905–06, the composer Arnold Schönberg had decided to try painting as a means of supplementing his meager income from music. Having possibly met Gerstl at a Mahler concert in December 1905, he sought assurances from Gerstl's new professor, Heinrich Lefler, regarding the 22-year-old artist. Thus in spring 1906, Schönberg invited Gerstl into his apartment at 68/70 Liechtensteinstraße, in Vienna's ninth district, next door to that of Mathilde's older brother, Alexander Zemlinsky, so that the young artist could teach both Schönberg and Mathilde to paint. Gerstl soon undertook a large-scale portrait of the composer, seated in a favorite pose of Schönberg on his chaise longue in the living room. Gerstl composed the work in a relatively realistic, representative style, perhaps at Schönberg's request. In portraying his subject with characteristically piercing eyes and powerful, strong hands, however, Gerstl not only remains faithful to the image of Schönberg as revered by his closest circle, but also retained his own artistic individuality. Moreover, the portrait betrays some of the influence that Van Gogh's work had begun to have on Gerstl, not least in the free and expressive brushwork used for Schönberg's brown suit, the somewhat undefined outline of his body and the elements of Pointillism displayed in the background.

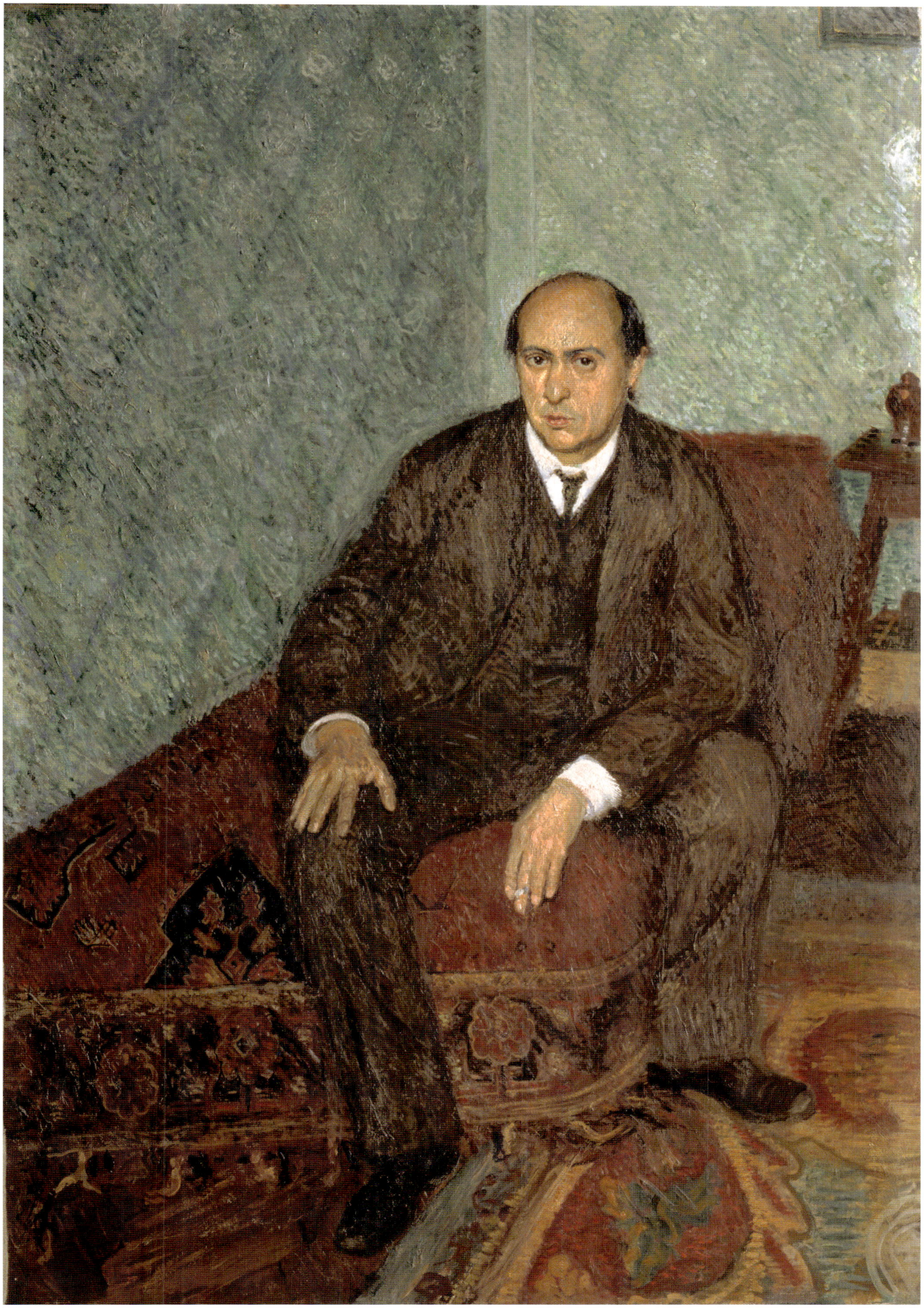

16

WOMAN WITH CHILD (MATHILDE SCHÖNBERG WITH HER DAUGHTER GERTRUD)/ FRAU MIT KIND (MATHILDE SCHÖNBERG MIT TOCHTER GERTRUD), June 1906

Oil on canvas
160.5 x 108 cm (63 1/8 x 42 1/2 in.)
Belvedere, Vienna****

Gerstl painted *Woman with Child,* presumably after the *Portrait of Arnold Schönberg,* in the adjacent living room when Mathilde was some six months pregnant with their son Georg, born September 22, 1906. This may explain why Gerstl demurely concealed her advanced condition behind the table. Indeed, the double portrait can safely be ascribed to June 1906, for the family was on vacation in Rottach-Egern between July 2 and August 26, 1906; Mathilde then suffered difficulties in the latter stages of the pregnancy. The work follows much of the realistic characterization seen in Schönberg's portrait, although Gerstl could not resist adding small pointilist brushstrokes in the background and door. The two Schönberg paintings may also owe some debt to the Intimist style of Vuillard and Bonnard, which Gerstl would have observed at the 1903 Impressionist show at the Vienna Secession and which represented something of a bridge between the *Fey Sisters* and the series of domestic portraits that Gerstl painted thereafter. Schönberg appears to have approved of Gerstl's portrait of his wife and daughter, for it was hung prominently, first in the hall (see p. 51) and then in the living room of 68/70 Liechtensteinstraße, and may have led to Gerstl receiving several commissions within Schönberg's circle in subsequent months.

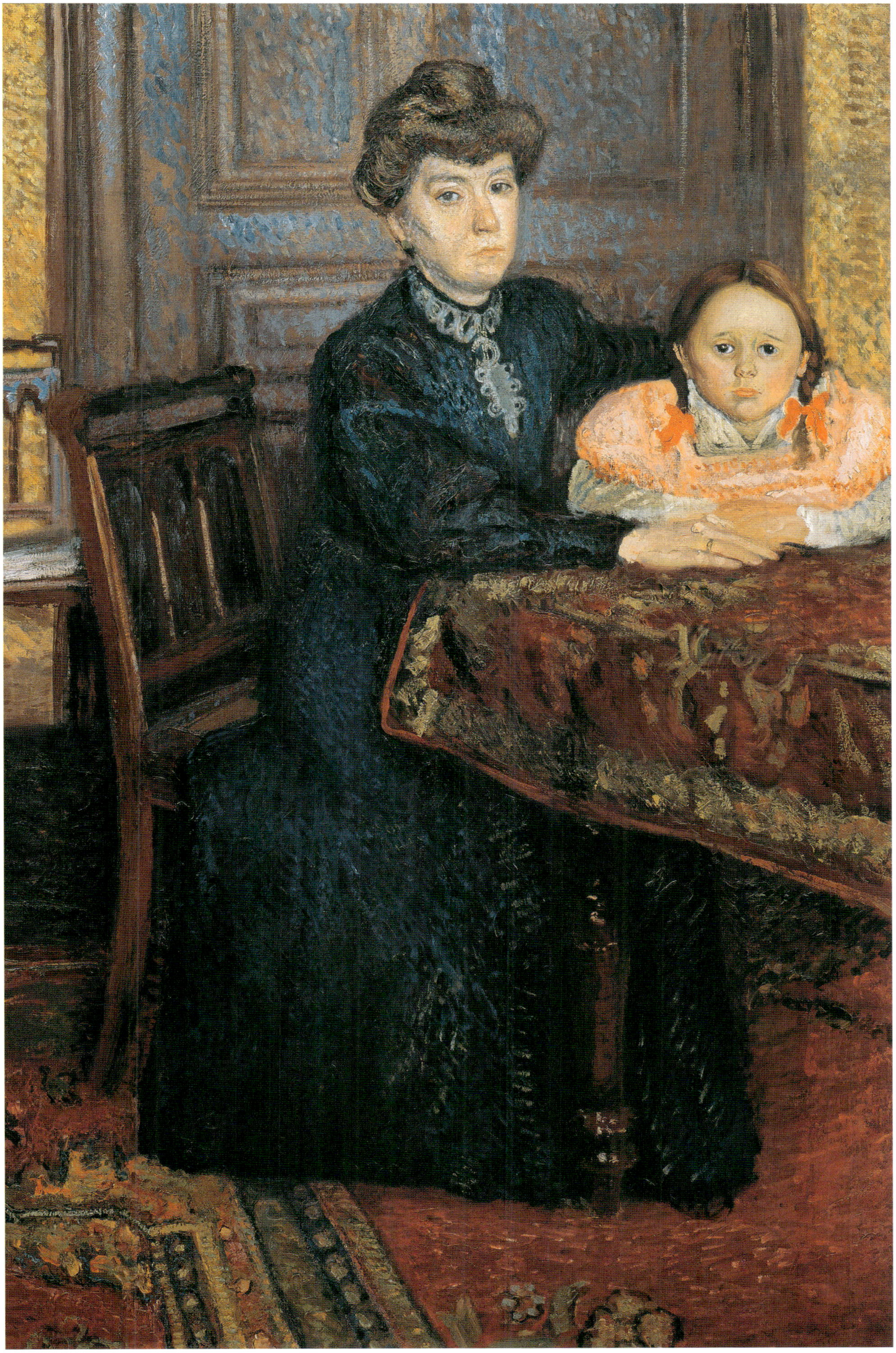

17

PORTRAIT OF A YOUNG WOMAN WITH A LIGHT BLUE DRESS AND FEATHER HAT/BILDNIS EINER JUNGEN FRAU IM LICHTBLAUEN KLEID MIT FEDERHUT), spring-summer 1906

Recto: *Seated Woman, Nude*, autumn 1908 [Cat. no. 87]
Oil on canvas
166 x 116 cm (65 3/8 x 45 5/8 in.)
Leopold Museum, Vienna**

Portrait of a Young Woman with a Light Blue Dress and Feather Hat is among three undated paintings of unknown female subjects [see also Cat. nos. 3 and 24] which, like the two Schönbergs, are each large-scale, "drawing-room" portraits displaying varying degrees of pointilism. This portrait also contains Gerstl's final known work, a nude study of Mathilde Schönberg [*Seated Female Nude,* Cat. no. 87], on the verso. While it could have been the first of the commissions introduced to Gerstl by Schönberg, it may equally have come in early 1906 following Van Gogh's show. Indeed, in its pose, setting, scale, and detail, this could have been a template for Schönberg, who may have insisted on viewing Gerstl's portraits before agreeing to his own. In either case, a dating of 1906 appears to be reasonable.

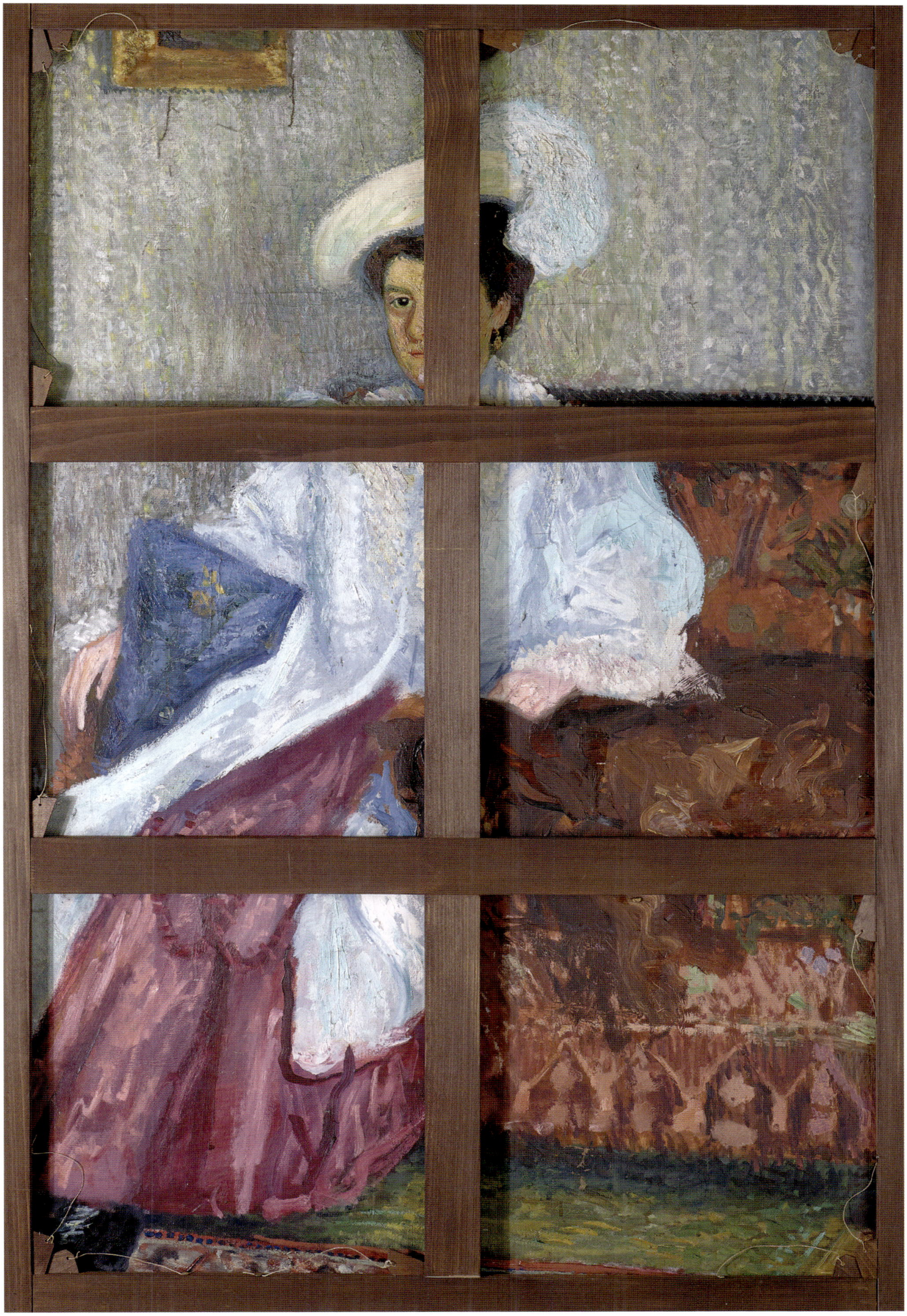

18

PORTRAIT OF THE ARTIST'S FATHER, EMIL GERSTL/BILDNIS DES VATERS EMIL GERSTL, summer 1906

Oil on canvas
211.1 x 150.3 cm (83 1/8 x 59 1/8 in.)
Leopold Museum, Vienna*

During the summer of 1906, Gerstl turned his attention to producing a meticulous, disciplined, and respectful portrait of his father, a man of independent means who had earned his fortune from stock exchange dealings. On a very large-scale canvas, Gerstl portrays Emil Gerstl at the age of 72 as an old, weary man, sitting in his study in the family's first-floor apartment at Nussdorferstrasse 35, with the sunny façade of the Säulengasse building opposite shown through the south-facing window. It is a brave work that confirms Gerstl's colorist leanings and acts as a powerful display of the Divisionist tendencies that Gerstl would have witnessed in both Segantini's works at the Vienna Secession in 1901 and Seurat's at the great 1903 Impressionist show and which, for a short time, dominated his painting. As his most ambitious pointilist work to date, Gerstl would, no doubt, have required several sittings from his elderly father, and much time to apply his newly developed techniques to the portrait. Having remained in Vienna while the Schönbergs were on vacation, he presumably had a plentiful supply of both at the time. The painting was plainly held in considerable esteem by the family, for it was shown to Nirenstein, although it was not exhibited at the 1931 show, presumably on Alois's instructions.

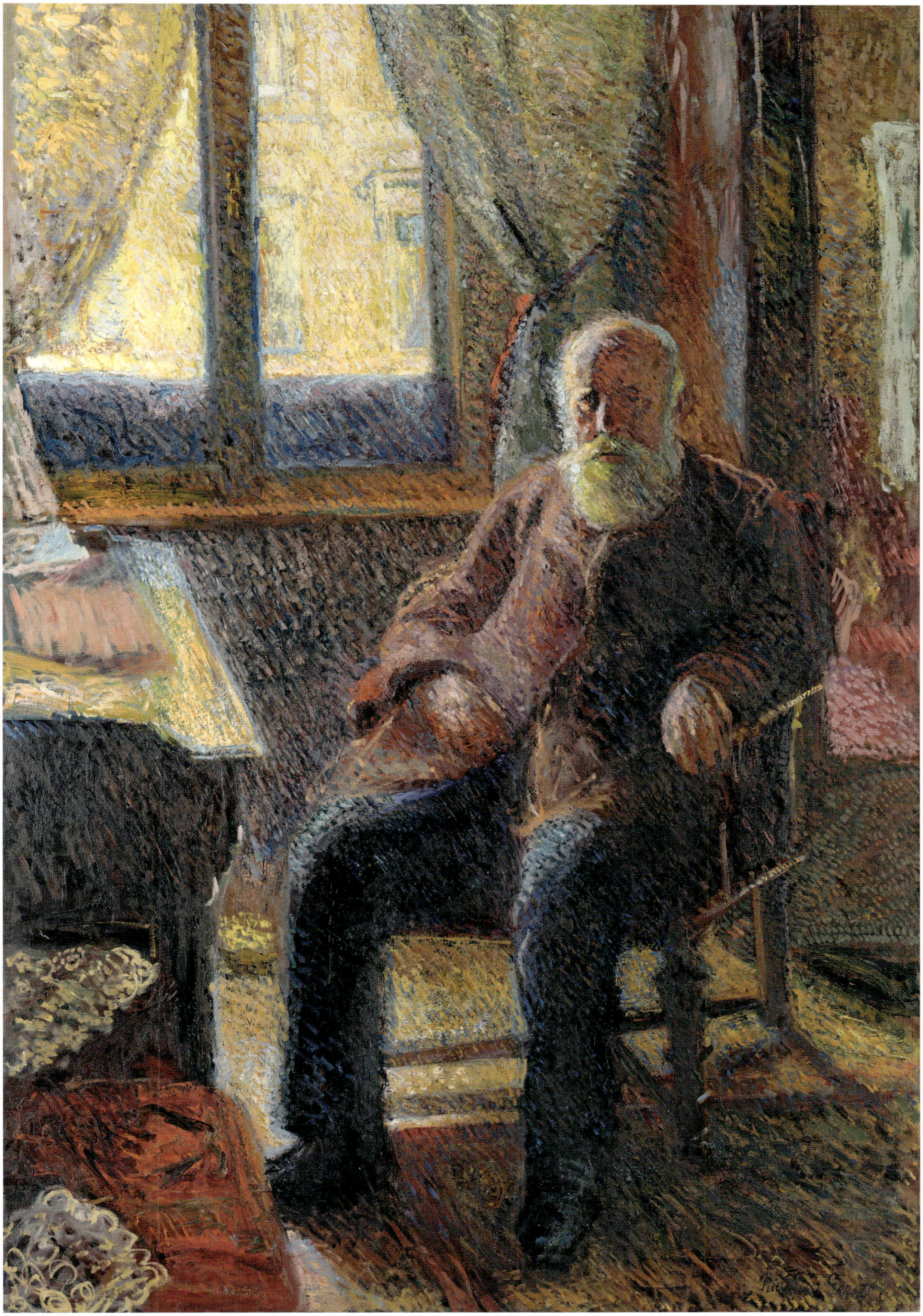

19

PORTRAIT OF THE RESERVE LIEUTENANT ALOIS GERSTL/BILDNIS DES RESERVELEUTNANTS ALOIS GERSTL, autumn 1906

Oil on canvas
153 x 130.2 cm (60 1/4 x 51 1/4 in.)
Leopold Museum, Vienna***

Alois insisted that his brother painted his portrait in the autumn of 1906, presumably at the family apartment, after he had been promoted to Lieutenant, adding that he did so *alla prima*—at the first attempt—with no preparation, and required at least ten sittings. *Portrait of Reserve Lieutenant Alois Gerstl* gives the impression of having been executed in two phases. Gerstl seems to have first composed the unequivocally pointilist dining room, whose east/south double aspect allowed sunlight to stream through the open window throughout the day. Against this background, he then appears to have painted the figure of Alois in a contrasting realistic style, almost as an afterthought, to the point that he never finished his legs. Indeed, while it remains unknown whether the original was cut by Gerstl himself or the family after his death; Nirenstein received the portrait as two separate vertical segments. He then waited three weeks after the opening of the 1931 show before incorporating the two sections as distinct works: *Interieur* (*Interior*), which would certainly have highlighted its "Van Gogh" affinities, and *Bildnis eines Leutnants* (*Portrait of a Lieutenant*). The work was later restored to its present form, with Alois's legs painted by another hand.

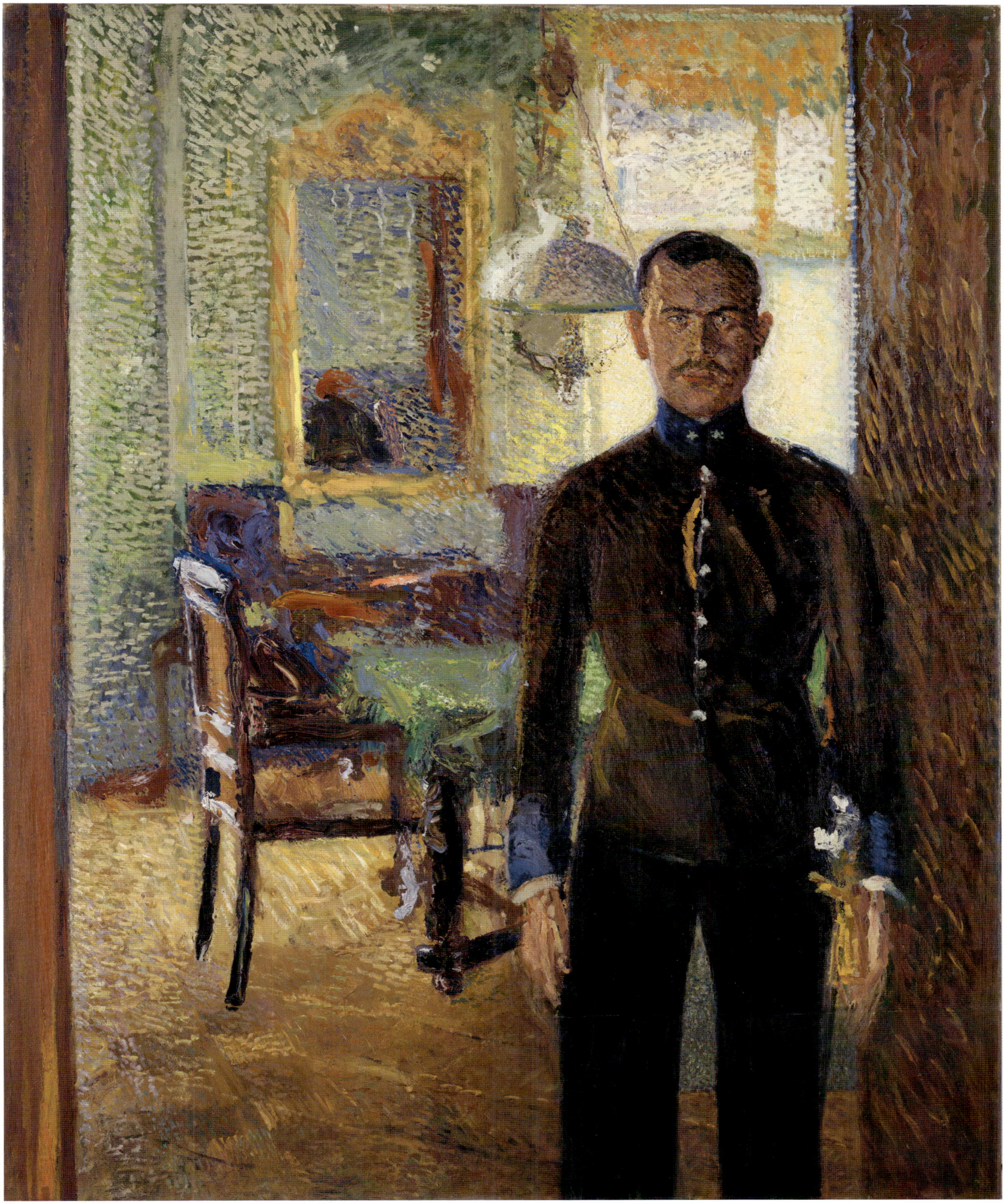

19

20

ERNST DIEZ II, 1906

Technique and size unknown
Whereabouts unknown

21

PROFESSOR ERNST DIEZ/
PROFESSOR ERNST DIEZ, autumn 1906

Tempera and oil on canvas
184 x 74 cm (72 ½ x 29 ⅛ in.)
Belvedere, Vienna**

Professor Ernst Diez is one of two portraits that Gerstl painted of the art historian and first cousin of Schönberg's student, Anton Webern, in the autumn of 1906 after Diez's return from a summer in Rome. The commission was arranged by Schönberg, who, no doubt aware of Klimt's success as a society portraitist, had apparently decided to act as Gerstl's "agent" so as to introduce similar commissions to his new friend from within his circle. Diez recalled that his two portraits, of which one is now lost, were painted in Gerstl's temporary studio, close to the Secession, probably above Café Sperl at Gumpendorferstrasse 11 in Vienna's sixth district, where art societies, including the Hagenbund, met. Many art historians find affinities between *Ernst Diez* and reproductions of Munch's *Marcel Archinard* and *Hermann Schlittgen,* which had recently been published. However, Gerstl's unusual use of tempera and a freer, lighter hand, coupled with Hammer's assertion that he knew nothing of Munch's influence on Gerstl, suggest that, rather than the influence of the Norwegian artist, this was another example of a subject asserting his preferences as with *Schönberg*, and that Diez may have demanded a pose reflecting his expertise in antiquities and Egyptian art. Sadly, Diez had no funds to pay for the commission, so the work remained with Gerstl's family until the 1931 show.

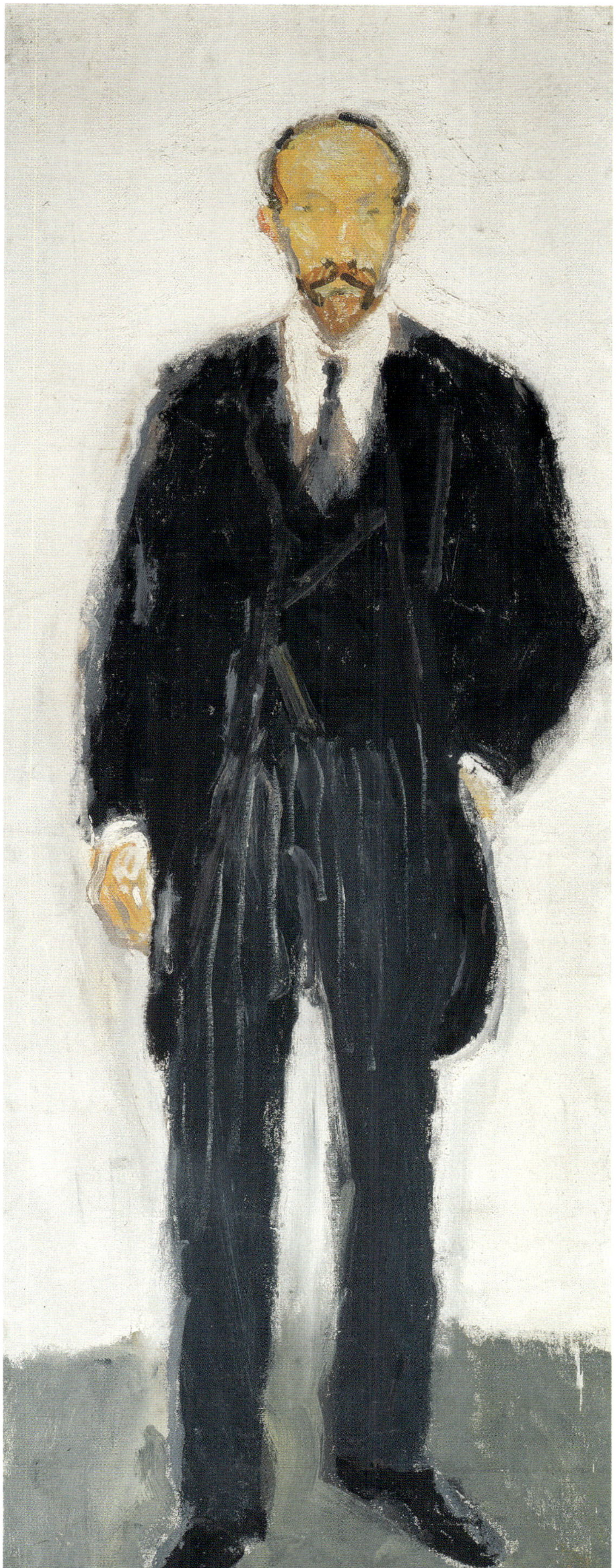

21

22

SMARAGDA BERG, late 1906

Oil on canvas

195 x 137 cm (76 3/4 x 53 7/8 in.)

Private Collection*

Gerstl and his portraiture quickly found favor among Schönberg's circle, and he was soon invited to paint Smaragda, the sister of one of Schönberg's young students, Alban Berg. Indeed, Gerstl and Smaragda, a talented pianist and musician herself, seem to have enjoyed each other's company in the Bergs' fashionable city villa in Hietzing during the several sittings that the large-scale work must have required to complete. *Smaragda Berg* can be ascribed to late 1906; before Christmas 1906 and ahead of her wedding on April 21, 1907. Smaragda, who later came out as a lesbian, had circulated an official engagement photo in which she wears the same dress and ring that Gerstl depicts in her portrait. *Smaragda Berg*, therefore, may have been a celebration of her betrothal, painted from life in her mother's villa, almost certainly before Christmas 1906, when the photograph would have been taken. Once again, however, some concession may have been made towards its subject's preferences, for, although Gerstl now employed a pointilist technique far freer than the one that characterized the meticulous brushwork in his father's portrait, he also made some compromise, perhaps ironically, by drawing on the Secessionist styles of Klimt and Carl Moll.

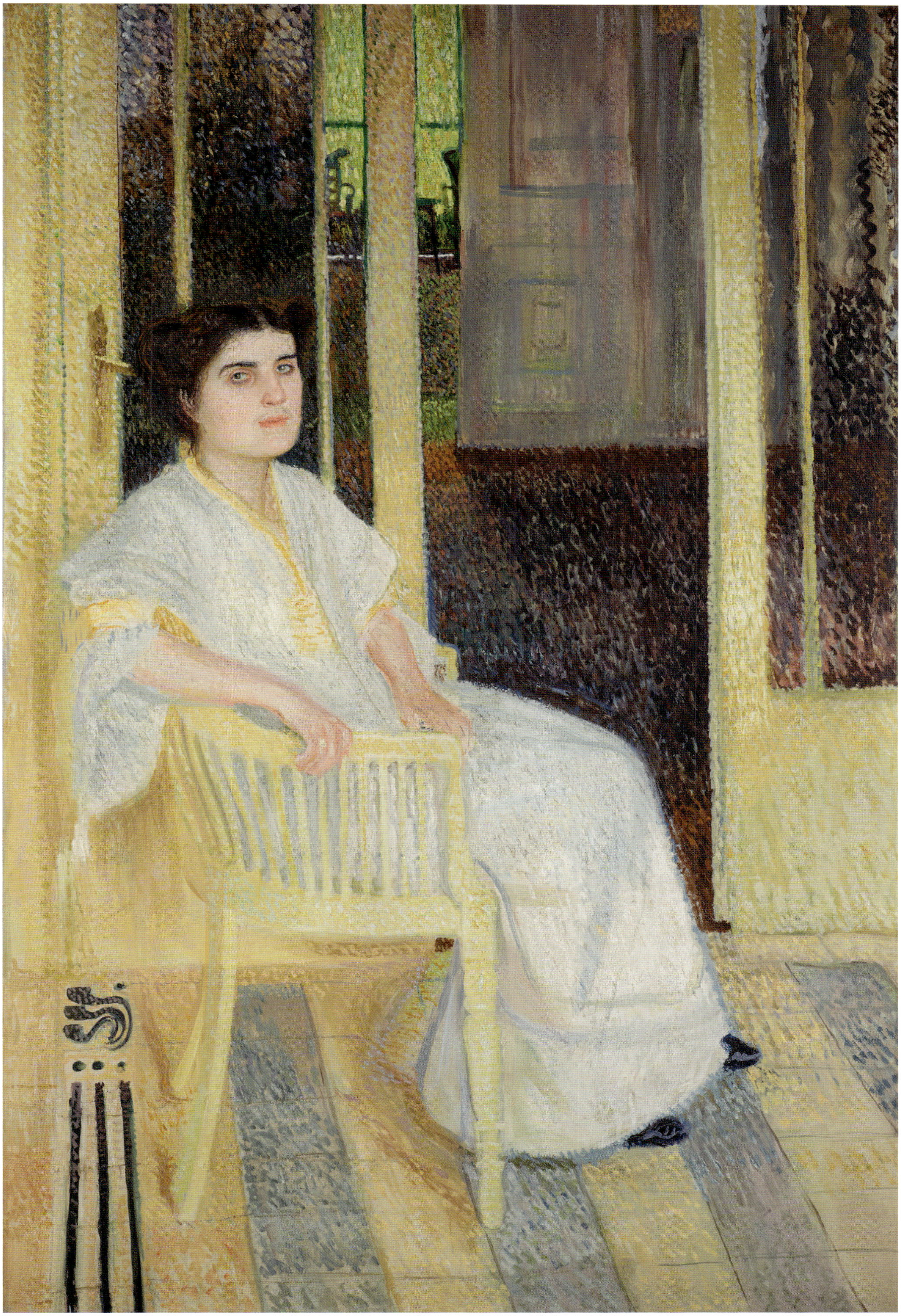

23

MOTHER AND DAUGHTER/MUTTER UND TOCHTER, late 1906

Oil on canvas

145.7 x 120.5 cm (57 ⅜ x 47 ½ in.)

Wien Museum, Vienna*

While the identities of its sitters remain unknown, *Mother and Daughter* was most likely another of the intimate domestic "commissions" that Schönberg appears to have introduced to Gerstl after the artist had been so readily welcomed into the composer's close circle during the winter of 1906–07. The term "commission," however, although used throughout, may need generous interpretation, for many of Gerstl's portraits remained, not in his subjects' possession, but in Gerstl's, perhaps because according to Hammer, "no one found his paintings any good." Stylistically, the work must have been painted around the time of *Smaragda Berg*, and therefore after the double portrait of *Mathilde Schönberg with her Daughter Gertrud*, with whose subject matter and composition it shows obvious correlations. Indeed, Gerstl now displays a much stronger debt to both Van Gogh and the artists that clearly made such a strong impression on him at the 1903 Impressionist show. Puzzlingly, Nirenstein excluded the work from the Neue Galerie's 1931 show for reasons that remain unclear.

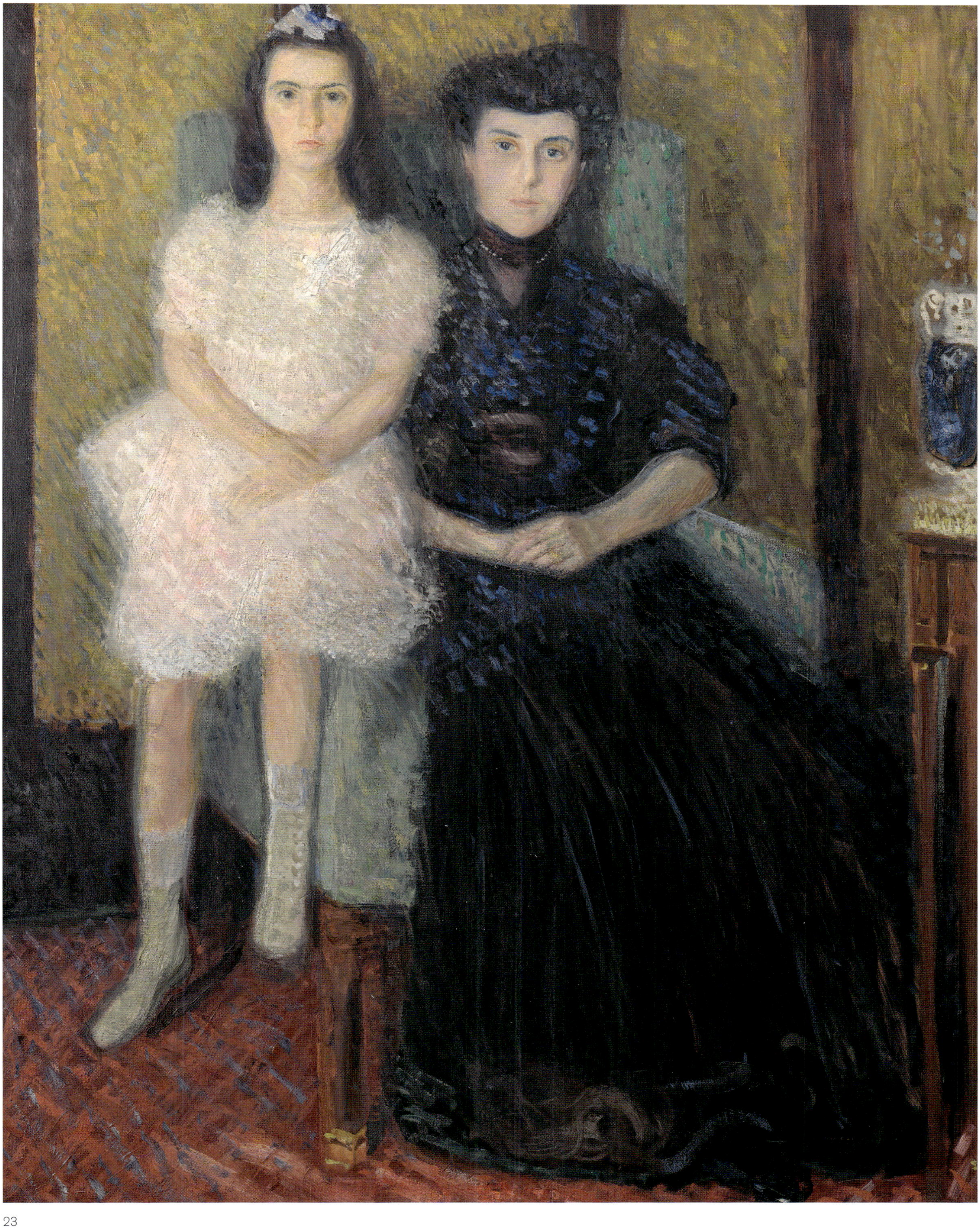

24

WOMAN IN A FEATHER HAT/BILDNIS EINER DAME MIT FEDERHUT, early 1907

Oil on canvas
98.7 x 79.3 cm (38 7/8 x 31 1/4 in.)
Private Collection****

While its subject is again unidentified, *Woman in a Feather Hat* can be considered to be amongst the later domestic commissions from the Schönberg circle that Gerstl completed in the months after he first met the composer. Probably executed in early 1907, the work shows a transitional progression to others from the time: in the outline of the subject's body and hands, Gerstl begins to dematerialize form, a technique which, together with the freer brushwork and color application evident in the work, would come to fruition in the Gmunden summer of 1908 as an example of what Jane Kallir describes as "pointillism's expressive potential." Kallir best expresses its significance: "The small, erratic brushstrokes animate the form, conveying a sense of nervous anticipation that is at odds with the sitter's elegant demeanor. The conventions of the society painter are violated through the aggressive intrusion of the painter's own personality. Gerstl's use of pointillism in this and other works from the same period proved crucial to his future development." Such an insight not only highlights how Gerstl may have vented his antipathy to Klimt and the Secessionist ideal through the medium of portraiture, but also the path that his subjective adoption of Impressionist techniques would take him.

25

THE SINGER, HELENE OBERLÄNDER/DIE SÄNGERIN HELENE OBERLÄNDER, spring 1907

Oil on canvas
184.5 x 90.5 cm (72 5/8 x 35 5/8 in.)
Destroyed during World War II***

Among other later commissions that appear to have been completed during the first year of Gerstl's relationship with Schönberg and the members of his inner circle, was a pointilist-style life-size portrait of the soprano, Helene Oberländer as Tosca. It was exhibited by Nirenstein in 1931 as *Die Sängerin Oberländer*, but destroyed in World War II after Alois lent it out. It is likely that Zemlinsky was instrumental in facilitating the work, for Oberländer sang the role in *Tosca's* Vienna première, given by Zemlinsky at the Volksoper on May 4, 1907. If so, the work may have been one of the last in the sequence of commissions associated with Schönberg that Gerstl painted before their joint holiday in Gmunden in 1907.

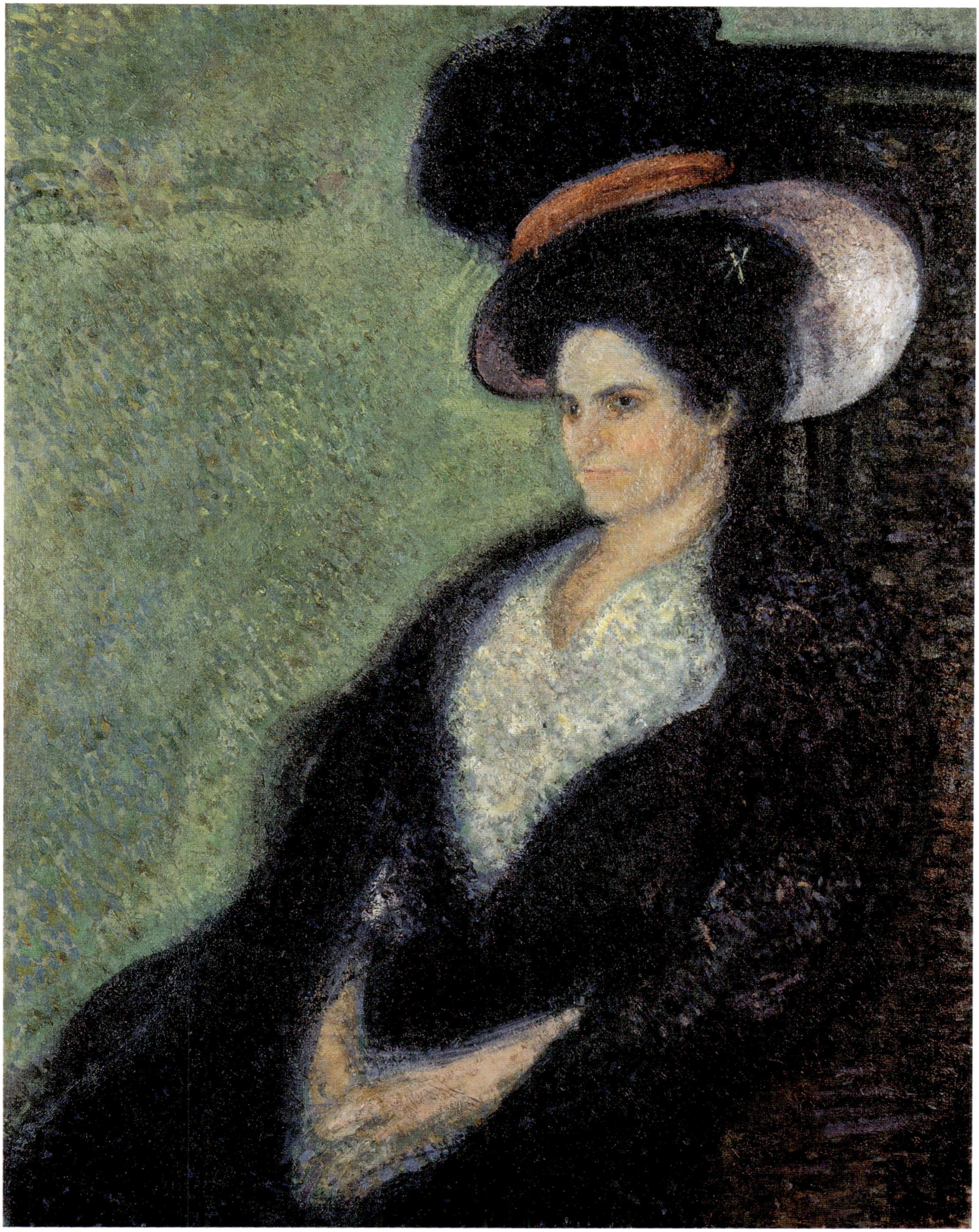

26

SELF-PORTRAIT/SELBSTBILDNIS, winter 1906–07
India ink on paper
45 x 31.5 cm (17 ¾ x 12 ⅜ in.)
[Schirn has 44.9 x 31.4 cm]
The Albertina Museum, Vienna**

27

SELF-PORTRAIT/SELBSTBILDNIS, winter 1906–07
India ink on paper
34.6 x 26 cm (13 ⅝ x 10 ¼ in.)
Private Collection**

28

SELF-PORTRAIT/SELBSTBILDNIS, winter 1906–07
India ink on paper
34.5 x 26 cm (13 ⅝ x 10 ¼ in.)
Private Collection, Courtesy Galerie St. Etienne, New York****

29

SELF-PORTRAIT/SELBSTBILDNIS, winter 1906–07
Pen and ink on cream wove paper
45 x 31.5 cm (17 ¾ x 12 ⅜ in.)
Private Collection, Courtesy Galerie St. Etienne, New York**

Even though Gerstl seems to have been content producing commissions of the various members of Schönberg's circle, his favorite subject in the months after he met Schönberg proved to be himself, whom he portrayed using a variety of media. While very few of Gerstl's sketches survive [see Cat. nos. 26–29], among those that do are a series of four pointilist pen-and-ink self-portraits on paper, drawn in the winter of 1906–07, which stand as vivid examples of Gerstl's Divisionist mindset around that time. Heinrich Jalowetz's wife, Johanna, firmly recalls that it was in the winter of 1906–07 when Gerstl gave her husband a gift of an India ink self-portrait on white paper [Cat. no. 26], which she described as extraordinarily lifelike. Moreover, she confirmed that, at the same time, Gerstl painted a commission of Jalowetz, a life-size, knee-length, entirely pointilist oil portrait, which she indicates was lost after being left in safe custody in Vienna when the Jalowetzes emigrated to the United States in 1938. Jalowetz was a very close friend of Anton Webern, as well as being a member of Schönberg's closely-knit band of students. Johanna Jalowetz's recollections and Gerstl's gift to her husband provide a compelling insight into his swift integration into Schönberg's circle, which appears to have warmly welcomed him into its midst. Moreover, according to Jalowetz's daughter, Lisa and Zemlinsky's second wife, Louise, they apparently had a high regard for his artistic talent, too.

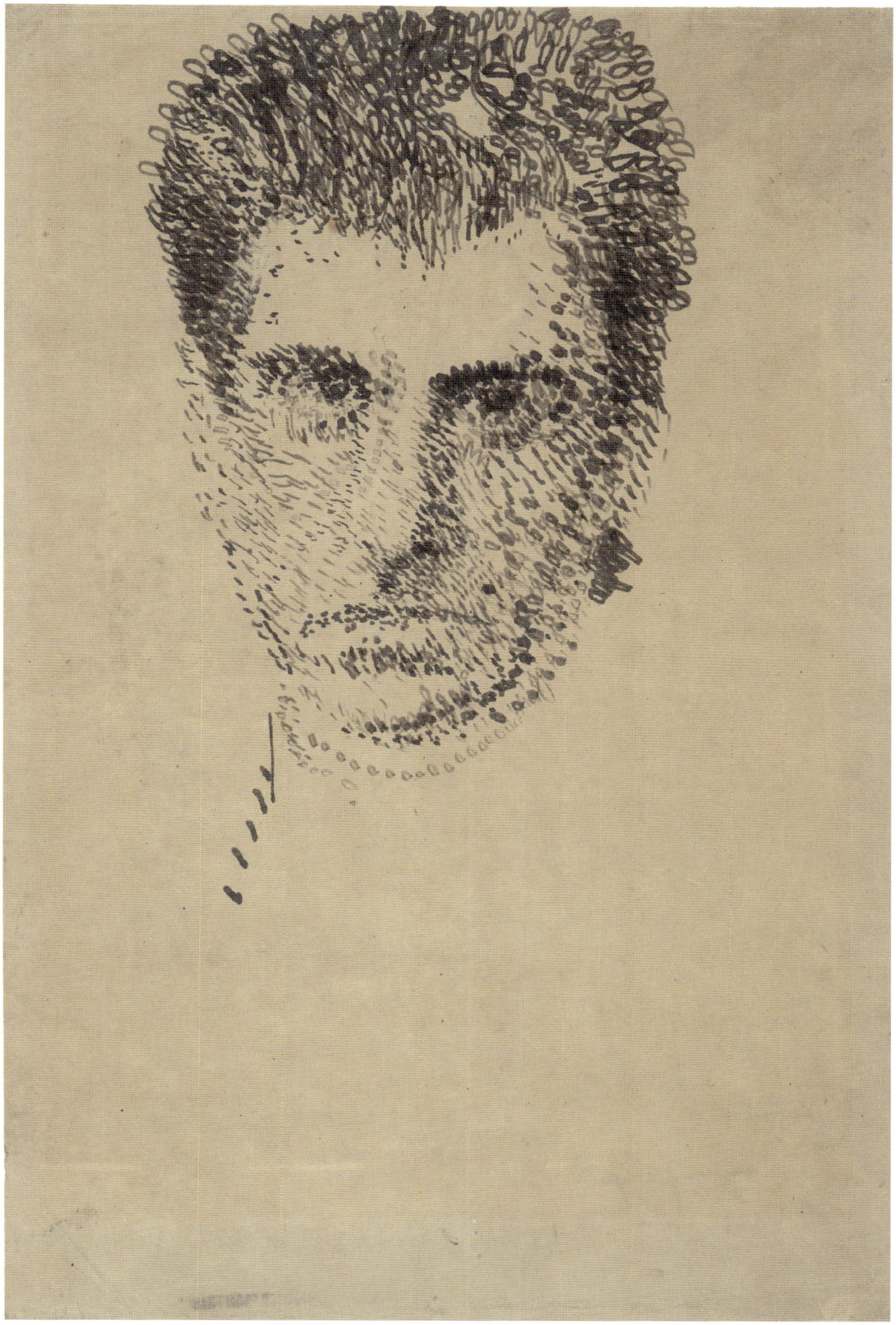

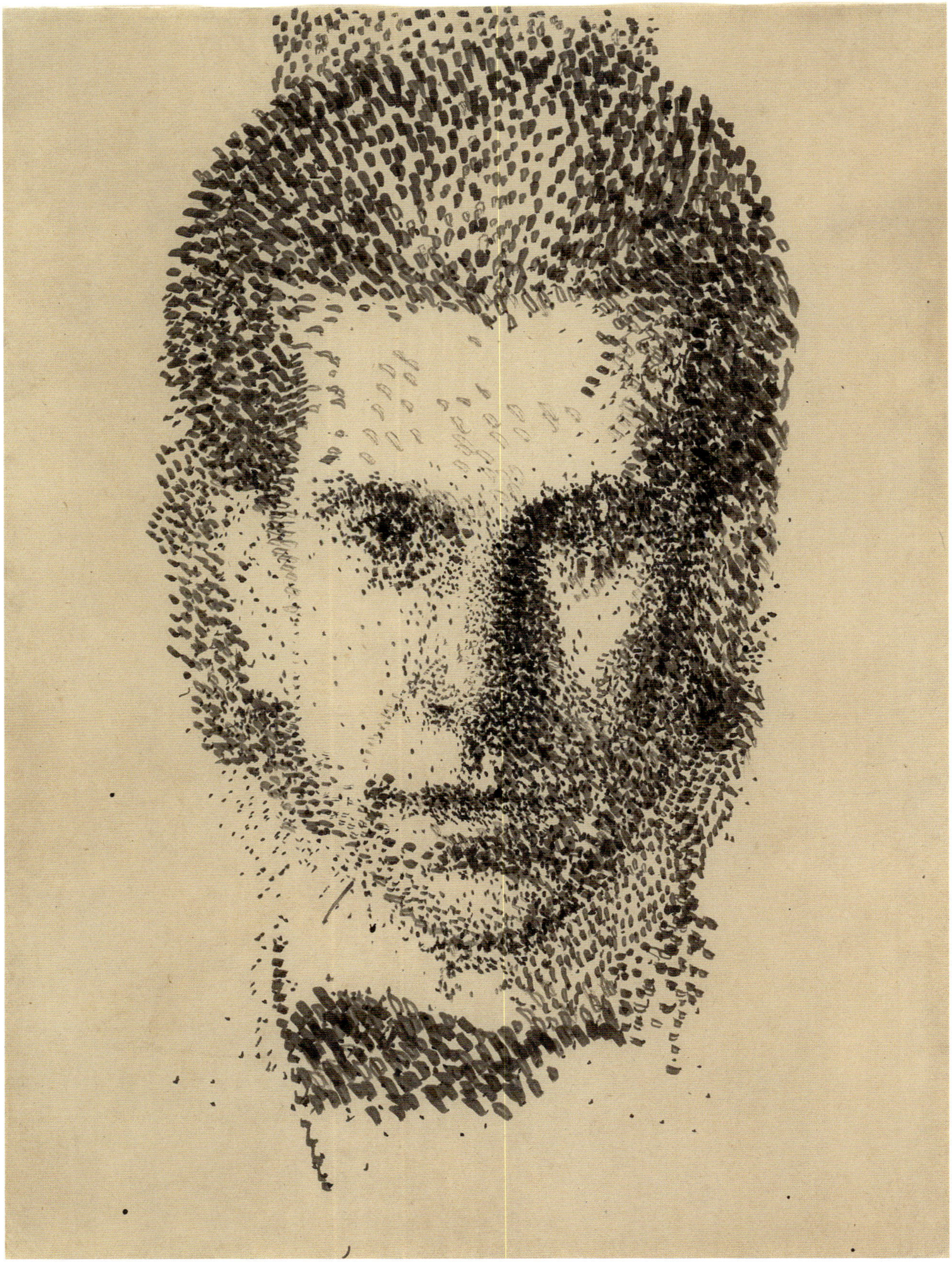

27

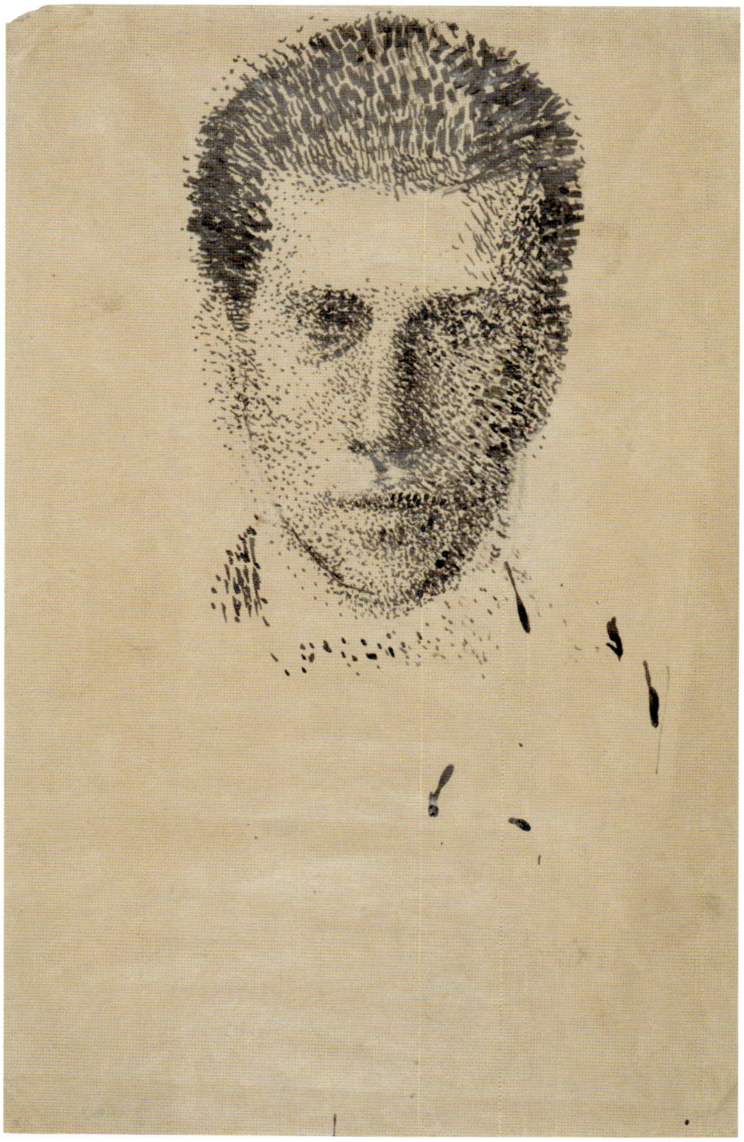

28

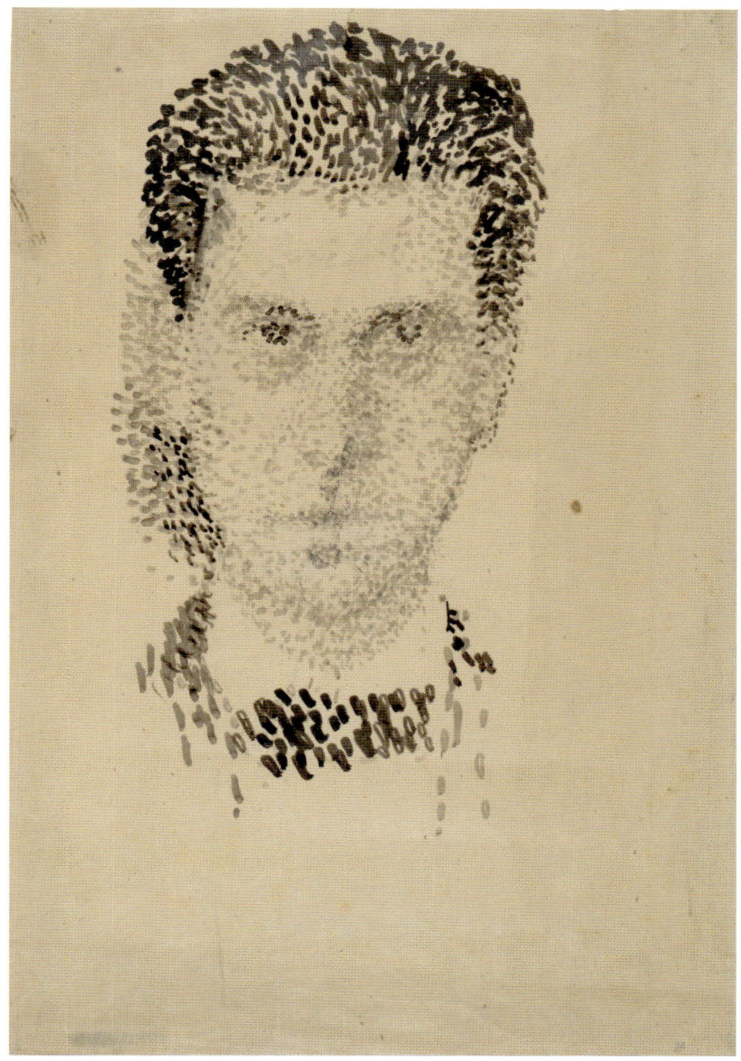

29

30

SELF-PORTRAIT (STUDY)/SELBSTBILDNIS [STUDIE], winter 1906–07

Recto: *Self-Portrait in front of a Stove*, winter 1906–07 [Cat. no. 33]
Distemper on canvas
69 x 55 cm (27 ⅛ x 21 ⅝ in.)
Neue Galerie New York**

On being invited by Lefler to join his Special School of Landscape Painting in March 1906, Gerstl, probably to appease his notorious reticence and well-documented dislike of anyone viewing his work, had demanded and received his own individual studio in the Academy where he painted several self-portraits during the winter of 1906–07. One, *Self-Portrait (Study)*, is found entirely within the stretcher on the reverse of *Self-Portrait in front of Stove* [see Cat. no. 33], for which it may have been a preliminary study. The two share a similar direction of light and since it is highly likely that the front of the canvas had already been designated for the main work, Gerstl's use of quick-drying distemper here may have been intentional so that he could proceed quickly to the half-portrait that became the final version.

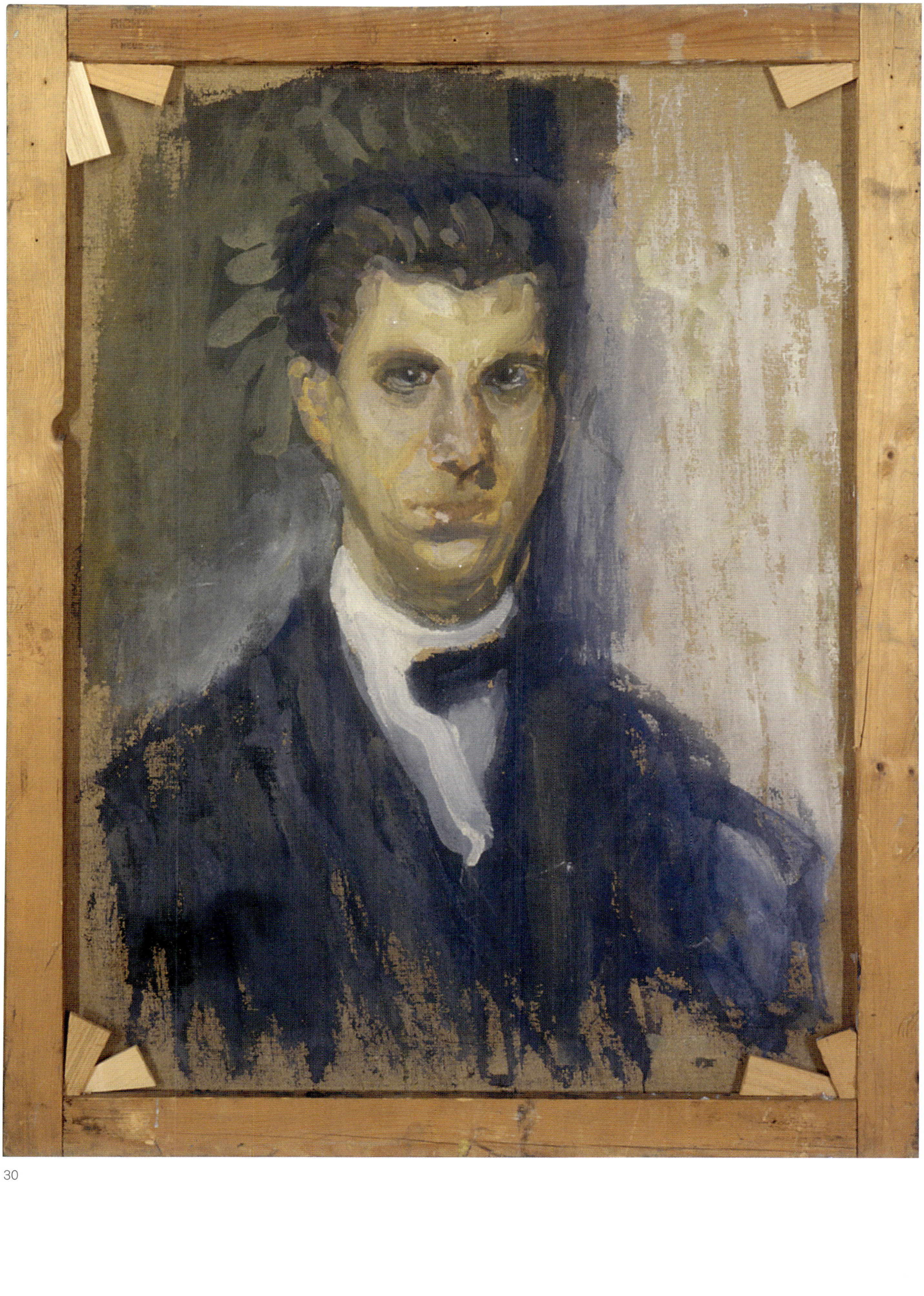

31

SMALL SELF-PORTRAIT/KLEINES SELBSTBILDNIS, winter 1906–07

Verso: *Head of a Woman*, ca. 1902 [Cat. no. 3]
Oil on canvas
47 x 37 cm (18 ½ x 14 ⅝ in.)
Kunsthaus Zug, Stiftung Sammlung Kamm**

Self-Portrait (Study) [Cat. no. 30] and *Small Self-Portrait,* found on the recto of *Head of a Woman* [Cat. no. 3], bear obvious similarities to each other. However the latter, although unfinished, is an oil, in which, as in his portrait of his brother, Alois, Gerstl again applied impasto colors onto unprimed canvas. Interestingly, as compared to the proud demeanor he displays in other self-representations from his first period at the Academy, Gerstl chose to present himself in both this and *Self-Portrait (Study)* in a less attractive and, in the case of the latter, even slightly grotesque manner. They perhaps represent a more honest expression of the unease that he would always harbor with regard to his looks and physique.

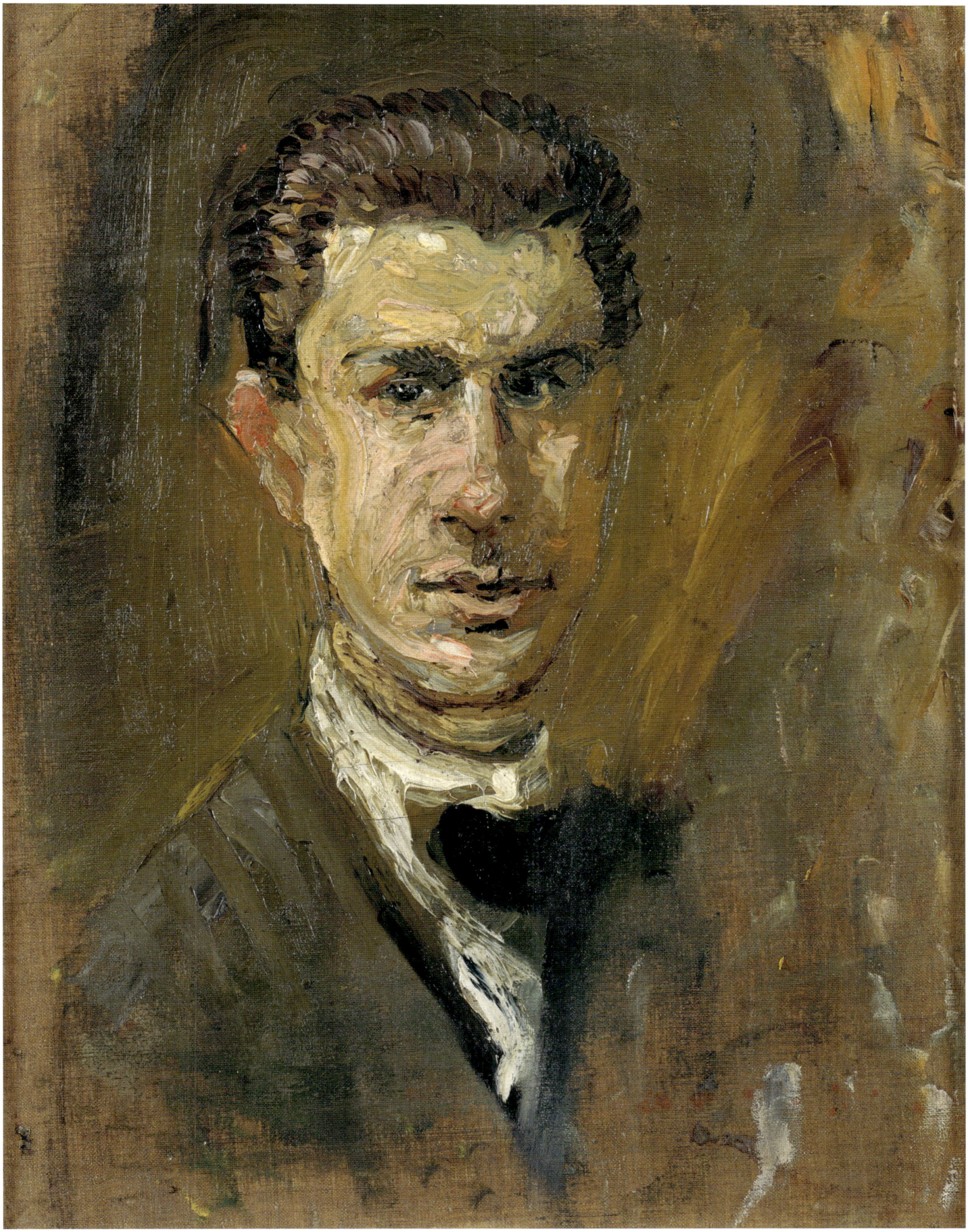

32

SELF-PORTRAIT WITH PALETTE/SELBSTBILDNIS MIT PALETTE, winter 1906–07

Oil on canvas
186.5 x 58.5 cm (73 3/8 x 23 in.)
Wien Museum, Vienna**

Gerstl's rapid integration into Schönberg's circle does not necessarily assume that he had exchanged his withdrawn, confrontational traits for gregarious, sociable ones. Nonetheless, there is reason to suppose that he gained a degree of confidence from being amongst his new, musically oriented young friends, as well as a desire to represent himself as an artist. In his life-size, narrow format *Self-Portrait with Palette*, Gerstl depicts a reverse image of himself, reflected in his beloved long mirror that followed him to every studio, holding a clutch of brushes in his left hand while resting a palette on his forearm as he dabs with the other hand. Smartly attired with a bow-tie and well groomed, Gerstl is surrounded by his paraphernalia; his *Semi-Nude Self-Portrait* [Cat. no. 6] hangs behind him, giving the impression of one whose new social and academic environment had endowed in him the determined and self-assured demeanor of a serious, even professional artist. The work is also the only self-portrait onto which Gerstl inscribed his name and address on the stretcher, but since the canvas was attached after this was applied, the frame may have been intended for a commission, but was then used by Gerstl for himself.

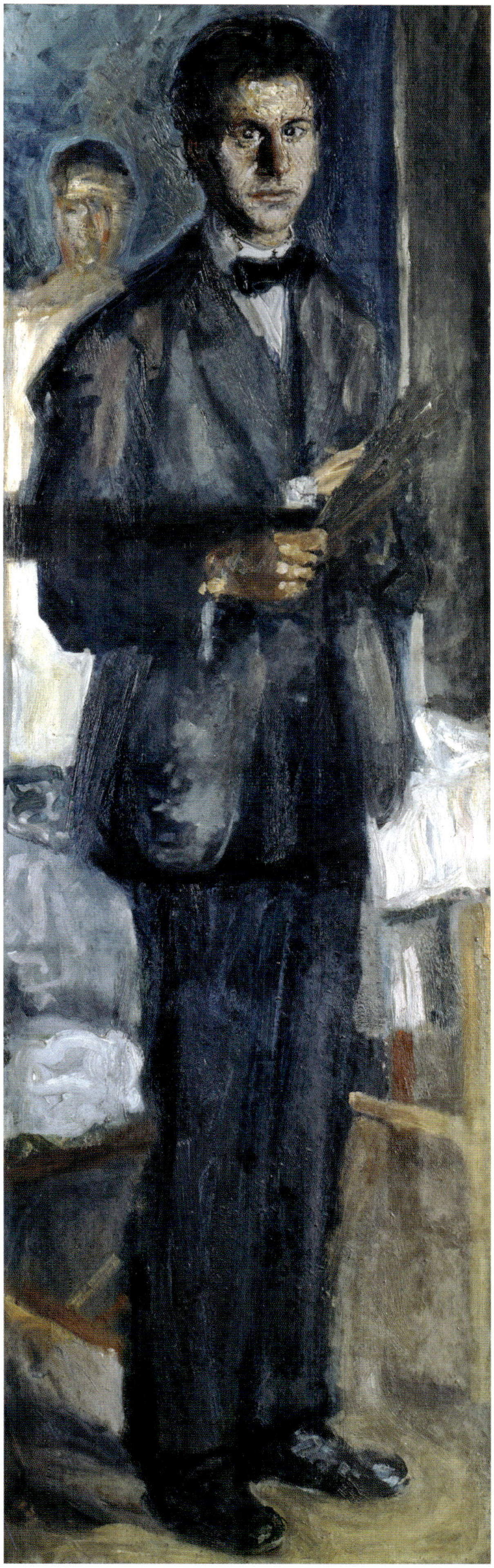

33

SELF-PORTRAIT IN FRONT OF A STOVE/ SELBSTBILDNIS VOR EINEM OFEN, winter 1906–07

Verso: *Self-Portrait (Study)*, winter 1906–07 [Cat. no. 30]
Oil on canvas on mounted board
69 x 55 cm (27 1/8 x 21 5/8 in.)
Neue Galerie New York**

The presence of *Professor Ernst Diez* [Cat. No. 21] hanging behind him in *Self-Portrait in front of Stove* confirms that Gerstl painted the work after the autumn of 1906, probably in early 1907. Compared to *Self-Portrait with Palette*, it is a more nuanced work, particularly in its use of light and shade and the greater detail and expressive intricacy with which Gerstl endows his facial features. While both were probably conceived in his new Academy studio, this suggests that *Self-Portrait in front of Stove* was the later work. Gerstl again presents himself in a fastidious, serious and intense manner, with long, wavy hair, a style that, although radically changed thereafter, he appears to have maintained for perhaps two years before summer 1907. It will be seen that both pictures also feature *Semi-Nude Self-Portrait* hanging on the wall, a clear indication of the importance that the work, painted while still a teenager, obviously held for the artist.

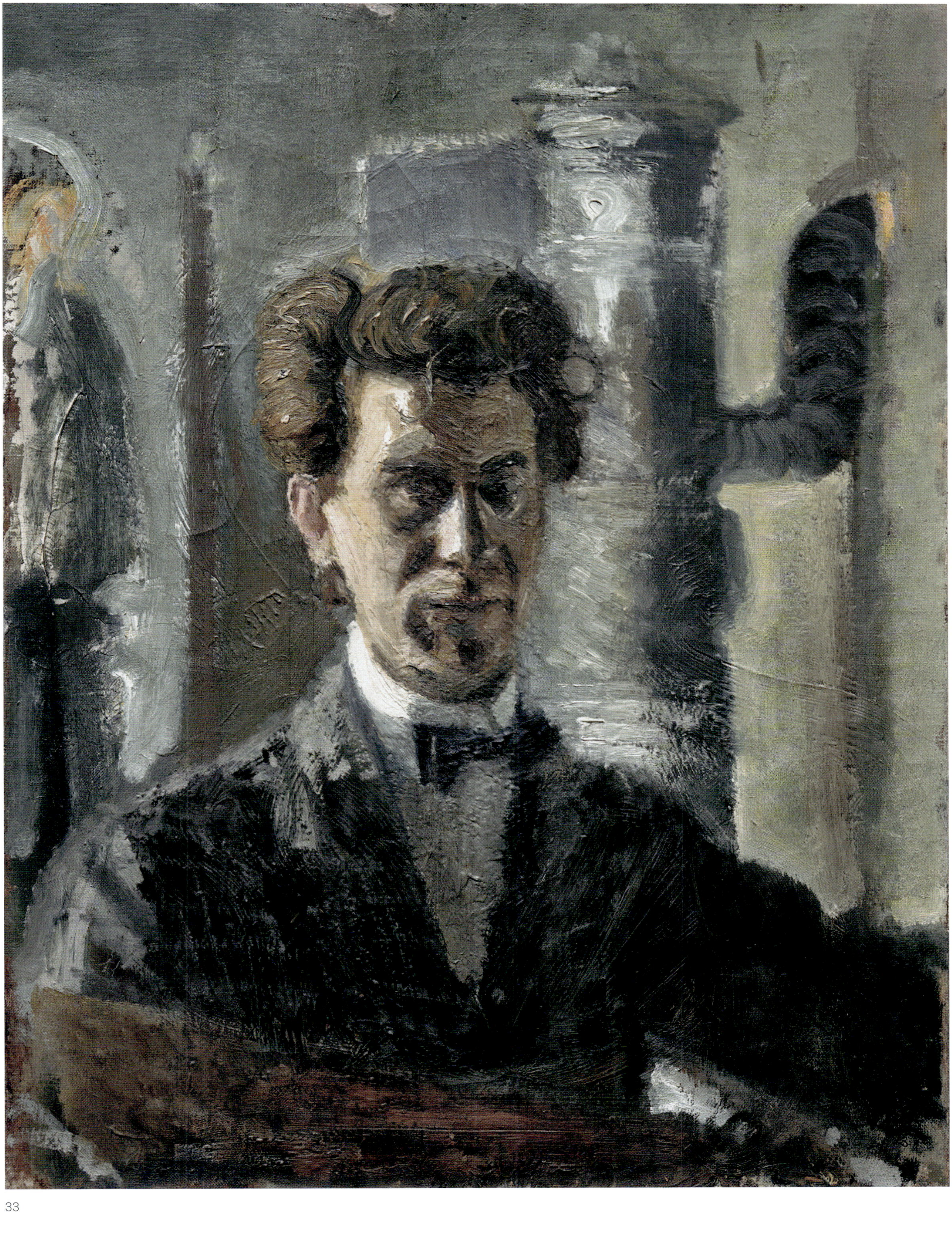

34

COGWHEEL RAILWAY TO THE KAHLENBERG/ TRASSE DER ZAHNRADBAHN AUF DEN KAHLENBERG, spring 1907

Oil on canvas
56 x 69.5 cm (22 x 27 3/8 in.)
Belvedere, Vienna**

While it might have been expected that Gerstl's first year at Lefler's Special School for Landscape Painting would have seen an outpouring of such images, the converse appears to be the case. Indeed, other than *Grinzing* [Cat. no. 14], just one other landscape from this period exists: Gerstl's *Cogwheel Railway to Kahlenberg,* a depiction of a nearly 1,600-feet-high hill that rises above the banks of the Danube. The railroad, which ceased operating in 1919, ran steeply from nearby Nussdorf, from where this was painted in spring 1907, in an area in Vienna's northernmost nineteenth district that Gerstl knew well from his time in neighboring Hohe Warte. Clearly owing much to Van Gogh and his depictions of the countryside that were exhibited at the 1906 Miethke show, the work not only displays a far more dexterous pointilism than *Grinzing*; it also predicts Gerstl's positive flurry of landscapes that emanated from Gmunden in summer 1907.

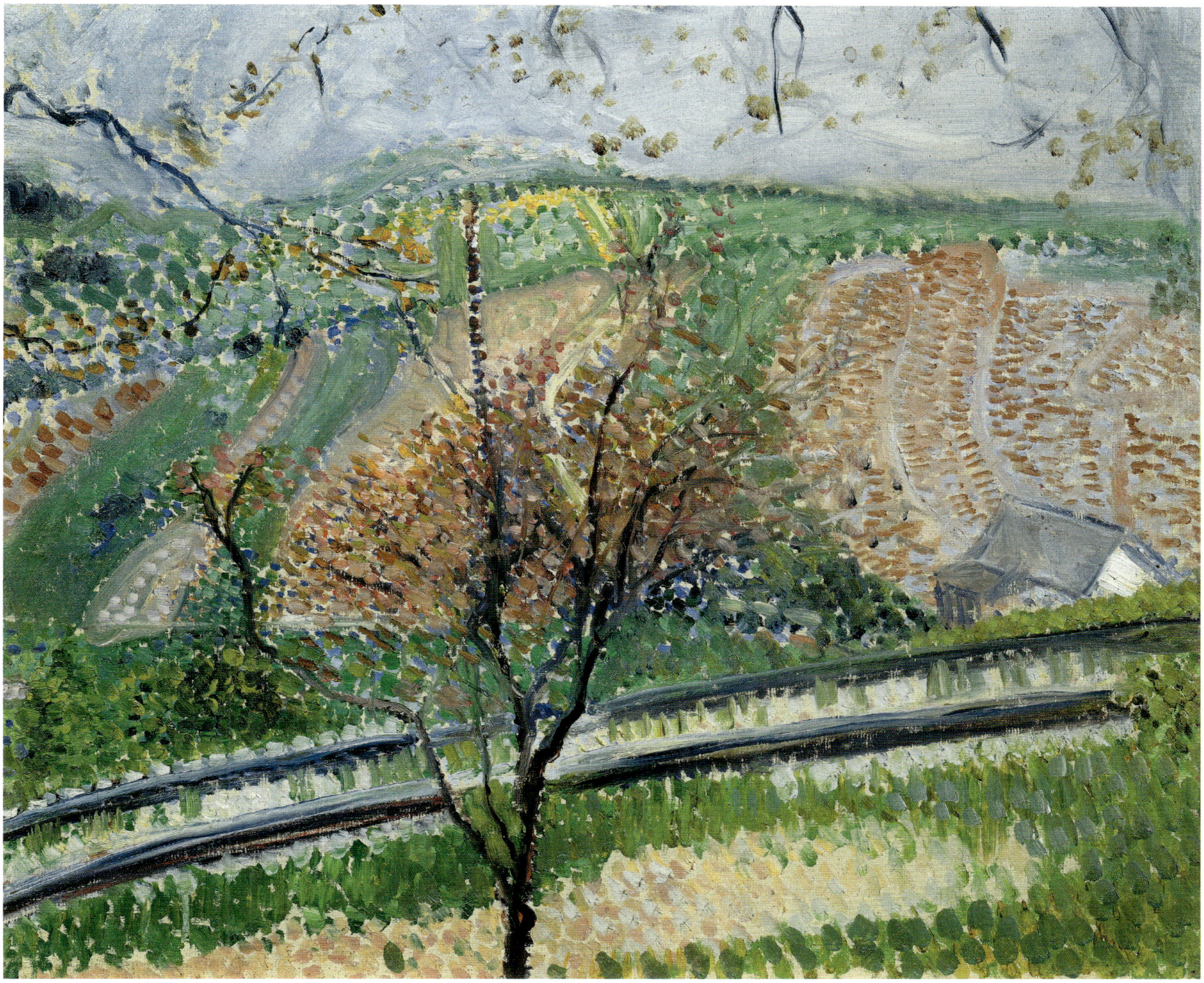

34

35

SELF-PORTRAIT IN FRONT OF A BLUE-GREEN BACKGROUND/SELBSTBILDNIS VOR BLAUGRÜNEM HINTERGRUND, spring-summer 1907

Oil on board
100 x 72 cm (39 3/8 x 28 3/8 in.)
Tiroler Landesmuseum Ferdinandeum***

For his *Self-Portrait in front of a Blue-Green Background*, Gerstl moved to a new medium. This is the first of ten extant works painted on artboard, an affordable, easily divided material that may have been selected in deference to his friend, the cash-strapped Schönberg, with whom he had started to share art supplies. For this confident self-representation, Gerstl uses the full dimensions of the board, leaving areas of its brown surface exposed to suggest the skin tone of his hands. The work can be attributed to early summer 1907, for Gerstl's appearance changed during his imminent Gmunden vacation with the Schönbergs, when he began to sport a shorn look and facial hair. Painted with a quick, free hand, the work shows a significant evolution in Gerstl's style. He abandons the Divisionism that had characterized his work in the previous months in favor of random dabs and flecks, which invest his imposing, brazen stance with the dynamic energy of a newfound certitude and self-assuredness. Whether this had been gained from Schönberg's holiday invitation, a successful year at the Academy, or even his rejection of Galerie Miethke's proposal to exhibit alongside Klimt's *Faculty Paintings*, Gerstl's direction here further anticipates the landscapes that he would produce in Gmunden.

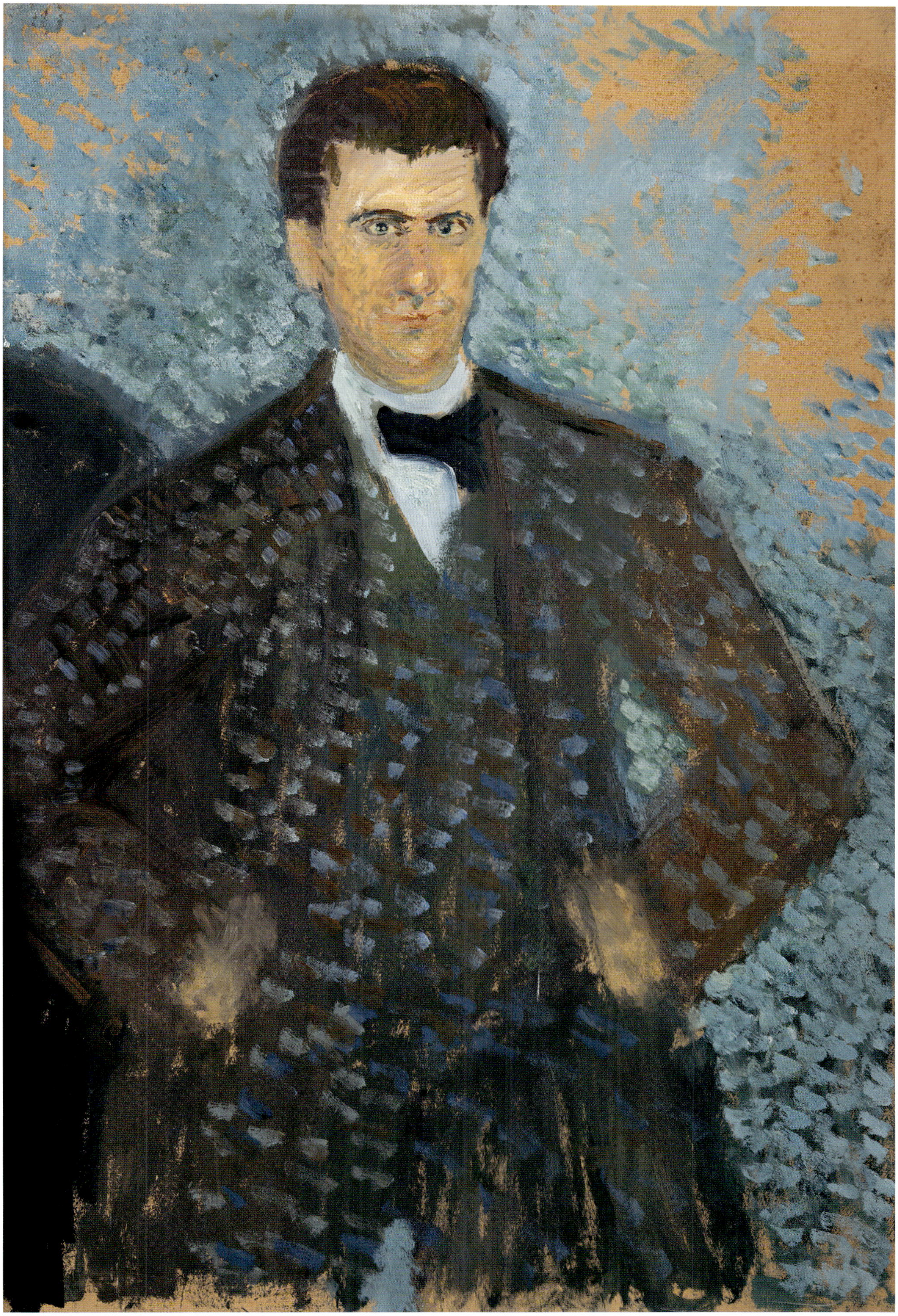

36

FRUIT TREE WITH SUPPORTS/OBSTBAUM MIT HOLZSTÜTZEN, summer 1907

Oil on canvas on board
35.5 x 20.5 cm (14 x 8 1/8 in.)
Kunsthaus Zug, Stiftung Sammlung Kamm**

37

FLOWER MEADOW WITH TREES/BLUMENWIESE MIT BÄUMEN, summer 1907

Oil on canvas on board
36 x 38 cm (14 1/8 x 15 in.)
Kunsthaus Zug, Stiftung Sammlung Kamm**

38

FRUIT GARDEN (SMALL GARDEN PAINTING)/ OBSTGARTEN (KLEINES GARTENBILD), summer 1907

Oil on canvas on board
35 x 34 cm (13 3/4 x 13 3/8 in.)
Ernst Ploil, Vienna**

39

MEADOW WITH FRUIT TREES/WIESE MIT BÄUMEN, summer 1907

Oil on canvas
44 x 34.7 cm (17 3/8 x 13 5/8 in.)
Leopold Museum, Vienna**

By mid-1907 Gerstl had become so established within Schönberg's circle that the composer invited him to join his family, friends and students in Gmunden, a beautiful spa town south of Salzburg, which lies on Austria's deepest glacier lake, the Traunsee. Here, in both 1907 and 1908, Schönberg and his group rented a number of farmhouses beneath the nearly 5,550 feet high Traunstein on the eastern bank of the lake, nearly 3 miles from the center of the town. Gerstl took up residence for the summer in Feramühle, a millhouse a quarter mile south along the lake road from the Schönbergs' farmhouse, Engelgut. July—his first month—was blighted by one of the rainiest in Gmunden's history. Presumably, once conditions had become more favorable, Gerstl set up his easel and, using *plein air* techniques that he had acquired from his two summers in 1900 and 1901 at Simon Hollósy's Nagybánya Malerschule (for example, see Hollósy's *Fall*), began to paint the hillside meadows and bankside around the Feramühle. The result was a series of landscapes and other works that saw an extraordinary acceleration in Gerstl's metamorphosis as an artist.

Gerstl painted 15 or more landscapes in Gmunden in 1907. The sole survivor of the five he painted on artboard is his *Fruit Tree with Supports*. Gerstl had reassured both his parents and Alois on July 26 that, not only were things "very good" with his new friends from Vienna, but also that he had executed a number of studies in his first days away. This might suggest that *Fruit Tree with Supports* and, indeed, others from the same time frame, may have been academic exercises set by Professor Lefler. Nonetheless, the work bears many of the advanced pointilistic ideas that Gerstl had developed since the Van Gogh show, as well as following the approach he took in his *Self-Portrait in front of a Blue-Green Background* [Cat. no. 35], namely allowing the brown tone of the board to create the background effect. The tree-supports are typical of the area and suggest that the fruit harvest was imminent. Since for some trees on the Traunsee this occurs in late July or early August, the fact would seem to reinforce the likelihood that Gerstl may not have been able to work outside beforehand. Indeed, by then, as Cat. nos. 37–39 vividly illustrate, the record monthly rainfall that had hitherto hindered him may also have caused the orchard meadows in the vicinity of Gerstl's lodgings to become lush and verdant.

It is evident from Gerstl's 1907 Gmunden landscapes that he had fully grasped Hollósy's *plein air* techniques. Moreover Van Gogh's paintings, especially, perhaps, those of woods and copses—for example, *The Grove,* exhibited as No. 26 at Miethke's 1906 show—had left a deep impression on him. Where Gerstl differs is in his synthesis of tones; in *Flower Meadow with Trees*, *Fruit Garden (Small Garden Painting)* and *Meadow with Fruit Trees* particularly, these create a sense of infinity, which is not readily apparent in later landscapes from that summer. These three, predominantly green works have been affectionately dubbed Gerstl's "*Spinat*" or "spinach" landscapes; they portray a hillside route to Feramühle, which bridged the mill gullies that brought logs down from the higher slopes to the lake. Taking the path it was possible to avoid detection on the lakeside road, and may, therefore, have been of advantage to Mathilde during her affair with Gerstl—although it is by no means certain whether this had started by this point. Conversely, had Gerstl already found himself drawn to Mathilde, there is the poignant possibility that these could be considered portraits without a subject, with the empty path, perhaps, expressing the artist's nascent feelings towards his closest colleague's wife.

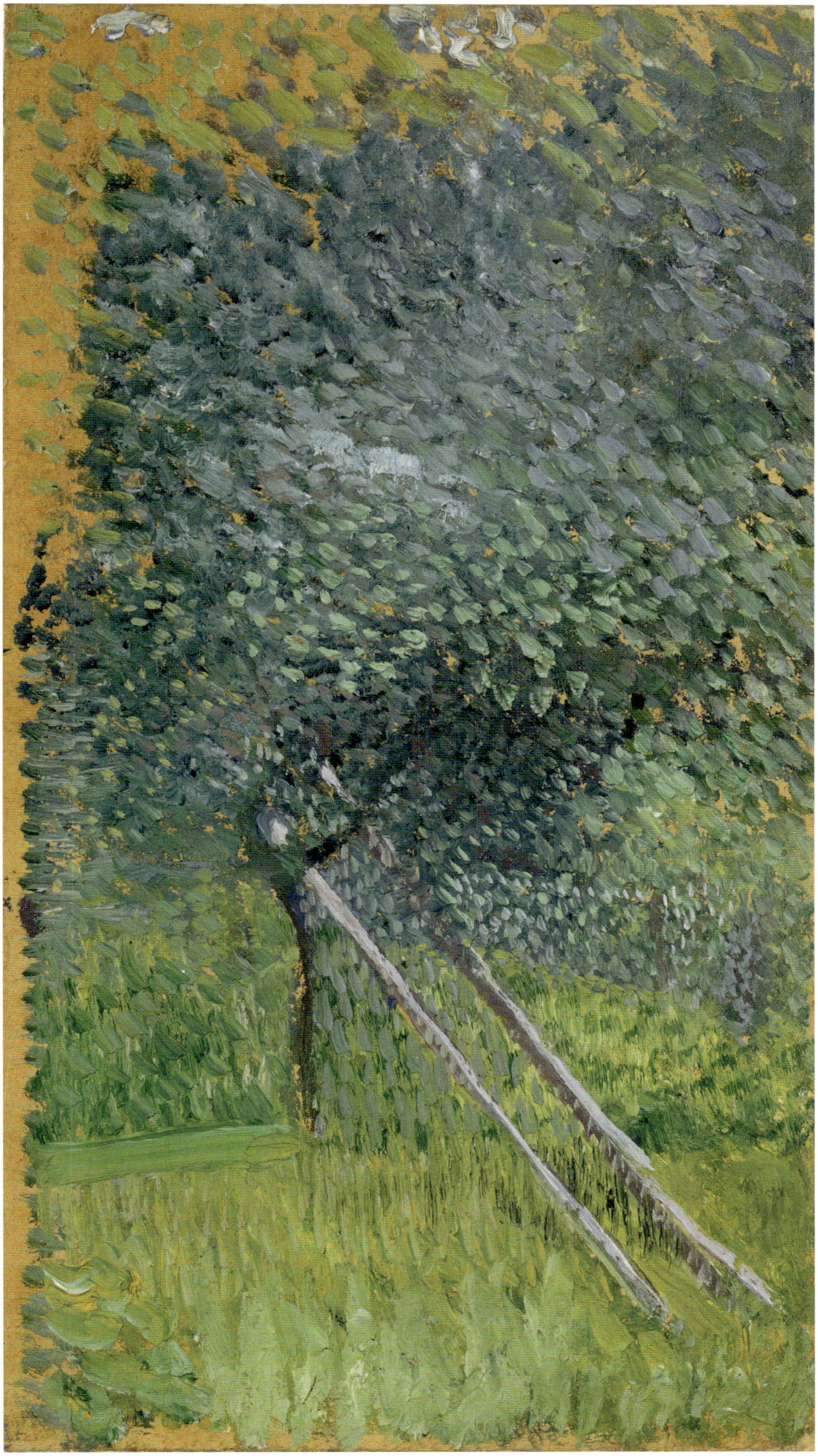

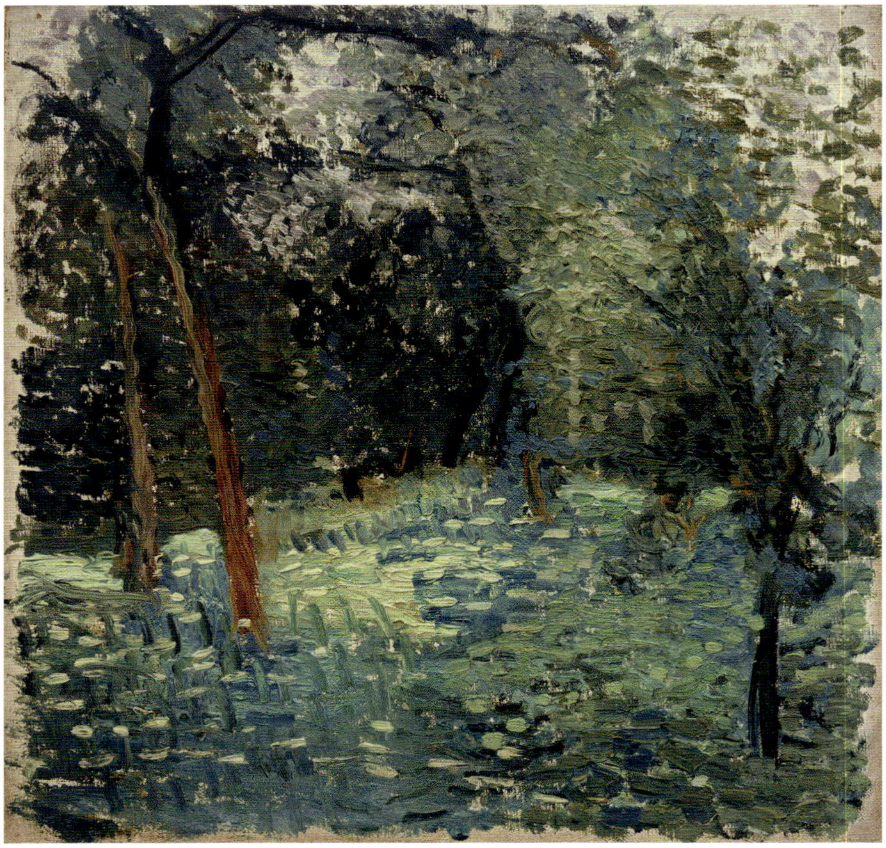

37

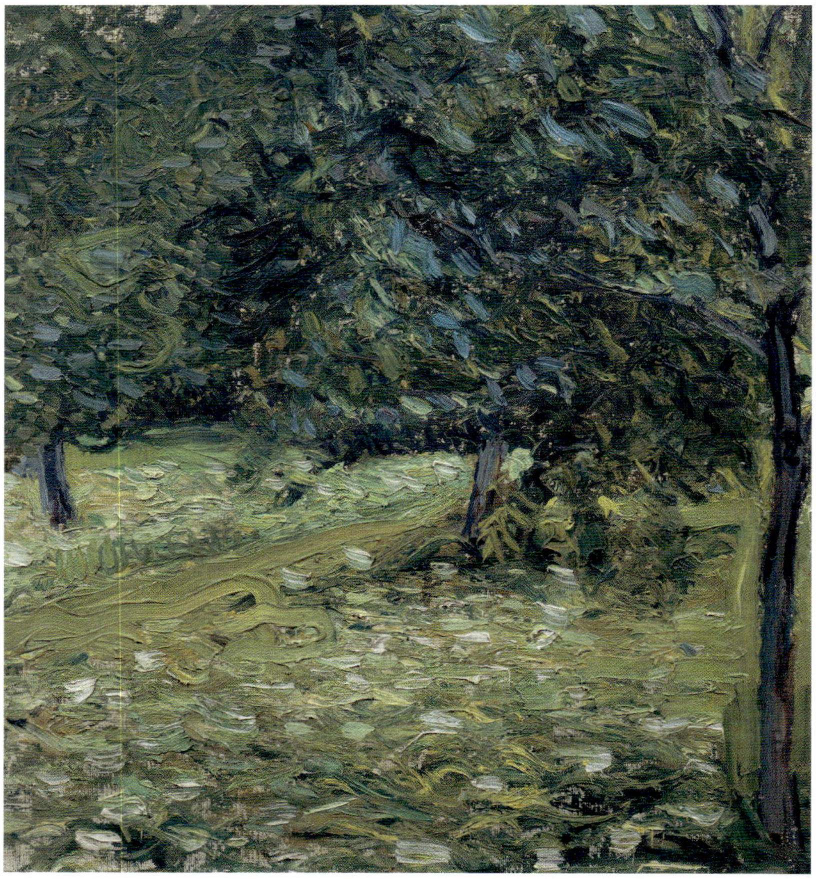

38

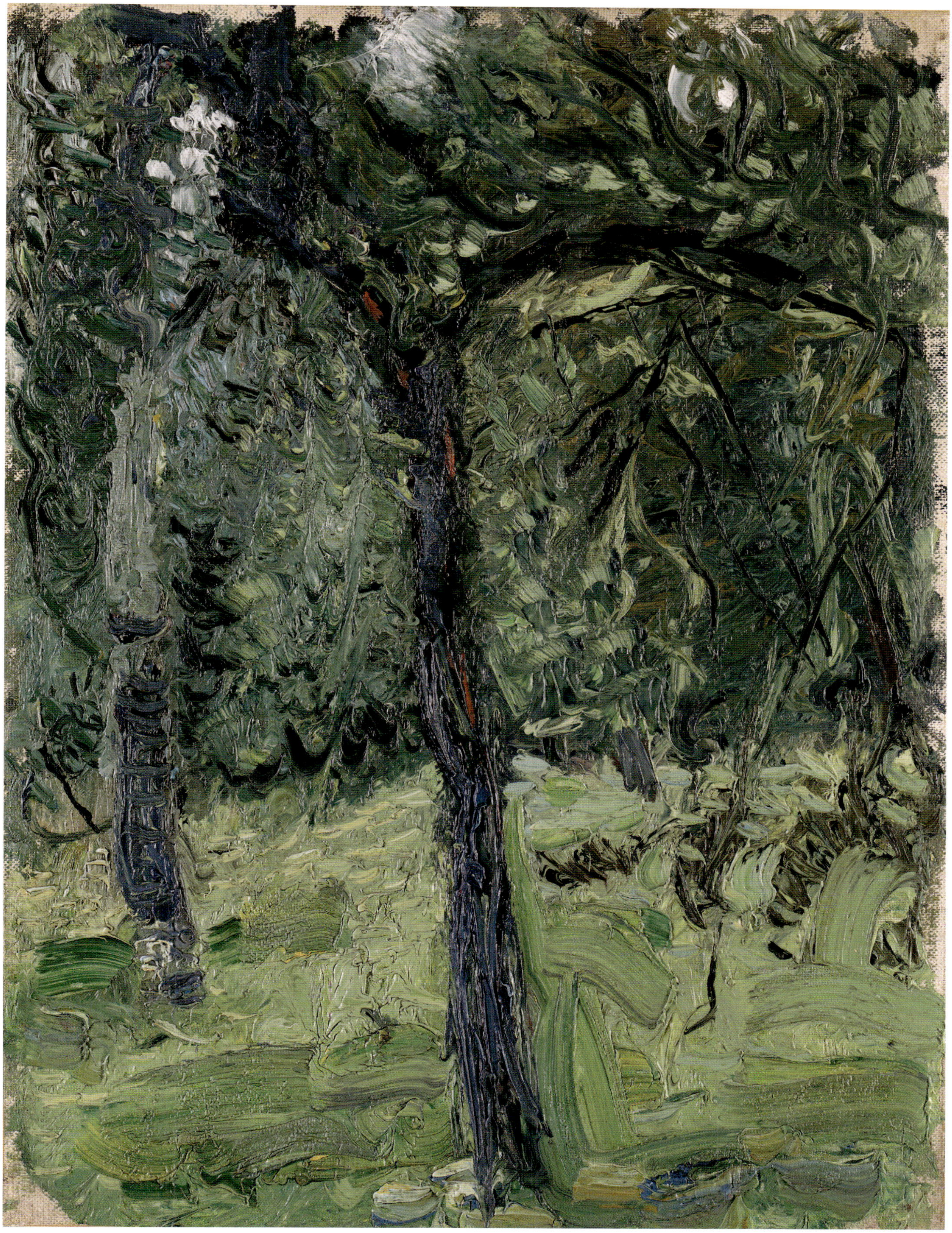

39

40

LAKESIDE ROAD NEAR GMUNDEN/UFERSTRASSE BEI GMUNDEN, summer 1907
Oil on canvas
32.3 x 33.2 cm (12 ¾ x 13 ⅛ in.)
Leopold Museum, Vienna**

41

FRUIT TREE/OBSTBAUM, summer 1907
Oil on canvas mounted on board
51.5 x 22.5 cm (20 ¼ x 8 ⅞ in.)
Richard Grubman and Caroline Mortimer

42

COUNTRY GARDEN WITH FENCE/ BAUERNGARTEN MIT ZAUN, summer 1907
Oil on canvas
36.7 x 51.2 cm (14 ½ x 20 ⅛ in.)
Leopold Museum, Vienna**

43

TREE WITH HOUSES IN THE BACKGROUND/BAUM MIT HÄUSERN IM HINTERGRUND, summer 1907
Oil on canvas
35 x 19.4 cm (13 ¾ x 7 ⅝ in.)
Leopold Museum, Vienna**

The square-format *Lakeside Road near Gmunden* depicts the embankment below Feramühle, looking east across the Traunsee to the Erlakogel peak. Stylistically it is the first of a series of lake views [see Cat. nos. 41–44] that demonstrate an extraordinary and accelerated evolution in Gerstl's technique. Here, however, in contrast to the comparative serenity of his slightly earlier meadow landscapes, Gerstl employed flecks and swoops to impart the essence of a windy day into the profuse branches of the bankside trees as they bend towards the unusually agitated waters of the lake. However, together with Gerstl's "spinach" pictures, *Lakeside Road near Gmunden* shows an absence of the bright primary colors that might be expected to distinguish Traunsee mid-summer, although Gerstl soon remedied this in three works that portray the hillside orchards and gardens in full bloom. Indeed, the weather was far sunnier and more amenable from the beginning of August 1907, so there is compelling reason to believe that most of Gerstl's landscapes from Gmunden in 1907 emerged in August and early September, and therefore after the inclement early weeks of his vacation and his letter to his parents of July 26. *Fruit Tree,* for example, one of three works portraying the hillside orchards and gardens in bloom around Feramühle, is almost certainly a pear tree planted on the meadows by the banks of the Traunsee. With the Traunstein lying to the east behind it, it would have borne fruit in August and, since it faces west towards the sun, its fruit often ripened red. This allowed Gerstl to apply dabs and flecks of paint generously to the foliage and fruits of the tree, which is supported by a strut. But he combined this with broad continuous brushstrokes that became a feature of the Expressionist works he produced during his second Gmunden holiday with the Schönbergs the following year.

Tree with Houses in the Background shares the same narrow format of *Fruit Tree*, so it was probably painted around the same time, although here Gerstl's jagged flecks are more evident in the green sunlit meadow and the smattering of pink blossoms that bedecks the branches. Gerstl's experimentation also extended to varying formats in his late summer-autumn canvases, which include the wider *Country Garden with Fence,* a work looking east, probably painted from the bank below Feramühle. Here, with the Traunstein in the background, the orchard verdant with foliage, and the garden in full bloom, Gerstl employs his quick hand and subjective eye to lace overlays of variegated greens with sharp yellows and intense reds. Such an array of bright, blooming colors contrasts starkly with the subtle hues of Gerstl's "spinach" landscapes, and suggests that this work, together with *Lakeside Road near Gmunden,* acts as something of a bridge to the later works [Cat. nos. 41–44] that can all be attributed to Gmunden in either late or, as is more likely in view of their distinctly autumnal feel, early September 1907.

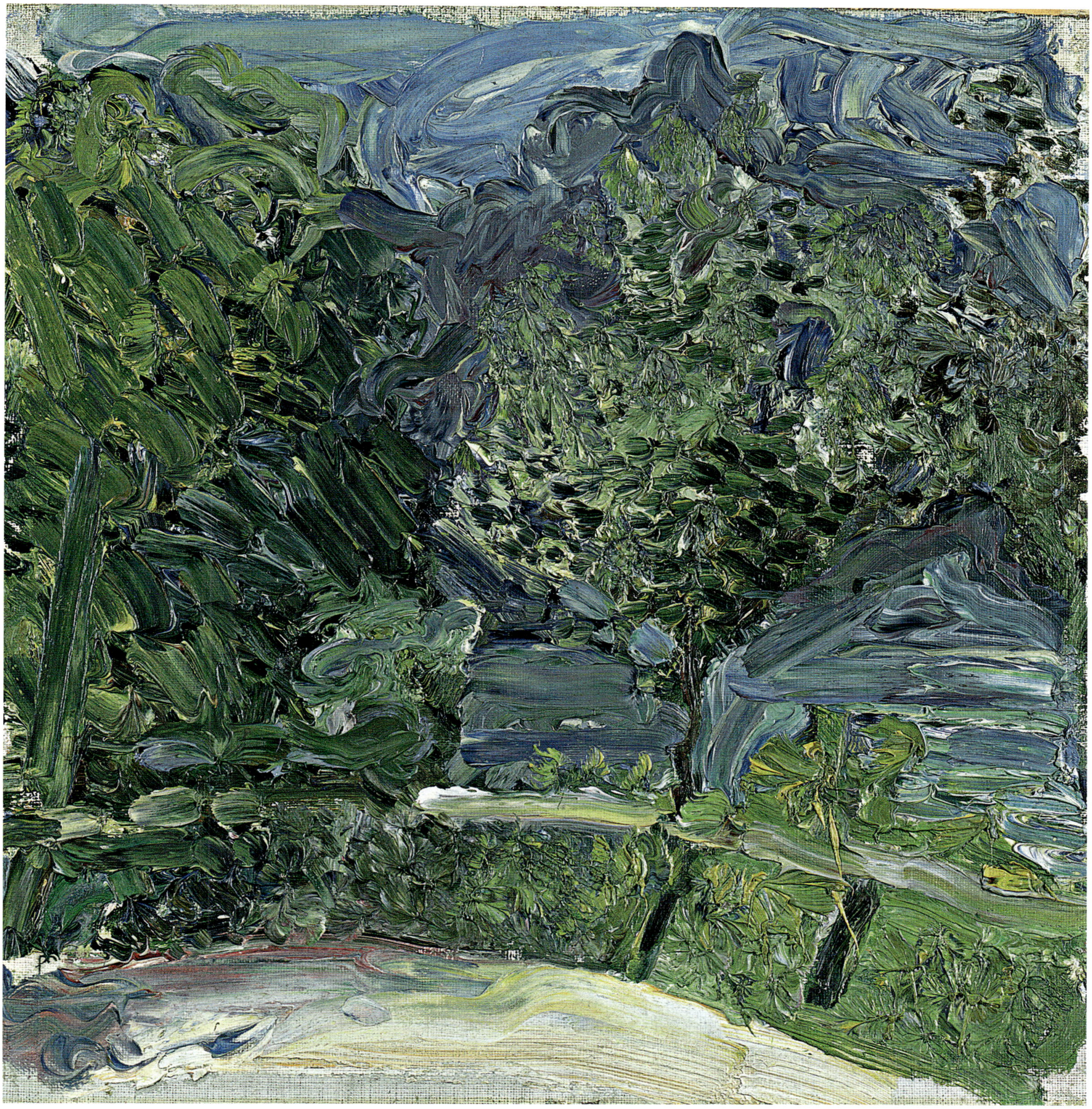

40

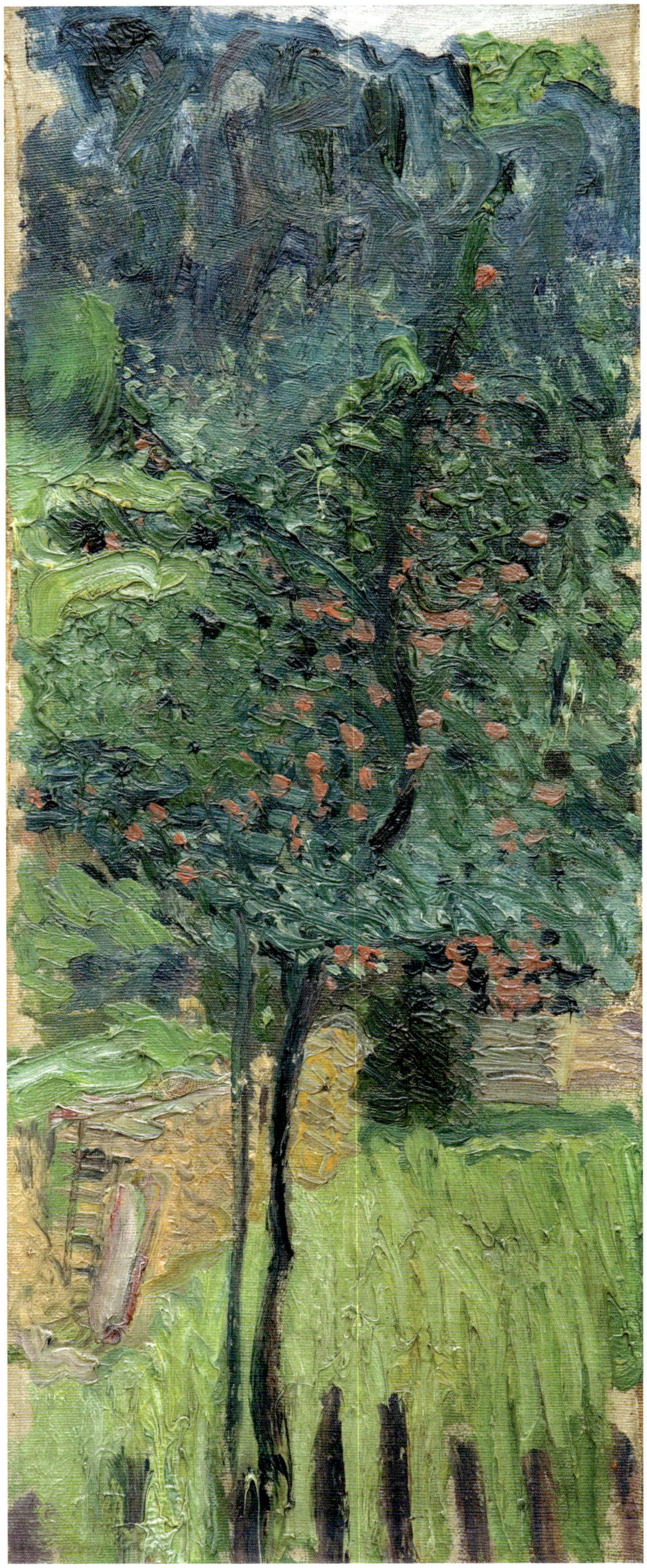

41

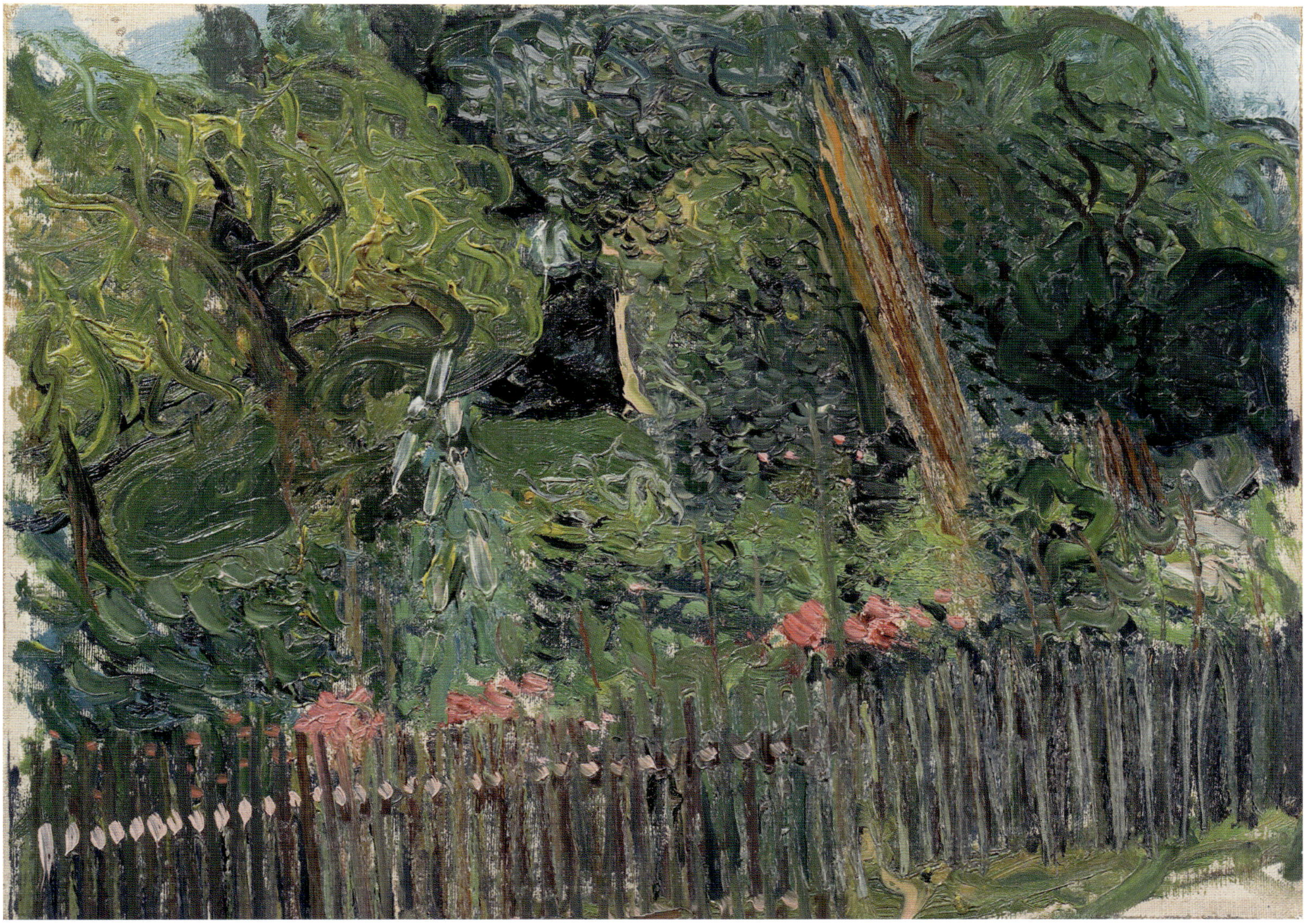

42

44

GARDEN/GARTEN, summer 1907

Oil on board

33.9 x 35 cm (13 3/8 x 13 3/4 in.)

Whereabouts unknown**

45

VIEW OF THE LAKE WITH THE TRAUNSTEIN/ SEEPARTIE MIT TRAUNSTEIN, summer 1907

Oil on board

36 x 50 cm (14 1/8 x 19 5/8 in.)

Whereabouts unknown**

46

STUDY OF THE VIENNA WOODS/ WIENERWALDSTUDIE, summer 1907

Oil on board

35 x 49 cm (13 3/4 x 19 1/4 in.)

Whereabouts unknown*

47

MEADOW WITH FRUIT TREES/WIESE MIT OBSTBÄUMEN, summer 1907

Oil on board

36.4 x 49.7 cm (14 3/8 x 19 5/8 in.)

Whereabouts unknown**

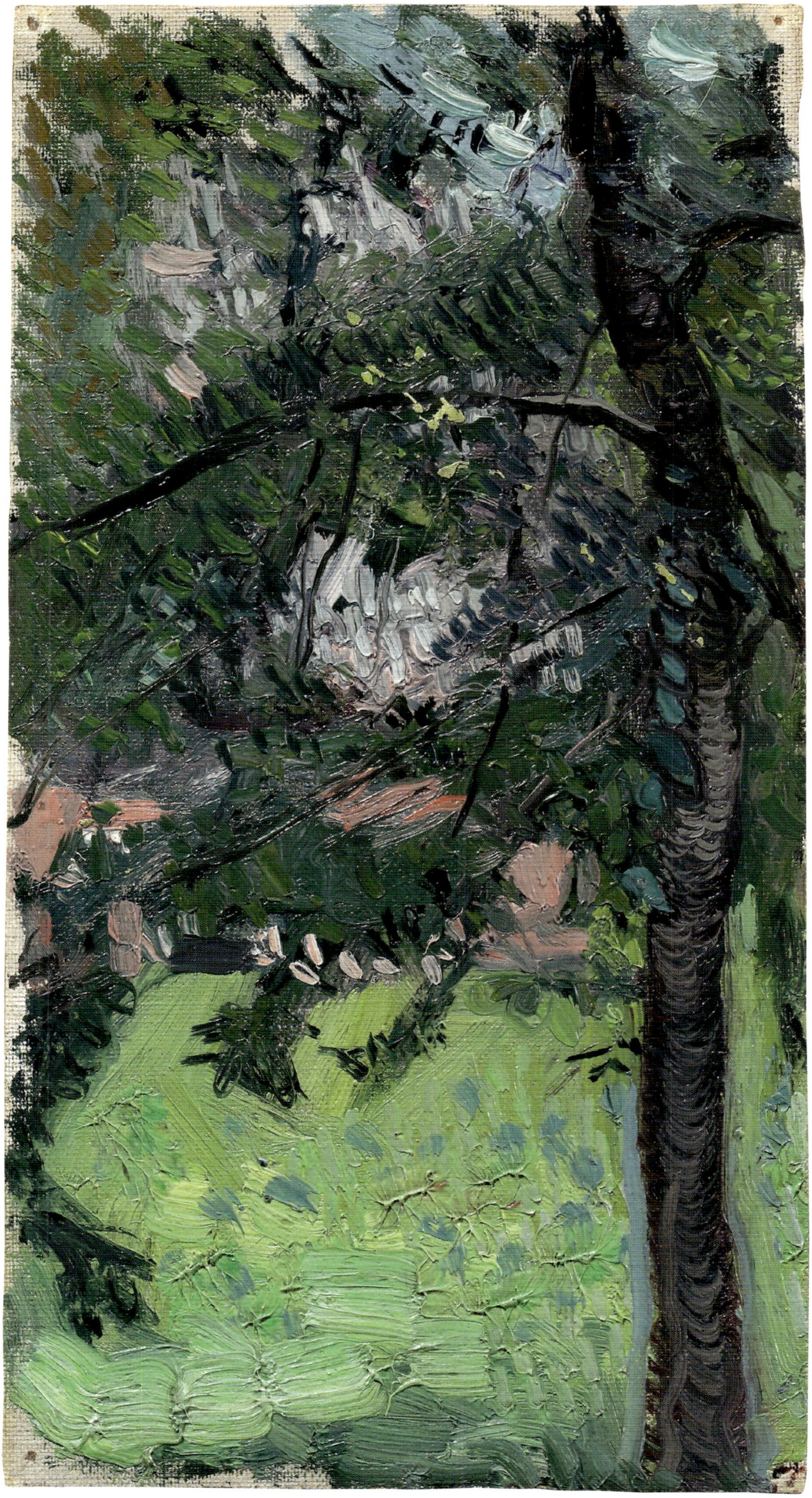

48
SMALL LANDSCAPE AT TRAUNSEE/KLEINE TRAUNSEELANDSCHAFT, August 1907
Oil on canvas
40.3 x 36.1 cm (15 7/8 x 14 1/4 in.)
Richard Grubman and Caroline Mortimer

49
TREE AT TRAUNSEE/BAUM AM TRAUNSEE, September 1907
Oil on canvas on board
38 x 51 cm (15 x 20 1/8 in.)
Kunsthaus Zug, Stiftung Sammlung Kamm**

50
TRAUNSEE WITH "SLEEPING GREEK WOMAN"/ TRAUNSEE MIT "SCHLAFENDER GRIECHIN," September 1907
Oil on canvas
37.7 x 39.3 cm (14 7/8 x 15 1/2 in.)
Leopold Museum, Vienna****

51
LANDSCAPE STUDY/LANDSCHAFTSSTUDIE, September 1907
Oil on canvas
37 x 51 cm (14 5/8 x 20 1/8 in.)
Private Collection**

While all of Gerstl's landscapes from Gmunden in 1907 display elements of his pluralistic approach of loops, long and short strokes, dabs, spirals and curls, it is only in those that came later in his vacation with the Schönbergs that he gradually dispensed with the pointilism that had vividly characterized his technique over the previous year or so. We sense from these later works that, as Schönberg's circle dispersed in late summer, Gerstl found time to take in a broader vista of the lake and his surroundings, beginning perhaps with *Small Landscape at Traunsee.* Here, against the background of the Traunsee and, on its western bank, the Sonnstein, a mountain through which runs a rail tunnel connecting the rest of the Salzkammergut, Gerstl utilizes swirls and flecks and random dabs and streaks to depict the rush of lakeside vegetation that greeted his view from Feramühle.

Then, in *Tree at Traunsee*, Gerstl's view moves across the lake to the hills a few degrees to the north. It is dominated, however, by the interwoven branches of darkening foliage whose yellow streaks, also seen in *Small Landscape at Traunsee,* recall the fading vestiges of summer, while the deep blue of the tree bark in both of these pictures echoes the trunks that frame Gerstl's "spinach" paintings of the meadow path. The third picture, *Traunsee with "Sleeping Greek Woman,"* refers to the Erlakogel, a peak that sits further to the south of the lake. Here Gerstl depicts the long-established lime works that operated at the base of the mountain at that time and whose sailing ships, seen in the center of the lake, transported the output across the Traunsee to the ports on its western banks and the single-track railway that ran across the Salzkammergut. Interestingly, this particular outlook is not easily reached from Gerstl's farmhouse on the eastern shore, so it is likely that Gerstl either sketched or painted it from a boat or steamship while on the lake itself. It should be noted that this is the only Gmunden landscape that was not later adhered to board by Otto Nirenstein and was only first exhibited in 1966. Finally, perhaps the last and most evocative of Gerstl's autumnal works, *Landscape Study*, merges the colors of the seasonal change in the meadows above the Traunsee as they climb towards the Traunstein and its glowering skies in the background. It was in this and, to a lesser extent, in *Traunsee with "Sleeping Greek Woman,"* that Gerstl's flecks and daubs were replaced by the broad, almost abstract brushstrokes that evolved into the fierce techniques characteristic of the resolutely Expressionist and unapologetically challenging portraits of his second joint holiday in Gmunden with the Schönbergs one year hence. Thus it is here, in these late landscapes from Gmunden in 1907, that the extraordinary swift transition that had occurred in Gerstl's technique during that summer became complete.

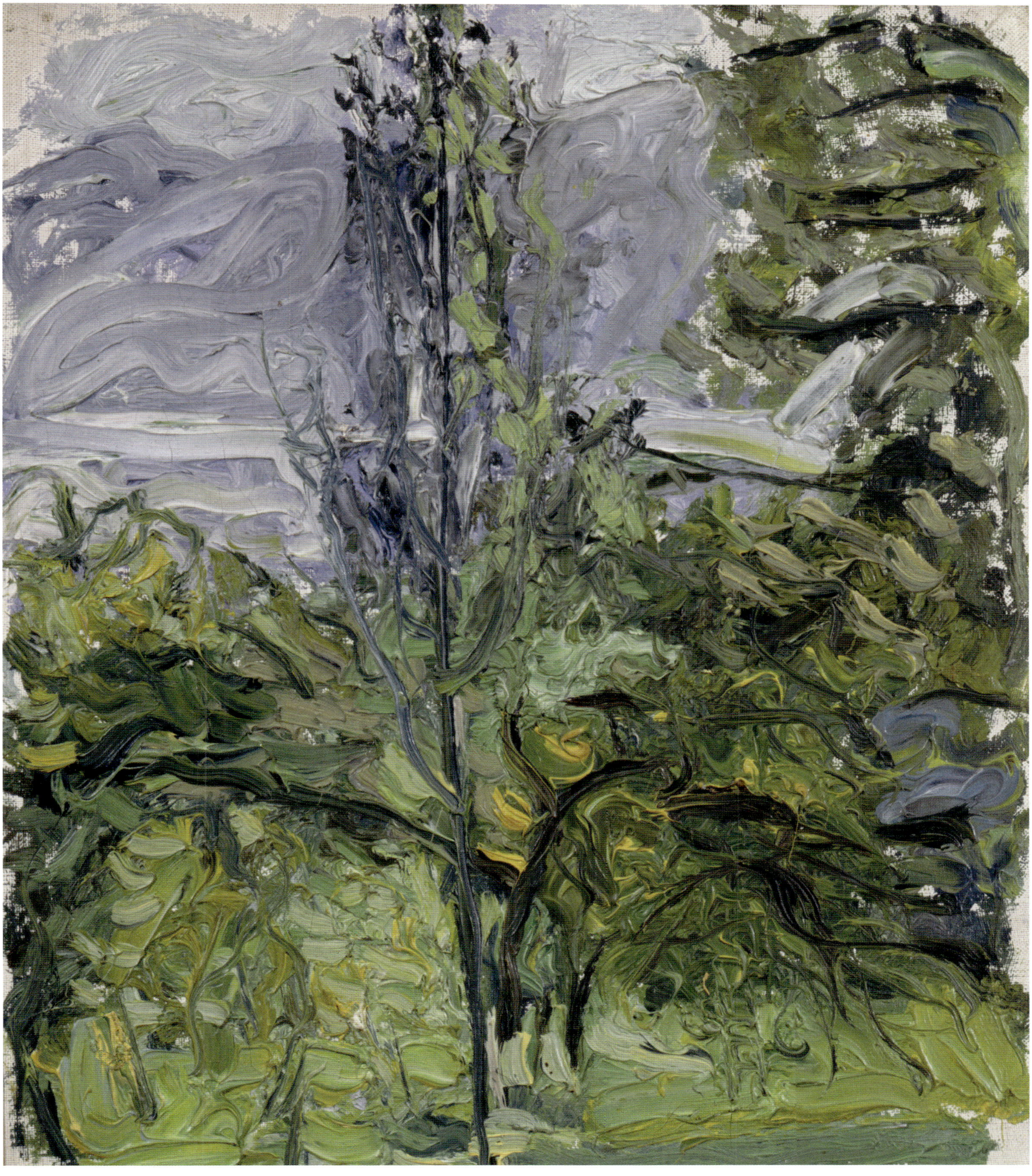

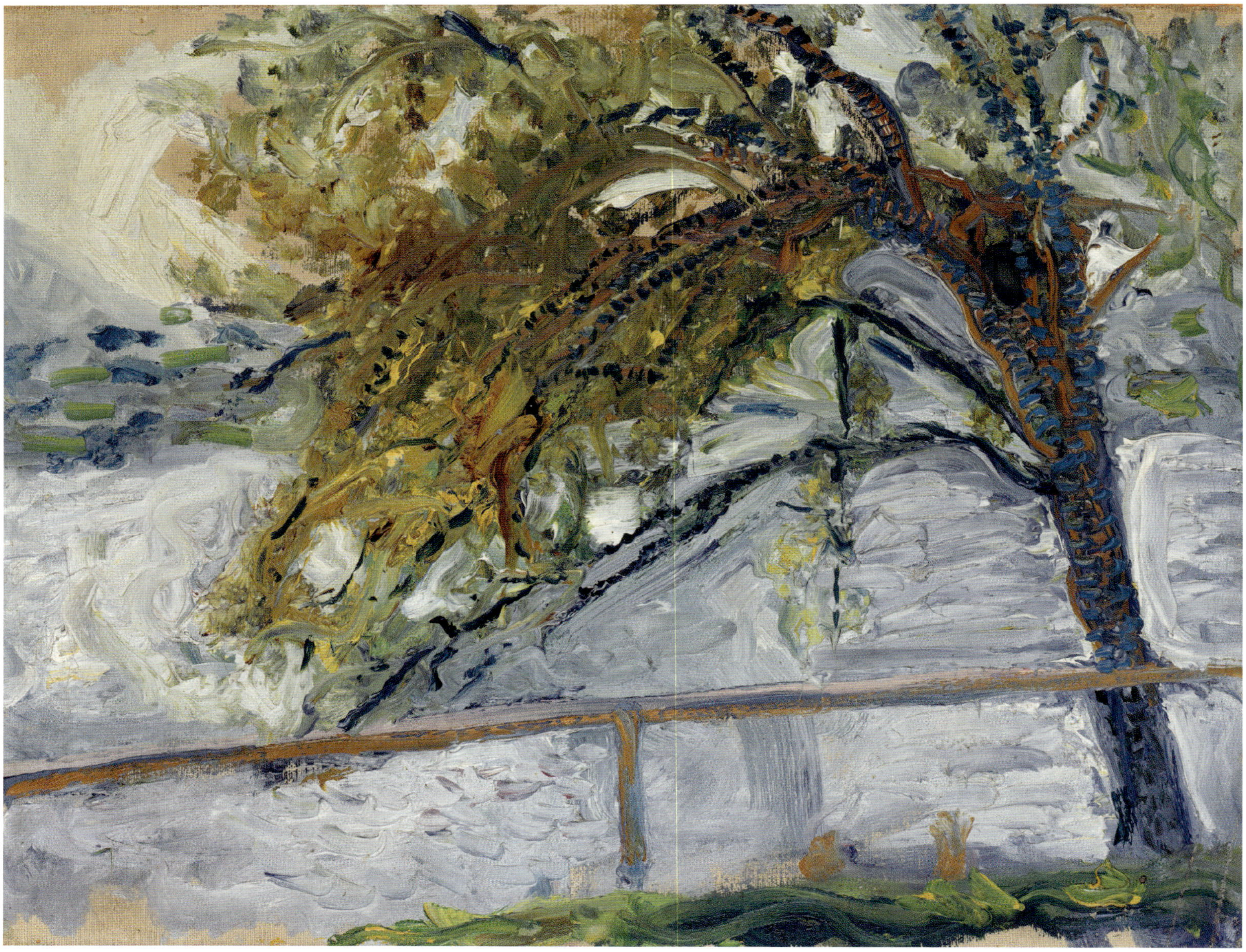

49

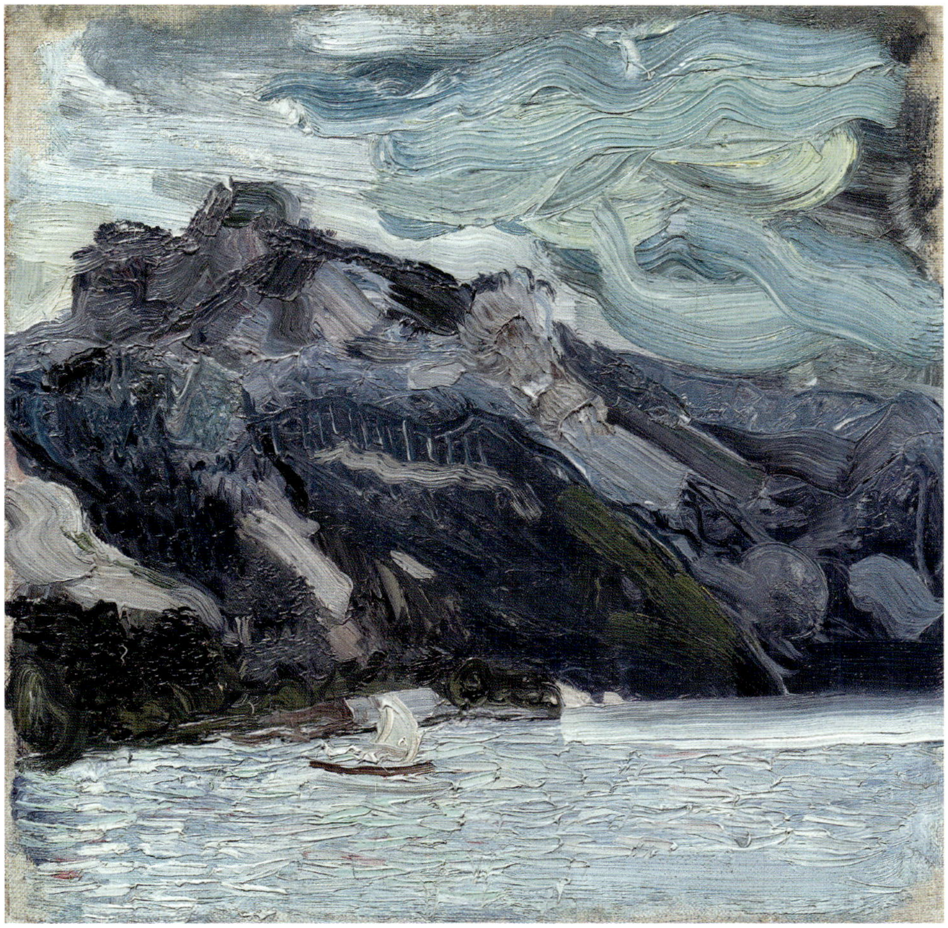
50

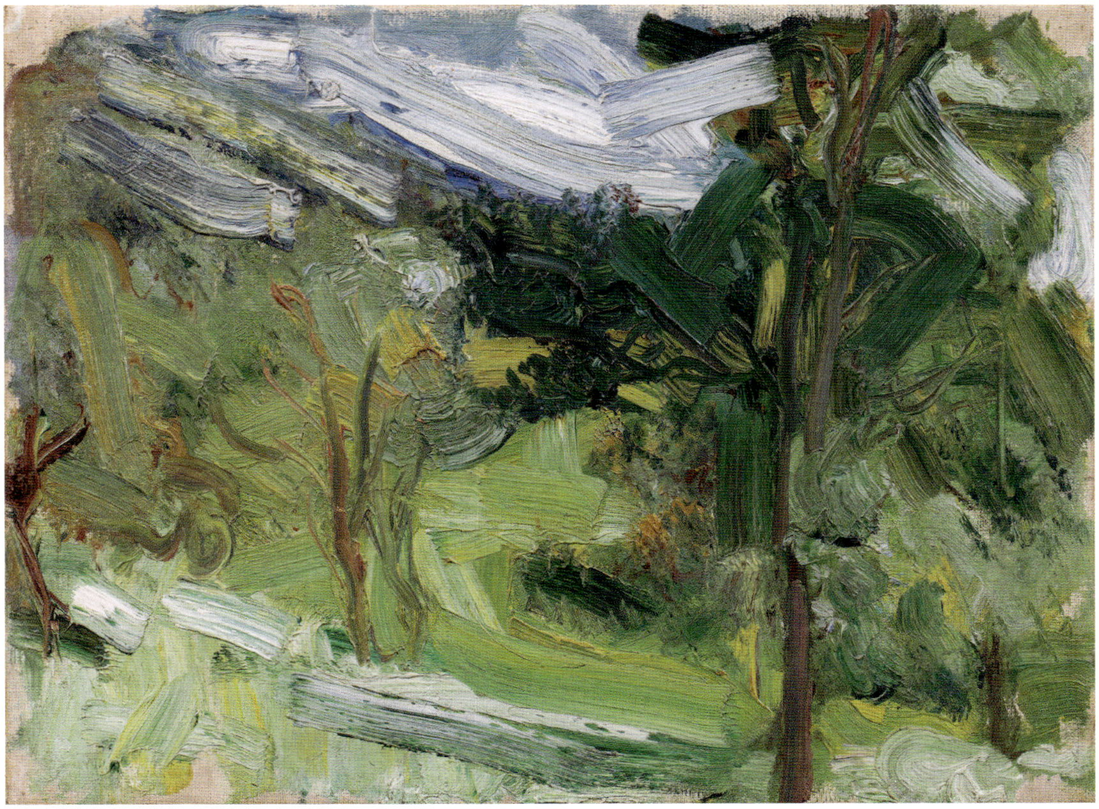
51

52

PORTRAIT OF JOHANN GEORG PRILLINGER/ BILDNIS JOHANN GEORG PRILLINGER,

summer 1907

Oil on board
50 x 36 cm (19 ⅝ x 14 ⅛ in.)
Private Collection****

Whether Gerstl's multiple landscapes from Gmunden in 1907 were in part an academic exercise set by his teacher, Heinrich Lefler, or simply a personal pursuit to depict, à la Van Gogh, the nature that he found around him, he did not desert portraiture entirely. Indeed, as with the *Portrait of Carl Zentzytzki* of five years earlier, he painted the landlord of his summer farmhouse and owner of Feramühle, Johann Georg Prillinger. The work, inscribed by the artist, "Richard Gerstl Traunstein 1907" on the reverse, was likely a gift of appreciation to his hosts, although probably not painted until Gerstl had been in residence for a few weeks and had become more familiar with the family, who were apparently pleased enough to retain it thereafter. Using a flecking technique that has stylistic affinities to other works painted around the same time, including *Self-Portrait in front of a Blue-Green Background,* Gerstl nonetheless portrays Prillinger in a surprisingly realistic style, perhaps in deference to his 48-year-old landlord's wishes. The work's dimensions at 19 ⅝ x 14 ⅛ inches represent a quarter of a standard 39 ⅜ x 28 ⅜ inches sheet of artboard [see Cat. no. 32], which suggests that Gerstl may well have brought his supplies with him ready cut from Vienna.

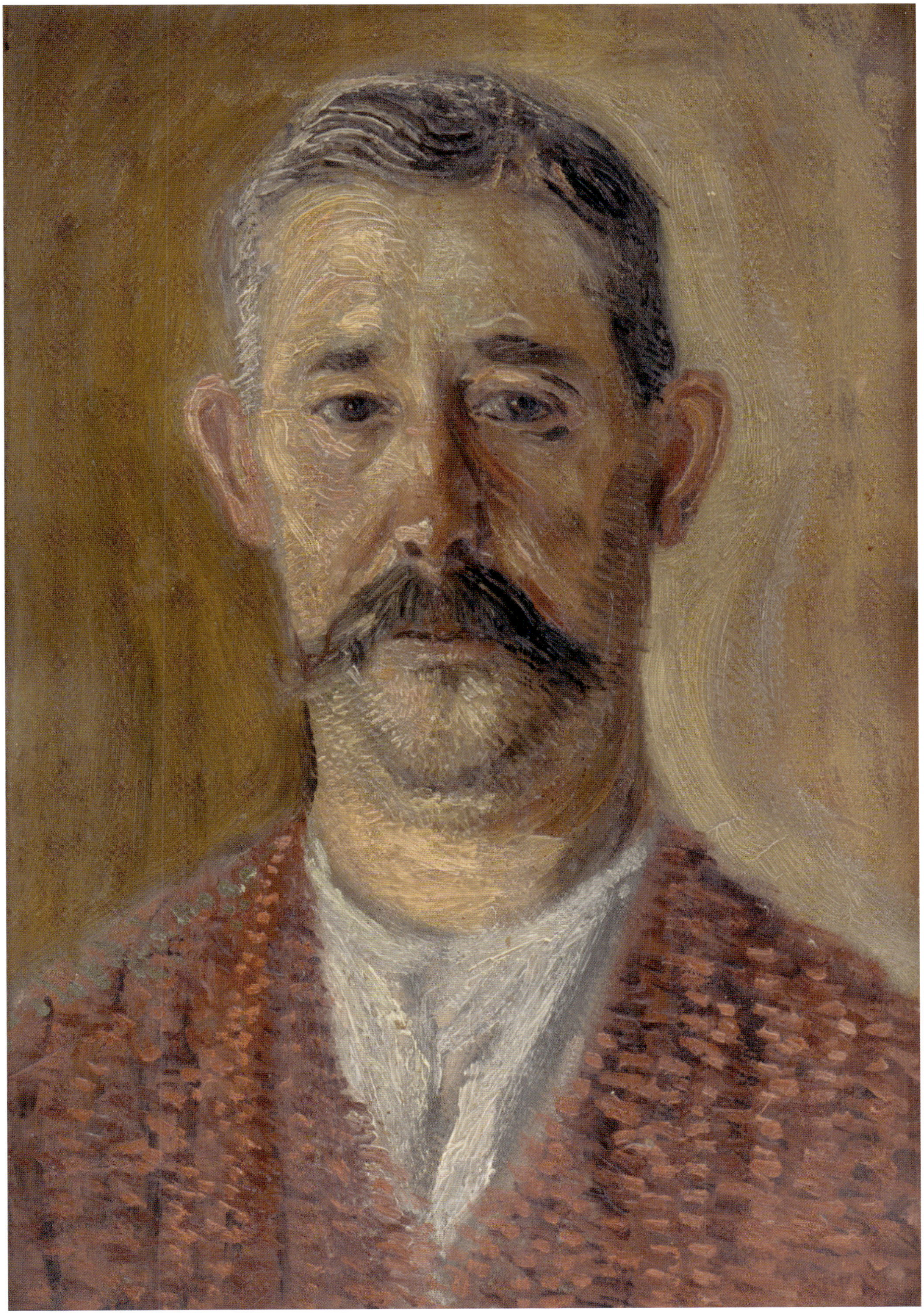

53

MATHILDE SCHÖNBERG, summer 1907

Tempera on canvas
95 x 75 cm (37 3⁄8 x 29 1⁄2 in.)
Belvedere, Vienna***

Mathilde Schönberg was a tiny woman who readily embraced *Reformkleidung,* a modern, emancipatory concept of woman's attire. This is how Gerstl portrayed her both here and later in *Portrait of Mathilde Schönberg in the Studio* [Cat. no. 67]. The present picture, however, is a summer painting, set against background colors typical of those found on the roughly plastered walls of Salzkammergut farmhouses at the time and which provide a vivid setting for Gerstl's almost sketch-like representation of his subject. As elsewhere, perhaps knowing that it would come under Schönberg's scrutiny, Gerstl portrays the demurely seated Mathilde respectfully. Moreover, in using tempera and rough, effective brushwork, he would presumably have executed the portrait quickly, possibly to avoid intrusions, or simply to seize the pose, which, with her deliberately sparse features, catches something of the "mousy and withdrawn" impression she apparently made. The room detail bears little relation to the floor plans of Preslgütl, the Schönbergs' 1908 accommodation, so, while it obviously cannot be excluded that Gerstl could have painted the portrait in Feramühle, it is more likely to have been executed in the Schönbergs' 1907 farmhouse, Engelgut, the previous summer.

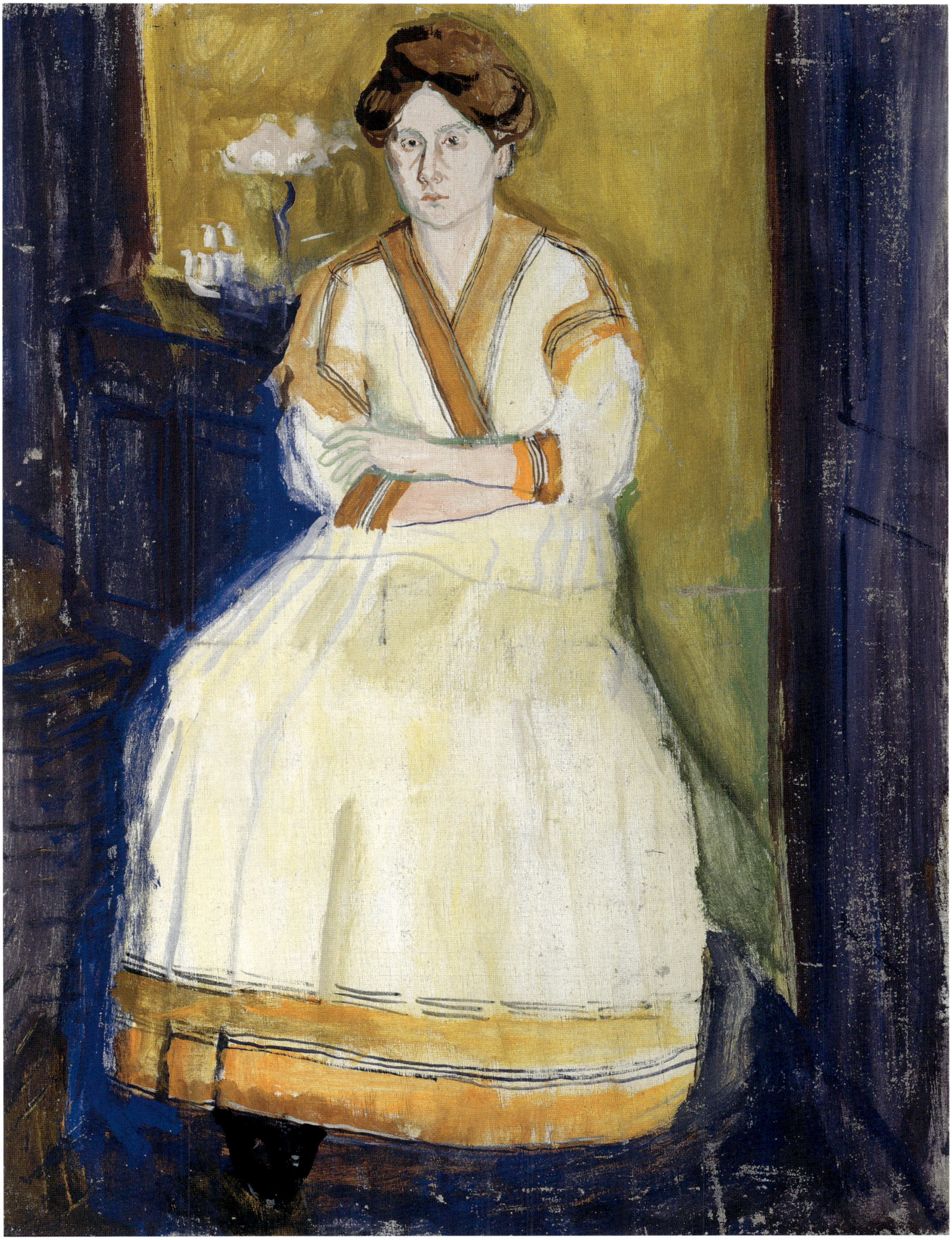

54

SELF-PORTRAIT, LAUGHING/SELBSTBILDNIS, LACHEND, summer-autumn 1907

Oil on canvas

40 x 30.5 cm (15 ¾ x 12 in.)

Belvedere, Vienna**

Self-Portrait, Laughing shows Gerstl using his flecking technique to new and dramatic effect, creating a fluid, agitated background that somehow amplifies the artist's nightmarish laugh and gawky, dishevelled look. It resonates with similar works throughout the ages, notably by Rembrandt, Hals, Corinth and others. Here, however, Gerstl deserts his typical piercing and disconcerting glare, leaving his eyes animated and uneven in a vulnerable, almost pleading gaze. In doing so, Gerstl portrays himself in direct contrast to the taciturn, tight-lipped image conveyed by many of his previous self-representations. Indeed, here, this is replaced by a manic spontaneity that suggests a sense of bipolarity and confirms Hammer's recollection that Gerstl's mockery of his own appearance was "the laughter of despair." This work can be stylistically attributed to the late summer or autumn of 1907 and was probably done in Gmunden. Gerstl's appearance and degree of hirsuteness correspond to a portrait of him painted by William Clarke Rice, who was visiting his brother-in-law, Alexander Zemlinsky, at the resort that summer. Some scholars have suggested that this was Gerstl's final self-portrait, and thereby indicative of his pre-suicidal frame of mind. Yet Alois clearly stated that *Nude Self-Portrait* [Cat. no. 86] was his brother's last self-portrait, so such conclusions can only be considered as speculation at best.

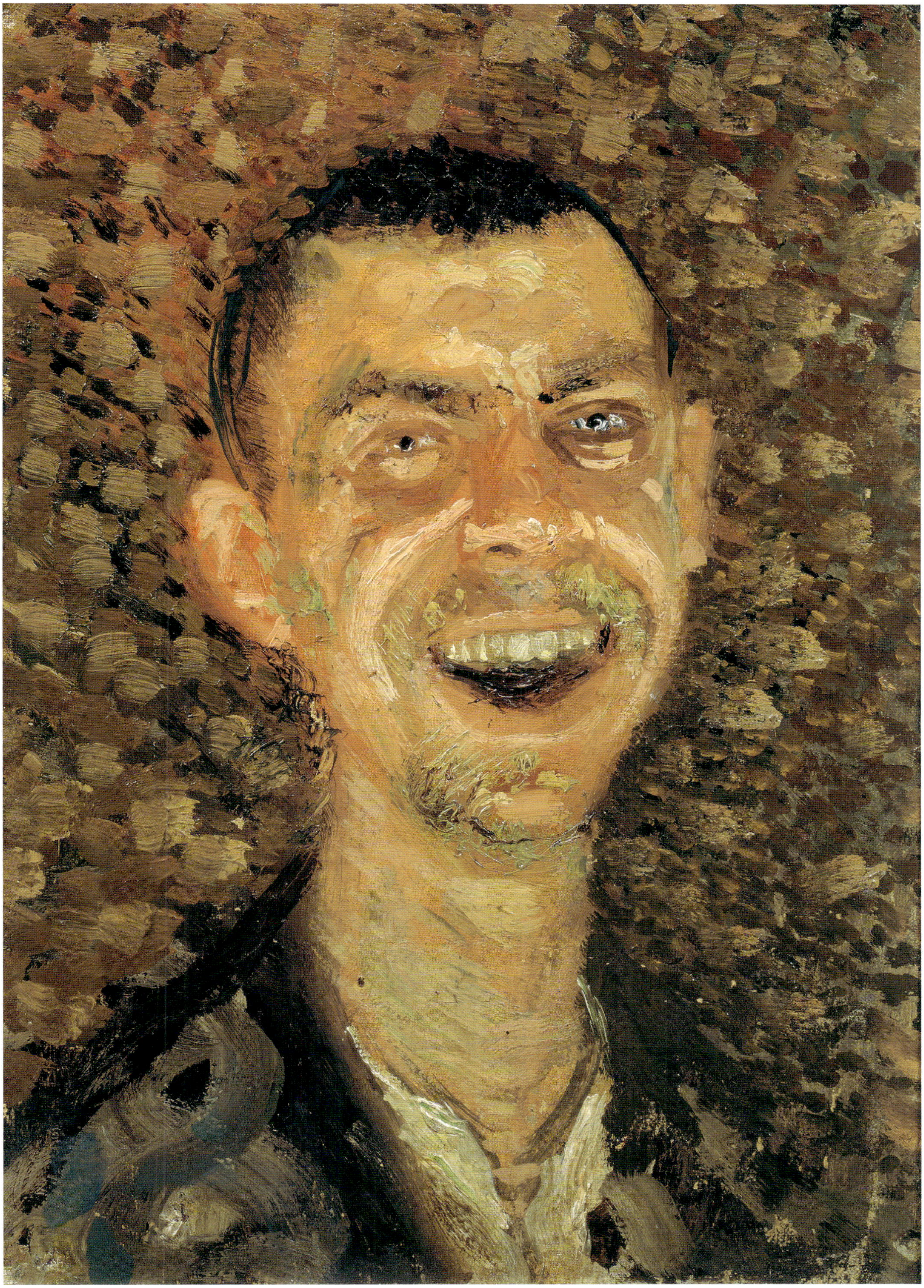

55

VILLAGE CHURCH/DORFKIRCHE, autumn 1907

Oil on canvas

42.2 x 53 cm (16 ⅝ x 20 ⅞ in.)

Whereabouts unknown

56

BEND IN THE STREET (MOTIVE FROM NUSSDORF WITH A VIEW TOWARD THE KAHLENBERG)/ STRASSENBIEGUNG (MOTIV AUS NUSSDORF MIT DEM BLICK ZUM KAHLENBERG), autumn 1907

Oil on canvas

50.5 x 63 cm (19 ⅞ x 24 ¾ in.)

Museum der Moderne Salzburg

57

ATRIUM OF PALAIS LIECHTENSTEIN IN VIENNA/ VORHOF DES PALAIS LIECHTENSTEIN IN WIEN, autumn 1907

Oil on canvas

55.5 x 68.8 cm (21 ⅞ x 27 ⅛ in.)

Wien Museum, Vienna**

58

ON THE DANUBE CANAL/AM DONAUKANAL, autumn 1907

Oil on canvas

63.5 x 47.5 cm (25 x 18 ¾ in.)

Leopold Museum, Vienna**

Having returned to Vienna from his first summer in Gmunden with Schönberg, Gerstl's winter term at the Academy was marred by the loss of his studio following a damaging disagreement with Lefler concerning Emperor Franz Josef's Diamond Jubilee parade, to which Gerstl had refused to contribute the previous term. Gerstl, however, continuing his penchant for *plein air* painting, transferred many of the techniques from his Gmunden countryscapes to producing autumnal images of the city and its environs, of which three have survived and one, *Village Church*, painted in oil on canvas and measuring 16 ⅝ x 20 ⅞ inches, is lost. These constitute Gerstl's largest landscapes, being somewhat bigger than those from Gmunden in 1907, to which they display a direct relationship, although, even here, there is a sense of development in Gerstl's style, as though the artist was in a transient state of flux as to how to move forward with his individualistic brushwork techniques.

The first of the series may well have been *Bend in the Street,* an area that Gerstl knew well and to where he eloped with Mathilde Schönberg in late August 1908. It is evident that Gerstl did not abandon his pointilistic tendencies so soon after his Gmunden sojourn, with the result that he superimposed his favored dabs and spots enthusiastically, albeit purposefully, over the more freely painted, broader brushwork of the background

The largest of the series is *Atrium of Palais Liechtenstein in Vienna*, a landmark that was situated in the Alsergrund area of Vienna's ninth district, conveniently close to his home. Here, Gerstl depicts the forecourt and side of the palace, again employing a mixture of styles, but still strongly featuring the flecks and dabs that characterised both *Bend in the Street,* and his works from the previous summer, notably in the late, lingering vegetation.

On the Danube Canal, perhaps the final work of the series, portrays examples of the new blocks of apartments and tenements that burgeoned during the modernization of Vienna at the turn of the twentieth century as its citizens aspired to move into middle-class accommodation and districts, including, incidentally, the ninth district where Schönberg and Gerstl lived. While the leaves and branches of the windswept treetops along the raised bank are executed using a jumpier, flecking technique, Gerstl appears to have moved on, for it is now difficult to detect many remnants of his earlier pointilism in the work. By contrast, in the façades of the buildings, the embankment, and also elsewhere in the picture, Gerstl uses broad, thick, impasto brush strokes, even employing the wooden handle of his paintbrush to create a brooding, animated mood against a gray, thinly painted, autumnal Viennese sky.

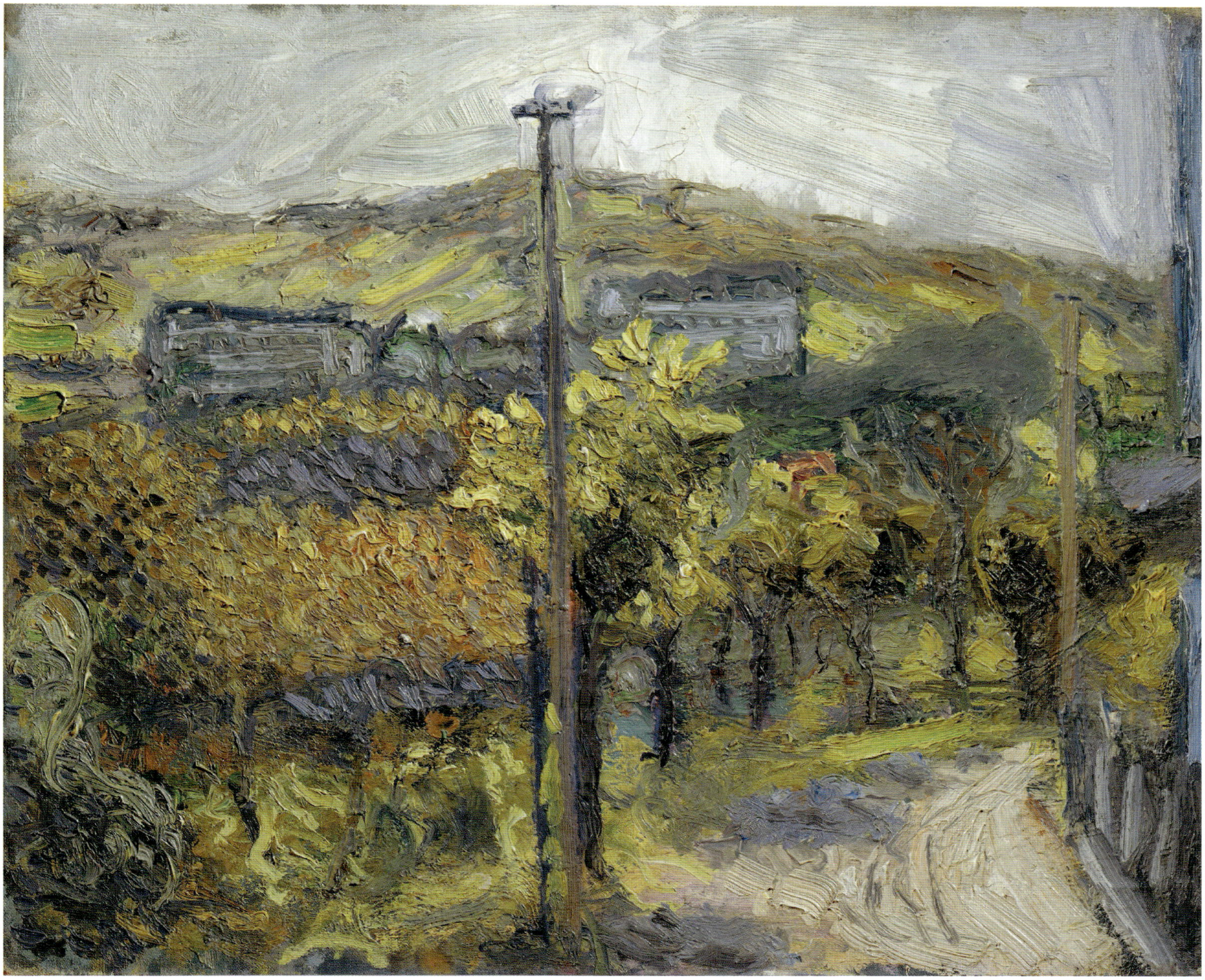

56

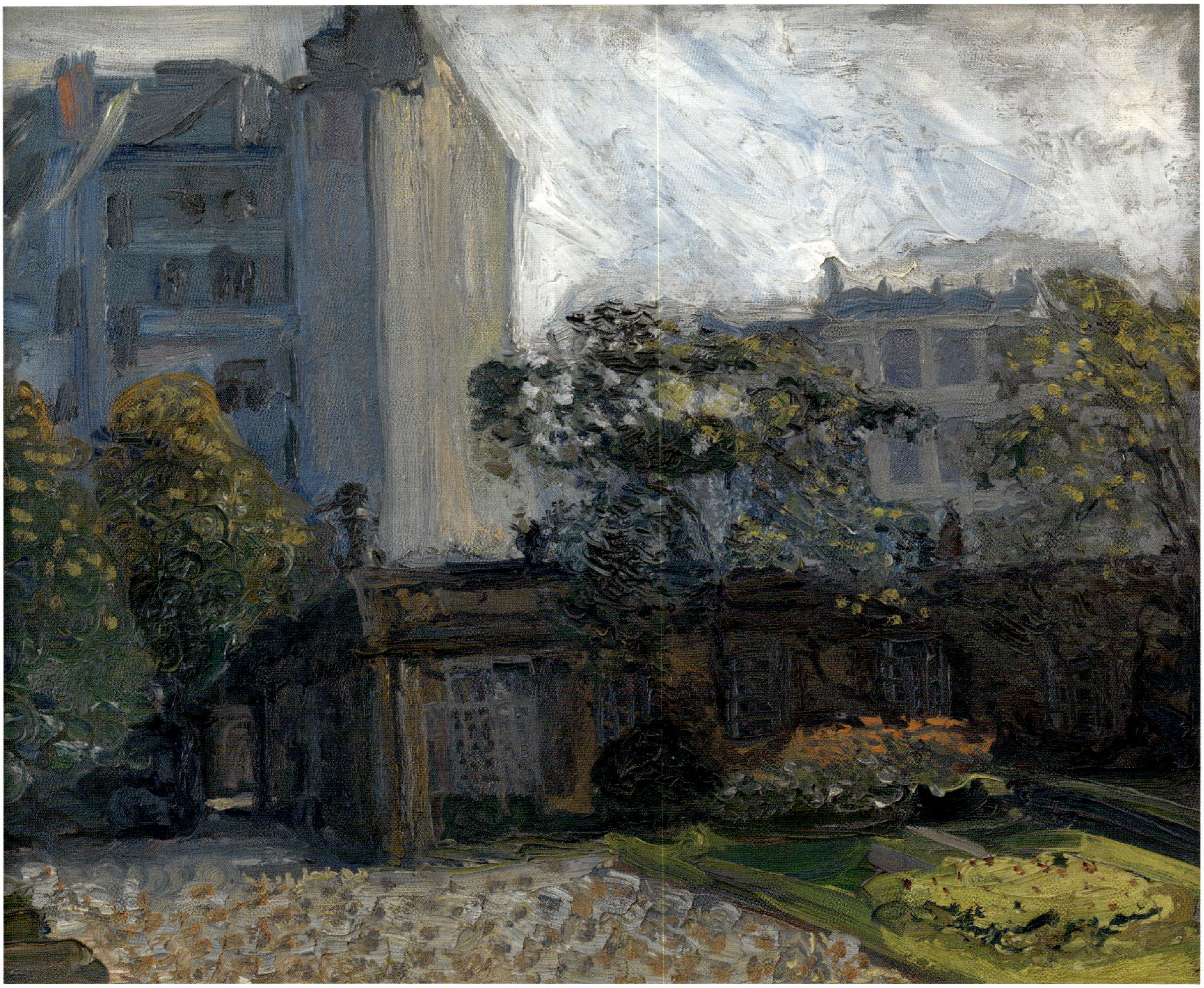

57

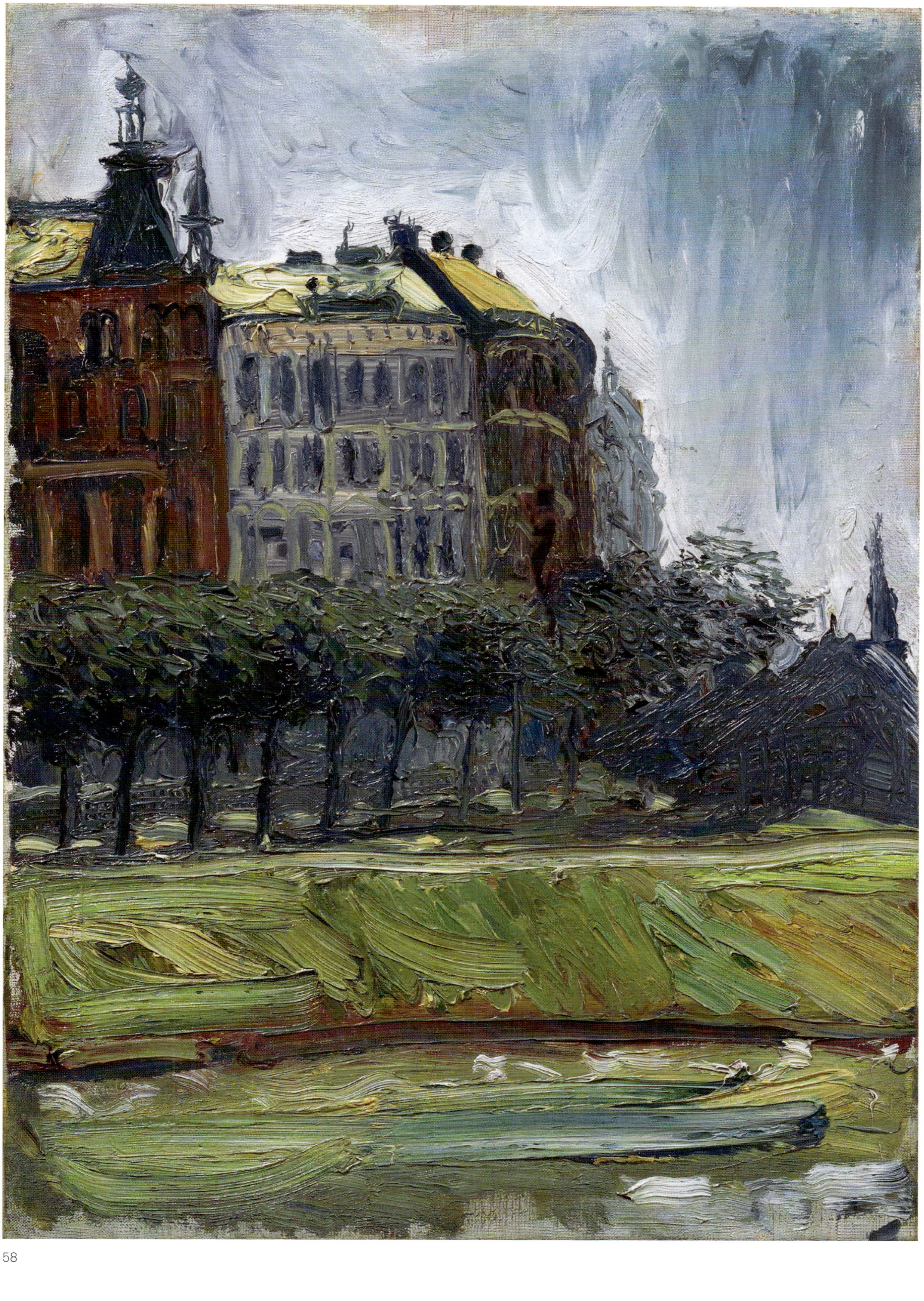

59

SELF-PORTRAIT/SELBSTBILDNIS, summer 1907 (?)

Recto: *Self-Portrait*, September 15, 1907 [Cat. no. 60]
Sepia on paper
40.2 x 30 cm (15 7/8 x 11 3/4 in.)
Wien Museum, Vienna**

60

SELF-PORTRAIT/SELBSTBILDNIS, September 15, 1907

Verso: *Self-Portrait* [Cat. No. 59], summer 1907
Pencil, charcoal, India ink on paper
40.2 x 30 cm (15 7/8 x 11 3/4 in.)
Wien Museum, Vienna**

61

SELF-PORTRAIT/SELBSTBILDNIS, September 29, 1907

India ink and brush on paper
40 x 29.7 cm (15 3/4 x 11 3/4 in.)
The Albertina Museum, Vienna**

62

SELF-PORTRAIT/SELBSTBILDNIS, September 29, 1907

Charcoal and washed ink on paper
40 x 29.5 cm (15 3/4 x 11 5/8 in.)
Private Collection, Courtesy Galerie St. Etienne, New York**

In addition to the four sketches from 1906–07 [see Cat. nos. 26–29], only four other Gerstl drawings are known to exist from what Alois described as his brother's entire graphic output. This was supposedly contained in a box of drawings and watercolors that was destroyed after Gerstl's death, evidently in an act of posthumous vengeance, by his oldest brother, August, whom young Gerstl apparently "hated" and described pointedly as "the monster."

Unusually, three of these four additional drawings are dated: one [Cat. no. 60], as "15 September" and two [Cat. nos. 61, 62], as "29 September." Regrettably, Gerstl failed to add a year, so it becomes tricky to conclude a precise date for them. Some clues are evident, though, and suggest that Gerstl's angst-ridden, sparsely defined drawings came at the time, or just after, his *Self-Portrait, Laughing,* which shows obvious similarities in his dress, shorn hairstyle and bristle. Even though these three are decidedly realistic and devoid of any recent pointilistic references, it nonetheless remains prudent to date all three to September 1907. Moreover, since it was probably at about the same time that Gerstl was ejected from his studio at the Academy perhaps causing him to sketch these in his family apartment, this may well have been reason enough for the reticent, shy artist to represent himself in such an introspective, stark and disturbing manner.

The first of the series [Cat. no. 59], however, may have come earlier, perhaps before Gerstl embarked on his joint vacation on the Traunsee. Indeed, in its shading and intensity, it appears also to have much in common with Gerstl's *Self-Portrait in front of a Blue-Green Background* [Cat. no. 35]. It was probably also painted in Vienna, before he departed for Gmunden, where his appearance changed dramatically. He was portrayed with cropped hair, first by William Clarke Rice in July 1907 (see p. 225) and then by Gerstl himself in *Self-Portrait, Laughing* a few weeks later. Equally, this particular drawing alone has considerable affinities with Gerstl's personal appearance in two nude self-portraits [Cat. nos. 85, 86] from September 1908, so it cannot be entirely excluded that, unlike the three other drawings illustrated here, this one was sketched in autumn 1908.

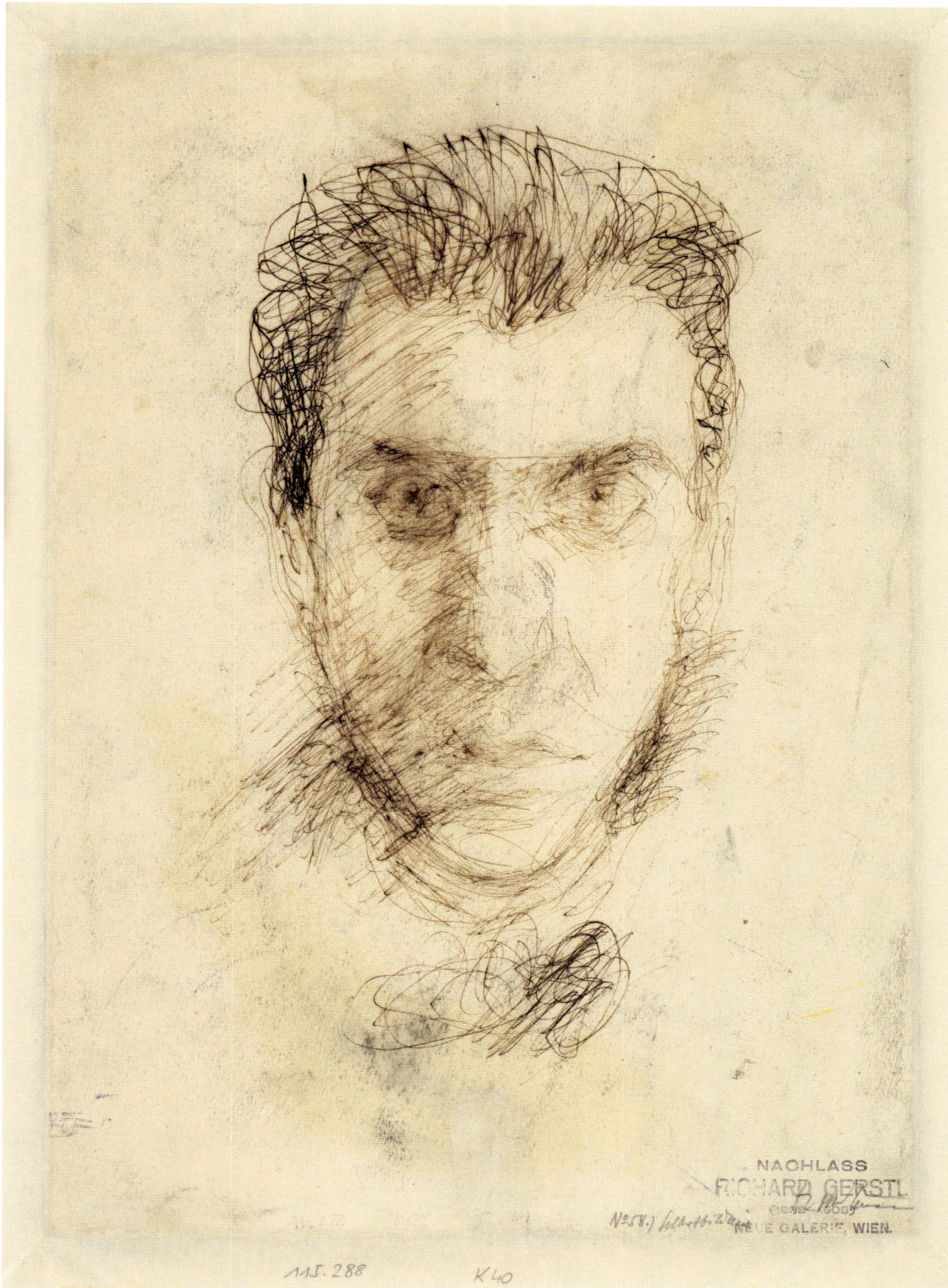

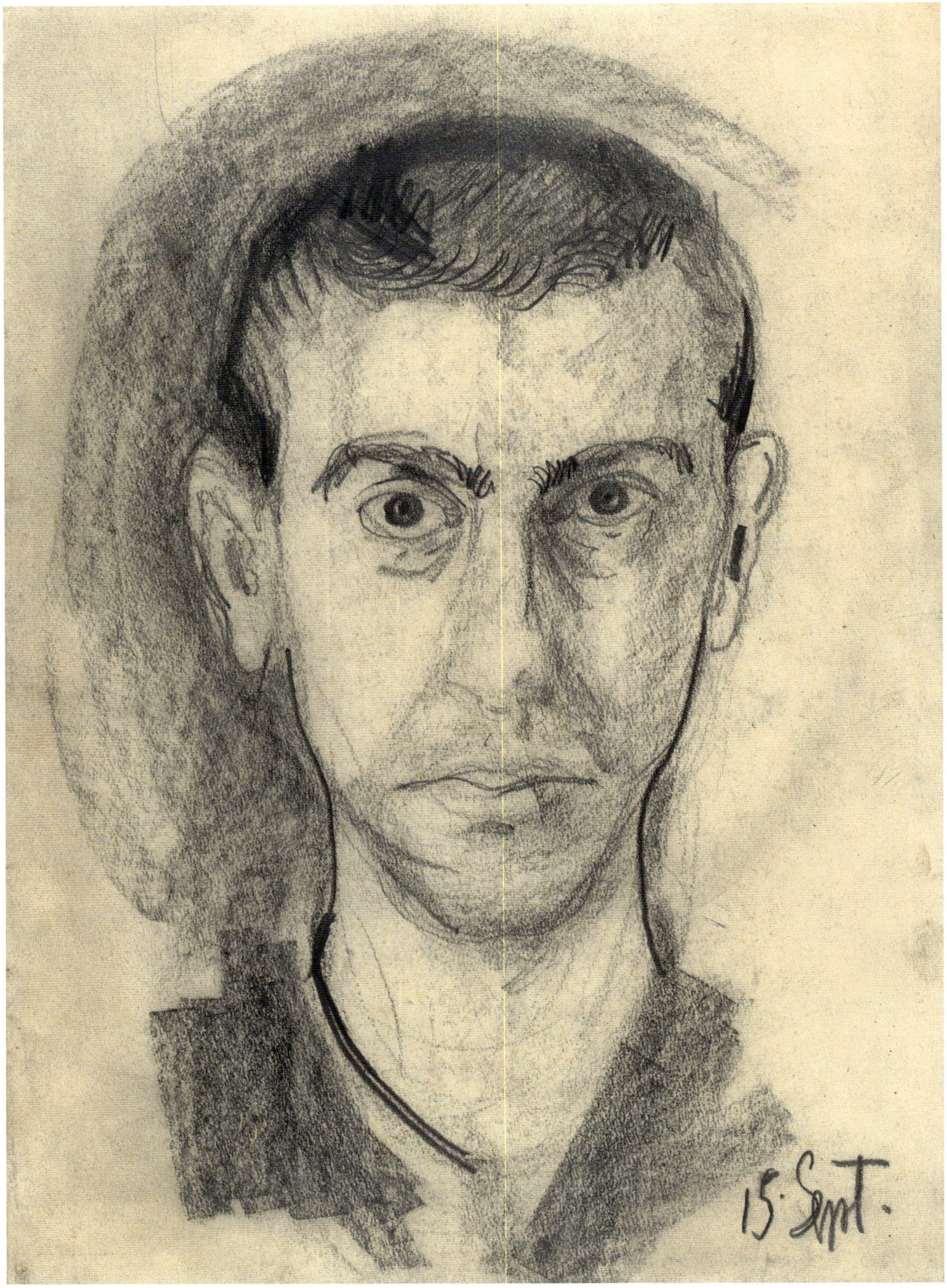

60

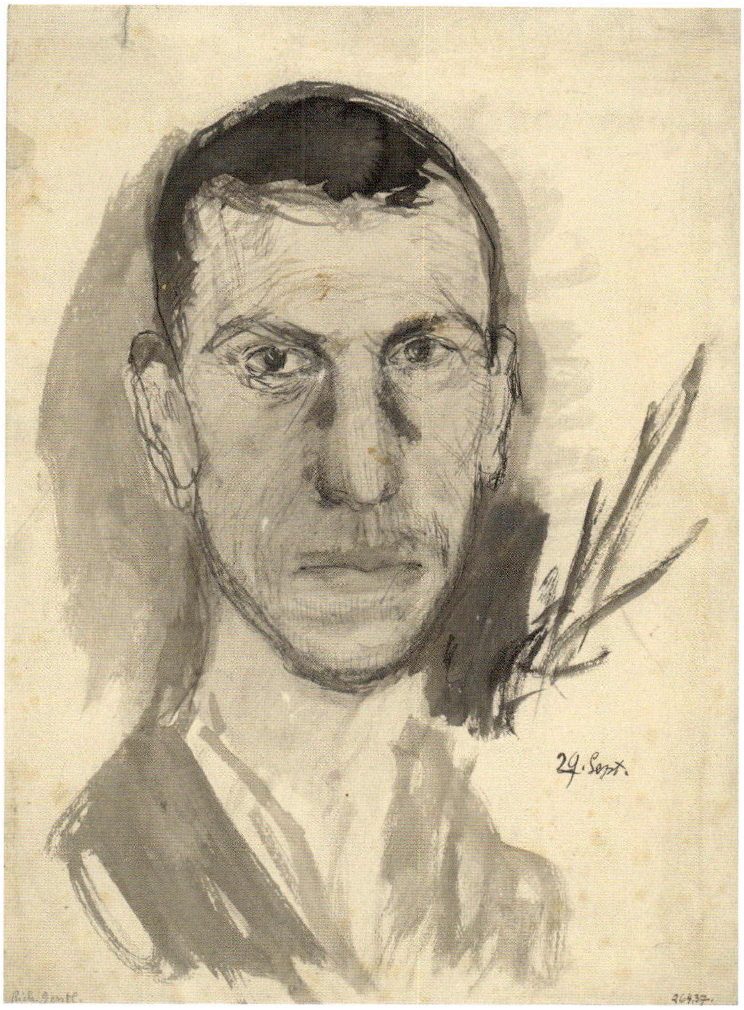

61

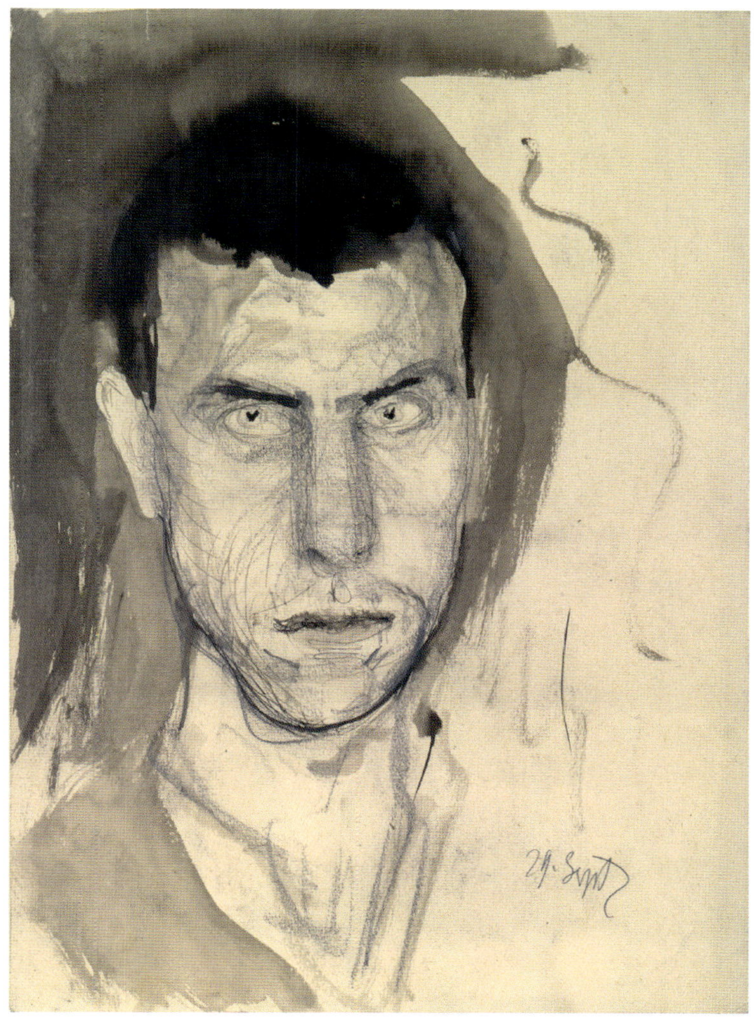

62

63
SELF-PORTRAIT/SELBSTBILDNIS,
winter 1907-spring 1908
Oil on canvas
41.7 x 39.2 cm (16 3/8 x 15 3/8 in.)
Leopold Private Collection, Vienna*

Nirenstein's 1931 description of this self-portrait was: "Kopf, Selbstporträt, Ausschnitt aus einem grossen Bild" (Head, self-portrait, detail of a larger painting). If this had originally been full-length, even life-size, it would explain the somewhat unexpected expanse of background encompassing the artist. Having previously cut other paintings [see Cat. no. 8], Gerstl himself is the most likely candidate to have done so in this instance. Nonetheless, *Self-Portrait* is a maturely painted, brutally honest self-representation, in which Gerstl unflatteringly depicts his high receding brow and weak chin, two features that apparently caused him lifelong disillusionment. Moreover, with its disconcerting, asymmetric glare and deliberate, menacing glint in the right eye, the work, as Lloyd and Winiarczyk perceptively observe, (see pp. 34–36), demonstrates a certain affinity with Van Gogh's psychologically searing self-portraits, several of which were painted from a comparable angle. Gerstl's appearance here, notably his shorter, unkempt hairstyle, is far more in keeping with his post-Gmunden 1907 look than the brushed, wavy style that he maintained for the previous two years. Furthermore, since the green background has much in common with his spring 1908 studio portraits [Cat. nos. 56–58], it is reasonable to attribute this newly found work to winter 1907 or, more likely, early spring 1908.

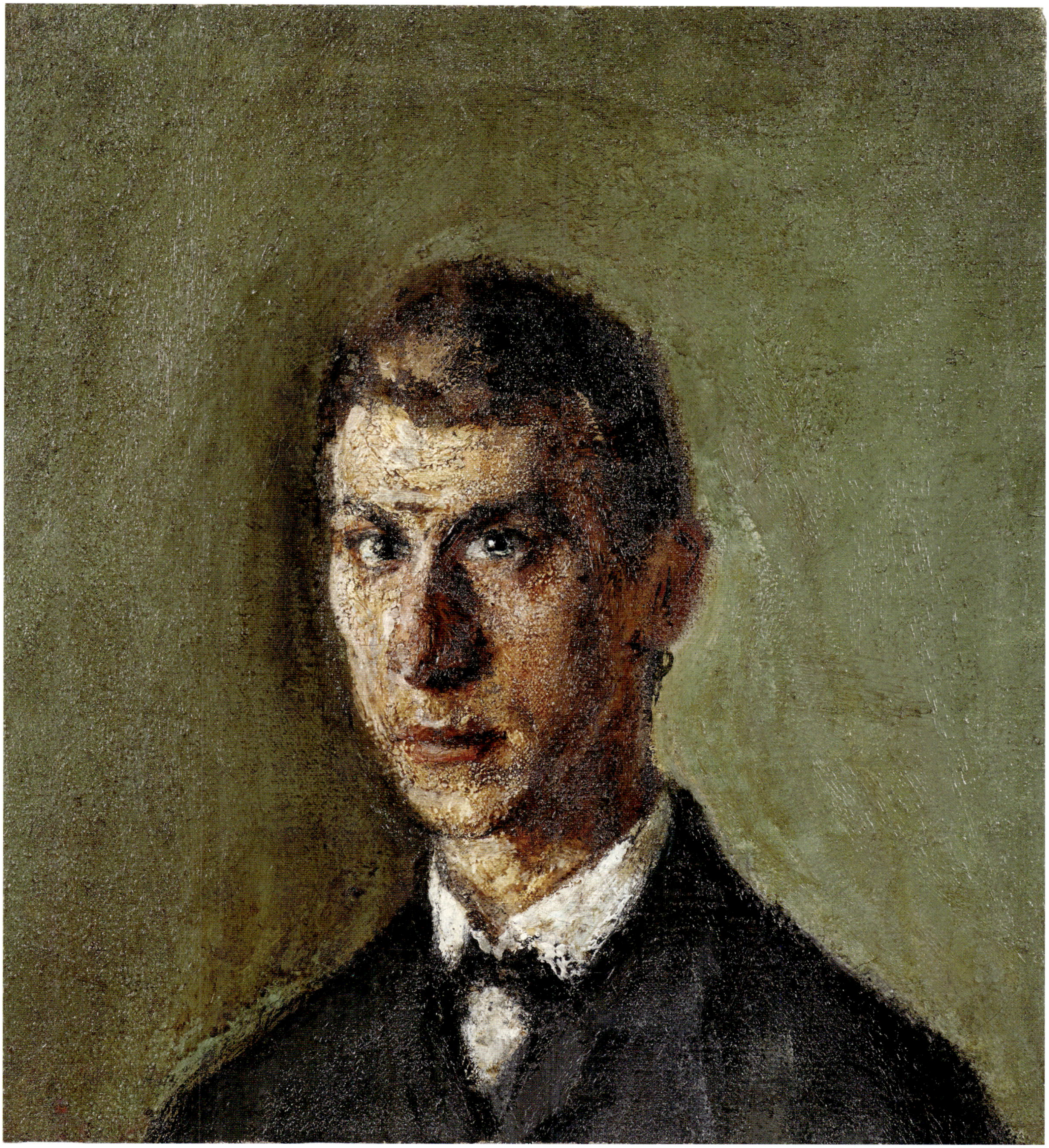

63

64

SEATED WOMAN IN A GREEN DRESS II/SITZENDE FRAU MIT GRÜNEM KLEID II, after February 1908

Oil on canvas
Size unknown
Whereabouts unknown

65

SEATED WOMAN IN A GREEN BLOUSE/SITZENDE FRAU MIT GRÜNER BLUSE, spring 1908

Oil on canvas
180.5 x 85.5 cm (71 x 33 ⅝ in.)
Leopold Museum, Vienna***

By winter 1907, Gerstl's bond with Schönberg and his circle had further strengthened. Not only was he among the group of the composer's students who bade an anguished farewell to Mahler when he departed for New York in December 1907, but the two men began sharing a studio, probably funded by Gerstl's father, at 68/70 Liechtensteinstraße in February 1908. While the tenement also housed Schönberg's apartment at the back of the building, the studio, which could be easily reached via a connecting staircase, was at the front, facing west towards Liechtensteinstraße itself, and so benefited from excellent light from midday. Here, Gerstl and the perpetually cash-strapped Schönberg pooled resources and shared materials, including, presumably, artboard, on which several of Schönberg's own works from the time were painted. Gerstl, however, returned to portraiture, painting the unidentified subject of the life-size *Seated Woman in a Green Blouse*, here sitting on a green chaise longue, twice. The second, depicting her lying on a sofa, was stolen around the time of the 1931 exhibition. Her profession—she was an actress—suggests that this was another commission that came from within Schönberg's circle, as with the portrait of *Professor Ernst Diez* [Cat. no. 21] that hangs to her right in a similar narrow format. For the portrait, Gerstl employs characteristic loops and broad, impasto strokes for her green jacket; a disintegration of form in her hands; contrasting, melding tones in her flowing skirt; and a subtle nod to Impressionism. His realistic representation, which was perhaps the actress's preference, and favored three-quarter pose, catch a coquettish, arguably thespian, moment that perfectly captures his subject's calling.

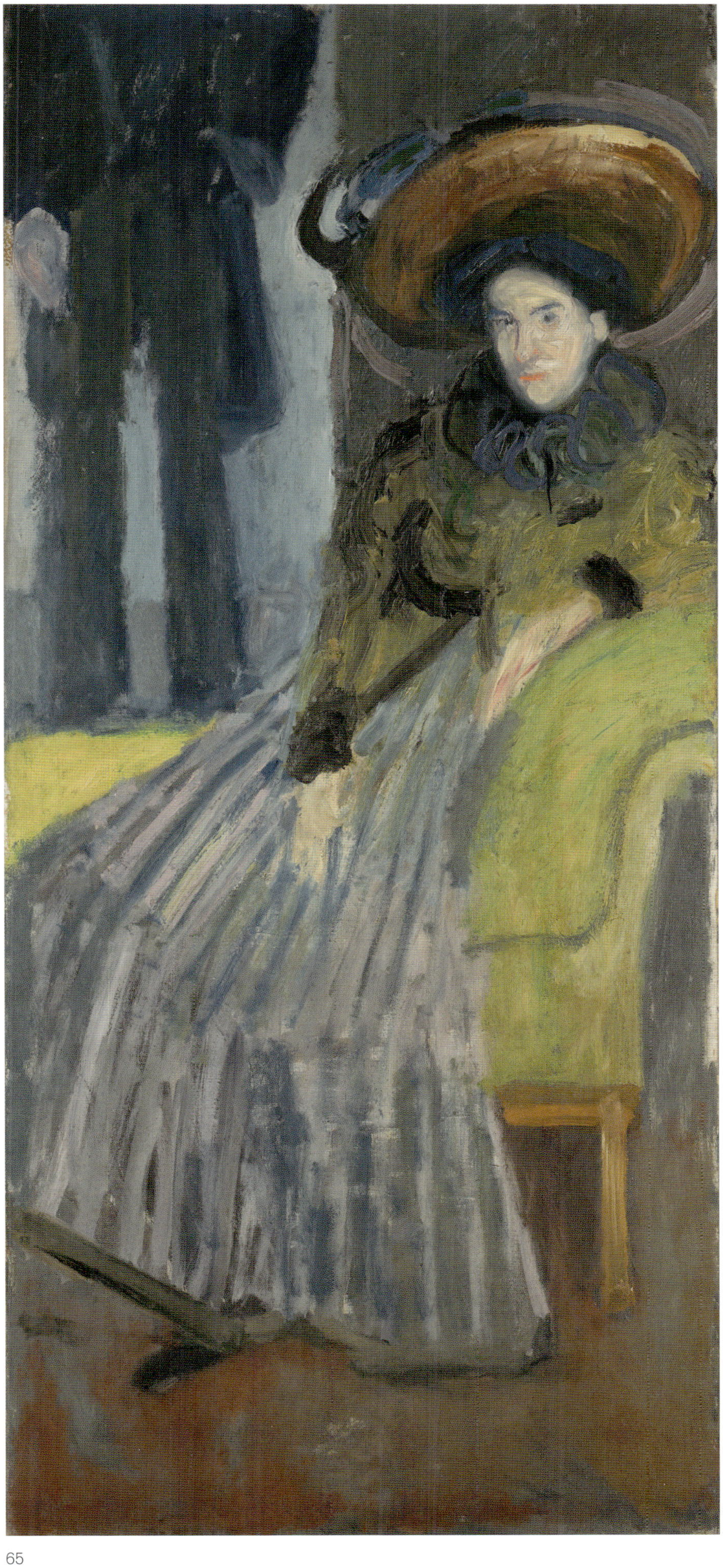

66

PORTRAIT OF A SEATED MAN/BILDNIS EINES SITZENDEN MANNES, spring 1908

Oil on canvas
130 x 100 cm (51 ⅛ x 39 ⅜ in.)
Private Collection**

Virtually nothing is known of *Portrait of a Sitting Man,* other than it was almost certainly painted in the same studio at 68/70 Liechtensteinstraße as *Seated Woman in a Green Blo*use, with Gerstl's green chaise longue against the wall and *Professor Ernst Diez* [Cat. no. 21] again on the wall behind, although here Gerstl's *Semi-Nude Self-Portrait* [Cat. no. 6] also hangs to the sitter's right. Breicha advanced the idea that this could be Gerstl's lost second portrait of Diez. However, while, according to Diez, this was indeed, "ein Portrait in dunkelblauem Anzug" (a portrait in a dark blue suit), the subject in *Portrait of a Sitting Man* appears older and bears little facial resemblance to him. While the portrait displays elements of the swirls and flecks that became typical of Gerstl's later works, here, as on previous occasions, he delivers a realistic depiction. Coming after his evolutionary time in Gmunden, this indicates how he adapted his style to possess a certain formality that perhaps reflected many of his sitters' expectations.

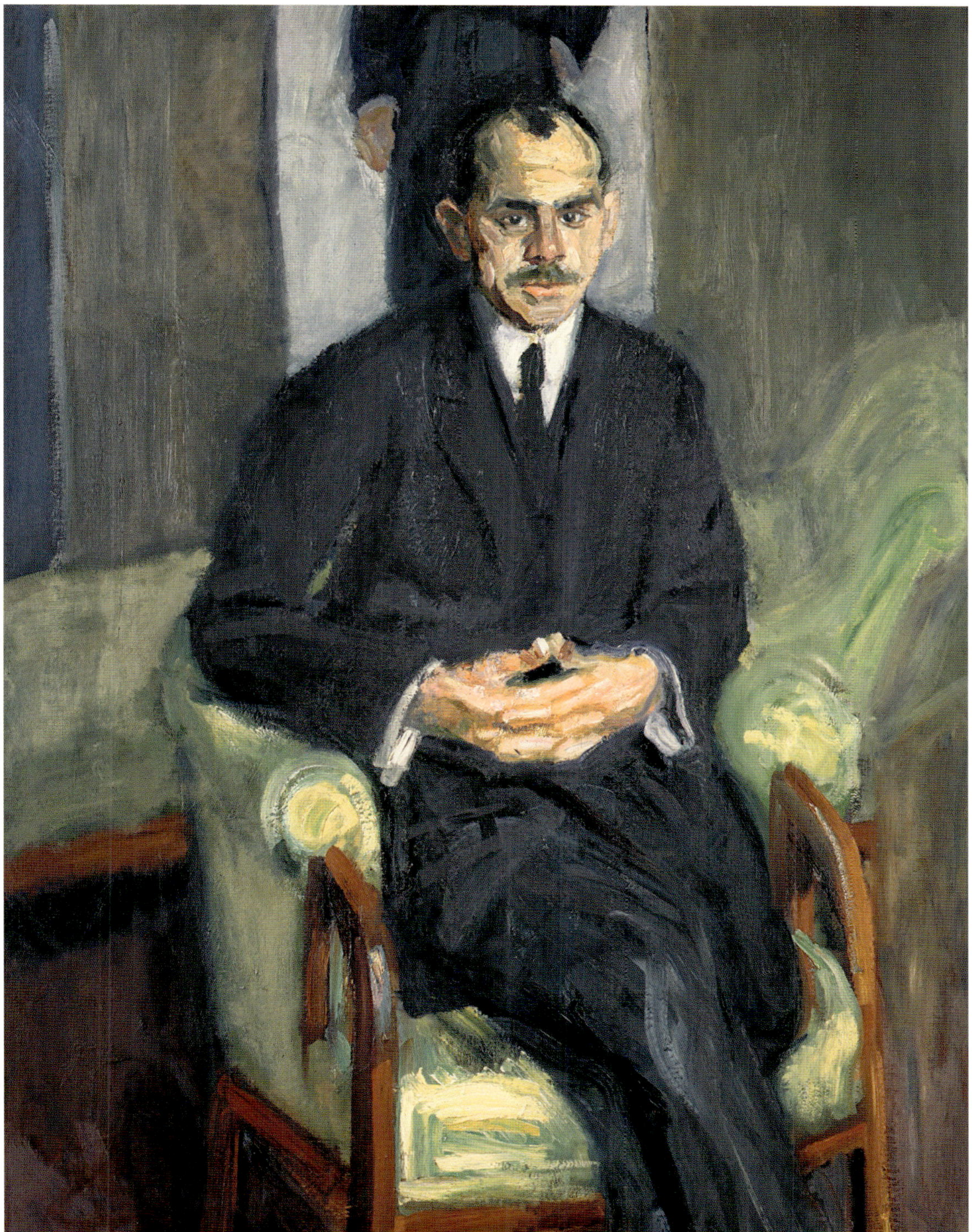
66

67

PORTRAIT OF MATHILDE SCHÖNBERG IN THE STUDIO/BILDNIS DER MATHILDE SCHÖNBERG IM ATELIER, spring 1908

Oil and mixed technique (possibly distemper) on canvas
171 x 60 cm (67 3/8 x 23 5/8 in.)
Kunsthaus Zug, Stiftung Sammlung Kamm***

For *Portrait of Mathilde Schönberg in the Studio*, Gerstl reverts to the flecks and dabs of his recent landscapes, choosing a life-size, narrow format to again depict Mathilde demurely, respectfully and smartly dressed in cool, modern attire, ready for a spring day. The work represents the best example of the influence of the French Intimists, recalling, in particular, Vuillard and Bonnard, the two most distinguished members of the Nabis movement. While only identified as Mathilde around 1957, presumably by Alois, in whose possession it had remained until then, the portrait acts as an indication that Mathilde was free to visit Gerstl's studio on the other side of the building without restriction. This strongly suggests that any liaison between them had not yet blossomed. Indeed, Gerstl was soon invited a second time to join the Schönbergs for their 1908 summer vacation, and by the end of June had left the city for Gmunden.

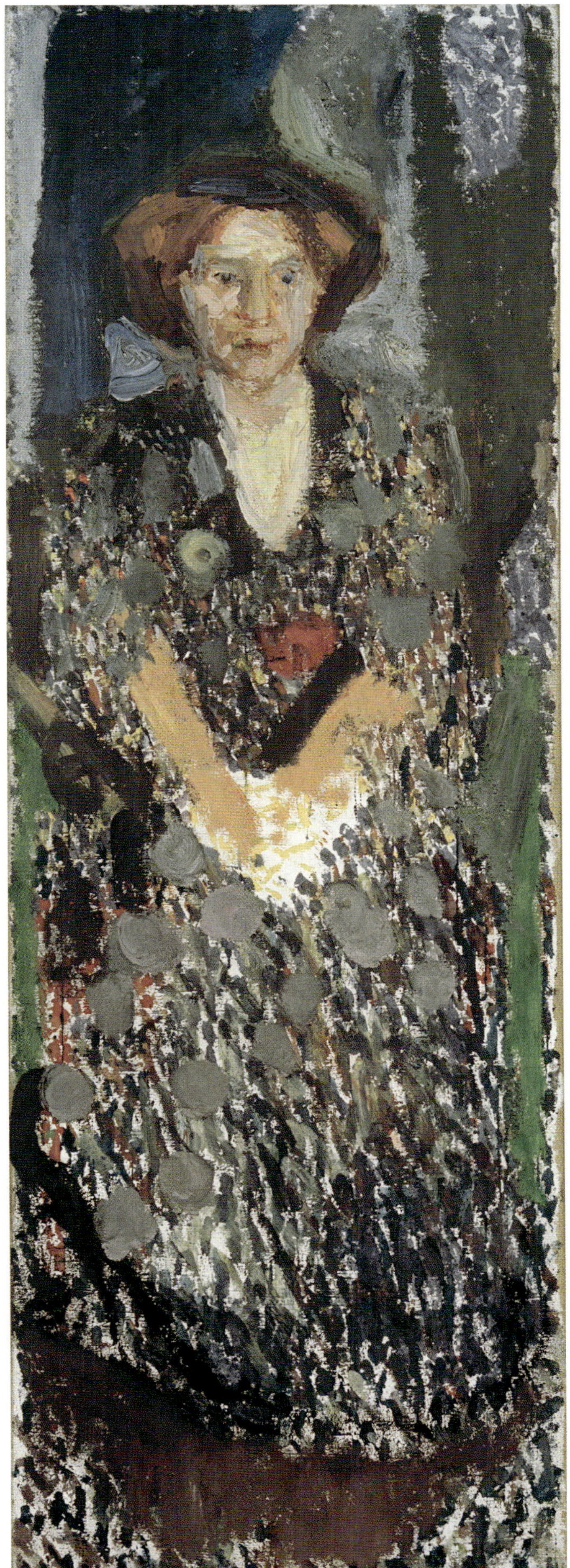

67

68

FEMALE DANCER IN A RED DRESS IN FRONT OF A YELLOW CURTAIN/TÄNZERIN IN EINEM ROTEN KLEID VOR EINEM GELBEN VORHANG, spring-summer 1908

Oil on canvas

67.8 x 54.6 cm (26 3/4 x 21 1/2 in.)

Whereabouts unknown**

69

SELF-PORTRAIT (STUDY)/SELBSTBILDNIS (STUDIE), spring-summer 1908

Oil on canvas

33.9 x 35 cm (13 3/8 x 13 3/4 in.)

Whereabouts unknown**

70

SELF-PORTRAIT/SELBSTBILDNIS, undated

Watercolor on paper

40 x 30 cm (15 3/4 x 11 3/4 in.)

Whereabouts unknown**

71

HALF-PORTRAIT OF MATHILDE SCHÖNBERG/ BILDNIS MATHILDE SCHÖNBERG ALS HALBFIGUR, spring-summer 1908

Oil on canvas

68 x 100 cm (26 3/4 x 39 3/8 in.)

Private Collection****

With its atypical horizontal format, there are indications in its lower edge that Gerstl's *Half-Portrait of Mathilde Schönberg* may have been another cut down, possibly from a life-size portrait of Mathilde Schönberg, who, despite never having been positively identified, can be safely assumed to be the subject. Certainly, her relaxed, seated pose, the air of domesticity, the picture frame hanging on an ochre background and its familiar composition all recall Gerstl's earlier double portrait of Mathilde and Gertrud Schönberg [Cat. no. 16]. It is highly likely that Gerstl produced this unusually large, oddly shaped and sharply defined image of Mathilde in the Schönbergs' apartment, rather than in the studio he shared with her husband in the same building. Here, in a work probably painted in spring or early summer 1908, Gerstl once again employs his color swirls, dabs, and impasto paint application. At the same time, Mathilde's cheek rouge matches her hat decoration, and the blue flecks on her dress endow the half-portrait with an intimate touch and even a soupçon of humor.

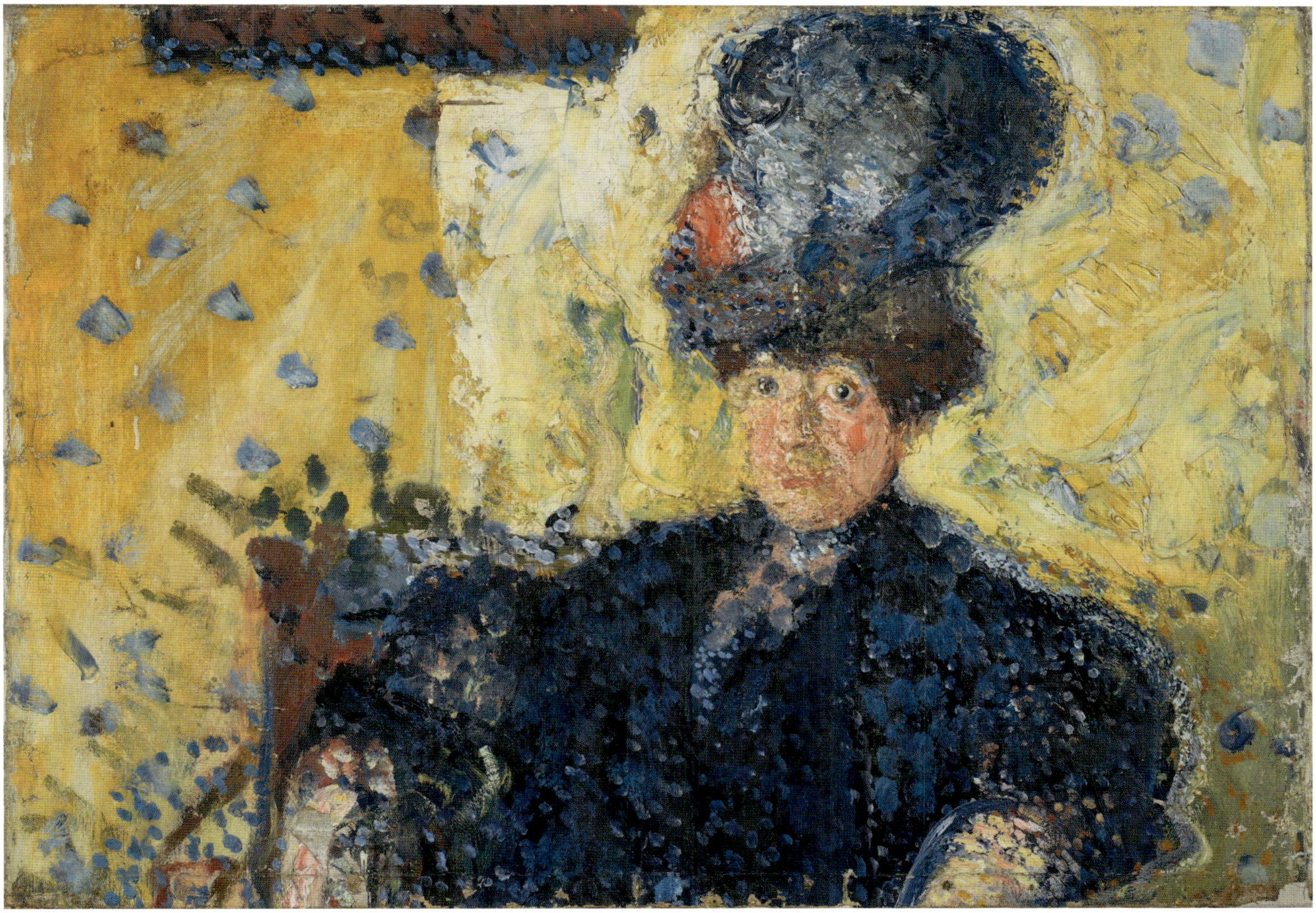

71

72

PORTRAIT OF HENRYKA COHN II/PORTRAIT HENRYKA COHN II, summer 1908

Oil on canvas
Size unknown
Whereabouts unknown

73

PORTRAIT OF HENRYKA COHN/BILDNIS HENRYKA COHN,
June 1908 (between June 1 and 27)

Oil on canvas
147.9 x 111.9 cm (58 ¼ x 44 in.)
Leopold Museum, Vienna*

Portrait of Henryka Cohn, artist, piano teacher and member of Schönberg's circle, was probably the last commission initiated by Schönberg that Gerstl ever painted. Since it bears clear, sardonic reference to Klimt's *Portrait of Fritza Riedler,* which was exhibited for the first time at the "Kunstschau 1908," which opened in June, *Henryka Cohn* stands as a calculated riposte to Klimt, Vienna's arch-portraitist, whom Gerstl openly scorned. This work can be ascribed to June 1908, as Gerstl departed for his ill-fated Gmunden vacation on the 27th, after which he unsurprisingly became *persona non grata.* Gerstl again adopts his favored three-quarter pose for Henryka, who sits dressed in white on a sofa in her home at Esterhazygasse 23, in Vienna's sixth district. Here, in a pointed rejection of the Secessionist aesthetic, Gerstl, in a work that can also be seen as a precursor to the primitive Expressionism that blossomed in Gmunden just weeks later, purges the decorative ornamentation of *Fritza Riedler* with disintegrative, jagged brushwork, an unsettling, abstract background and an enveloping, mesmerizing mesh of black and red flecks to define the sofa. Moreover, the demure, almost virginal quality that suffused Gerstl's similarly composed domestic portraits, is here supplanted by an erotic undertow with which Gerstl imbues his elegant, stern subject, depicting her suggestively with a stray, tumbling ringlet, lips slightly pouted, eyes angled seductively, and a hand falling unnaturally on her gossamer gown. Her portrait was inscribed on the reverse with Gerstl's return address and, indeed, remained in Alois's hands for the next 50 years.

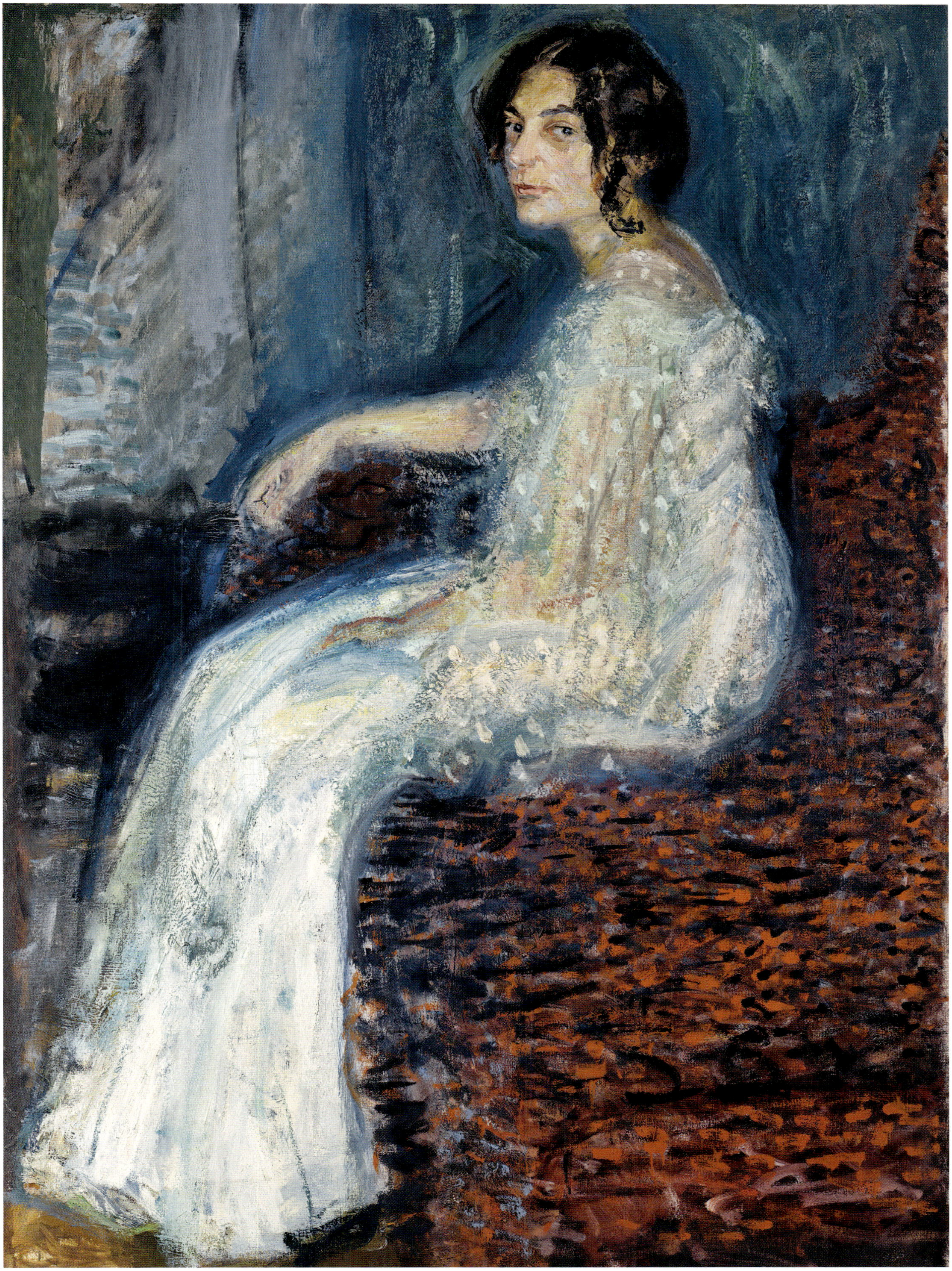

74

PORTRAIT OF A MAN (GREEN BACKGROUND) [PORTRAIT OF A MAN IN THE MEADOW]/ HERRENBILDNIS (GRÜNER HINTERGRUND) [BILDNIS EINES MANNES IN DER WIESE], summer 1908

Oil on canvas
109.5 x 90.2 cm (43 ⅛ x 35 ½ in.)
Private Collection***

Before Gerstl left for Gmunden in 1908, he had already been practicing with yard-long brushes in order to find a more effective and expressive way of painting his subjects from a distance. It was a technique that he may have tried out in *Henryka Cohn* as well as *Portrait of a Man (Green Background)/Portrait of a Man in the Meadow*, which has long been conjectured to portray Alban Berg. Certainly, Berg's tall, languid physique fits that of the subject, and the work was indeed exhibited at the 1956 Venice Biennale as *Ritratto A.B*, and in Brussels in 1961 as *Portrait de Alban Berg.* Having already portrayed his sister, it would have been surprising if Gerstl had not offered to paint his friend's portrait too. Since Berg spent the entire summer of 1908 at his summerhouse in Villach, this could only have been painted in Vienna before Gerstl left on vacation. Nonetheless, the work has clear affinities with the works that Gerstl produced there, notably in its broad brushstrokes and subject representation, although here he employs a rather thinner application of paint than the heavy deposits seen in his Gmunden portraits. The work, therefore, can be ascribed to June 1908, and was possibly painted in Vienna's Stadtpark. Berg had recently moved and was living near that park, which would have provided the perfect green, garden-like backdrop, similar to those seen later in Gmunden, for Gerstl to paint his friend.

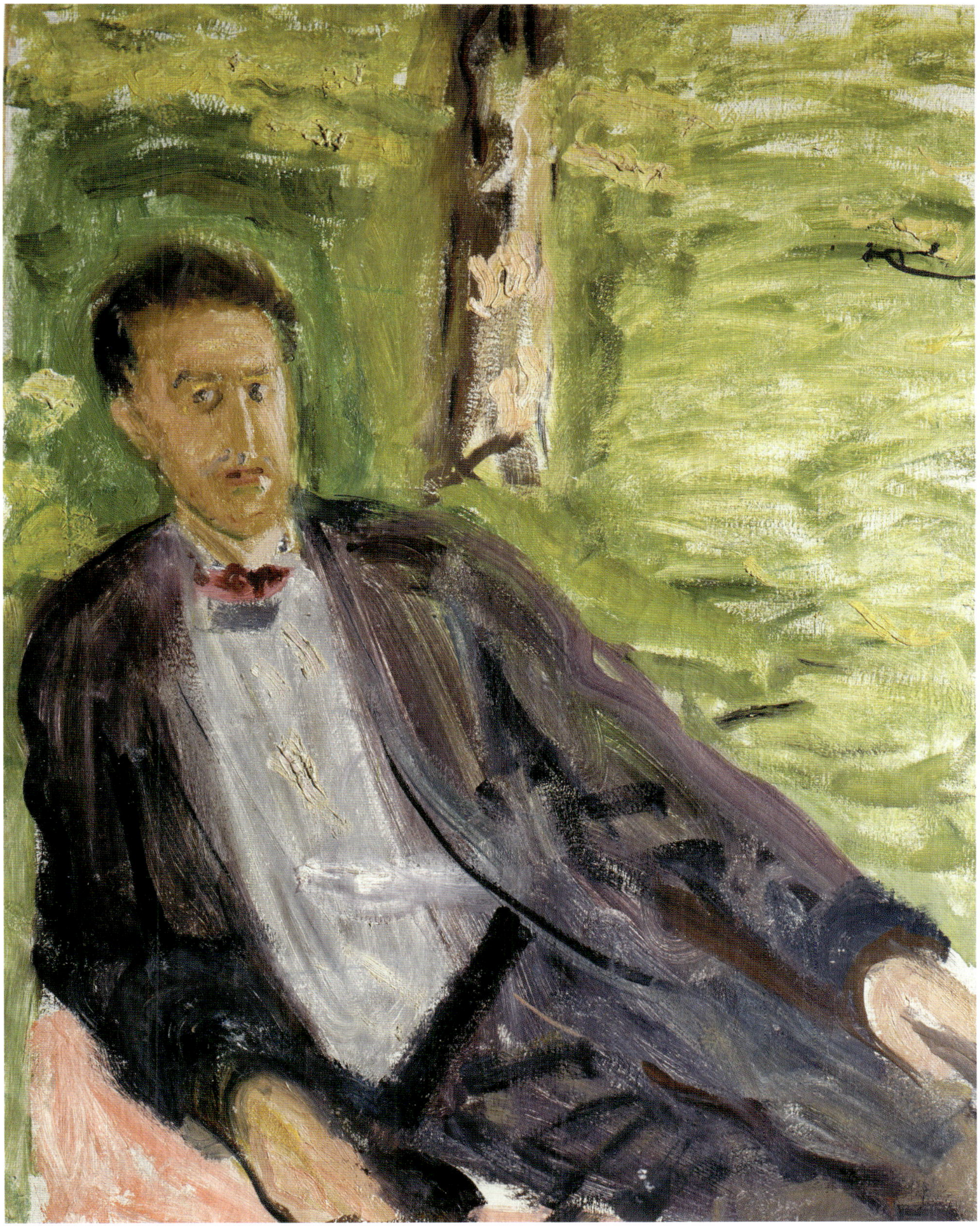

75

TRAUNSEE LANDSCAPE/ TRAUNSEELANDSCHAFT, July 1908

Oil on canvas

Approximately 100 x 50 cm (39 3/8 x 19 5/8 in.)

Whereabouts unknown

76

COUPLE IN A FIELD/PAAR IM GRÜNEN, July 1908

Oil on canvas

111.2 x 90.7 cm (43 3/4 x 35 3/4 in.)

Leopold Museum, Vienna**

As a sign of their strengthening bond, Schönberg again invited Gerstl to join him in Gmunden in the summer of 1908. Gerstl duly arrived on June 27 and settled in again at Feramühle, just over a quarter mile from Preslgütl, the Schönbergs' new farmhouse accommodation. Unlike the previous year, Gmunden experienced fine weather during July 1908, so that while the Schönbergs enjoyed a family vacation, Gerstl soon began producing a series of *plein air,* life-size portraits, the first of which may have been *Couple in a Field.* The couple's identity remains unknown, although there are unconfirmed suggestions that the woman might be Mathilde. The verdant greens of the meadow, hedge and orchard differ here from the bright yellow backgrounds of other portraits from Gmunden in 1908, although the painting's broad, expansive brushwork and dramatic swirls and loops remain consistent with Gerstl's later approach there. Moreover, although the subjects are seated rather than standing, the composition of *Couple in a Field* bears affinities to Van Gogh's *Lovers in the Poet's Garden*, which Gerstl would have viewed as No. 41 at the Galerie Miethke's show in January 1906, especially in the pose, the dress and hat, the tender, poignant mood, and the couple's proximity.

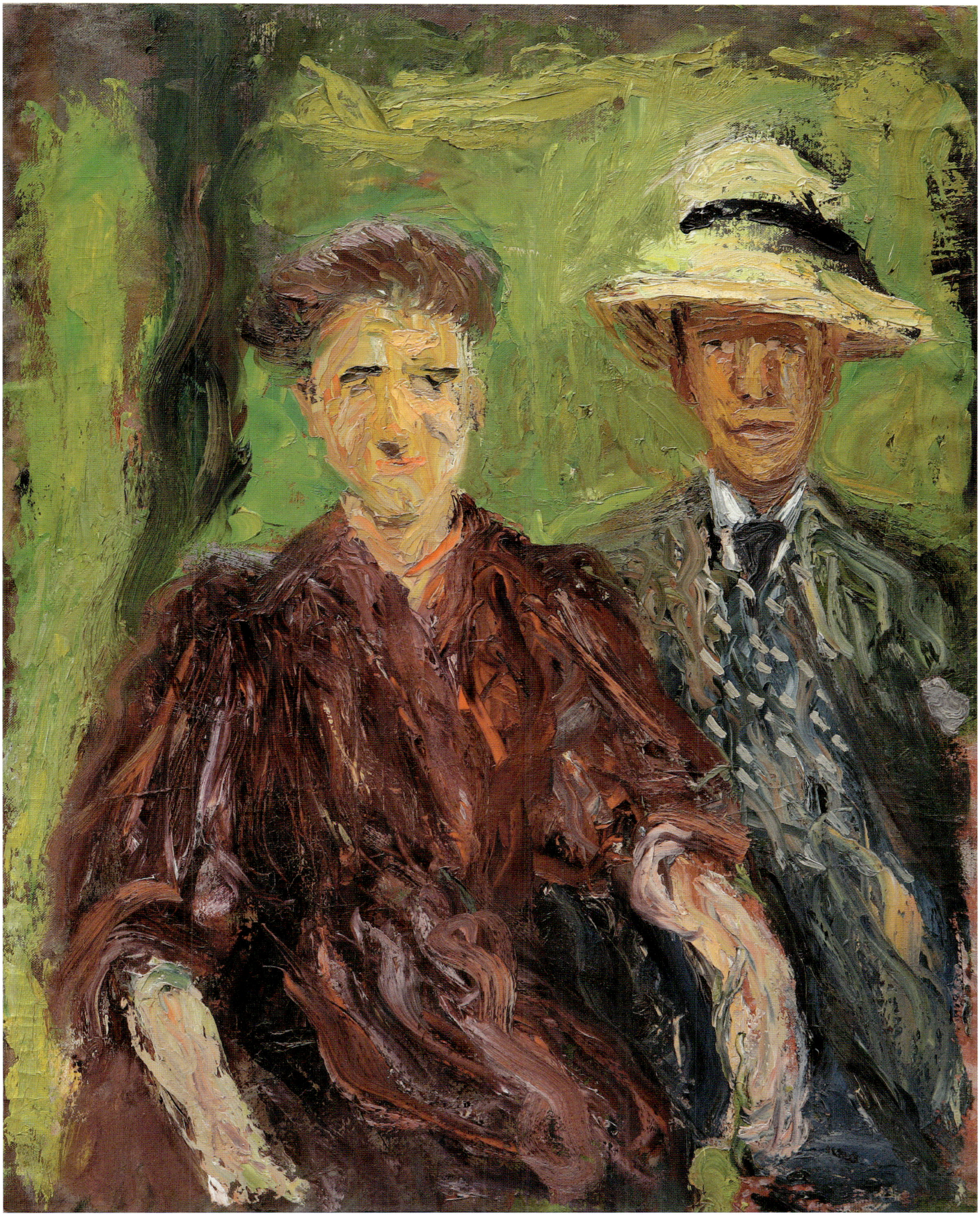

77

PORTRAIT OF ALEXANDER ZEMLINSKY/BILDNIS ALEXANDER VON ZEMLINSKY, July 1908

Verso Upturned: *Fragment of a Full-Length Self-Portrait, Laughing,* ca. 1904, [Cat. no. 11]. The narrower half was used by Gerstl for *Mathilde Schönberg in the Garden*, July 1908 [Cat. no. 78].
Oil on canvas
170.5 x 74.3 cm (67 ⅛ x 29 ¼ in.)
Kunsthaus Zug, Stiftung Sammlung Kamm**

Seizing an opportunity to capture Zemlinsky on the bank outside his 1908 farmhouse, Engelgut, Gerstl portrays the diminutive composer life-size with a touch of vanity, a downcast look and a ghostly halo, reminiscent of his *Semi-Nude Self-Portrait* [Cat. no. 6]. Walking stick at the ready and his sun-hat protecting him in the morning glow, Zemlinsky may not have had the patience to pose for long, so Gerstl painted him quickly, the glistening Traunsee waters merging with his legs, the left side of his body dissolving into the background, and his left hand barely a shadow against his pristine white suit jacket. Using the reverse of the larger, upturned half of the bisected *Fragment of a Full-Length Self-Portrait, Laughing* [Cat. no. 11], and applying the white background by palette knife directly from the tube, Gerstl's broad, almost sketch-like brushstrokes and loops achieve a corporal translucence and a near-dissolution of boundaries, which the darkened ocher tone in the face and hands merely emphasizes. Equally, Gerstl's minimal representation of Zemlinsky's facial features appears to be a continuation in a process that saw him obliterate them almost completely in the other extraordinary portraits that he executed in the three weeks before the end of July, shortly after which Zemlinsky joined the Mahlers in Tolbach.

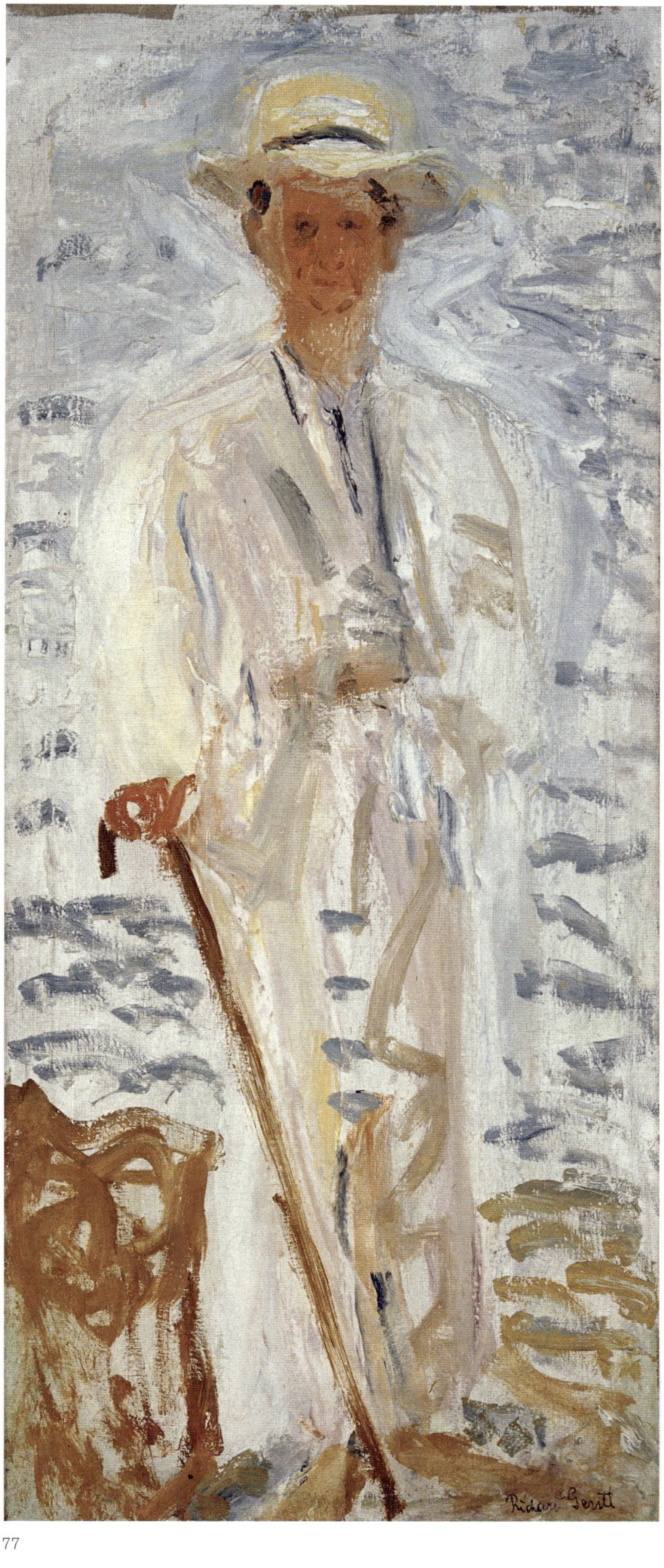
Richard Gerstl

78

MATHILDE SCHÖNBERG IN THE GARDEN/ MATHILDE SCHÖNBERG IM GARTEN, July 1908

Verso: The narrower half of the bisected canvas was used for *Fragment of a Full-Length Self-Portrait, Laughing*; the wider half was used for *Portrait of Alexander Zemlinsky*, July 1908 [Cat. no. 77]
Oil on canvas
171 x 61 cm (67 ⅜ x 24 in.)
Leopold Museum, Vienna**

Painted verso the narrow half of the bisected *Fragment of a Full-Length Self-Portrait, Laughing* [Cat. no. 11], *Mathilde Schönberg in the Garden* has, as with the portrait of Alexander Zemlinsky, a marked air of spontaneity, with Mathilde seemingly caught in motion, oblivious to the presence of the artist, going about her day on the grounds of Preslgütl. The work catches the sense of the freedom that Gerstl plainly enjoyed within Schönberg's circle in Gmunden 1908, for blades of grass are embedded near its base, indicating that Gerstl painted Mathilde *in situ*, presumably resting the life-size stretcher on the ground to do so. Here, Gerstl lightens Mathilde's hands with thick, elegant strokes, but again employs heavy ocher-brown skin tones for the face. He hardly hints at Mathilde's eyes and mouth, yet as with her brother Alexander's portrait, somehow retains recognition of the subject, a technique seen to greatest effect in the later group portraits. Indeed, *Mathilde Schönberg in the Garden* can be seen as a staging post to these, for it not only displays a style of *Reformkleidung* dress seen just days later in the group portrayals, but also the same broad, almost disdainful brushstrokes of possibly unthinned yellows and greens that Gerstl used to create their determinedly non-specific backgrounds.

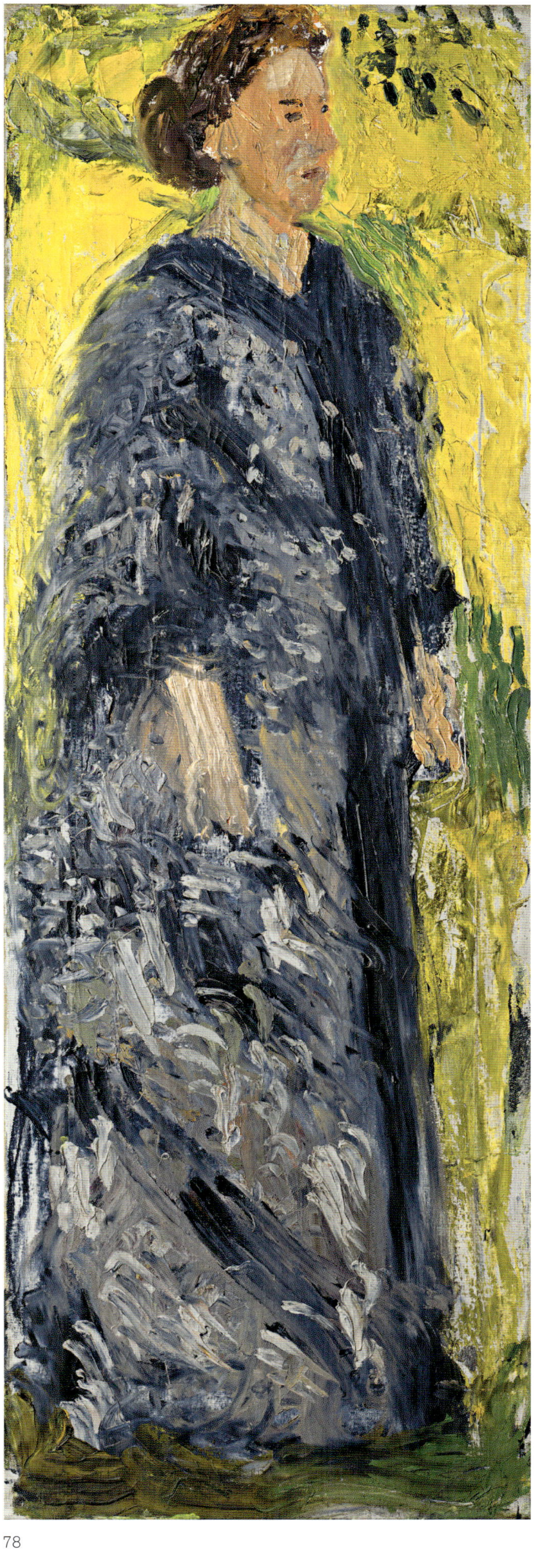

79

THE SCHÖNBERG FAMILY/DIE FAMILIE SCHÖNBERG, late July 1908

Oil on canvas
88.8 x 109.7 cm (35 x 43 ⅛ in.)
Museum moderner Kunst Stiftung Ludwig Wien, Gift of the Kamm Family, Zug 1969**

Gerstl painted *The Schönberg Family* over a Traunsee seascape (see illustration p. 233 bottom), and clearly intended to allow segments of the blue water of the original to show through, creating, perhaps deliberately, the craquelure in the surface of the work. He sets the Schönbergs against a summer garden of cracked greens and yellows, persisting with his characteristic thick swirls, whirls and spirals to lift the warm pinks of Trudi's dress, the pristine white of Görgi's smock, the white/rose of Schönberg's summer suit and the blue dress that Mathilde also wears in *Mathilde Schönberg in the Garden.* It is, however, Trudi's striking red bows that draw the eye to the hierarchic order of the family—Arnold and Mathilde sit close to one another with a protective arm around each child. The obscuring of the subjects' faces has been formed close-up, again by Gerstl sculpting colors directly from the tube, while darker areas on the parents' left cheeks hint at sunlight coming over the artist's right shoulder. With a dab for an eye, a smear for the lips, and a mere trace for other features, Gerstl nonetheless maintains the likenesses, so that, rather than a marriage in collapse, he purveys a warm, even affectionate vision of a tight nuclear family unit and a further example of the friendly co-operation of his fellow holidaymakers as he portrayed them in the late July Gmunden sunshine.

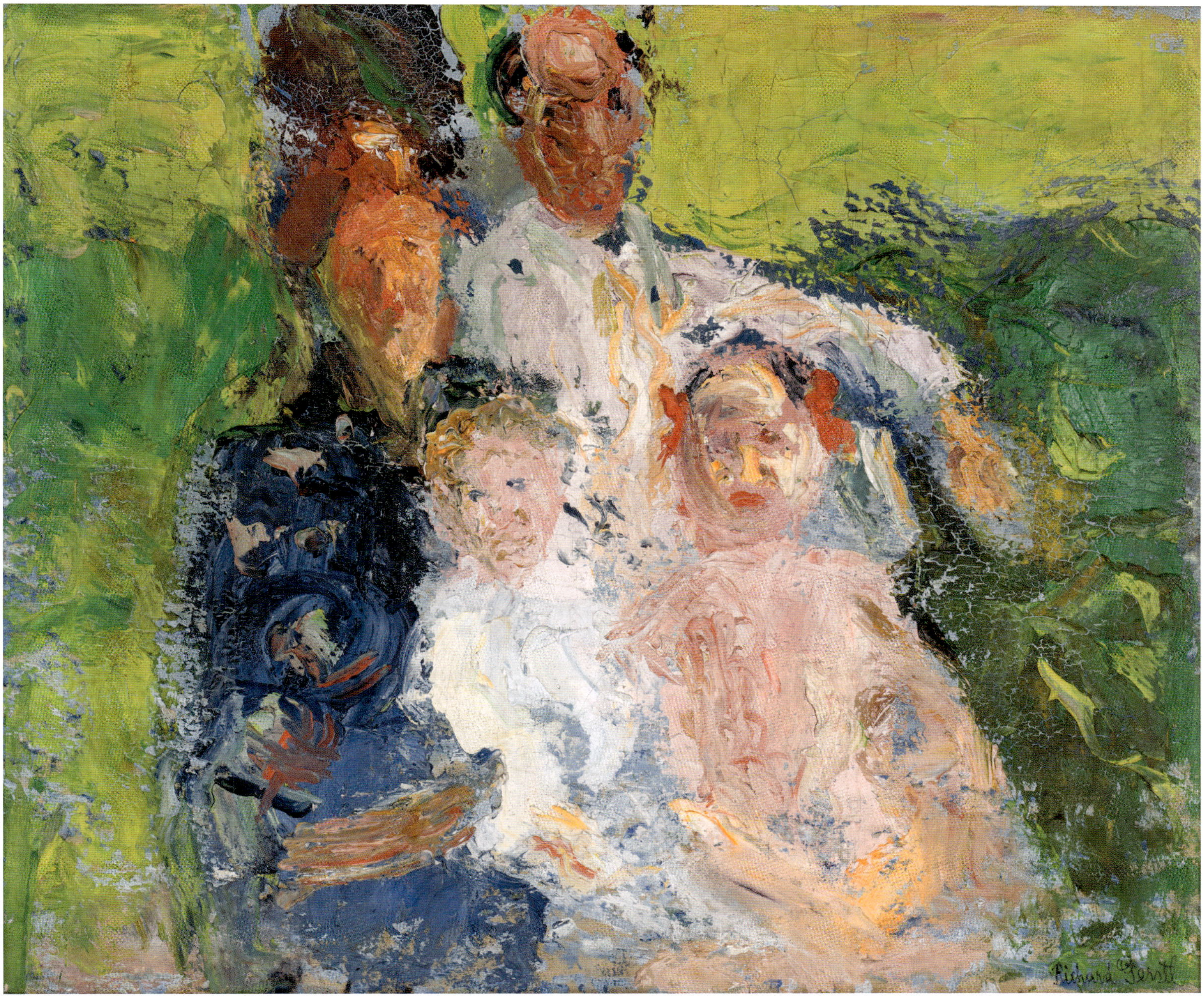

79

80

GROUP PORTRAIT WITH SCHÖNBERG/ GRUPPENBILDNIS MIT SCHÖNBERG, late July 1908 (ca. July 23, 1908)

Oil on canvas
169 x 110 cm (66 ½ x 43 ¼ in.)
Kunsthaus Zug, Stiftung Sammlung Kamm**

Gerstl's *Group Portrait with Schönberg* stands at the vanguard of early Austrian Expressionism. Here, in a culmination of Gerstl's rapid and dramatic progression first seen in his landscapes the previous summer, Schönberg stands top left with Zemlinsky seated below him next to his wife, Ida, and Mathilde Schönberg to her right. The third couple were probably Schönberg's student, Karl Horwitz and his wife, Mizzi, who were on honeymoon. Finished around July 23, 1908, the group's pose, although ostensibly structured, is asymmetrical, suggesting an impromptu moment amongst friends, a depiction of kinship in which the only one missing is the artist himself. A sun-strewn backdrop, applied with a palette knife, shares the rich, pastose ochers and greens that typified Gerstl's Gmunden portraits in 1908. However, as Gerstl stretched his dematerializing techniques to the extreme, this work touches on the grotesque, creating a paradoxical experience, wherein, despite his wild, sweeping, savage brushwork, bodies and dress contrive to remain representational, and the subjects' faces, distorted and indistinguishable close up, become gradually recognizable as the viewer draws back. Of the six, however, Gerstl took the most trouble over Schönberg, and, despite the black hollows for his eyes and mouth, portrays him in kindly fashion, even respectfully. Indeed, whereas the features of the rest are nearly obliterated, Schönberg's identity is preserved, with the result that, although the eye is initially drawn to the pink androgynous figure of Horwitz, it is Schönberg, Gerstl's friend and colleague, who, as its father figure, dominates the group.

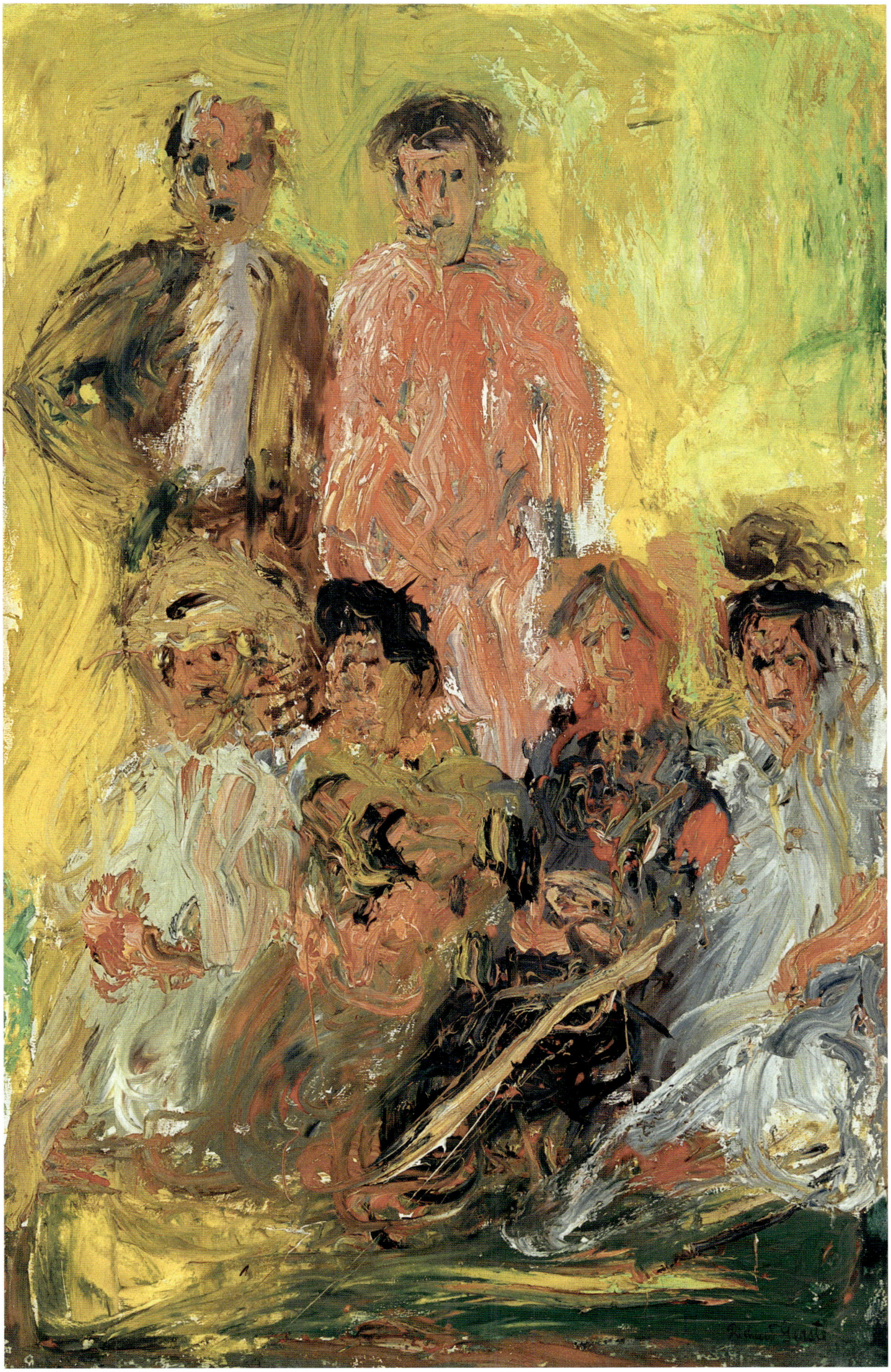

81

NUDE IN THE GARDEN/AKT IM GARTEN, July 1908

Oil on canvas
121.1 x 99 cm (47 ⅝ x 39 in.)
Private Collection, Courtesy Galerie St. Etienne, New York**

Although the colors in *Nude in the Garden* are applied flatter and the yellow/green tones are more subdued, it displays affinities to other paintings from the 1908 summer in Gmunden, such as the innovative brushwork and common location. Its figures, however, are barely defined and their facial features indiscernable, echoing the near-abstraction of the *Group Portrait with Schönberg.* It may be Gerstl's final known work of the vacation, as well as the most enigmatic. For example, Nirenstein, presumably without Alois's positive identification, entitled it simply *Composition.* Others suggest that the white ball under the central figure's right arm might be laundry, or that it was a study for a later nude self-portrait. Another theory is that this was a nude depiction of Mathilde inserted into a garden scene. What is most likely, however, is that the tall, slim main subject was Gerstl himself, standing with a palette in his left hand, and a white easel behind him, in the midst of faceless, distracted onlookers, who exhibit no interest in the figure before them, naked or not. If this is so, *Nude in the Garden* may be Gerstl's Ensor-like nightmarish view of himself working *plein air* at a typical social gathering of Schönberg's Gmunden entourage, probably in late July 1908.

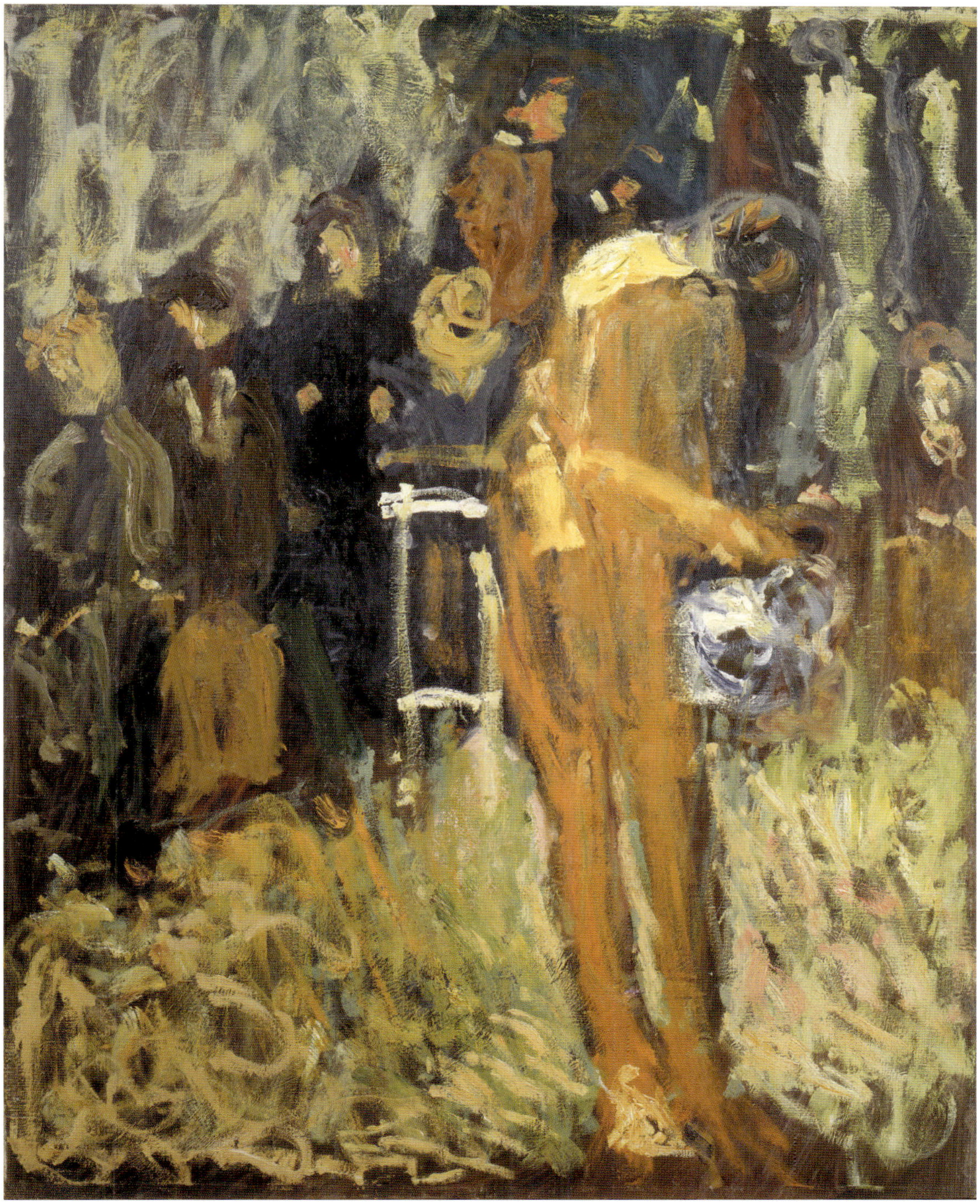

81

82

VIEW TO A STREET (SMALL STREET SCENE)/BLICK IN EINE STRASSE (KLEINES STRASSENBILD), early September 1908

Oil on board

35.3 x 29 cm (19 5/8 x 13 3/4 in.)

Private Collection***

On August 26, 1908, Gerstl and Mathilde were found *in flagrante delicto* and, after a confrontation with Schönberg, eloped to a pension in Nussdorf, where they spent three nights together before Schönberg tracked Mathilde down and she returned to the family home. His love affair at a temporary end, *persona non grata* amongst Schönberg's circle and once again excluded from the Academy, Gerstl returned to his family's home at Nussdorferstraße 35 in Vienna, from where he produced a number of works. Amongst these was his *View to a Street*, painted on artboard, again cut from a standard 19 5/8 x 13 3/4 inch sheet, for which Gerstl partly uses a palette knife to achieve broad, thick strokes. The view is from the overhanging balcony of the first-floor apartment at the corner of Nussdorferstraße and Säulengasse, whose buildings opposite are detailed on the right-hand edge of the cityscape. From there, Gerstl was able to look south down Nussdorferstraße towards the nearly completed, distant gray apartment block on Bindergasse, a street that, ironically, Gerstl would have taken on his short walk to Liechtensteinstraße, where Schönberg had his apartment. Closer are the shops and cafés of Nussdorferstraße, with their awnings. Gerstl's use of light and shadow suggests that they are shown bathed in the afternoon sun of the cloudless and warm spell that Vienna enjoyed in early September 1908.

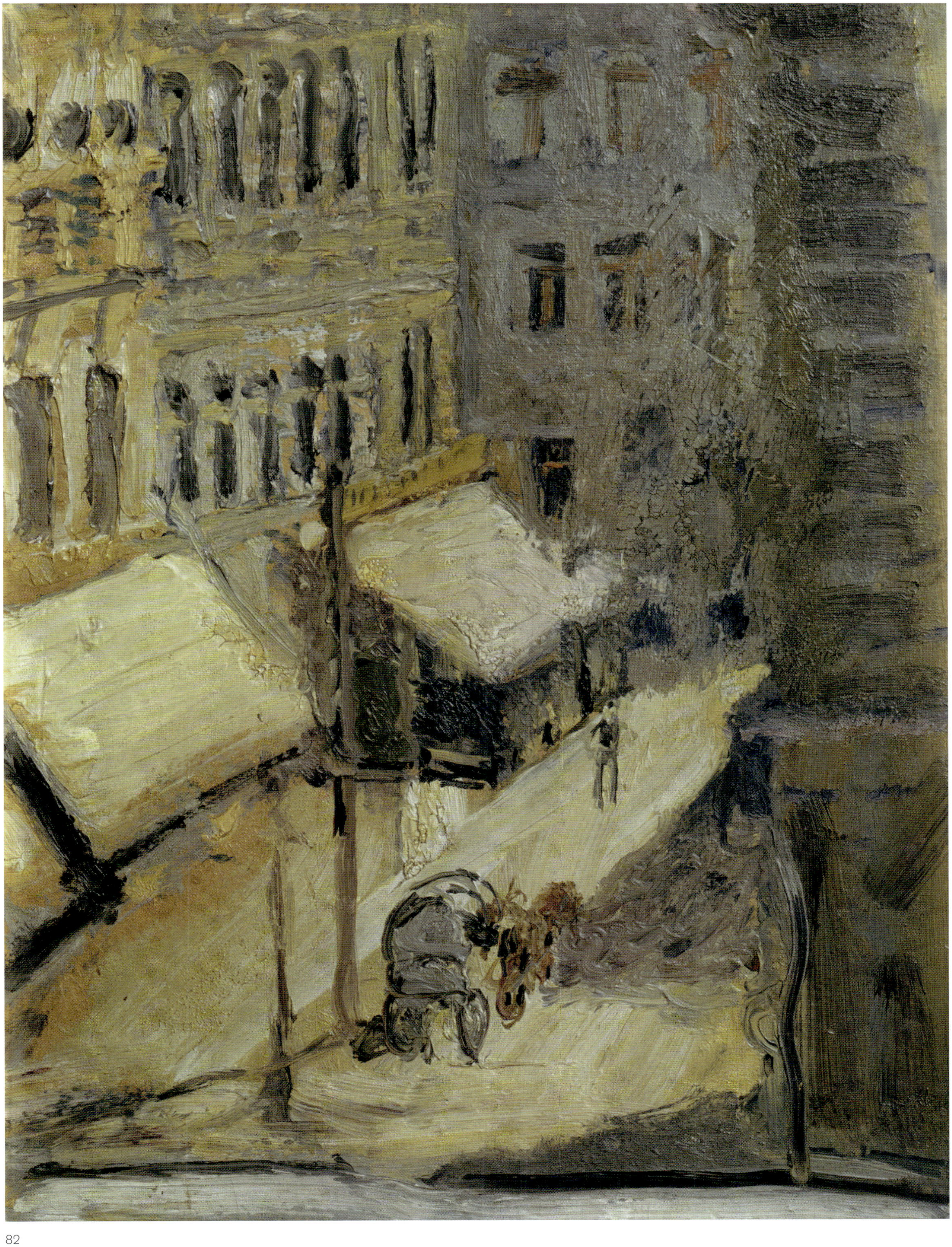

83

INTERIOR WITH THONET CHAIR (ROOM)/ INTERIEUR MIT THONETSTUHL (ZIMMER), autumn 1908

Oil on board
49.8 x 35 cm (19 ⅝ x 13 ¾ in.)
Private Collection, Vienna**

For *Interior with Thonet Chair,* Gerstl used almost exactly one quarter of a sheet of artboard to depict a Thonet bentwood chair, perhaps one of the most iconic symbols of middle-class domesticity in 1900 Vienna. As might be deduced from its shadow, it stands beside a dressing table with mirror. The work is the closest that Gerstl came to painting a still-life; its techniques can be compared with those used in his *View to a Street,* although here, Gerstl varies his brushstrokes freely, alternating longer applications of muted color with flecks and twists in the mirror and curls on the walls. Gerstl contrives to create an oasis of family calm and normality in a setting that may show the bedroom of his mother, Maria, far removed from the turbulence into which his life had recently fallen.

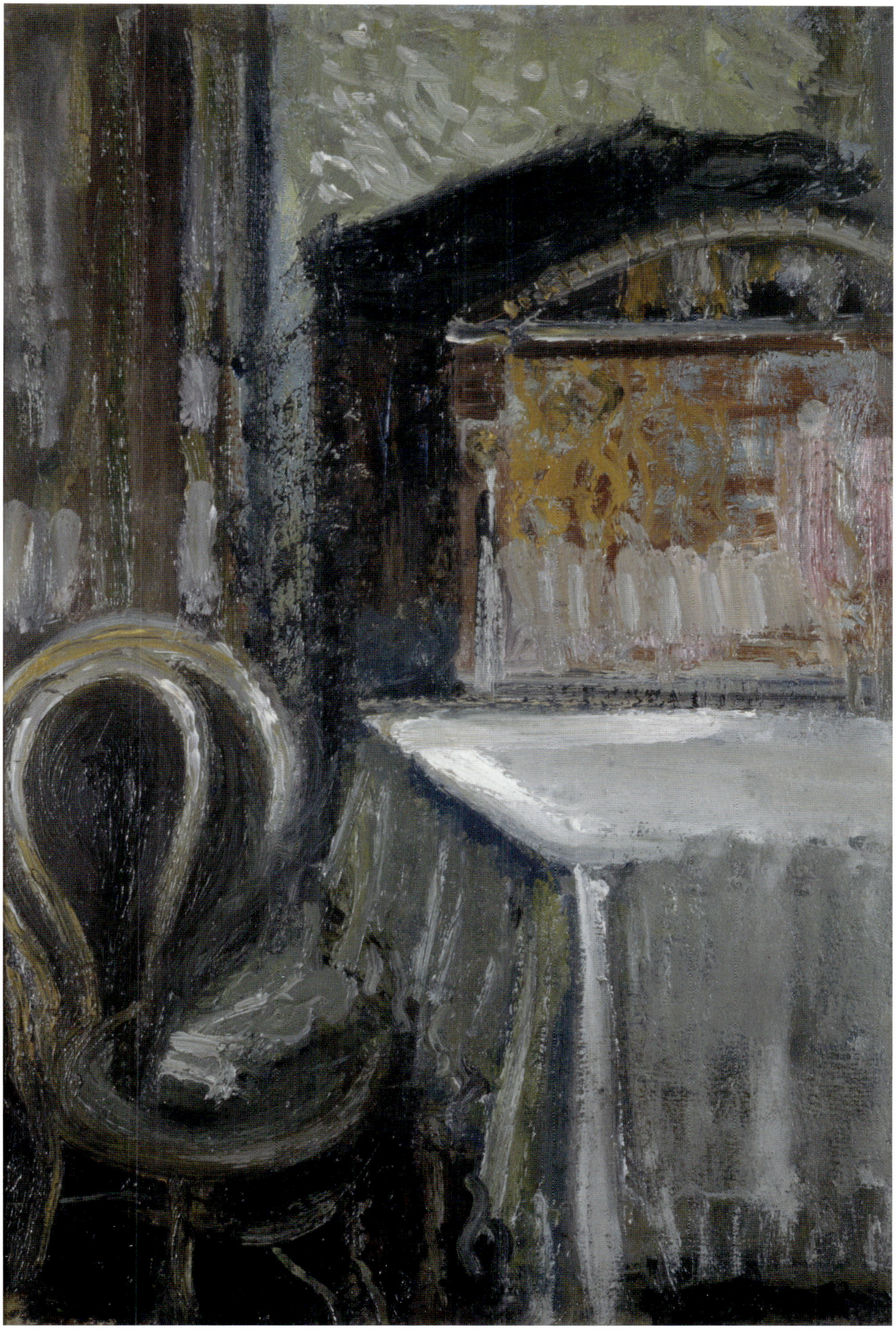

84

PORTRAIT OF THE ARTIST'S MOTHER MARIE GERSTL/BILDNIS DER MUTTER MARIE GERSTL, probably autumn 1908

Oil on board
49 x 35 cm (19 ⅝ x 13 ¾ in.)
Kunsthaus Zug, Stiftung Sammlung Kamm**

Almost certainly painted in the family's Nussdorferstraße apartment in the fall of 1908, Gerstl's portrait of his mother, Maria, is of almost identical dimensions to the *Interior with Thonet Chair* and so may have been cut from the same sheet of artboard. Gerstl was unquestionably close to his mother, who, unlike his father, was sympathetic towards her son's artistic and temperamental nature. Indeed, so strong were his feelings for her and so great his disappointment in his perceived inability to catch her true likeness that, according to his brother Alois, he could not bring himself to finish her portrait in the weeks before his death, even though comparison with a much younger Maria indicates that Gerstl had achieved a reasonable resemblance. Setting aside his understandable desire to produce a perfect, idealized image, Gerstl portrays his mother lovingly with a benign smile and warm, gray eyes, adorning her with the swirls and dabs that he delighted in painting at that time.

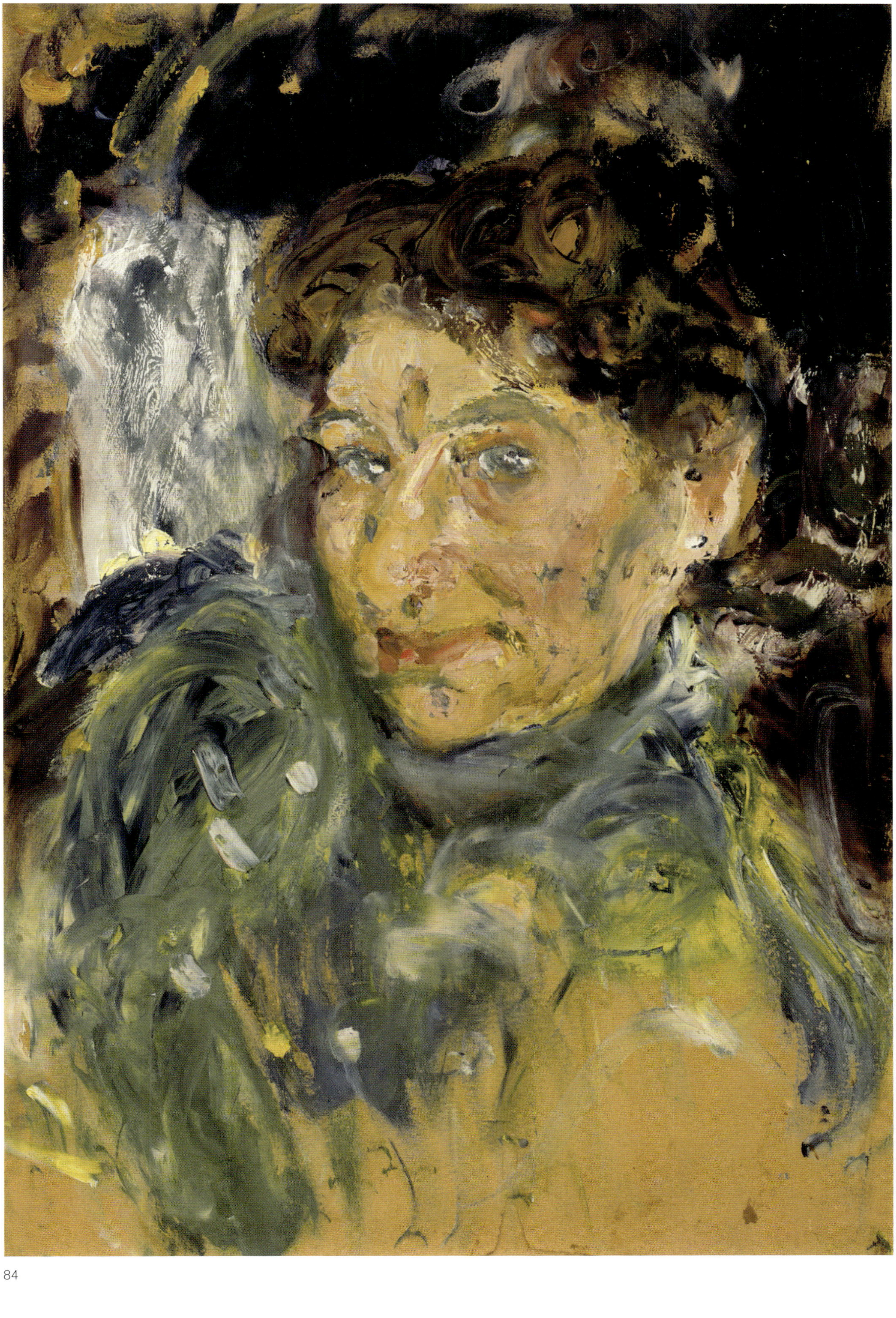

85

FRAGMENT OF A NUDE SELF-PORTRAIT/ FRAGMENT EINES SELBSTAKTES, September 1908

Oil on canvas
Size unknown
Whereabouts unknown**

Little is known about Gerstl's *Fragment of a Nude Self-Portrait,* whose black and white photograph, taken by Nirenstein, bears obvious affinities to his full-length *Nude Self-Portrait,* for which it may have been a study. Nirenstein exhibited the work in his 1931 Gerstl show. However, he did not draw immediate attention to its similarities, for while *Nude Self-Portrait* was hung prominently in Salon 1 and would have been the first works that visitors viewed as they entered the Neue Galerie in Vienna, *Fragment of a Nude Self-Portrait* was shown in Salon 2, some distance away. It was probably painted around the same time, and was most likely an oil on canvas, although of unknown dimensions. It sold at a very early stage of the exhibition, and was replaced soon thereafter by *Self-Portrait* [Cat. no. 63]. The current whereabouts of the canvas remain unknown.

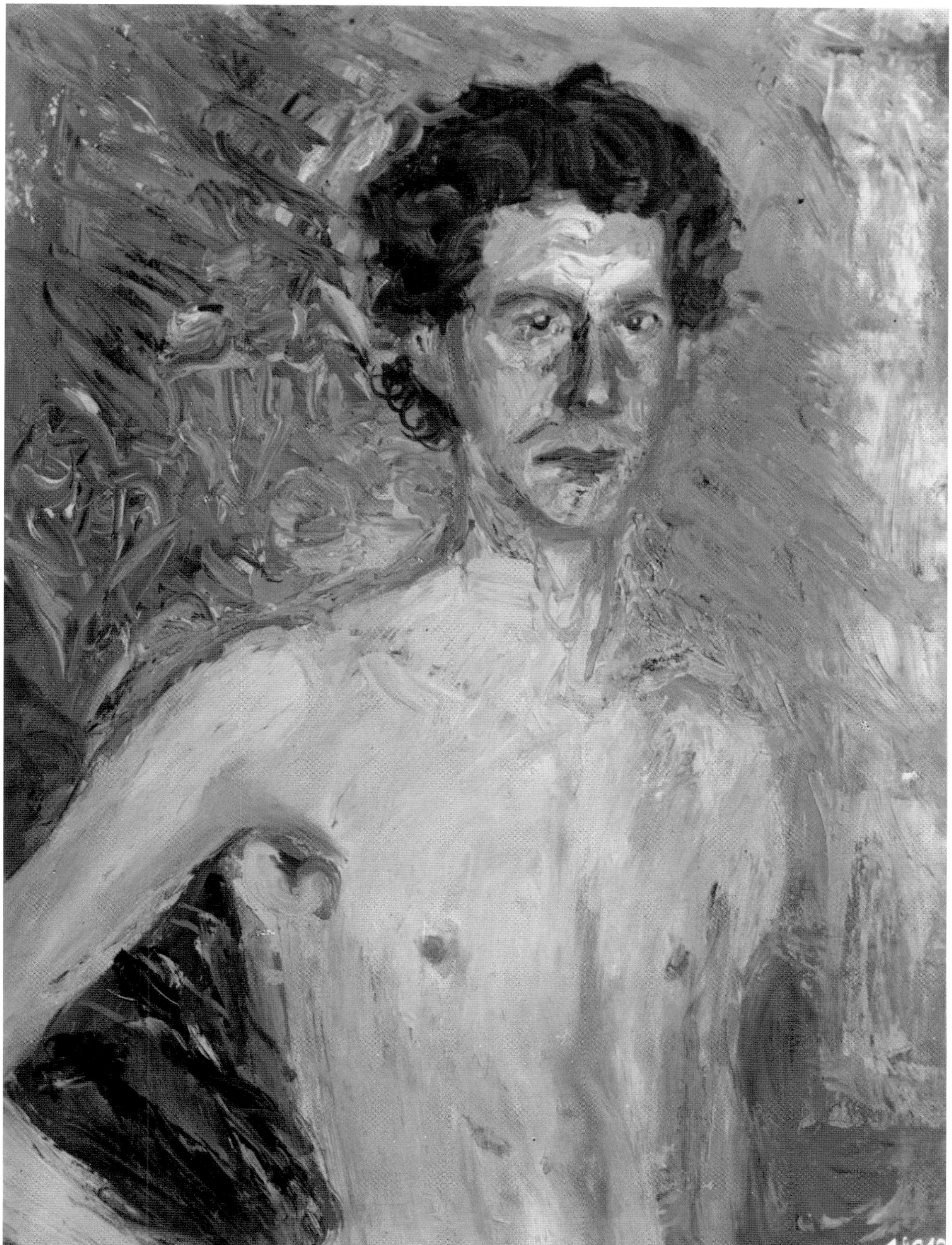

85

86

NUDE SELF-PORTRAIT/SELBSTBILDNIS ALS AKT, September 12, 1908

Oil on canvas
139.3 x 100 cm (54 7/8 x 39 3/8 in.)
Leopold Museum, Vienna**

According to Alois, his brother's full-length *Nude Self-Portrait,* was the last that Richard painted of himself. It was also the only one that Gerstl dated precisely, inscribing it as "12 September 1908," just two weeks after he had returned to his parents' apartment, where it was painted and hung in the brothers' bedroom until their disapproving father insisted that it be removed. While Gerstl defines his apartment with the swirls of a possible sofa on the left and perhaps a doorway to the right, opportunities to pose nude there would have been limited, so the jagged, intense, elongated brushwork that characterizes the work may reflect the speed with which it was conceived and executed. At the same time, the sharper definition of Gerstl's features suggests a momentary retreat from the developing abstraction of his recent Gmunden paintings. Moreover, in painting himself in mirror-image against a blue background, possibly a mirror, this may be a conscious reference to his 1902–04 *Semi-Nude Self-Portrait* [Cat. no. 6]. There, still a youth, Gerstl chose to cover his nakedness, whereas here, now a man, he did not, so that the two works can be seen as bookends in the artist's inveterate search for self-representation and sexual self-awareness. Equally, in delineating his upper body in the same eerie blue glow, he insulates himself, as in the earlier work, within a ghostly aura. In the earlier work he portrays himself as thin, but in this one he is positively emaciated, his ribcage visible, his waist pinched and his arms spindly. Moreover, his legs are disproportionately long, so that the effect of cropping them at the calf is to bring Gerstl's sex to the center of the canvas. This was plainly his intention since, as with the blur of his paint brushes in his hand, he painted it in a far deeper hue than the rest of his painfully pale torso. Some scholars find pre-suicidal tendencies in the work; however, Gerstl's *Nude Self-Portrait* may be interpreted to represent the emotions of an artist who is crowing at his potency, having slept with the wife of a man who was not only his friend, but a father figure, too.

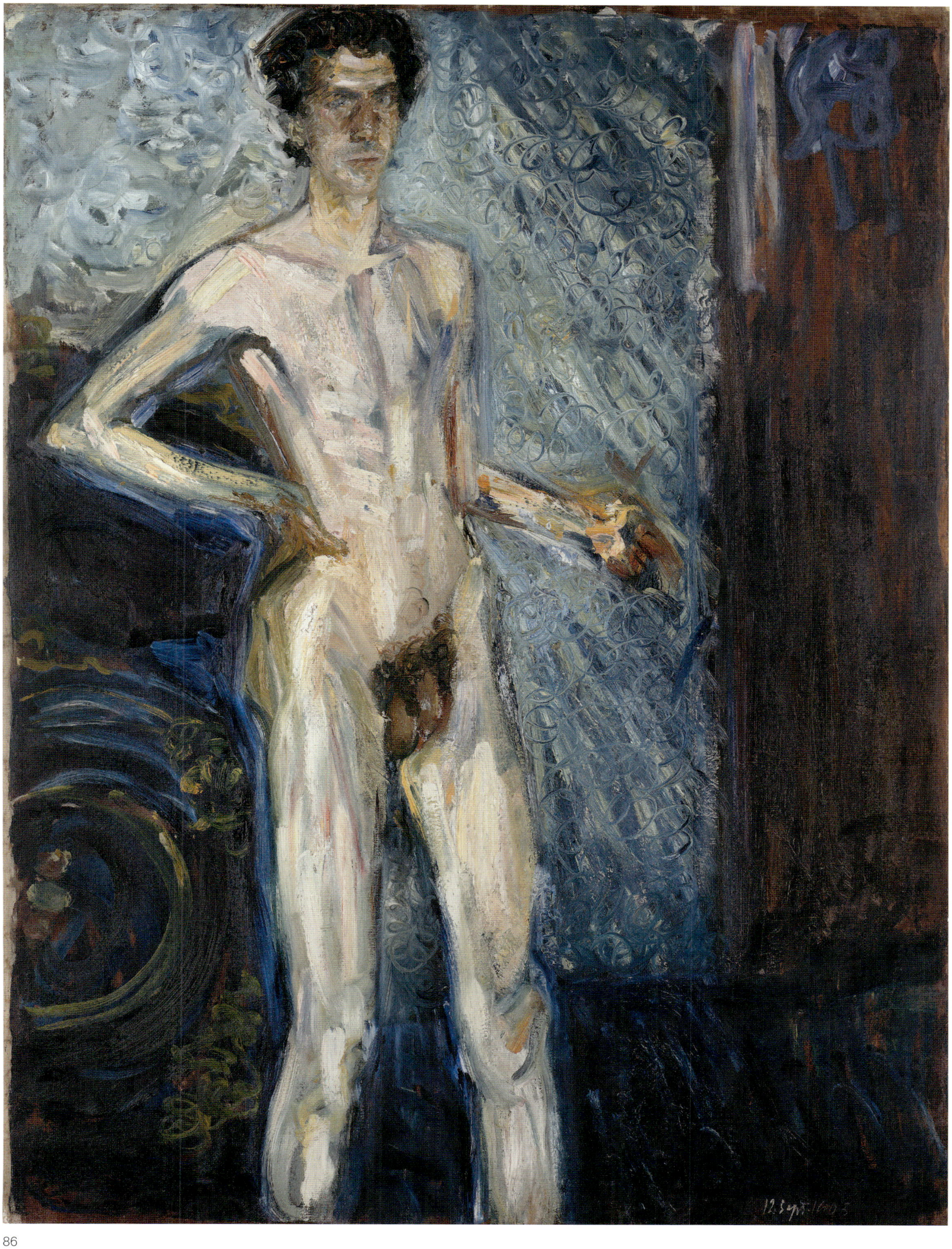

87

SEATED FEMALE NUDE/SITZENDER WEIBLICHER AKT), autumn 1908

Recto: *Portrait of a Young Woman in a Light Blue Dress and Feather Hat*, spring-summer 1906 [Cat. no. 17]
Tempera on canvas
166 x 116 cm (65 3/8 x 45 5/8 in.)
Leopold Museum, Vienna**

Gerstl moved into a commercial loft atelier in Liechtensteinstraße 20, in Vienna's ninth district, on October 18, 1908, with the intention to establish himself as a professional artist. At the same time, there is evidence that his affair with Mathilde had rekindled and that she visited his new studio, where he probably painted this life-size *Seated Female Nude* of her. The description of Mathilde by her son-in-law, Felix Greissle in 1970 is aptly repeated here: "She was not a beautiful woman, but was very attractive in her behavior; she had a very good figure, she was flirtatious." Presumably to avoid detection, the painting was executed quickly, using quick-drying tempera, applied thinly and speedily against a patchy background and the reflection of Gerstl's mirror. Moreover, the subject's face has been left either deliberately unfinished or obliterated, perhaps to prevent recognition. However, it is plain from the anecdotal recollections from Alois and his circle that that the subject was indeed Mathilde Schönberg and, moreover, that this was Gerstl's last work. This proved to be the case, for, on November 4, 1908, following Mathilde's return to her husband, Gerstl was excluded from a concert of Schönberg's students. The young artist, just 25 years of age, stabbed and hung himself, without warning, in front of his mirror in his new studio. His premature end brings a deep poignancy, for despite two of his final portraits being of the women he most loved, Gerstl, for separate reasons, failed to complete either.

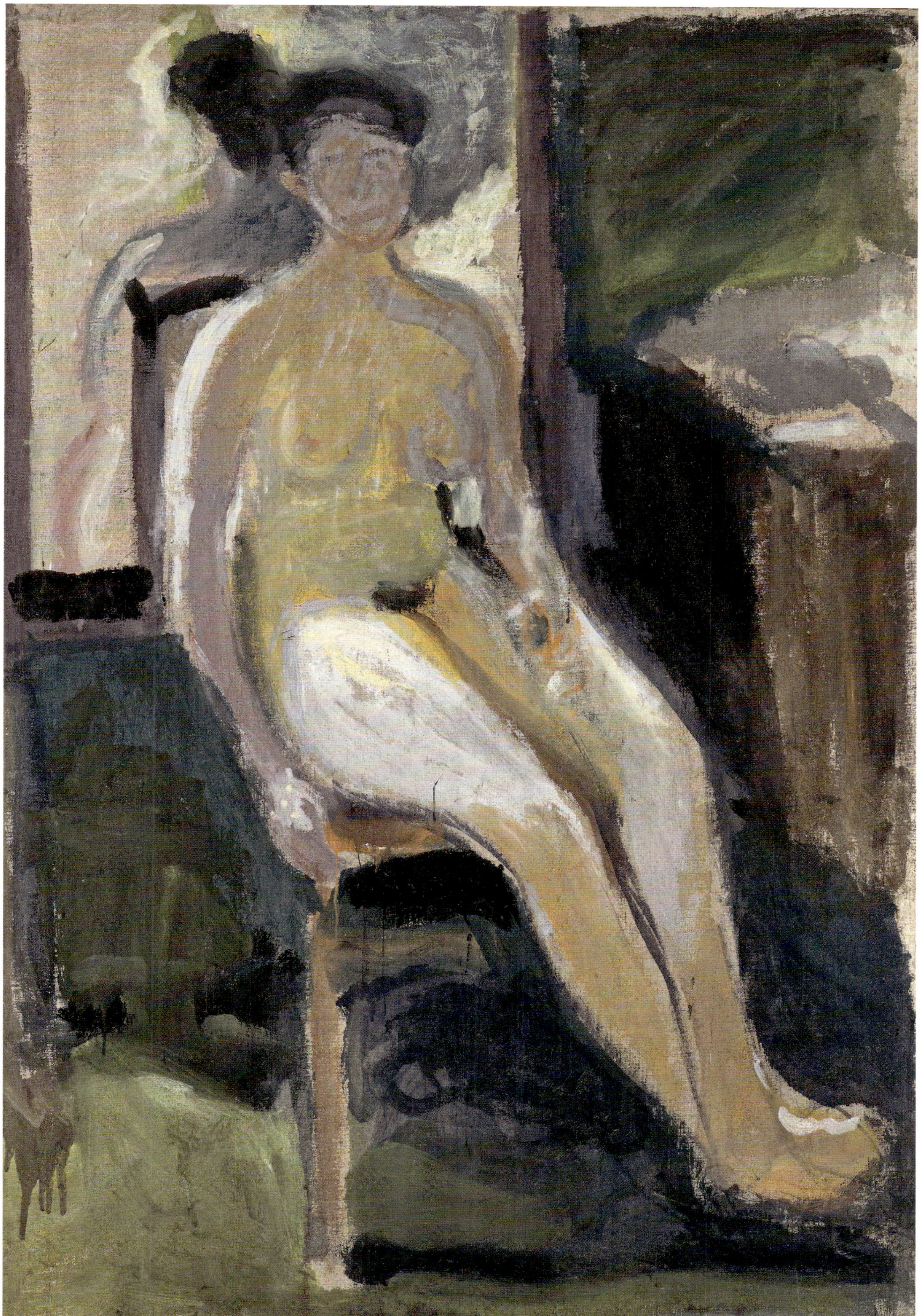

COMPARATIVE WORKS

Jill Lloyd

1

Gustav Klimt (1862–1918)

THE BLACK FEATHERED HAT, 1910

Oil on canvas

79 x 63 cm (31 ⅛ × 24 ¾ in.)

Private Collection

Richard Gerstl was determined to rebel against Gustav Klimt—the father figure of modern Viennese art—to the extent that he refused to exhibit his own paintings alongside Klimt's at the Galerie Miethke. Nevertheless, Klimt was also an unavoidable point of reference. Klimt set the standard for society portraiture, and in Gerstl's commissioned work in this genre, most notably in his depictions of musicians and friends in Arnold Schönberg's circle, he aimed to achieve a new expressive vitality. Klimt's *The Black Feathered Hat*, painted in 1910, shows the elder artist turning away from his ornamental and so-called "Golden Style" evident in portraits such as *Adele Bloch-Bauer I* of 1907, to explore a simplified, modern aesthetic he admired in French artists such as Henri Toulouse-Lautrec. Although he would have been unaware of Gerstl's work, Klimt was not unaffected by the innovations of the younger generation of Expressionists whose work was shown in Vienna at the 1909 "Internationale Kunstschau" at Klimt's behest. While Klimt clearly defines his subject with finely chiseled contours, by contrast Gerstl's pointillist brushwork dissolves the boundaries between his sitters and the surrounding space.

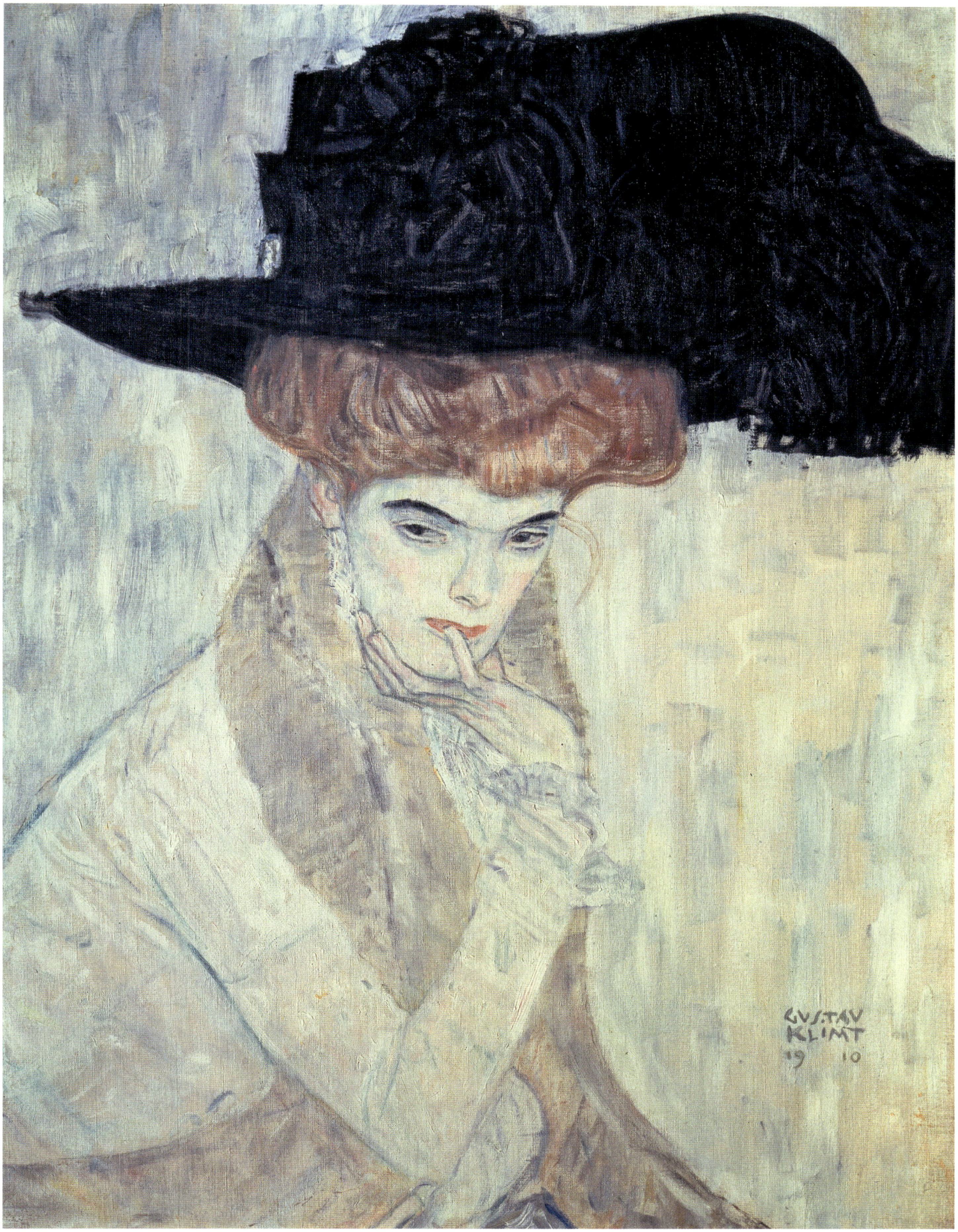

1

2
Oskar Kokoschka (1886–1980)
RUDOLF BLÜMNER, 1910
Oil on canvas
80 x 57.5 cm (31 ½ x 22 ⅝ in.)
Private Collection

Kokoschka's portrait of the avant-garde actor Rudolf Blümner is a superb example of the direction that Expressionist portraiture took in Vienna following Gerstl's death. In this instance, Kokoschka's combination of bold, painterly brushwork, vivid colors, and scratch marks made on the surface of the canvas with the end of his brush show the artist using every stylistic means at his disposal to heighten the painting's expressive impact. Although Gerstl's commissioned portraits are more restrained, his radically experimental paintings from the summer of 1908 depicting the Schönberg family and their circle clearly foreshadow and even surpass Kokoschka's expressive style. It is these works that justly earn Gerstl the title of first Austrian Expressionist.

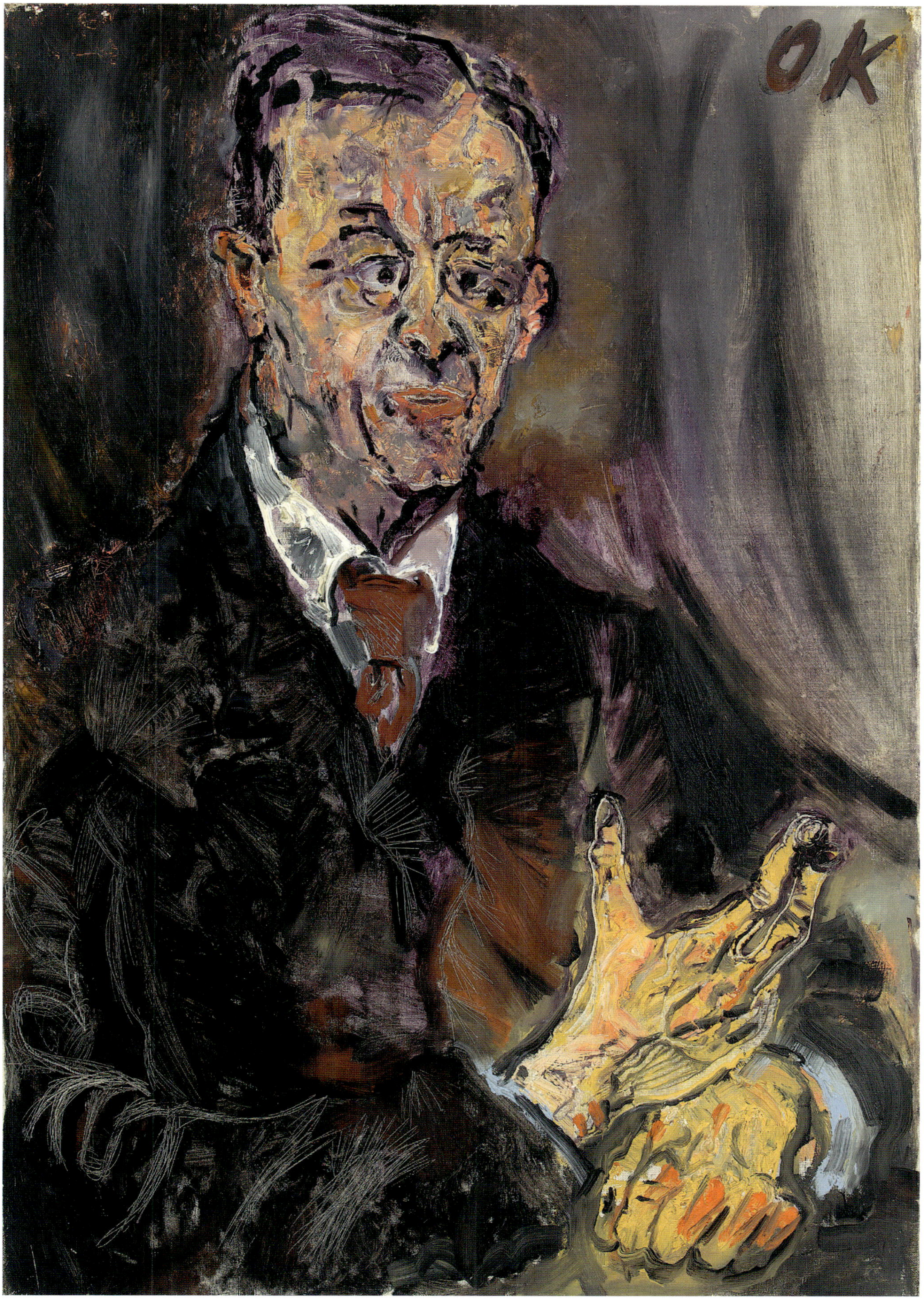

2

3

Egon Schiele (1890–1918)

PORTRAIT OF THE COMPOSER ARNOLD SCHÖNBERG, 1917

Watercolor, gouache and black crayon on paper
45.7 x 29.2 cm (18 x 11 ½ in.)
Private Collection

Arnold Schönberg's central position in the Viennese avant-garde is underscored by the many portraits that exist of the revolutionary musician created by various leading artists, including Richard Gerstl, Oskar Kokoschka, Max Oppenheimer, and Egon Schiele. Schönberg's gaunt, intense physiognomy in Schiele's colored drawing from 1917 bears only a tenuous relationship to the composer's actual appearance at this date, although it eerily predicts his features in old age. The drawing is nevertheless executed in the newly realistic style that Schiele adopted during the war years. The liberties Schiele takes with Schönberg's appearance allow him to focus on the inner man, and enable him to project his own gaunt features empathetically onto his subject. This confirms Schiele's strong personal identification with Schönberg as a leading protagonist of Viennese modernism.

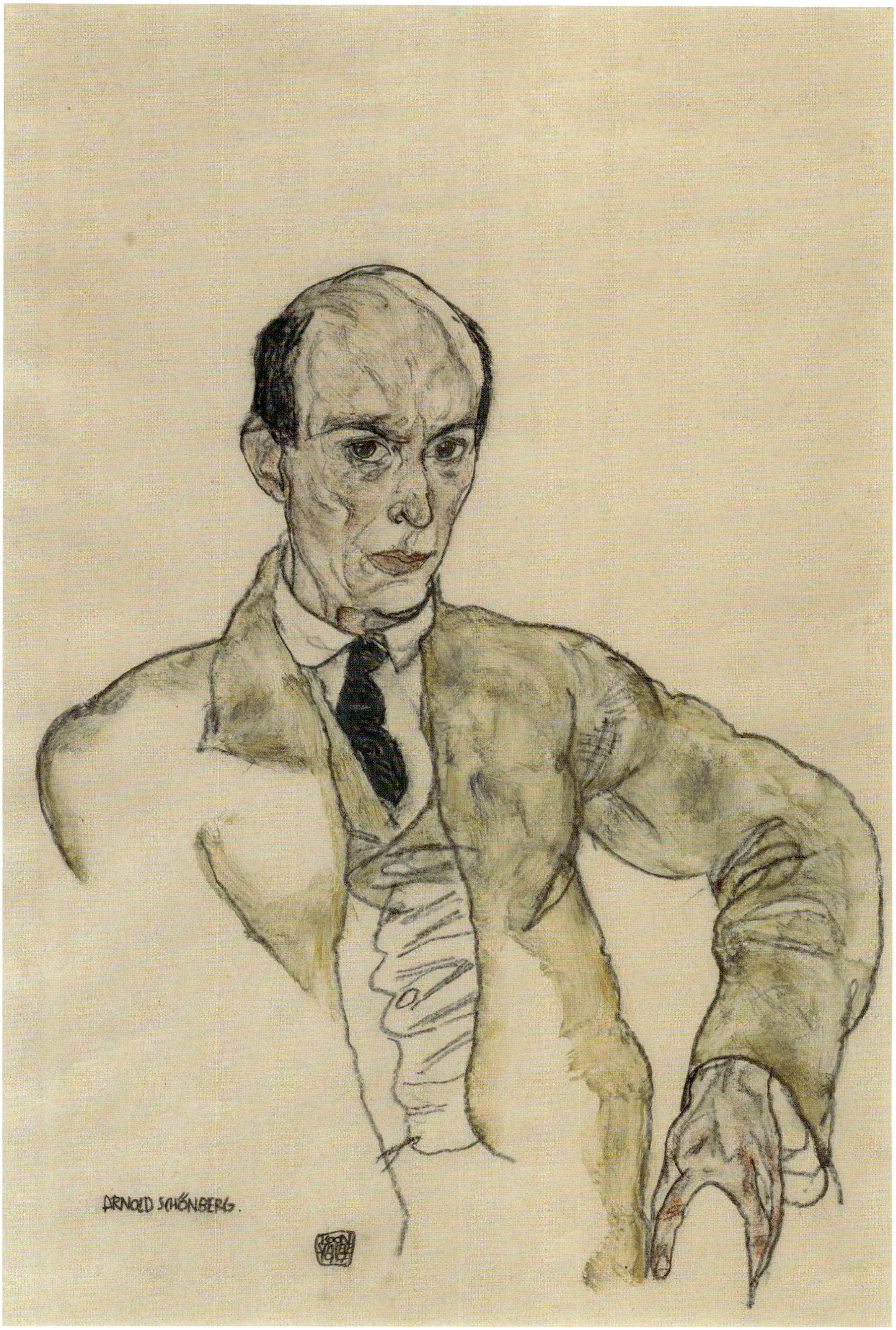

3

4
Arnold Schönberg (1874–1951)
SELF-PORTRAIT, ca. 1908
Watercolor, brush and ink on paper
39.8 x 29.9 cm (15 ⅝ x 11 ¾ in.)
Belmont Music Publishers, Pacific Palisades, Courtesy Arnold Schönberg Center, Vienna

5
Arnold Schönberg (1874–1951)
SELF-PORTRAIT, December 26, 1908
Brush, pen and ink
39.9 x 31.7 cm (15 5/8 x 12 ½ in.)
Belmont Music Publishers, Pacific Palisades, Courtesy Arnold Schönberg Center, Vienna

6
Arnold Schönberg (1874–1951)
SELF-PORTRAIT, 1910
Oil on board
33.9 x 22.2 cm (13 3/8 x 8 3/4 in.)
Belmont Music Publishers, Pacific Palisades, Courtesy Arnold Schönberg Center, Vienna

Self-portraiture was Arnold Schönberg's principal focus as a visual artist. Although his main period of activity in this regard lasted just five years, from 1906 (when he met Richard Gerstl) until 1911, he created self-portraits at important junctures throughout his lifetime. Given that Gerstl introduced Schönberg to painting, and they shared a studio in 1908, it is likely that he also transmitted his own predilection for self-portraiture. Indeed, Gerstl's self-portrait drawings from 1906–07, where he starkly confronts his face and barely indicates his shoulders, are a clear precedent for this similar series by Schönberg dating from around 1910. The two artists' mutual fascination with "severed" heads was possibly inspired by Edvard Munch, whose similarly decapitated *Portrait of Stanislaw Przybyszewski* (see p. 30) was shown in Vienna in 1906 at Hugo Heller's bookshop and gallery, where Schönberg himself exhibited in 1910. Like Munch, both Gerstl and Schönberg focus on the intense expressive potential of the head and gaze in their self-portraits. In his *Blue Self-Portrait,* Schönberg employs non-realistic color to convey mood and expression, while *Red Gaze* moves a step further away from realism, echoing Munch's famous symbolic image of *The Scream,* and reducing the composer's features to little more than his haunted, red-rimmed eyes. Art historian Jean Clair suggests that Schönberg's emotive self-portrait series was an attempt on the composer's part to come to terms with the trauma of Gerstl's suicide.

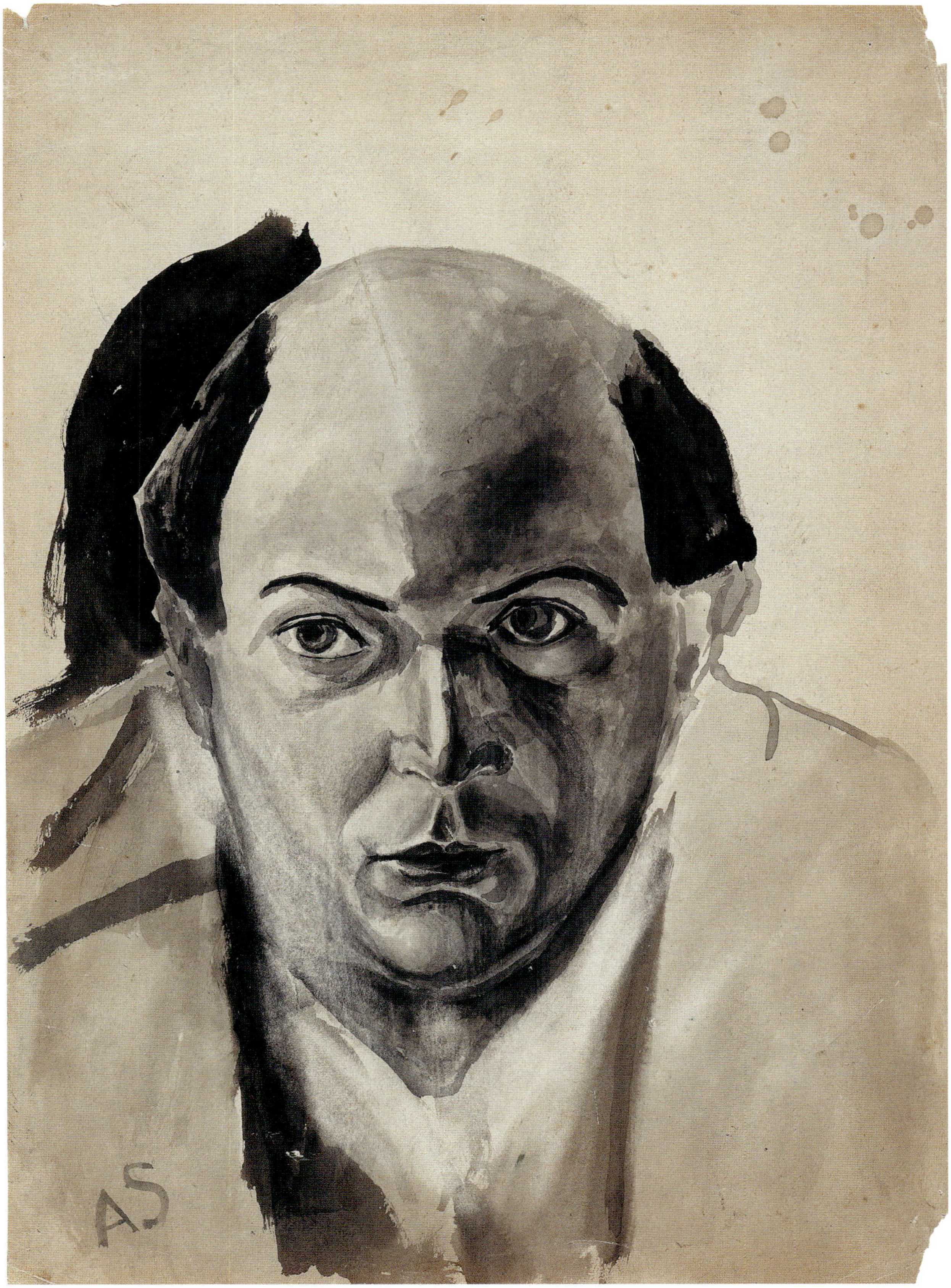

4

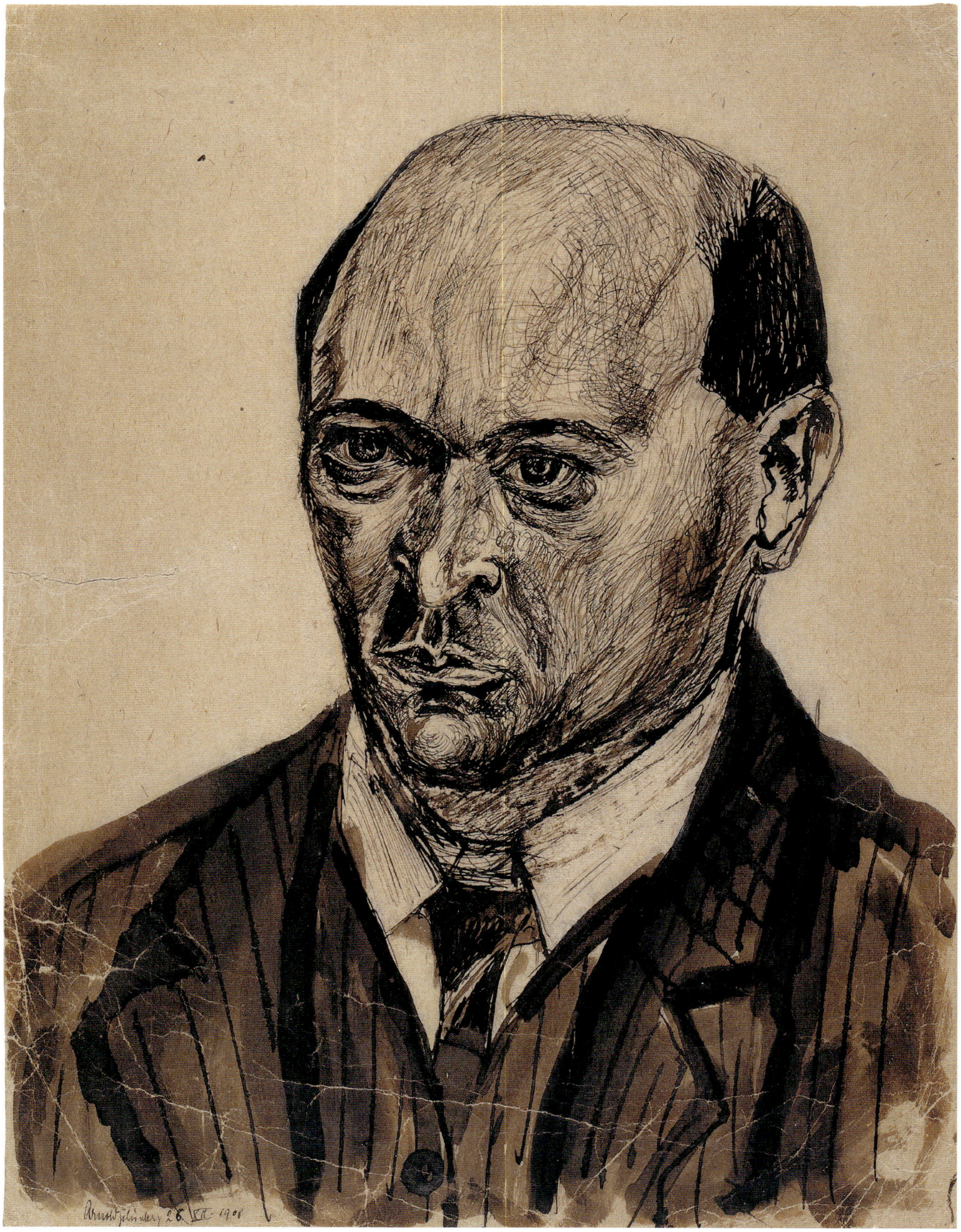

5

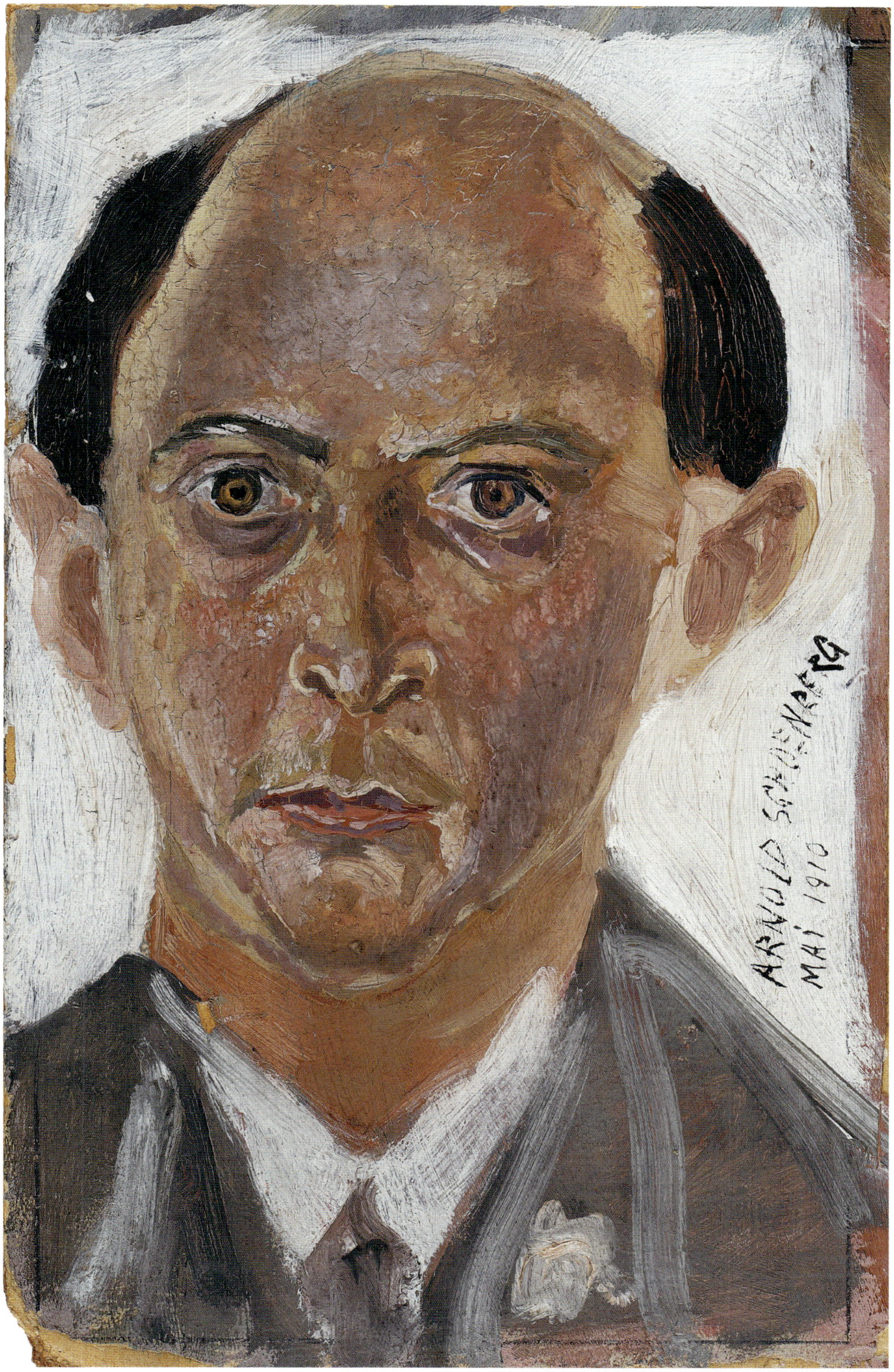

6

7
Arnold Schönberg (1874–1951)
GREEN SELF-PORTRAIT, 1910
Oil on board
33.2 x 24.7 cm (13 ⅛ x 9 ¾ in.)
Belmont Music Publishers, Pacific Palisades, Courtesy Arnold Schönberg Center, Vienna

8
Arnold Schönberg (1874–1951)
BLUE SELF-PORTRAIT, 1910
Oil on three-ply panel
31.1 x 22.9 cm (12 ¼ x 9 in.)
Belmont Music Publishers, Pacific Palisades, Courtesy Arnold Schönberg Center, Vienna

9
Arnold Schönberg (1874–1951)
GAZE, 1910
Oil on board
32.2 x 24.6 cm (12 ⅝ x 9 ⅝ in.)
Belmont Music Publishers, Pacific Palisades, Courtesy Arnold Schönberg Center, Vienna

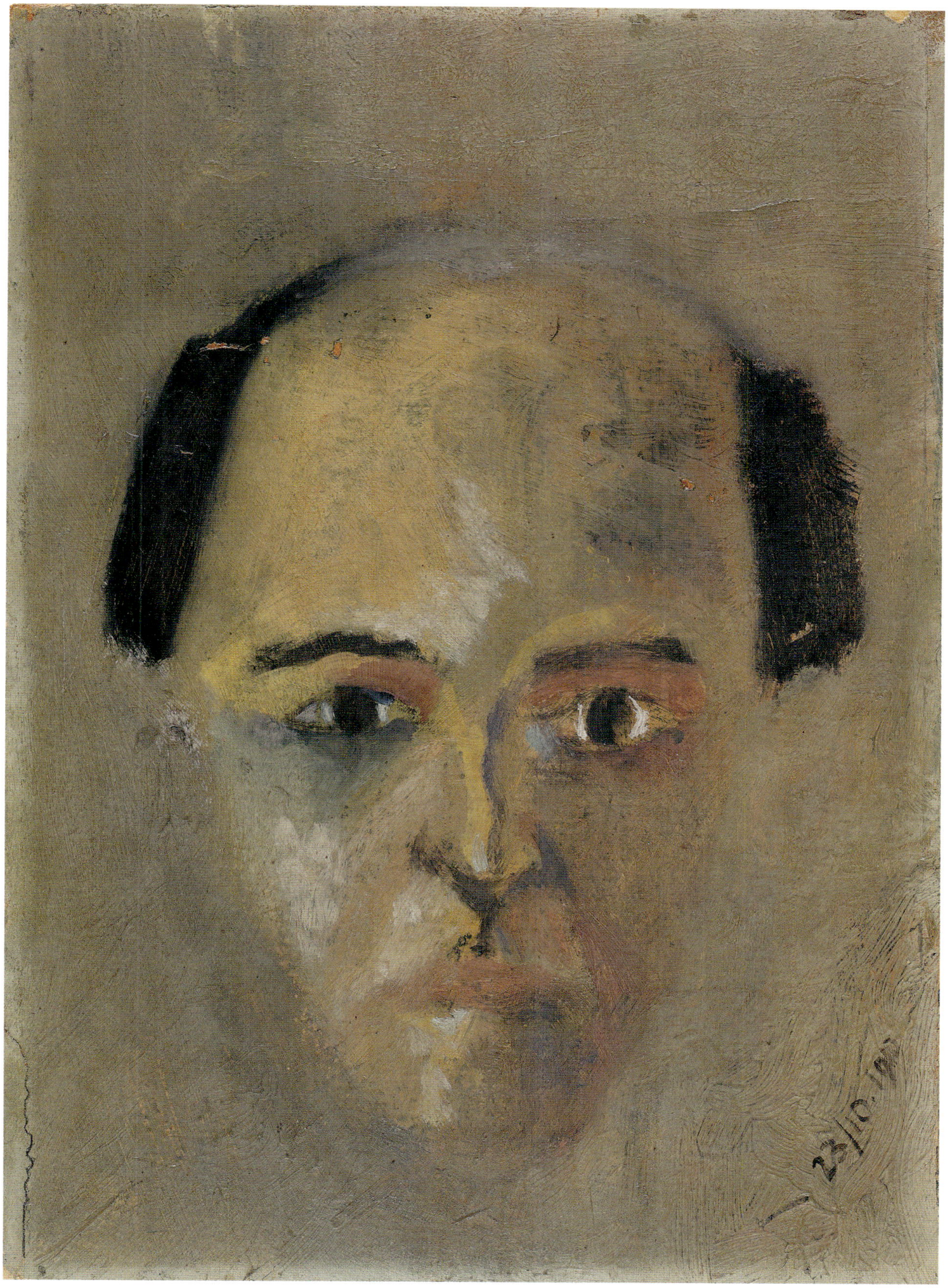

7

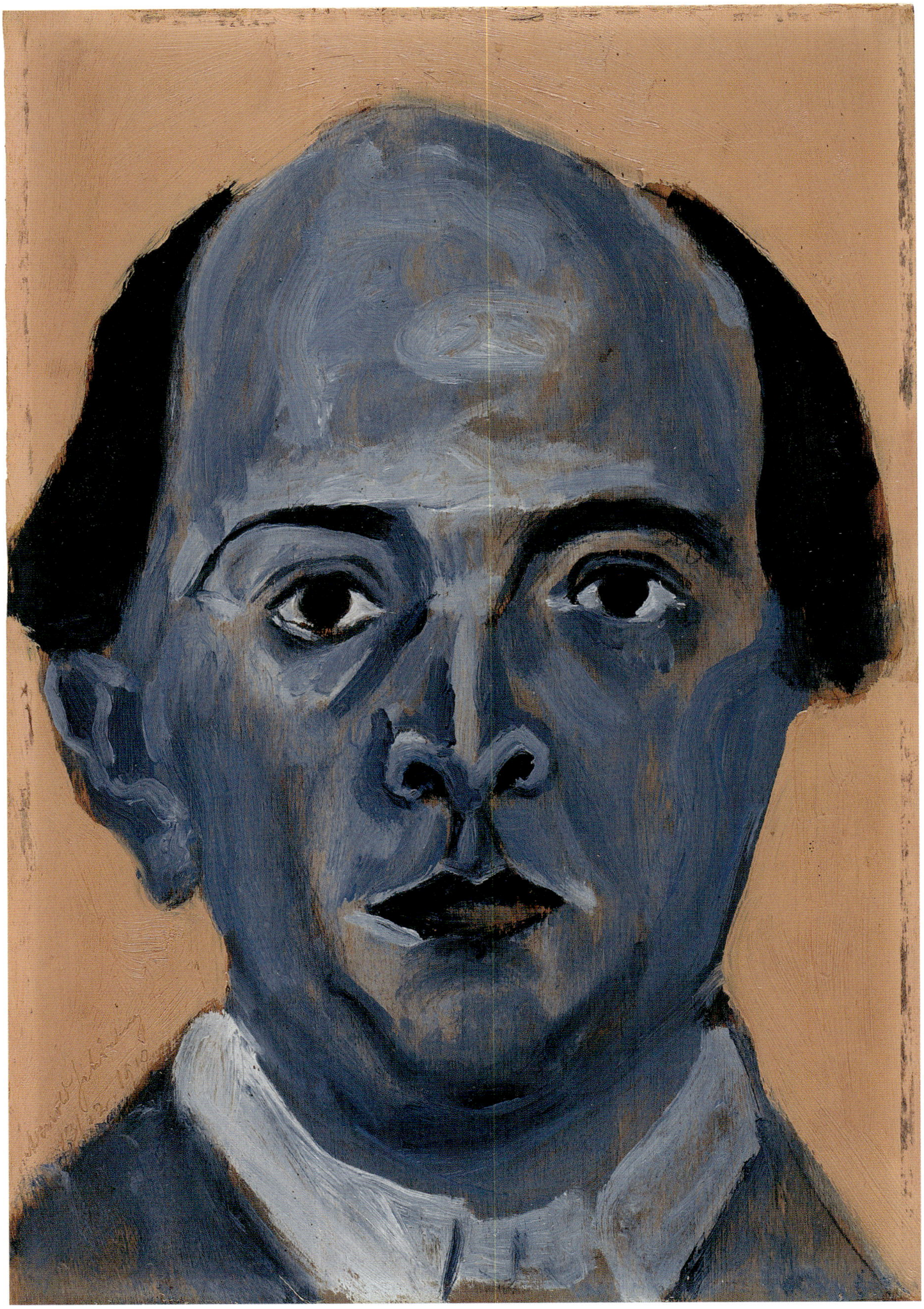

8

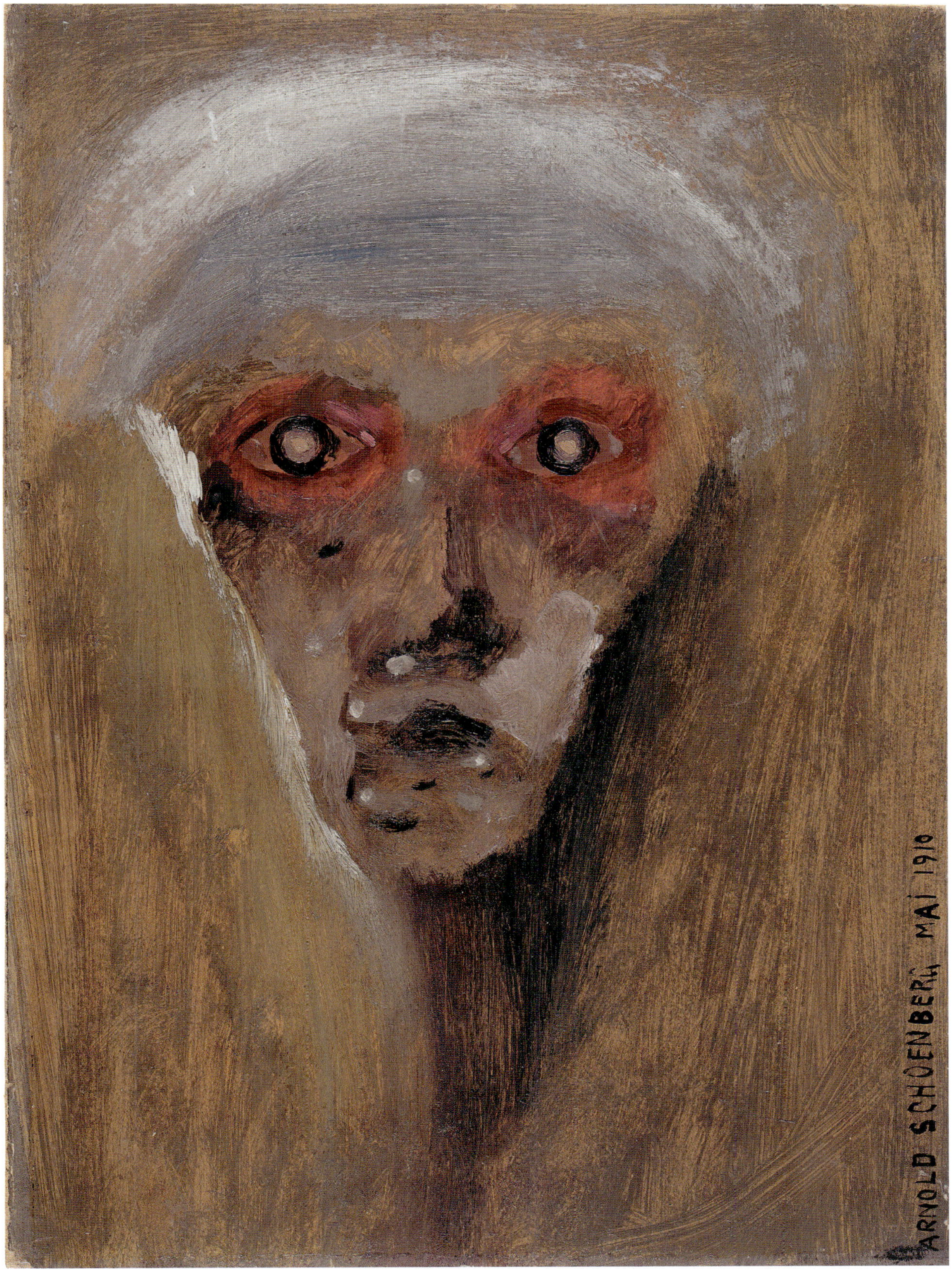

9

10
Arnold Schönberg (1874–1951)
SELF-PORTRAITS WITH MATHILDE SCHÖNBERG, ca. 1907–09
Brush, ink and pencil on paper
25.8 x 31.9 cm (10 ⅛ x 12 ⅝ in.)
Belmont Music Publishers, Pacific Palisades, Courtesy Arnold Schönberg Center, Vienna

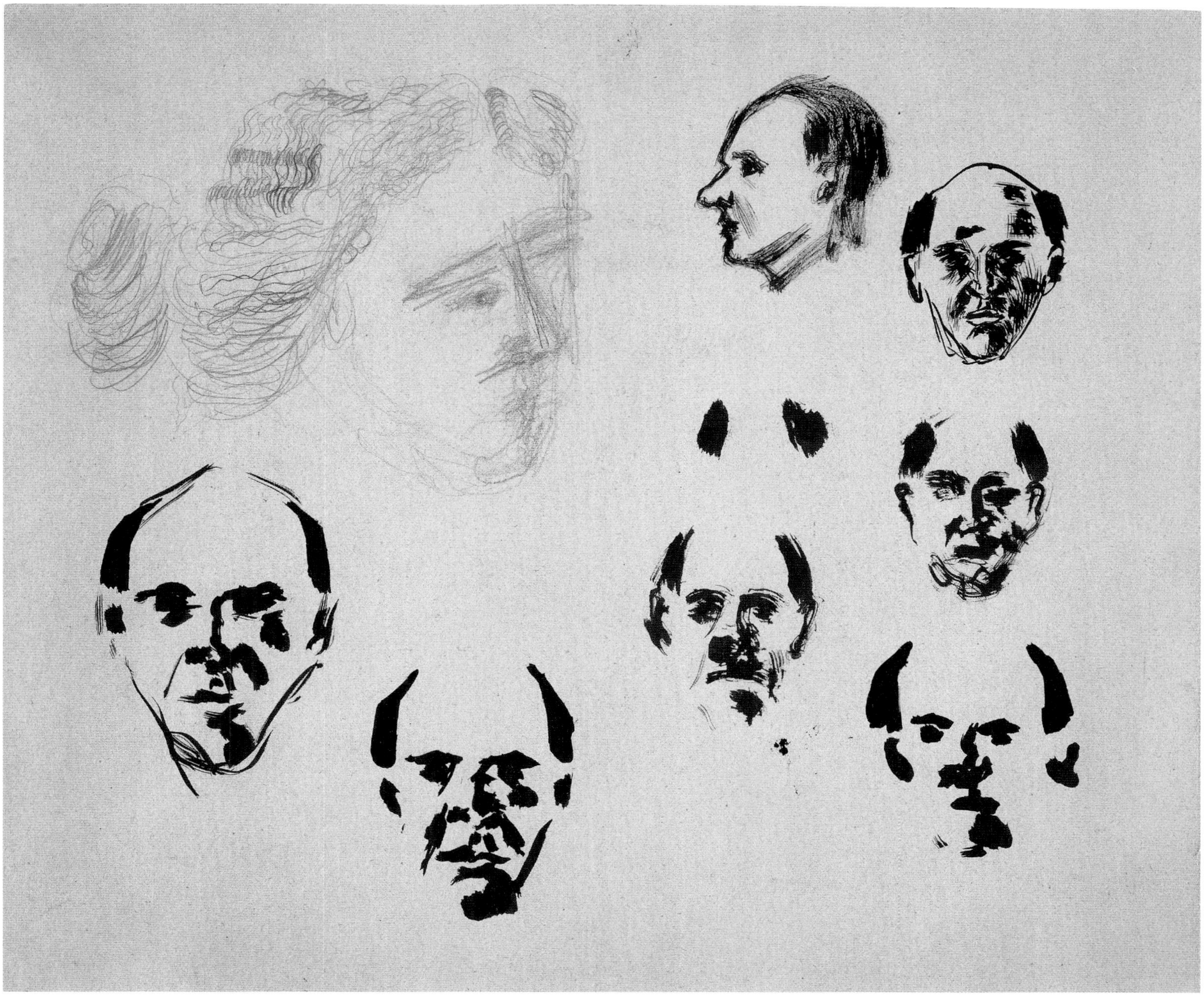

10

11

Arnold Schönberg (1874–1951)

ERWARTUNG, OP. 17, ca. 1911

Watercolor, pastel, brush and ink on paper
31.4 x 45 cm (12 ⅜ x 17 ¾ in.)
Belmont Music Publishers, Pacific Palisades, Courtesy
Arnold Schönberg Center, Vienna

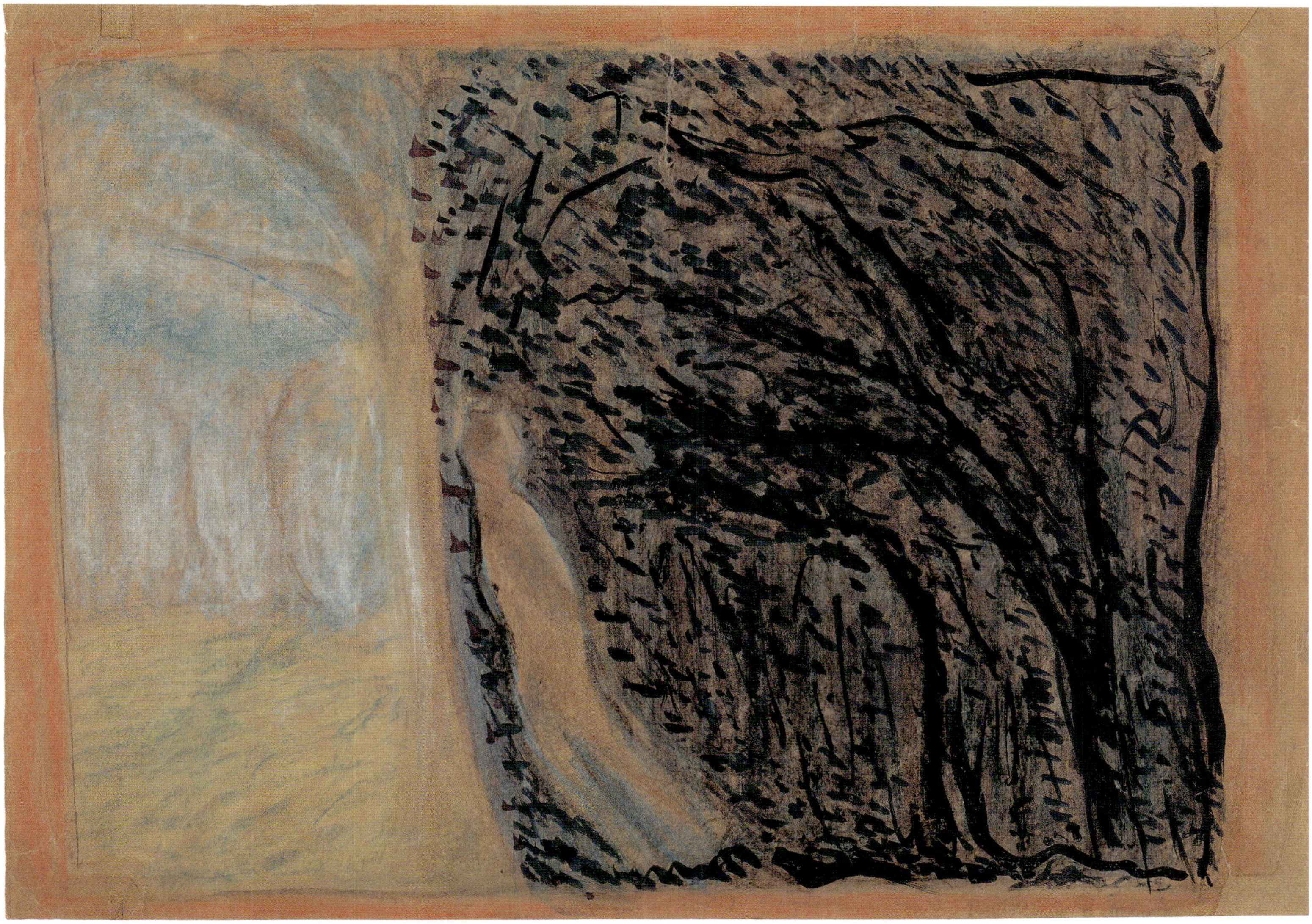

11

12

Arnold Schönberg (1874–1951)

NOCTURNE III, ca. April 1911

Oil on panel

21 x 20 cm (8 ¼ x 7 ⅞ in.)

Belmont Music Publishers, Pacific Palisades, Courtesy Arnold Schönberg Center, Vienna

Schönberg explored expressive effects in scenographic works closely related to his musical compositions. For example, his evocative drawing *Erwartung* from around 1911 refers to his one-act monodrama in four scenes, which Schönberg wrote in 1909. Schönberg depicts his female protagonist lost in the forest, where she searches for her lover, eventually finding him dead and wandering off alone into the night. Like his contemporary series of *Nocturnes,* this imaginary scene illustrating Schönberg's Opus 17 invokes an atmosphere of menace and solitude by juxtaposing darkness with bright light, offsetting the mysterious mood that dominates the scene.

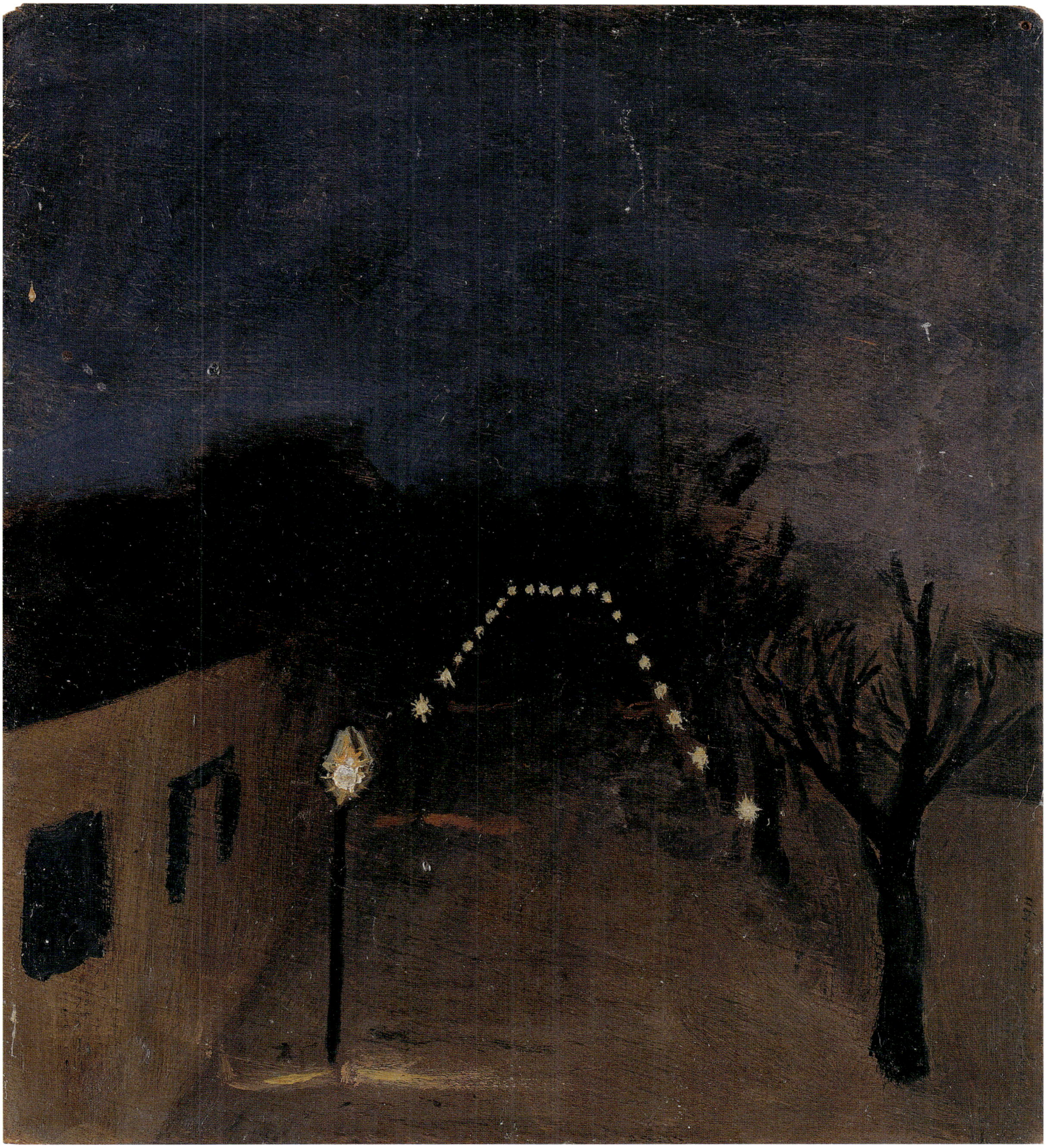

12

13
Arnold Schönberg (1874–1951)
MEMORY OF OSKAR KOKOSCHKA, 1910
Oil on board
31.3 x 35.5 cm (12 ⅜ x 14 in.)
Belmont Music Publishers, Pacific Palisades, Courtesy Arnold Schönberg Center, Vienna

14
Arnold Schönberg (1874–1951)
RED GAZE, 1910
Oil on board
28 x 22 cm (11 x 8 ⅝ in.)
Belmont Music Publishers, Pacific Palisades, Courtesy Arnold Schönberg Center, Vienna

15
Arnold Schönberg (1874–1951)
TO THINK, before October 1910
Oil on board
22.3 x 25.1 cm (8 ¾ x 9 ⅞ in.)
Belmont Music Publishers, Pacific Palisades, Courtesy Arnold Schönberg Center, Vienna

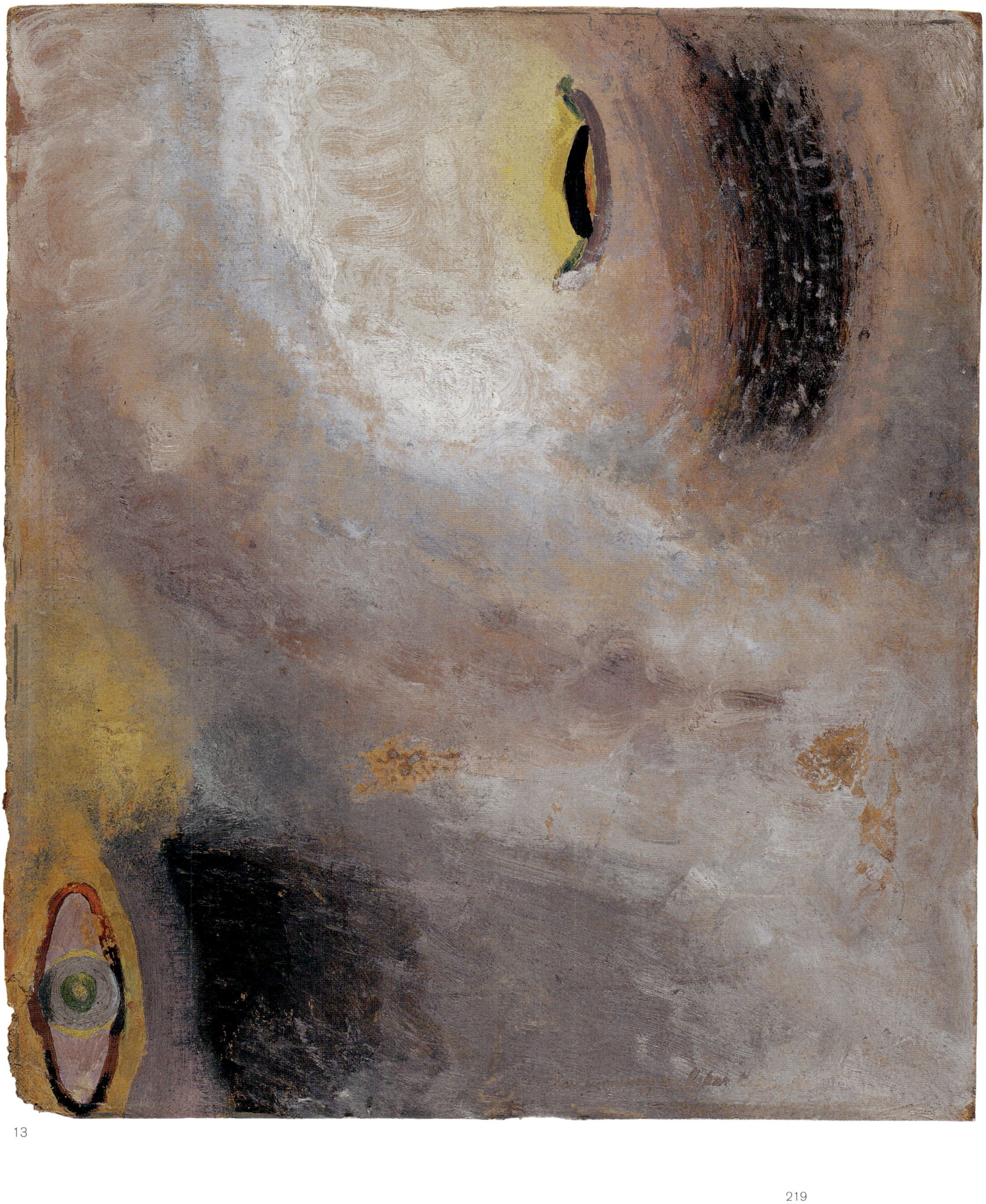

13

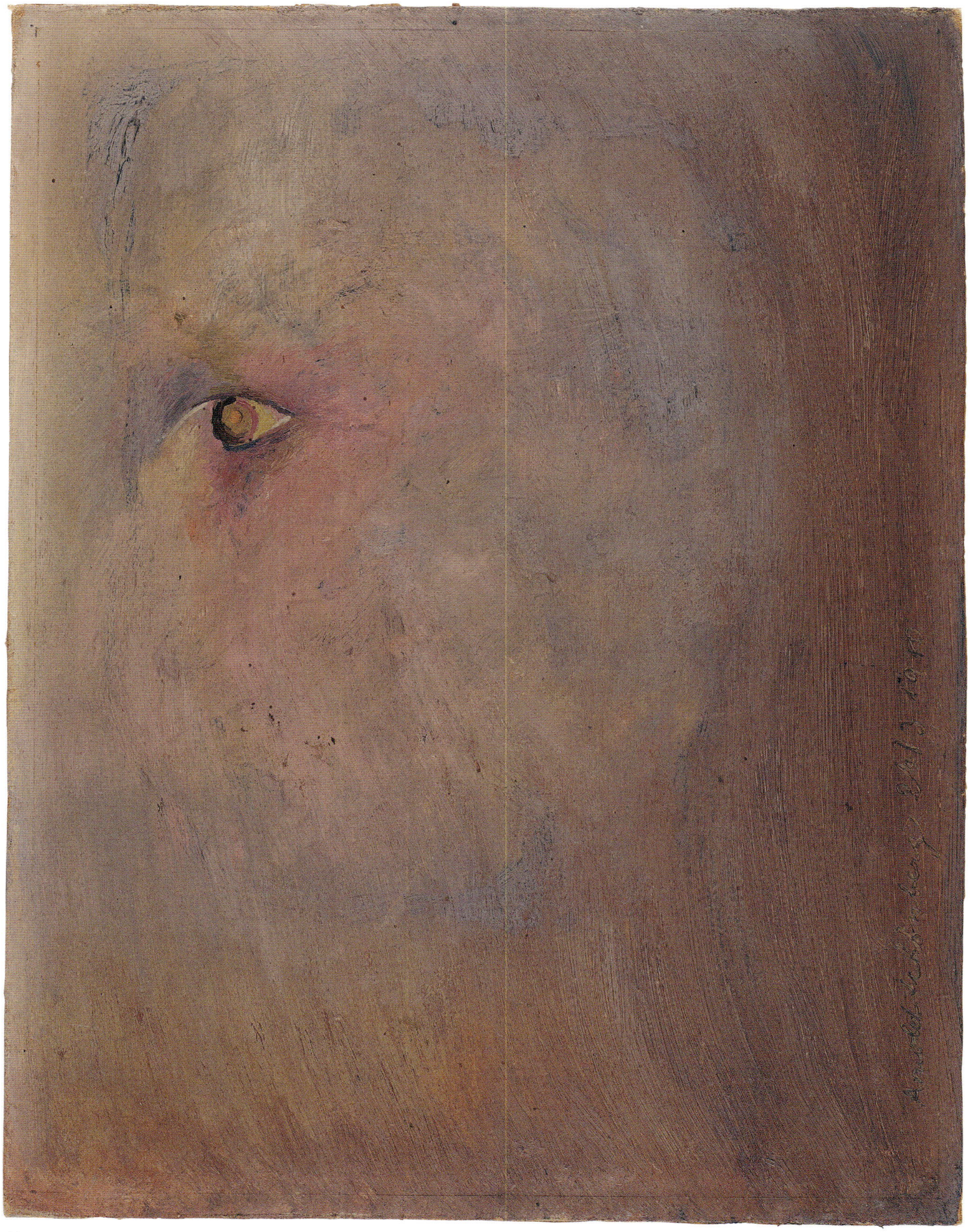

14

15

16
Arnold Schönberg (1874–1951)
VISION (MATHILDE), 1923
Oil on canvas
59 x 46 cm (23 1/4 x 18 1/8 in.)
Courtesy Galerie St. Etienne, New York

Before World War I, Schönberg's work was celebrated by the Expressionist avant-garde and included in key exhibitions, such as the first Blaue Reiter show held in 1911. The following year, 23 works by Schönberg were displayed alongside works by Egon Schiele and Oskar Kokoschka at the exhibition "Neukunst Wien" (New Art from Vienna) held in Budapest.

Schönberg's *Visions*, sometimes referred to as "Impressions" and "Fantasies," were the most experimental aspect of his work, which Vasily Kandinsky associated with expressions of a spiritual state that had not found a musical form. In *To Think* and *Memory of Oskar Kokoschka,* Schönberg pushes toward the brink of abstraction while he simultaneously composed radical musical compositions that feature the absence of traditional keys and tonal centers, such as *Erwartung* (1909), *Die glückliche Hand* (1910–13) and *Pierrot Lunaire* (1912). Raymond Coffer convincingly describes Gerstl's role in Schönberg's artistic development. The young artist's extraordinary creative advances spurred the composer to finish his Second String Quartet, Opus 10, in the summer of 1908. It is likely that Gerstl's attack on pictorial harmony in favor of a radical dissolution of form also influenced Schönberg's strange formal dislocations in his *Visions*. The final work in this series, *Vision (Mathilde)* was painted after his wife's death in 1923.

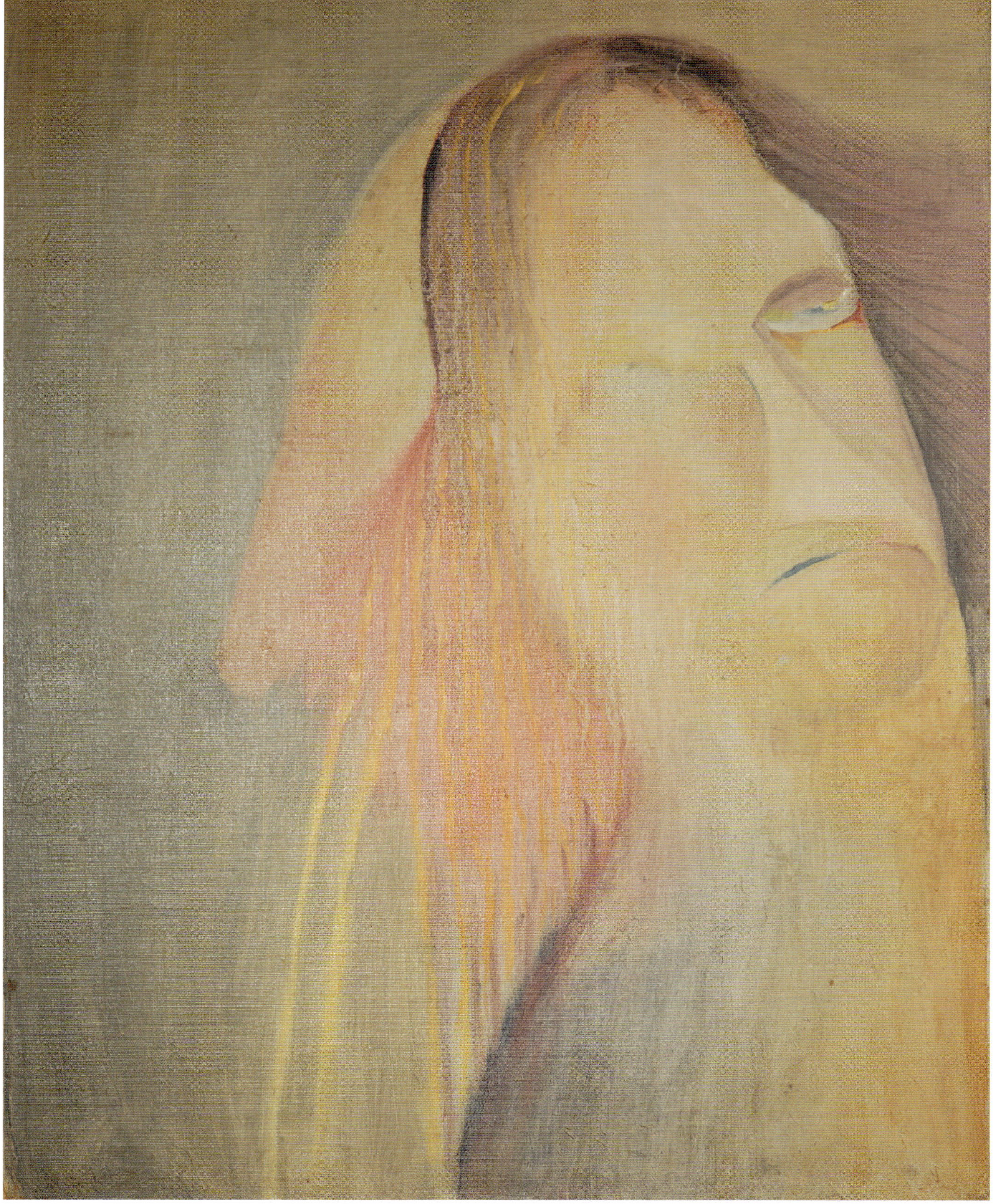

16

17

William Clarke Rice (1875–1928)

PORTRAIT OF RICHARD GERSTL, 1907

Oil on canvas
66 x 52.1 cm (26 x 20 ½ inches)
Private Collection, Courtesy Galerie St. Etienne

American artist and illustrator William Clarke Rice painted the only known surviving portrait of Richard Gerstl. The two men met in the holiday resort of Gmunden, where Gerstl spent the summer of 1907 along with Arnold Schönberg and his circle. Rice joined the group with his wife Melanie to celebrate a belated honeymoon. Melanie Guttmann-Rice was a Viennese opera and concert soprano who had previously been engaged to Alexander Zemlinsky. She developed a successful career in New York and married Rice in 1905. Rice portrayed Gerstl with a sober expression and formally attired in a shirt, tie, and jacket; Gerstl frequently depicted himself in similar dress in various self-portraits, including *Self-Portrait in front of a Stove* (winter 1906–07 [Cat. no. 33]) and *Self-Portrait* (winter 1907–spring 1908 [Cat. no. 63]). Raymond Coffer posits that the artist's short hair and beard suggest that Rice's portrait can be dated as consistent with his *Self-Portrait, Laughing* (summer–autumn 1907 [Cat. no. 54]). Nonetheless, Gerstl's manic expression and disheveled dress in this latter work contrasts starkly with the reserved formality of this work.

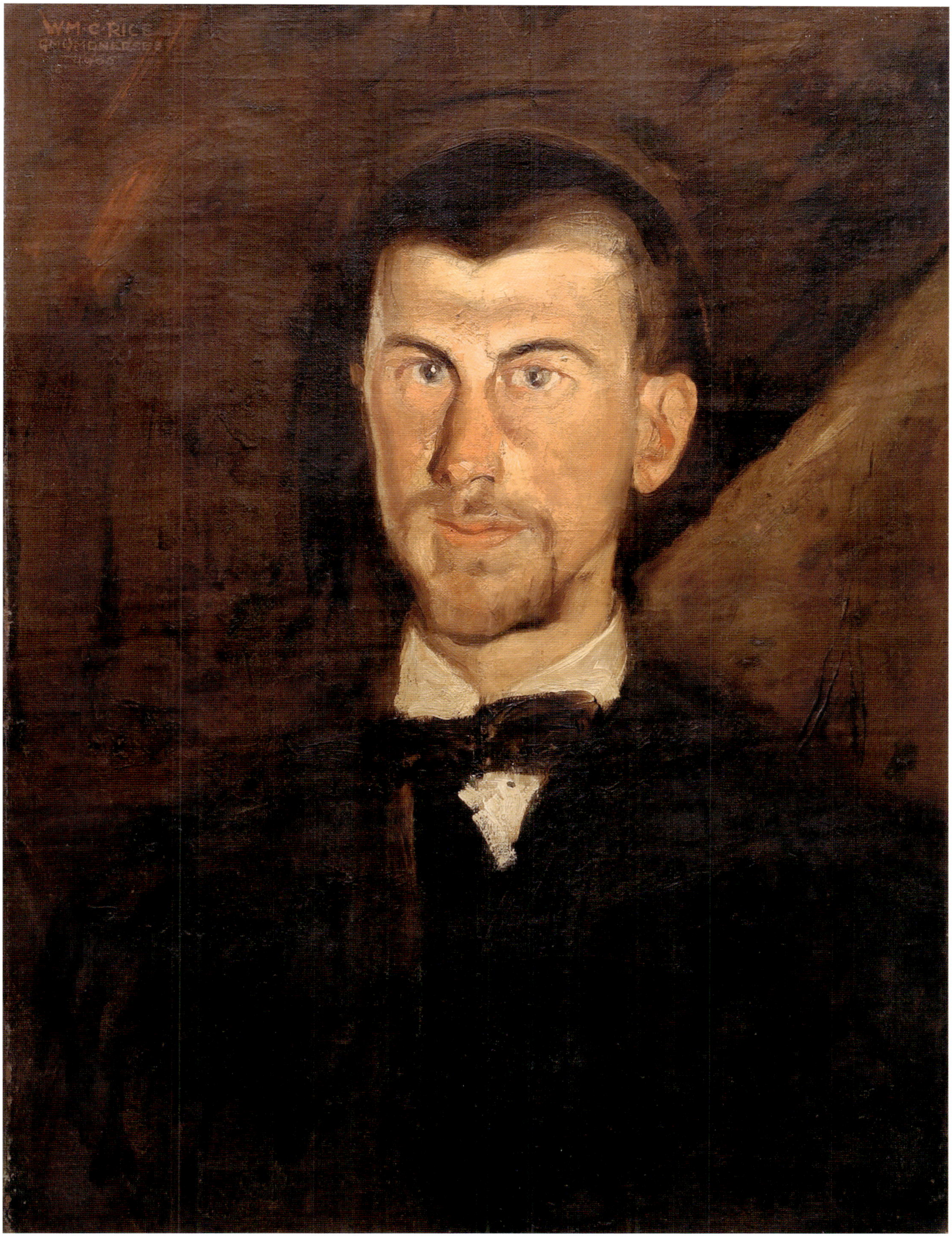

17

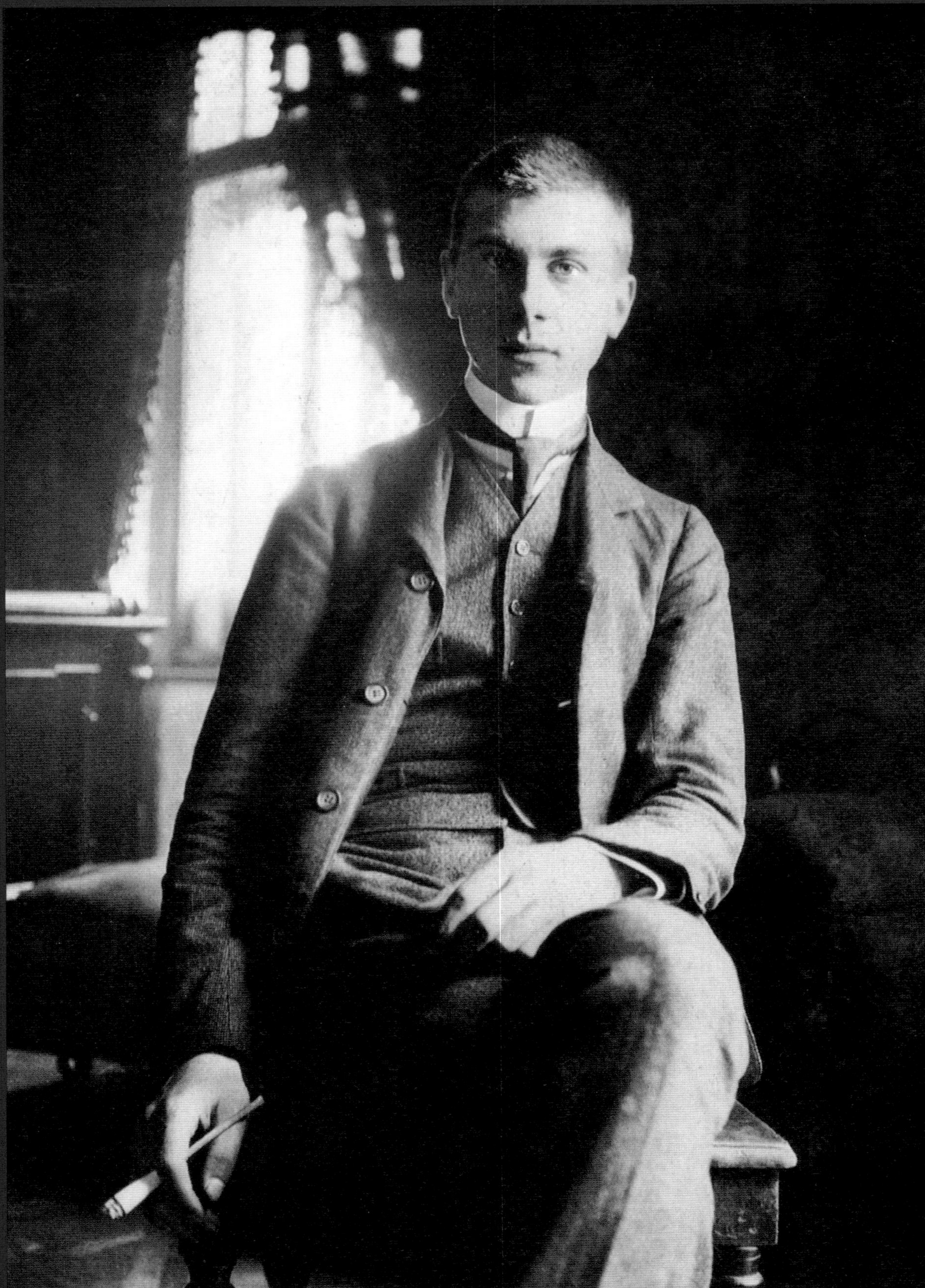

MARIA SITTE

Chronology

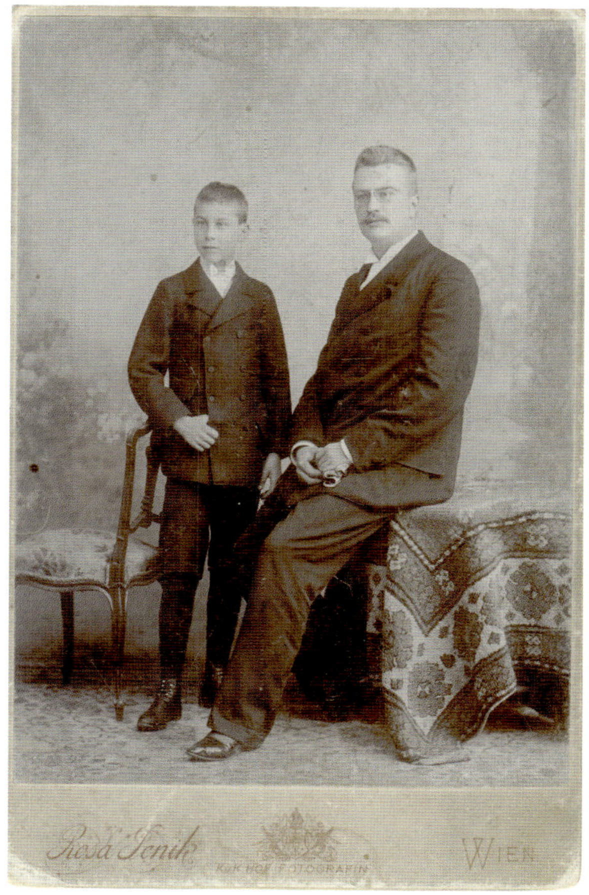

Richard Gerstl with his sponsor Dr. Karl Weihsböck, May 26, 1896. Archiv Otto Breicha, Vienna

1883

Richard Gerstl was born in Vienna on September 14, 1883. He was the youngest of three sons born to Maria (née Pfeiffer, 1857–1910) and Emil Gerstl (1834–1912).

Gerstl's father was a native of Nyitra in what was then Hungary (now Nitra, Western Slovakia). He was a businessman of Jewish descent who amassed a substantial fortune, thus ensuring financial security and an upper-middle-class standard of living for his family. Gerstl's mother, whose ancestors came originally from Kaplitz, near Budweis (now České Budějovice, Czech Republic), was a Christian. She insisted that her son be baptized into the Roman Catholic Church.

After completing his primary eductation, Gerstl spent two years at the Maria Treu Gymnasium, a prestigious secondary school run by the Piarists in Vienna, before transferring to the Meixner Private School in 1897. While still a student, he took drawing lessons from Otto Frey, who was enrolled at the Akademie der bildenden Künste (Academy of Fine Arts).

1898

During the summer, Gerstl attended classes at the Aula drawing school under the direction of Ladislaus Rohsdorfer in preparation for the admissions examination for the Academy in Vienna.

Gerstl was accepted by the Academy at the age of fifteen and enrolled in the Allgemeine Malschule (General School of Painting) headed by Professor

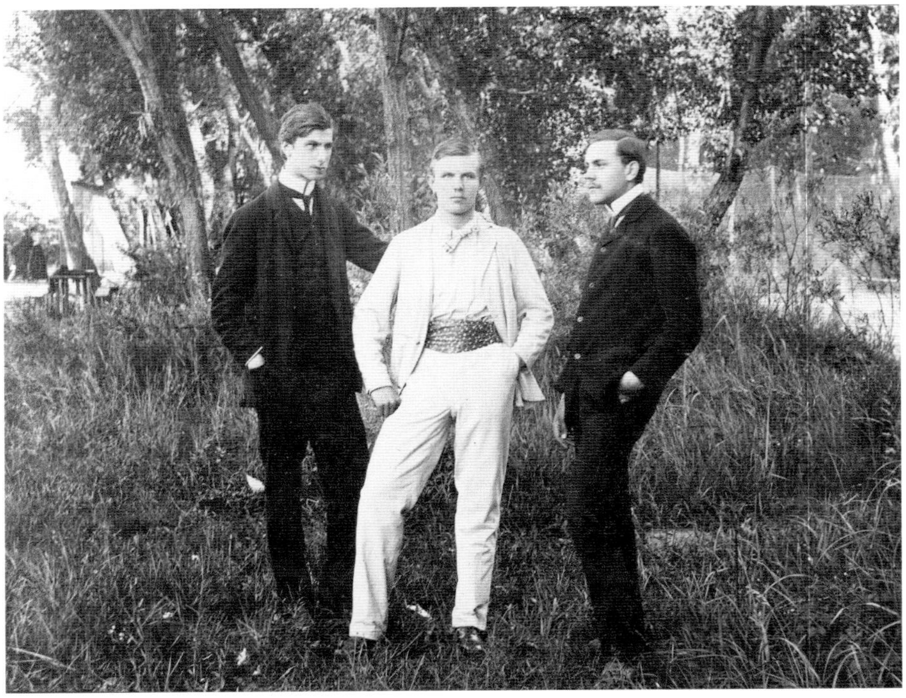

Richard Gerstl, Waldemar Unger and Alois Gerstl, around 1900. Archiv Otto Breicha, Vienna

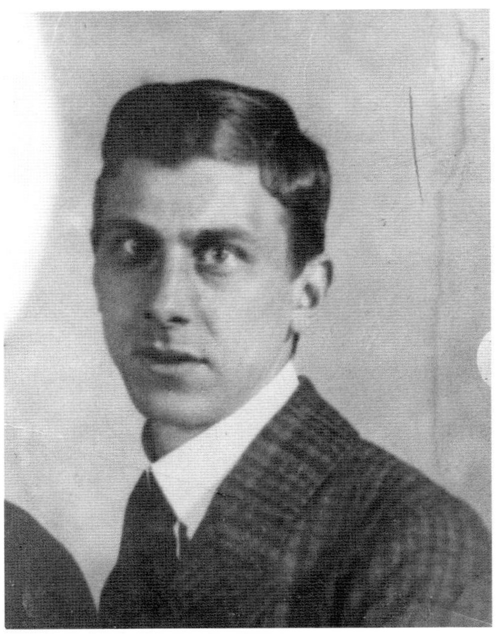

Richard Gerstl. Archiv Otto Breicha, Vienna

Christian Griepenkerl, eight years before Egon Schiele first attended the same school. Gerstl received financial support from his family throughout his lifetime. His mother encouraged his artistic ambitions, while his father expressed skepticism.

1900-01

Gerstl spent the summer at the free painting school operated by the Hungarian painter Simon Hollósy in Nagybánya. The local artists' colony was regarded as a center of modern art around the turn of the century and became a gathering point for young international artists, who were attracted to its unusually progressive teaching methods. In keeping with the colorist style of French Impressionism, *plein air* painting was taught in Nagybánya, based on aesthetic principles that clashed with Griepenkerl's conservative manner of teaching.

1901

The relationship between Griepenkerl and Gerstl as teacher and student was plagued by constant tensions. Gerstl was discouraged after receiving the grade of "satisfactory," and felt that his work was not appreciated. Consequently, he interrupted his studies for three years. Gerstl left the Academy in July of 1901. A transcript of Gerstl's course of study at the Academy since 1898 was issued in October.

1902–04

Gerstl rented his first studio on Haubenbiglgasse in Döbling before moving to the Therese-Krones-Haus on Hohe Warte 37 in Heiligenstadt. He continued to study as an autodidact and learned Italian and Spanish with the aid of the Langenscheidt method. An avid student of philosophy and literature, he was particularly interested in the writings of Otto Weininger and Sigmund Freud's *The Interpretation of Dreams*, as well as the plays of Henrik Ibsen and Frank Wedekind. Gerstl also pursued intensive studies in music theory and attended opera performances and symphony concerts in Vienna every week.

Gerstl maintained few close personal contacts during this period. Aside from members of his family, he was close only to Waldemar Unger, a friend from his youth and a prospective attorney, and fellow student Victor Hammer, who was about the same age as Gerstl. (Hammer left the Academy shortly after Gerstl's departure.) There is no evidence of ties to artists' circles in Vienna. His brother Alois, to whom he was also very close, recalled that Gerstl did not think much of contemporary Viennese painters.

According to Alois, Gerstl painted his first self-portrait, in which he appears nude against a blue background, at the age of nineteen [Cat. no. 6]. This work occupies a prominent place in the artist's oeuvre by virtue of its interpreted symbolic character.

1904-05

In October, Gerstl resumed his attendance in Griepenkerl's class. He completed the basic course for the General School of Painting and was compelled to leave Griepenkerl's course permanently after two semesters, shortly before the winter term of 1905–06.

Gerstl met Gustav Mahler, Director of the Wiener Hofoper (Royal Opera of Vienna), whom he greatly admired, and asked to paint his portrait. Regrettably, Mahler denied the request.

1906

Gerstl took a temporary studio at Gumpendorferstrasse 11, which he may have shared with Victor Hammer, who had already transferred to Professor Heinrich Lefler's Systemisierte Spezialschule für Landschaftsmalerei (Systematized Special School of Landscape Painting) at the Academy. Lefler, a co-founder of the Hagenbund (an association of Austrian artists), was regarded as one of the most progressive members of the Academy faculty at the time.

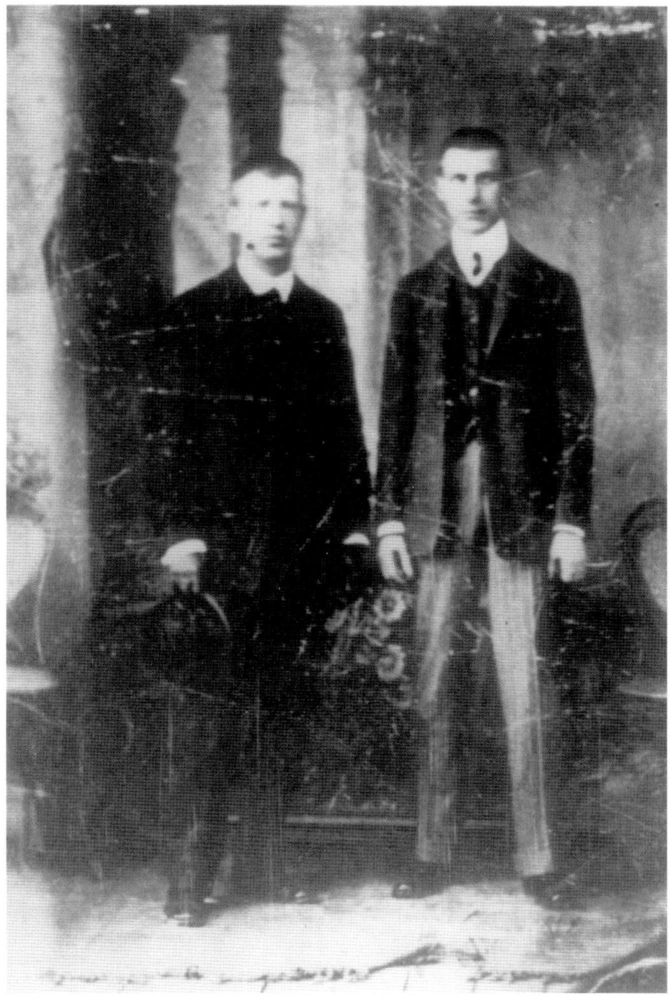

Victor Hammer and Richard Gerstl. Archiv Otto Breicha, Vienna

Arnold Schönberg in the family apartment, Liechtensteinstraße 68/70. Gerstl's *Portrait of Mathilde Schönberg* hangs in the background. Private Collection/Courtesy Arnold Schönberg Center, Vienna

Mathilde Schönberg in the family apartment with Gertrud (Trudi) and Georg, Liechtensteinstraße 68/70. Gerstl's *Portrait of Mathilde Schönberg* hangs in the background. Private Collection/Courtesy Arnold Schönberg Center, Vienna

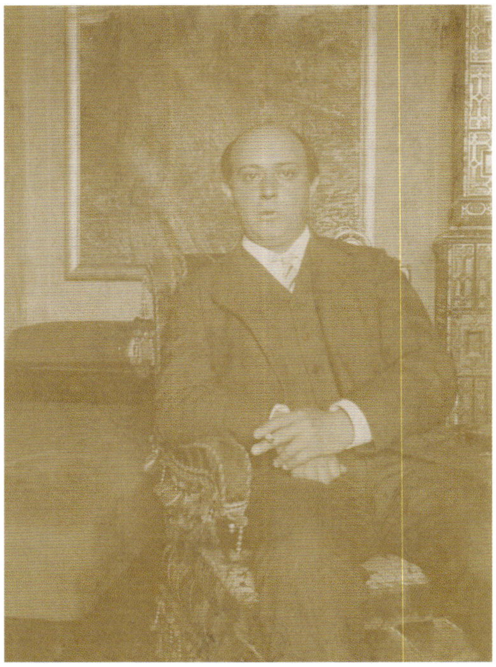

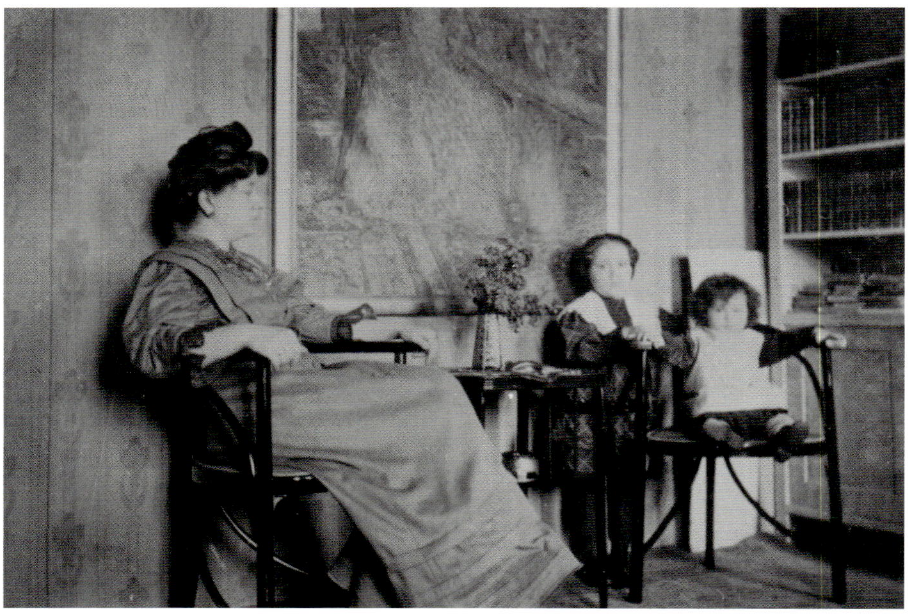

Lefler invited Gerstl to join his class in March after seeing his painting entitled *The Sisters Karoline and Pauline Fey* [Cat. no. 12]. Gerstl accepted on the condition that he be given his own studio at the Academy. His fellow students included Franz Wacik, Ignaz Schönfeld, Victor Hammer, and Anton Kolig.

That spring, Gerstl became acquainted with the composer Arnold Schönberg (1874–1951) and his wife Mathilde (1877–1923), to whom he gave private lessons in painting.

He painted Arnold Schönberg's portrait [Cat. no. 15] early that summer and completed the first of eight portraits of Mathilde, in this case with her daughter [Cat. no. 16], during June 1906.

Gerstl was admitted immediately to the so-called "Schönberg Circle," a close-knit group of musicians, composers, and students of Schönberg's, many of whose portraits Gerstl would subsequently paint. Through Schönberg, Gerstl met the composer's brother-in-law, the conductor and composer Alexander Zemlinsky, art historian Ernst Diez, pianist Smaragda Berg, and composers Alban Berg, Anton Webern, Egon Wellesz, Heinrich Jalowetz, and Victor Krüger. Gerstl even briefly considered embarking on a career as a music critic.

1907

Gerstl accepted Schönberg's invitation to spend the summer months with his group in Gmunden on the Traunsee. There, Gerstl devoted himself to landscape and *plein air* painting and completed his largest series of landscapes [Cat. nos. 36-51]. In addition to the Schönberg family, four of Schönberg's students, namely Victor Krüger, Heinrich Jalowetz, Anton Webern, and Karl Horwitz, were also there. The friendship between Gerstl and Mathilde Schönberg evolved into a clandestine love affair. When this commenced is unknown.

1908
The once close relationship between Lefler and Gerstl deteriorated due to disagreements on cultural policy. Gerstl questioned his teacher's commitment in support of the parade held on June 12, 1908, in honor of the 60th anniversary of Emperor Franz Josef's accession to the throne. Gerstl expressed harsh criticism of the exhibition planned by the Hagenbund.

Lefler briefly considered exhibiting Gerstl's works at the Hagenbund, but the idea was ultimately abandoned for fear of scandal. Gerstl rejected the offer of an exhibition proposed by Dr. von Wymetal, the President of the Ansorge-Verein, for reasons unknown. Gerstl's plan to take part in a presentation at the Galerie Miethke, which was managed by Carl Moll, came to nothing because Gerstl refused to exhibit his work alongside that of Gustav Klimt.

Gerstl moved into a second studio in the Schönbergs' house on Liechtensteinstraße 68/70 in February. He joined the Schönbergs in Gmunden at Traunsee again at the end of June.

Clearly upset by recent events, Gerstl sent a letter (see p. 17) to the Ministry of Culture and Education on July 22 in which he complained that his paintings had not been presented at the Academy exhibition that opened on July 19. That, he wrote, had robbed him of the chance to win the special school prize, which was awarded to fellow student Ignaz Schönfeld. The reaction of his professors to this letter, which was forwarded by the Ministry to the Principal of the Academy, was one of dismay and denial.

While vacationing on the Traunsee, Gerstl painted the two group portraits of the Schönberg family [Cat. nos. 78-79], both of which are characterized by a highly gestural painting style and a correspondingly high level of abstraction. In late August, Arnold Schönberg was painfully confronted by the affair between his wife and Gerstl. Leaving

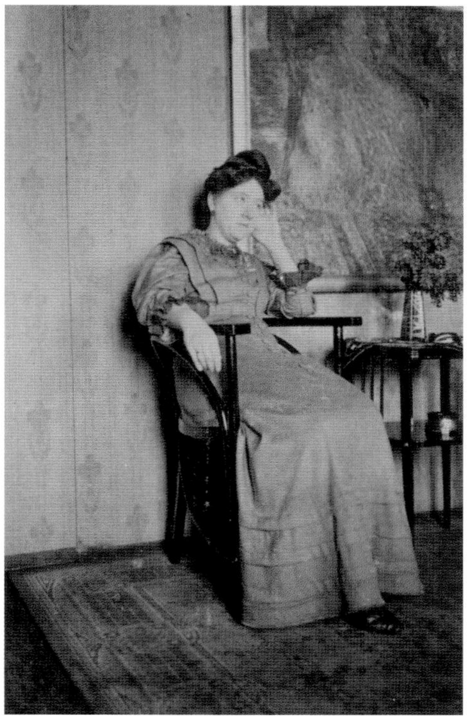

Mathilde Schönberg, 1907. Private Collection/Courtesy Arnold Schönberg Center, Vienna

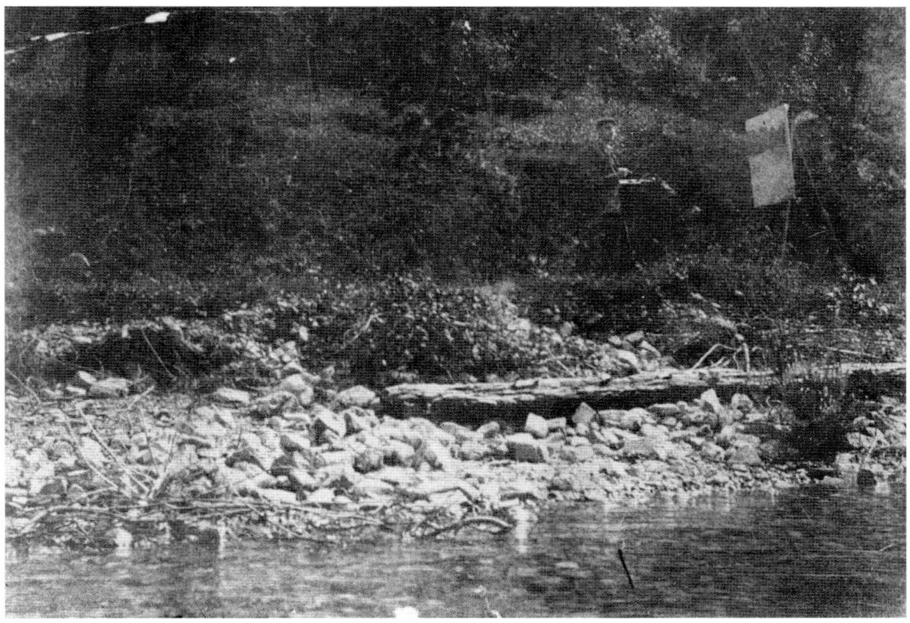

Gerstl painting on the shore of the Traunsee, summer 1908. Archiv Otto Breicha, Vienna

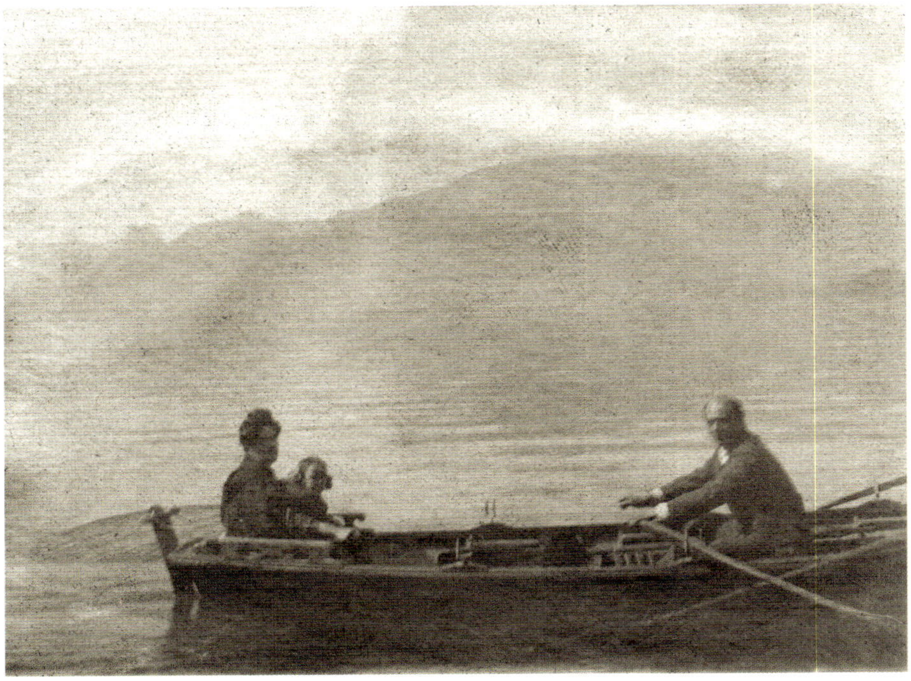

Mathilde, Gertrude, and Arnold Schönberg in a rowboat on the Traunsee, 1907. Private Collection/Courtesy Arnold Schönberg Center, Vienna

her family behind at Traunsee, Mathilde travelled to Vienna with Gerstl in late August, only to return to Schönberg several days later.

The incident put an immediate end to Gerstl's relationship with the Schönberg Circle, and the artist was once again in a state of social isolation. Shaken by these events, Gerstl abandoned his studio at Liechtensteinstraße 68/70 and worked from his family's home, where he realized his final self-portrait, the expressive *Nude Self-Portrait* [Cat. no. 86]. In mid-October, he moved into a loft atelier at Liechtensteinstraße 20, nearby the Schönbergs' home, where his final work, *Seated Female Nude* [Cat. no. 87], marks the radical endpoint in the artist's oeuvre.

After reputedly destroying all of his letters and documents, Gerstl hanged and stabbed himself in the early evening of November 4. Gerstl's suicide coincided with an important concert presented by Schönberg's students in the Great Hall of Vienna's Musikverein; available evidence indicates that Gerstl had not been invited. To avoid scandal, Gerstl's family kept his suicide secret. His affair with Mathilde was also concealed and not revealed to the public until fifty years later. A certificate of insanity issued by a physician assured Gerstl a Christian burial, which took place at the cemetery in the Sievering district of Vienna on November 7. The works left behind after his death were stored at the Rosin & Knauer shipping company.

1931–35

In 1931, Alois Gerstl approached Otto Nirenstein (later Kallir), an art dealer and owner of Vienna's Neue Galerie, for the purpose of having his brother's works appraised. Nirenstein was so impressed by the paintings that he organized a first solo exhibition under the title of "Richard Gerstl, ein Malerschicksal" (Richard Gerstl: A Painter's Fate). Between 1932 and 1935, the show traveled to Munich, Berlin, Cologne, Aachen, and Salzburg.

1956
Gerstl was represented by ten paintings in an exhibition at the Austrian Pavilion of the Biennale in Venice curated by Werner Hofmann.

A number of paintings from the estate were purchased by the Galerie Würthle and eventually added to the Kamm Collection in Switzerland, which now holds the world's third-largest collection of works by Gerstl.

1983-84
In honor of the artist's 100th birthday, the Historisches Museum of the City of Vienna (now the Wien Museum) hosted an extensive exhibition.

1993
A major retrospective was presented at the Kunstforum Bank Austria in Vienna in September and at the Kunsthaus Zürich in March of the following year.

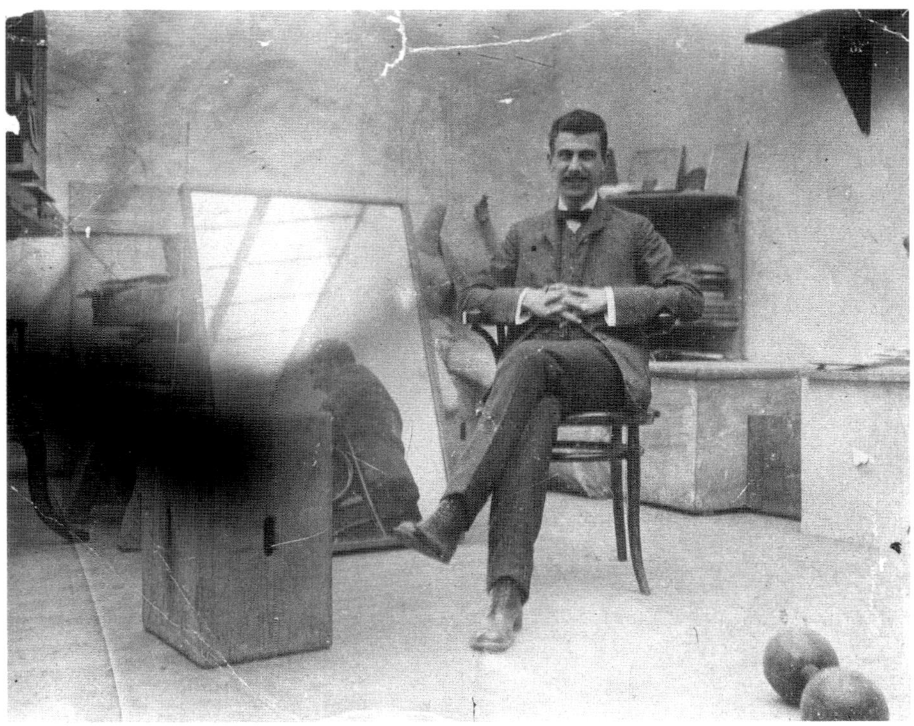

Richard Gerstl in his studio, ca. 1907–08.
Archiv Ottc Breicha, Vienna

INDEX

This book was published in conjunction with
the exhibition

RICHARD GERSTL

Neue Galerie New York
June 29–September 25, 2017
and at the Schirn Kunsthalle Frankfurt
February 24–May 14, 2017

Edited by Jill Lloyd and Ingrid Pfeiffer
in collaboration with Raymond Coffer

Curator (New York): Jill Lloyd
Exhibition Design: Peter de Kimpe

Director of Publications: Scott Gutterman
Managing Editor: Janis Staggs
Editorial Assistance: Liesbet Van Leemput

Book design: Judith Hudson
Typefaces: Berthold Akzidenz Grotesk and Neue

Project supervision for Hirmer: Kerstin Ludolph
Project coordination for Hirmer: Karen Angne, Sabine Frohmader
Copy-editing for Hirmer: Jane Michael, Munich
Translation from the German (Essays Pfeiffer, Leopold, Sitte): John Southard, Groß-Umstadt
Production: Hannes Halder
Origination: Repromayer Medienproduktion GmbH, Reutlingen
Printing and binding: Firmengruppe Appl, aprinta druck GmbH, Wemding

Printed in Germany

Published by
Hirmer Verlag
Nymphenburger Straße 84
80635 Munich
Germany
Tel. +49-89-12 15 16 0
Fax +49-89-12 15 16 10

Bibliographic information published by the
Deutsche Nationalbibliothek
The Deutsche Nationalbibliothek lists this publication in the Deutsche Nationalbibliografie; detailed bibliographic data is available on the Internet at http://www.dnb.de.

ISBN 978-3-7774-2943-4 (English museum edition)
ISBN 978-3-7774-2754-6 (English trade edition)

www.hirmerpublishers.com

Printed on the FSC-certified paper
Galaxi Supermatt

PHOTOGRAPH AND COPYRIGHT CREDITS

We wish to thank the museums, galleries, and individuals named in the captions of plates and text illustrations for supplying the photographic material in this publication.

Photograph credits:

© 2017 Kunsthaus Zurich: p. 32 bottom
Academy of Fine Arts, University Archive, Vienna: p. 17
akg-images, photo: akg-images: pp. 14, 21 right, 21 bottom, 35, 57, 132 top, 175, 181
akg-images, photo: Erich Lessing: p. 151
akg-images / MPortfolio / Electa: p. 25 right
The Albertina Museum, Vienna: pp. 115, 157
Archiv Otto Breicha, Courtesy Leopold Museum, Vienna: pp. 1, 2, 11, 18 left, 50 right, 226, 227, 228, 229, 231 bottom, 233
Arnold Schönberg Center, Vienna: pp. 50 left, 51, 54, 55, 60, 205, 206, 207, 209, 210, 211, 213, 215, 217, 219, 220, 221, 230, 231 top, 232
Auktionshaus im Kinsky GmbH, Vienna: p. 143 bottom
Belmont Music Publishers, Pacific Palisades, Courtesy Arnold Schönberg Center, Vienna: pp. 205, 206, 207, 209, 210, 211, 215, 217, 219, 220, 221
Belvedere, Vienna: pp. 25 left, 28, 33 left, 48, 91, 99, 107, 127, 147, 149, cover
BRUSEUM/Neue Galerie Graz, Universalmuseum Joanneum, Photo: Klaus Eschen: p. 46
Christie's Images Ltd – ARTOTHEK: p. 34 left
Courtesy Galerie St. Etienne, New York: pp. 12, 62, 64 bottom, 65, 93, 95, 117, 141, 145, 157, 183, 185, 187, 191, 223, 225 / Photo: Kretchy: p. 64 top
Courtesy W&K – Wienerroither & Kohlbacher: p. 136
Ernst Ploil, Vienna: p. 132 bottom
Galli & Thierry, Mailand: p. 83
Kunsthaus Zug, Photo: Alois Frommenwiler: pp. 79, 89, 121, 131, 142, 189
Leopold Museum, Vienna: pp. 4, 20, 21 left, 22, 32 right, 40, 43 top and bottom right, 85, 101, 103, 105, 109, 133, 135, 137, 139, 143 top, 153, 159, 161, 169, 173, 177, 193, 195
Munch museum: pp. 30, 32 left
Museo Nacional del Prado: p. 33 right
Museum moderner Kunst Stiftung Ludwig Wien, Gift of the Kamm Family, Zug: pp. 56, 179
Neue Galerie New York: pp. 119, 125
Oberösterreichisches Landesmuseum, Photo: Ernst Grilnberger: p. 81
Photo: Jürgen Diemer: p. 43 bottom left
Photo: Norbert Miguletz: p. 167
Tiroler Landesmuseum Ferdinandeum: pp. 34 right, 129
Universität für angewandte Kunst Wien, Kunstsammlung und Archiv, Oskar Kokoschka-Zentrum: p. 19 right
Wien Museum: pp. 19 left, 42, 97, 111, 123, 152, 155, 156
Wiener Stadt-und Landesarchiv, Historische Meldeunterlagen, K11: Gerstl Richard, 14.9.1883: p. 58

Page 1
Richard Gerstl in his studio, ca. 1907–08. Archiv Otto Breicha, Vienna

Page 2
Richard Gerstl, ca. 1905. Archiv Otto Breicha, Vienna

Page 4
Richard Gerstl, *Self-Portrait*, winter 1907– spring 1908, oil on canvas. Leopold Private Collection, Vienna

Page 228
Richard Gerstl, ca. 1905. Archiv Otto Breicha, Vienna